P9-DDT-538

Fodor's

PUERTO RICO

4th Edition

**Where to Stay and Eat
for All Budgets**

**Must-See Sights
and Local Secrets**

Ratings You Can Trust

Fodor's Travel Publications   New York, Toronto, London, Sydney, Auckland
www.fodors.com

FODOR'S PUERTO RICO
Editor: Douglas Stallings

Editorial Production: Evangelos Vasilakis
Editorial Contributors: Mark Sullivan
Maps: David Lindroth, *cartographer*; Bob Blake and Rebecca Baer, *map editors*
Design: Fabrizio La Rocca, *creative director*; Guido Caroti, *art director*; Melanie Marin, *senior photo editor*
Production/Manufacturing: Angela L. McLean
Cover Photo: (Buye Beach near Cabo Rojo): José Azel/Aurora

COPYRIGHT

Fourth Edition

ISBN-10: 1–4000–1710-6

ISBN-13: 978–1–4000–1710-2

ISSN: 1531–0396

SPECIAL SALES

This book is available for special discounts for bulk purchases for sales promotions or premiums. Special editions, including personalized covers, excerpts of existing books, and corporate imprints, can be created in large quantities for special needs. For more information, write to Special Markets/Premium Sales, 1745 Broadway, MD 6-2, New York, New York, NY 10019, or e-mail specialmarkets@randomhouse.com.

AN IMPORTANT TIP & AN INVITATION

Although all prices, opening times, and other details in this book are based on information supplied to us at press time, changes occur all the time in the travel world, and Fodor's cannot accept responsibility for facts that become outdated or for inadvertent errors or omissions. So **always confirm information when it matters,** especially if you're making a detour to visit a specific place. Your experiences—positive and negative—matter to us. If we have missed or misstated something, **please write to us.** We follow-up on all suggestions. Contact the Puerto Rico editor at editors@fodors.com or c/o Fodor's at 1745 Broadway, New York, NY 10019.

PRINTED IN THE UNITED STATES OF AMERICA

10 9 8 7 6 5 4 3 2 1

Be a Fodor's Correspondent

Your opinion matters. It matters to us. It matters to your fellow Fodor's travelers, too. And we'd like to hear it. In fact, we *need* to hear it.

When you share your experiences and opinions, you become an active member of the Fodor's community. That means we'll not only use your feedback to make our books better, but we'll publish your names and comments whenever possible. Throughout our guides, look for "Word of Mouth," excerpts of your unvarnished feedback.

Here's how you can help improve Fodor's for all of us.

Tell us when we're right. We rely on local writers to give you an insider's perspective. But our writers and staff editors—who are the best in the business—depend on you. Your positive feedback is a vote to renew our recommendations for the next edition.

Tell us when we're wrong. We're proud that we update most of our guides every year. But we're not perfect. Things change. Hotels cut services. Museums change hours. Charming cafés lose charm. If our writer didn't quite capture the essence of a place, tell us how you'd do it differently. If any of our descriptions are inaccurate or inadequate, we'll incorporate your changes in the next edition and will correct factual errors at fodors.com *immediately*.

Tell us what to include. You probably have had fantastic travel experiences that aren't yet in Fodor's. Why not share them with a community of like-minded travelers? Maybe you chanced upon a beach or bistro or B&B that you don't want to keep to yourself. Tell us why we should include it. And share your discoveries and experiences with everyone directly at fodors.com. Your input may lead us to add a new listing or highlight a place we cover with a "Highly Recommended" star or with our highest rating, "Fodor's Choice."

Give us your opinion instantly at our feedback center at www.fodors.com/feedback. You may also e-mail editors@fodors.com with the subject line "Puerto Rico Editor." Or send your nominations, comments, and complaints by mail to Puerto Rico Editor, Fodor's, 1745 Broadway, New York, NY 10019.

You and travelers like you are the heart of the Fodor's community. Make our community richer by sharing your experiences. Be a Fodor's correspondent.

Happy traveling!

Tim Jarrell, Publisher

CONTENTS

MAPS

ABOUT THIS BOOK

Our Ratings

Sometimes you find terrific travel experiences and sometimes they just find you. But usually the burden is on you to select the right combination of experiences. That's where our ratings come in.

As travelers we've all discovered a place so wonderful that its worthiness is obvious. And sometimes that place is so unique that superlatives don't do it justice: you just have to be there to know. These sights, properties, and experiences get our highest rating, **Fodor's Choice**, indicated by orange stars throughout this book.

Black stars highlight sights and properties we deem **Highly Recommended**, places that our writers, editors, and readers praise again and again for consistency and excellence.

By default, there's another category: any place we include in this book is by definition worth your time, unless we say otherwise. And we will.

Disagree with any of our choices? Care to nominate a place or suggest that we rate one more highly? Visit our feedback center at www. fodors.com/feedback.

Budget Well

Hotel and restaurant price categories from ¢ to $$$$ are defined in the opening pages of each chapter. For attractions, we always give standard adult admission fees; reductions are usually available for children, students, and senior citizens. Want to pay with plastic? **AE, D, DC, MC, V** following restaurant and hotel listings indicate whether American Express, Discover, Diner's Club, MasterCard, and Visa are accepted.

Restaurants

Unless we state otherwise, restaurants are open for lunch and dinner daily. We mention dress only when there's a specific requirement and reservations only when they're essential or not accepted—it's always best to book ahead.

Hotels

Hotels have private bath, phone, TV, and air-conditioning and operate on the European Plan (aka EP, meaning without meals), unless we specify that they use the Continental Plan (CP, with a continental breakfast), Breakfast Plan (BP, with a full breakfast), or Modified American Plan (MAP, with breakfast and dinner) or are all-inclusive (including all meals and most activities). We always

list facilities but not whether you'll be charged an extra fee to use them, so when pricing accommodations, find out what's included.

Many Listings

★	Fodor's Choice
★	Highly recommended
⊠	Physical address
↔	Directions
⌂	Mailing address
☎	Telephone
🖷	Fax
⊕	On the Web
✎	E-mail
🖅	Admission fee
☉	Open/closed times
▶	Start of walk/itinerary
Ⓜ	Metro stations
▭	Credit cards

Hotels & Restaurants

🏨	Hotel
⇆	Number of rooms
⌂	Facilities
⦿	Meal plans
✕	Restaurant
⌂	Reservations
🏛	Dress code
⤡	Smoking
🕮	BYOB
✕🏨	Hotel with restaurant that warrants a visit

Outdoors

🏌	Golf
⛺	Camping

Other

☺	Family-friendly
🔢	Contact information
⇨	See also
⊠	Branch address
☞	Take note

WHEN TO GO

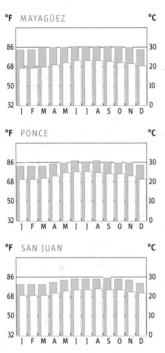

High season runs from mid-December through mid-April. Winter hotel rates are as much as 25% higher than off-season rates, and hotels tend to be packed. San Juan is also a commercial town, and hotels, except for the short season around Christmas and New Year's, are busy year-round with international business travelers. This doesn't mean the island won't have rooms in winter—rarely is space completely unavailable—but if you plan to beat that winter sleet in Duluth, make arrangements for flights and hotel space at least a few weeks ahead of time. A fun and often less expensive time to visit is during the "shoulder" seasons of fall and spring. The weather is—still—perfect, and the tourist crush is less intense.

You can always visit Puerto Rico during the less busy summer season, when temperatures are hot and hurricanes more likely. And you might even find some added bargains at this time of the year. Given its proximity to the East Coast of the United States and relatively large number of flights, Puerto Rico can be an excellent hurricane-season option for the Caribbean. This kind of trip works best when you can visit at the last minute, when you'll be able to watch the weather report and know a hurricane isn't about to strike; it's also nice if you can get a bargain airfare, which might very well happen on a summer weekend. Know that business travel—not to mention the fact that San Juan serves as a major hub for American Airlines flights to the rest of the Caribbean—keeps the flights to Puerto Rico fairly full from Monday through Friday all year long.

Climate

Puerto Rico's weather is moderate and tropical year-round, with an average temperature of about 82°F (26°C). Essentially, there are no seasonal changes, although winter sees cooling (not cold) breezes from the north, and temperatures in higher elevations drop by as much as 20 degrees. Hurricane season in the Caribbean runs July through November.

The following are average daily maximum and minimum temperatures.

🅕 Forecasts **Puerto Rico Weather** ☎ 787/253-4586. **The Weather Channel** ⊕ www.weather.com.

UNITED
STATES

Miami

Key West

Nassau

The Bahamas

Havana

Cuba

Turks and
Caicos Islands

*Little
Cayman*

George
Town

*Cayman
Brac*

*Grand
Cayman*

Puerto Plata

Haiti   **Hispaniola**

Port-au-Prince

Montego Bay

Ocho Rios

Santo
Domingo

Jamaica

Kingston

G R E A T E R

Greater Antilles

C a r i b b e a n   S e a

0   200 mi

0   200 km

COLOMBIA   Maracaibo

Cartagena

Caribbean

A T L A N T I C   O C E A N

Dominican Republic

San Juan

Puerto Rico

St. Thomas

St. John

Tortola

Virgin Gorda

St. Maarten

St. Martin

St. Croix

Anguilla

St. Barthélemy

Saba

St. Eustatius

Barbuda

St. Kitts

Nevis

Antigua

Montserrat

Guadeloupe

Marie Galante

Dominica

Martinique

Fort-de-France

L E E W A R D   I S L A N D S

A N T I L L E S

Leeward Islands

W I N D W A R D   I S L A N D S

St. Lucia

St. Vincent

Bequia

The Grenadines

Carriacou

St. George's

Grenada

Barbados

Bridgetown

Tobago

L E S S E R   A N T I L L E S

Aruba

Curaçao

Bonaire

Willemstad

Islas Los Roques

La Guaira

Caracas

VENEZUELA

Port of Spain

Trinidad

Windward Islands

Puerto Rico

Pta.
Agujereada

Isabela

Hatillo

Puerto de
Tortuguero

Pta.
Borinquén

Vega
Baja

Bahía de
Aguadilla

2

Quebradillas

Camuy

Arecibo

22

2

**Playa
Crashboat**

Aguadilla

Bosque
Estatal
Guajataca

129

10

Manati

Maricao

Pta.
Gorda

Aguada

Rincón

115

San
Sebastián

111

Utuado

Jayuya

149

Bahía de Añasco

2

Mayagüez

105

Maricao

Adjuntas

Bosque
Estatal
Toro Negro

Coamo

102

2

Bosque Estatal
Maricao

Juana Díaz

14

Joyuda

Cabo
Rojo

San
Germán

102

10

52

**Balneario
Boquerón**

101

La
Parguera

116

Guánica

Guayanilla

Ponce

Santa
Isabel

Bahía
de Rincón

Boquerón

El Combate

Bahía
Salinas

Bahía
Sucia

Bahía
Fosforescente

**Playa
Santa**

Ensenada
Las Pardas

**Playa
Ballena**

Caja de
Muertos

Pta.
Jagüey

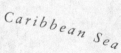

C a r i b b e a n   S e a

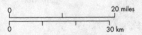

0   20 miles

0   30 km

ATLANTIC OCEAN

Bahía de
San Juan

Old
San
Juan

**Ocean
Park**

**Isla
Verde**

Dorado

Cataño

Piñones

**Balneario de
Luquillo**

Reserva
Natural las
Cabezas

Cayo
Icacos

**Playa
Flamenco**

✈ San Juan

Loíza

Luquillo

Bayamón

Carolina

Canóvanas

**Aeropuerto
Internacional
Luis Muñoz Marín**

191

Fajardo

987

**Balneario
Seven Seas**

Sonda de Vieques

Dewey

**Playa
Zoni**

Naranjito

3

Ceiba

Culebra

El Yunque

Caguas

Naguabo

Barranquitas

*Bosque
Estatal
Carite*

San Lorenzo

Humacao

Vieques

Cayey

1   52

184

Yabucoa

3

◆ **Palmas del Mar
Resort**

Esperanza

*Bahía
Mosquito*

**Playa
Sun Bay**

Guayama

Patillas

Puerto Yabucoa

Salinas

Maunabo

*Puerto
Patillas*

*Puerto
Arroyo*

KEY
✦ *Rainforest*

WHAT'S WHERE

SAN JUAN

Few places remain in the Caribbean where you can see what captivated the conquistadors. Strolling through Old San Juan's crimson-colored Puerta de San Juan, one of the five original gateways into the city, you will find yourself on the same cobblestone streets walked by Juan Ponce de León. This is the magical part of San Juan. The rest of the city is less magical, but with the renovation of some older resorts already in the works, it's certainly beginning to shake off a slightly down-at-the-heels feel that it's had since the late 1980s. Come to San Juan if you want to sample the city's excellent restaurants or shop in myriad designer boutiques, especially for clothing by Puerto Rico's more daring designers. And, naturally, choose San Juan if you want to party; there are few places in the Caribbean that have as varied and dynamic a nightlife scene as you'll find here. The city's beaches are nice, but you'll have to look further afield to find the island's finest. Don't choose San Juan if you want a quiet, get-away-from-it-all experience; the city's resorts, for all their good points, aren't really the best places if you want to while away your hours in solitude.

EL YUNQUE & THE NORTHEAST

The most popular day trip from San Juan, El Yunque, doesn't disappoint. There are more than a dozen hiking trails through this tropical forest, leading down to hidden pools and up to mountaintop observatories. If you're pressed for time, you can even experience it from your car; the waterfall called Cascada La Cola is so close to the road that you may get wet if you leave your windows rolled down. Don't miss beachfront Luquillo, which has one of the island's best-known beaches and a string of *kioskos* (food stands) selling all types of seafood. West of Luquillo, the coastline gets wilder. The Reserva Natural Las Cabezas de San Juan, with its miles of mangrove forest, is one of the island's most remote nature reserves. The only real city, Fajardo, won't win any beauty contests, but it does make a good base for exploring the region.

VIEQUES & CULEBRA

Although the rest of Puerto Rico rings with the adrenaline rush of Latin America, this pair of palm-ringed islands has the laid-back vibe of the Caribbean. It's understandable when you realize that Vieques and Culebra, off the main island's northeastern coast, are also a stone's throw from St. Thomas and St. Croix. Most famous is Vieques, in the headlines for years when protests led to the shutdown of a much-derided U.S. military base. Development is coming in fits and starts, with boutique

hotels and trendy eateries that wouldn't be out of place in Miami Beach. Culebra is even more off the beaten path. It's lack of infrastructure—only one of the lodgings has more than a dozen rooms—means its never gets too crowded. This is good news, because it keeps beaches like Playa Flamenco—one of the most beautiful in the world—pristine.

PONCE & THE SOUTHERN COAST

Puerto Rico's southern coast is drier than other parts of the island, and cacti are abundant. Here you'll find tropical dry forests such as the Bosque Estatal de Guánica, one of the island's most popular destinations for hikers. It's also one of the best places for bird-watching, as there are more than 100 types species, including the the pearly eyed thrasher, the lizard cockoo, and the nightjar. Don't worry, though, because beaches are always close at hand. They can be crowded, especially on holiday weekends, since this is a favored destination for Puerto Rican families. The south also has some of island's most historic towns, including bustling Ponce, with its fascinating blend of neoclassical and art–deco buildings.

RINCÓN & THE PORTA DEL SOL

The jagged coastline of the Porta del Sol is known for its world-class surfing. There are awe-inspiring waves around Aguadilla and Isabella, but these towns are still being discovered by travelers. Most surfers still head to Rincón, where dozens of beaches beckon those who hanker to hang ten. The place is a magnet for expats, so expect to run into a lot of gringos. The region known as Cabo Rojo, on the southwestern coast, attracts families, who pack the open-air terraces at seafood shacks along the beach at Joyuda. Flights to the airports at Aguadilla and Mayagüez make this regions a quick and easy trip from the northeastern United States.

THE CORDILLERA CENTRAL

The ridge running across the center of the island, called the Cordillera Central, is seldom explored by travelers. That's a shame because the scenery here is incomparable. Driving along the Ruta Panoramica, the "Panoramic Route" that traverses the heavily forested mountains, you catch glimpses of the island's northern and southern coasts. Some of the most remote nature reserves are found in the Cordillera Central. The cloud-covered Bosque Estatal de Toro Negro has waterfalls, natural pools, and the island's tallest mountain peak, Cerro de Punta. The drier Bosque Estatal de Maricao is known for its numerous species of birds. A casual, laid-back atmosphere is the norm in this region.

QUINTESSENTIAL PUERTO RICO

Coquis

The first time you hear the sound—*ko-kee, ko-kee*—you might mistake it for a bird. But then you realize that the sun has already set. This is the call of the coqui, the "little frog" that sings from dusk until dawn. They are indeed small, rarely measuring more than an inch and a half long. Although they are all called the "coqui," 16 different species live in Puerto Rico. They range in color from muddy brown to olive green to mustardy yellow. Unlike many frogs, they are not strong swimmers. In fact, since their young do not pass through a tadpole stage, there is not need for them to live near large bodies of water. Bring a flashlight if you're out walking at night—you might catch a glimpse of one of these shy creatures.

Mofongo

This dish, a favorite all over the island, couldn't be simpler: green plantains mixed with garlic and other flavorings and fried up in a pan. Served plain, it's often a side dish. But when it's stuffed with chicken, beef, or some other meat, mofongo becomes one of Puerto Rico's signature entrées. In the center of the island, it's often made with pork. On the coast, however, mofongo is almost always stuffed with fresh fish. Some restaurants are even known for what they put in their plantains. A neon sign outside Tino's, one of a long line of seafood restaurants in Joyuda, touts its signature dish: an earthenware goblet overflowing with plantains and seafood.

Rum

As you enjoy a piña colada—a cocktail served in nearly every bar on the island—lift your glass to Christopher Columbus. Although the explorer didn't invent the fruity cocktail, he did bring sugarcane to the Caribbean on his second voyage in

If you want to get a sense of contemporary Puerto Rican culture, and indulge in some of its pleasure, start by familiarizing yourself with the rituals of daily life. These are a few highlights—things you can take part in with relative ease.

1493. Juan Ponce de Léon, the island's first governor, planted vast fields of the stuff. The first sugar mill was opened in 1524, leading to the distillation of what was then called *brebaje*. Although rum was first exported in 1897, it took a bit longer for it become the massive industry it is today. The Bacardí family, fleeing Cuba, set up shop near Puerto Rico in 1959. Their company's product, lighter-bodied than those produced by most other distilleries, gained favor around the world. Today, Puerto Rico produces more than 35 million gallons of rum a year. You might say it's the national drink.

Salsa

Although it's the music most identified with Puerto Rico, salsa did not originate on the island. It was born in New York City, where there was a sizeable Puerto Rican community after World War II. (Puerto Rican–born Tito Puente, who helped popularize salsa, studied percussion at New York's Julliard School of Music.) Salsa blends the swing music that was popular at the time with the Afro-Caribbean rhythms of rumba, mambo, and merengue. The ensemble needed to perform salsa includes a huge array of percussion instruments, including maracas, bongos, and *güiros,* the gourds that the island's indigenous Taíno people once used to mark the beat. Today, more than 50 years after it was first created, salsa remains immensely popular in Puerto Rico.

IF YOU LIKE

Beaches

Sanjuaneros often pack the city's sandy stretches as well as such east-coast beaches as Luquillo. Those seeking solitude will find it on the outer islands, where the beaches are wide, spectacular, and often deserted. To the south, several strands are broad and inviting, with plenty of seaside bars and restaurants where you can while away the hours. The west coast near the town of Rincón is popular with surfers.

Balneario de Carolina, San Juan. There's a reason this spot is the site for some of the toniest resorts in San Juan—the beach, wide and warm and kissed by the surf, seems to go on forever.

Balneario Luquillo, Luquillo. This beautiful beach has all the trimmings—including lifeguards, changing rooms, and nearby kiosks where you can find tasty local cuisine and piña coladas.

Playa Crashboat, Aguadilla. The picturesque boats lining the shores here are just part of the appeal. The water has a shimmering, glassy look and is great for swimming and snorkeling.

Playa Flamenco, Culebra. Imagine a long curve of white sand and azure-tinted water. Palm trees wave in the wind. No one is there to claim the spot as theirs. It's the quintessential Caribbean beach.

Sun Bay, Vieques This crescent-shaped bay has one of the region's prettiest beaches. On weekdays, when the crowds are thin, you might also find wild horses grazing among the palm trees.

History

Puerto Rico has preserved much of its history, especially in Old San Juan, a UNESCO World Heritage Site. Walk down any cobblestone street and you'll get a sense of what it was to be here during the Spanish Empire. Nearly as fascinating is Ponce, whose boom in the 1930s brought wonderful art–deco buildings around the main square. For colonial splendor, there's San Germán and Guayama on the southern coast.

Capilla de Porta Coeli, San Germán. One of the oldest religious buildings in the Americas, this mission-style chapel now functions as a museum of religious art.

Casa Cautiño, Guyama. Dating from 1887, this elegant neoclassical home has a painstakingly restored exterior. You'll be swept back in time walking through the Victorian-era rooms.

Fuerte San Felipe del Morro, Old San Juan. El Morro is solid as a rock and even today seems impenetrable. Take a guided tour and see why San Juan was able to fend off invaders for 400 years.

Hacienda Buena Vista, Ponce. The grounds of this former coffee plantation are meticulously maintained. Take a guided tour to find out what it was like to be a settler taming the wilderness.

Museo de Arte de Puerto Rico, San Juan. The island's premier art museum scours the island for interesting pieces, displaying works by contemporary local artists as well as island masters like Rafael Tufiño.

Parque de Bombas, Ponce. This red-and-black striped structure has served as a firehouse since 1883. It's among the most photographed buildings in Puerto Rico.

Luxury Resorts

Most of Puerto Rico's luxury resorts are right on the beach, and those that aren't usually have a stunning view over the water. Although high-end hotels are scattered all over the island, most are along the northern and eastern coasts, which is not surprising, as these were the first places to see large-scale tourism.

El Convento Hotel, Old San Juan. You wouldn't recognize this as the Carmelite convent it was 350 years ago; today it's luxurious and hip, a fine example of sensitive planning and good decoration.

Horned Dorset Primavera, Rincón. This west-coast inn is the place to go to get away from it all in luxury. The two-story suites are impeccable.

Hacienda Tamarindo, Vieques. A tamarind tree rises up through three stories in the lobby, and the outdoor pool is touted as one of Puerto Rico's most beautiful. It's a formula for whimsical bliss.

Normandie, San Juan. One of the Caribbean's finest examples of art-deco architecture, this hotel hosted high-society types back in the 1930s. After a stem to stern renovation, it's ship-shape again.

Westin Río Mar Beach Golf Resort & Spa, Río Grande. Set on more than 500 acres, this sprawling resort is geared toward outdoor activities. The biggest draw is the 2-mi-long stretch of sand.

Outdoor Activities

Does it take more than a piña colada to get you going? Does the thought of lying on the beach for a week bore you to tears? Luckily, Puerto Rico has more than enough outdoor activities to keep you occupied. Whether you prefer your adventures in the forest, on the sea, or underground, the island has something to offer.

Kayaking in Bahía Mosquito, Vieques. The magnificence of gliding through the sparkling sea creatures at this bioluminescent bay is almost beyond description. Here nature beats special effects hands down.

Hiking in Bosque Estatal de Guánica, Guánica. This dry forest is an amazing site with its various forms of cacti and abundant bird life. Hiking here may not be for everyone—it's hot and arid—but you'll love it if you're interested in exotic flora and birds.

Soft-adventure Spelunking Parque de las Cavernas de Río Camuy, Arecibo. The tram ride down to the caves in the limestone karst just south of Arecibo—through wild bamboo and banana plants—is worth the price of admission alone. You'll soon see that Clara Cave de Empalme is a natural wonder.

Exploring El Yunque. With 100 billion gallons of precipitation annually, this protected area truly is a rain forest. Among its sights are 240 tree species and 68 types of birds, including the endangered Puerto Rican green parrot.

GREAT ITINERARIES

LIFE'S A BEACH

This itinerary takes you west to the best beaches of the Porta del Sol, along the island's west coast, and it will get you home in a week. You can easily combine this with one of the other itineraries if you want to see more of the island.

Day 1: Dorado
Head immediately to Dorado, one of the north coast's most stunning stretches of sand. This is a favorite weekend destination for *sanjuaneros*, so you won't have a problem finding a place to stay. One good choice is the Embassy Suites Dorado del Mar Beach & Golf Resort. There's a string of restaurants along the town's main drag, including El Ladrillo, a longtime favorite serving *zarzuela* and other traditional Spanish dishes.

Logistics: After arriving at San Juan's Aeropuerto Internacional Luis Muñoz Marín, pick up the rental car that you have arranged in advance. Take Route 165 west of San Juan, then head west on Route 693.

Day 2: Isabela & Rincón
Your destination for your second day is Rincón, on the western coast. There's no need to hurry, however. If it's a weekend, take a detour to Lago Dos Bocas, where you can have lunch at one of the waterfront restaurants. You'll have to take a boat across the lake, but we think that adds to the appeal. If it isn't a weekend, stop for a bite in Isabela, a small town that overlooks the rocky shoreline. Happy Belly's, on a stretch of shoreline called Playa Jobos, has great hamburgers. You'll probably arrive in Rincón in early afternoon, giving you plenty of time to hit the beach. If you've just received a large inher-

itance, you'll want to stay at the Horned Dorset Primavera. Otherwise, there are any number of inexpensive lodgings along the beach.

Logistics: From Dorado, drive south on 165, then west on Route 2. If you're in a hurry, save a bit of time by taking Route 22, a toll road that runs parallel to Route 2 until they meet near Arecibo. From Route 2, Route 115 takes you to Rincón.

Day 3: Cabo Rojo
The term Cabo Rojo is confusing, as "Red Cape" refers to a region, a town, and the tiny peninsula that juts off the southwestern tip of the island. The latter is where you are headed on your third day. Stop en route at Joyuda, known as the "Golden Mile" because of its string of seafood shacks. Make sure to stop at one for lunch. We like the food best at Tino's, even though it is one of the few places that doesn't have a view. Joyuda has no beachfront, so if you want to walk on the sand you'll have to head south to Boquerón. An even better idea is to continue on to El Combate. Here you'll find a less crowded beach near the neoclassical Cabo Rojo Lighthouse. (Be aware, though, that the rough road to the lighthouse is unpaved.) Stay overnight in El Combate, perhaps at the recently expanded Bahía Salinas Beach Hotel.

Logistics: From Rincón, Route 115 takes you back to Route 2. Head south on Route 2 until you reach the turnoff for Route 100, which leads to all the coastal communities in Cabo Rojo.

Day 4: Bosque Estatal de Guánica
From Cabo Rojo, it's an easy drive to the coastal town of Guánica. Drop your stuff

off at your hotel—either the expansive Copamarina Beach Resort or the intimate Mary Lee's by the Sea—and head to the Bosque Estatal de Guánica. There are several entrances to the state park, but take Route 334 because this route takes you past the park's ranger station, where you can pick up trail maps. This is a dry forest, so the scenery is different than anywhere else on the island. You'll see more than 700 species of plants ranging from the prickly pear cactus to the gumbo limbo tree. In the afternoon, head back to the hotel for some much-needed rest and relaxation. The beaches along the coast are beautiful, but you can also take a ferry to the offshore Gilligan's Island. The name may be a bit hokey, but the scenery is gorgeous. There's no better choice for dinner than the elegant dining room at Alexandra.

Logistics: From El Combate, head north on Route 100 until you reach the turnoff for Route 2. Follow it east until you reach Route 116, which leads south to Guánica. You can take the more direct route to Guánica, but the narrow roads won't save you any time.

Day 5: San Juan

If you have a flight home today, don't despair. The drive back to San Juan will take you less than two hours, so you can probably spend the entire morning by the beach or beside the pool.

Logistics: Route 2 takes you directly back to San Juan.

TIPS

❶ Book your hotels in advance. There are long stretches along the island's northern and western coasts that don't have any lodgings.

❷ This drive is especially nice with a convertible. Ask your rental company about rates—you may be surprised to find they cost only $20 or $30 more a day than a compact.

❸ The only traffic you're likely to encounter is in San Juan. If you're going to be driving through the city on a weekday morning or afternoon, add a half-hour to your estimated time of arrival.

GREAT ITINERARIES

COLONIAL TREASURES

More than almost any other island in the Caribbean, Puerto Rico has a treasure trove of well-preserved colonial cities. Old San Juan is the best known, and it's a must-see for anyone interested in the region's rich history. But the southern coast also has some gems, from the graceful square in Coamo to the churches of San Germán to the heady mix of neoclassical and art deco masterpieces in Ponce.

Day 1: Old San Juan

If you truly want to experience Old San Juan, make sure you stay within the city walls. El Convento, once a Carmelite convent, is Old San Juan's most luxurious lodging; Gallery Inn, whose mascot is a cockatoo named Campeche, has the most personality. After you drop off your suitcases, hit the cobblestone streets. Make sure to stroll along the city walls and visit one of the forts—most people pick Fuerte San Felipe del Morro, but the nearby Fuerte San Cristóbal is just as atmospheric. But Old San Juan isn't just for historical sightseeing. When the sun goes down, the streets of the historic district light up, becoming one of the city's nightlife centers. For dinner, head to Calle Fortaleza, where you'll find some of the city's best restaurants. Then you can while the night away at one of the happening bars or clubs.

Logistics: Believe us when we tell you that you don't want to worry about parking in Old San Juan. At San Juan's Aeropuerto Internacional Luis Muñoz Marín, take a *taxi turístico* (tourist taxi) to your hotel. The streets here were made for walking, and that's just what you should do. Wait and pick up your car when you're ready to leave town for the countryside.

Day 2: Coamo

If you get an early enough start, take a short detour to Guayama, where you'll find the gorgeous Casa Cautiño. This 19th-century manor house, transformed into a museum, is one of Puerto Rico's most beautifully restored colonial-era structures. Continue west to Coamo, best known for its thermal springs. The best place to stay is the Parador Baños de Coamo, a rustic retreat with hot and cold pools. On Coamo's lovely main square is the gleaming white Iglesia Católica San Blás, one of the island's oldest churches. In terms of distance, Coamo isn't so far from San Juan—only about 96 km (60 mi)—so you don't have to leave at the crack of dawn to have the better part of a day to explore the town.

Logistics: Ponce is reached by Route 52, a modern highway that heads south of San Juan. This is a toll road, so keep your change handy.

Day 3: Ponce

Your destination on your third day is Ponce, the "Pearl of the South." You'll know that you've arrived when you drive through the massive letters spelling the name of the city. The main square, the Plaza de las Delicias, is a delight. Here you'll find the Catedral de Nuestra Señora de Guadalupe, a church dating from 1835, and the Parque de Bombas, a firehouse from 1882 that is painted in bold red and black stripes. There are several museums around the city, but the most interesting is the small Casa Wiechers-Villaronga, a house built in 1911. In a city filled with neoclassical confections, this is one of the most elaborate. Don't forget to stroll

Caribbean Sea

around the downtown streets, as the combination of neoclassical and art deco architecture is fascinating. One of the great pleasures of going to Ponce is dining at Mark's at the Meliá, the city's best restaurant; happily, the restaurant also happens to be in the Ponce's best hotel, making your choice of lodging an easy decision.

Logistics: Ponce is reached by Route 52. To get downtown, take Route 1.

Day 4: San Germán
Less than an hour west of Ponce is San Germán, a must for anyone interested in the colonial era. The best place to start a tour of San Germán is Plazuela Santo Domingo, the small park in the center of the historic district. At the eastern edge of the park is the Capilla de Porta Coeli. This chapel, at the top of some steep stone steps, is now a museum of religious art. Stroll west past the delightful assemblage of buildings of every architectural style from mission to Victorian. Make sure to see the other gorgeous church, called the Iglesia de San Germán de Auxerre. There's a small hotel near the historic district, but the best lodging is Villa del Rey, a few miles outside of town.

Logistics: San Germán is easy to reach— simply take Route 2 west of Ponce. When you reach Route 122, head south.

Day 5: San Juan
If you have time on your way back to San Juan, stop for lunch at one of the open-air eateries near Cayey, a colonial town off Route 52. You can try *lechón,* whole suckling pig roasted on a spit.

Logistics: From San Germán, take Route 2 until you reach Ponce. Exit onto Route 52, a toll road takes you all the way to San Juan.

TIPS

❶ If you're staying in Old San Juan, pick up your rental car at one of the hotel desks. You'll avoid an expensive taxi ride to the airport.

❷ Bring comfortable shoes for exploring these colonial-era cities. You'll be glad you brought sneakers after a few hours traipsing the cobblestone streets.

❸ Old San Juan and Ponce are hillier than they first appear. Take advantage of the free public transportation to the most popular tourist sites.

GREAT ITINERARIES

ISLAND HOPPING

If you have a week for your trip, this itinerary will give you a taste of each of eastern Puerto Rico's highlights. However, if you are short on time, Puerto Rico is still the perfect destination. Nonstop flights from many U.S. cities mean that even a long weekend is a possibility, though after you see the beaches, you may not want to limit yourself to just a night or two on Vieques or Culebra.

Day 1: El Yunque

East of San Juan is El Yunque, the undulating rain forest that covers much of the eastern edge of the island. It's a highlight of any trip to Puerto Rico, but you can still have a memorable trip if you have but one day to spend there. Several of the trails can be done in an hour or less, including one leading to the spectacular waterfall called the Cascada La Mina. Spend the night in Río Grande; our favorite hotel along this stretch of shoreline is the Westin Río Mar Beach Golf Resort Spa, known for its seaside golf courses, lovely beach, and first-class restaurants.

Logistics: Take Route 3 east of San Juan, then head south on Route 191, which leads through El Yunque.

Day 2: Reserva Natural Las Cabezas de San Juan

Get an early start on your third day, because you've got to cover a lot of ground. Head to Fajardo, on the northeastern tip of the island. Drop your stuff off at your hotel—we prefer the smaller ones like the Fajardo Inn—then head out for a tour of the mangrove forests of the Reserva Natural Las Cabezas de San Juan. However, exploring this area isn't just a daytime experience. You may also want to head out at night to get a very different view of Las Cabezas; you

can paddle through the bioluminescent bay here in a kayak. Companies offer the trips nightly, though your experience will be heightened if there is no moon. And the experience here will give you a taste of what's in store when you get to Vieques, which has a much more dramatically beautiful bio-bay.

Logistics: Take Route 3, which leads all the way to Fajardo.

Days 3 and 4: Culebra

Culebra has some of the most beautiful, powdery soft beaches that you'll find in all of Puerto Rico. It's a small, quiet island, so you won't find much to do there except relaxation. But then that's the draw. You won't find any big hotels or fancy restaurants, just small guesthouses and some villas. If this sounds like too much of a get-away-from-it-all experience for your tastes, then skip Culebra and spend more time on Vieques, which has more resorts and better restaurants. If you visit both islands, it's usually to your advantage to visit Culebra before Vieques because the latter has more flights and better connections back to San Juan.

Logistics: Drop off your rental car in Fajardo—you'll want to rent a sturdier four-wheel-drive vehicle once you get to Culebra. Take a 90-minute ferry trip or 10-minute puddle-jumper flight to the island. We recommend taking the plane, as the views are spectacular. You can take a ferry from Culebra to Vieques on weekdays but not on weekends; it's also possible to fly, but have a reservation booked ahead of time.

Days 5 and 6: Vieques

Close—both in terms of atmosphere and geography—to the U.S. Virgin Islands, Vieques has an entirely different feel from the rest of Puerto Rico. If you've never

been to Vieques, we strongly recommend you spend at least one night there. The beaches are endless, the snorkeling remarkably varied, and the bioluminescent bay is one of nature's best shows. If you've seen Vieques—or if you aren't compelled, as so many visitors are, to return again and again—you might try Culebra alone.

Logistics: Make sure your flight to San Juan is headed to Aeropuerto Internacional Luis Muñoz Marín. If it is going to the San Juan's regional airport, Aeropuerto Fernando L. Rivas Dominici, you'll have to shuttle between the airports.

Day 7: San Juan

From Vieques, take a puddle-jumper flight back to San Juan. If you want to spend a day in Old San Juan, then take a flight into Aeropuerto Fernando L. Rivas Dominici, which is a short taxi ride from San Juan's colonial heart. If you are connecting to a flight back home, then all you have to do is switch planes and you'll be on your way.

Logistics: If you are just connecting to a flight back home, make sure your flight to San Juan is headed to Aeropuerto Internacional Luis Muñoz Marín. If it is going to the San Juan's regional airport, Aeropuerto Fernando L. Rivas Dominici, you'll have to shuttle between the airports.

TIPS

① Don't even think about taking your rental car to Vieques or Culebra. The cargo ferry runs at an erratic schedule, and may bump your vehicle at the last minute if there is no room. Besides, you need a 4x4 to navigate the island roads.

② Check to see if you have to reserve in advance for certain tours, such as the daily trip to Fajardo's Reserva Natural Las Cabezas de San Juan.

③ Vieques and Culebra are both popular weekend destinations for Puerto Ricans, so the ferries become crowded on weekends, and it's sometimes difficult to get on. If possible, plan your travel to the smaller islands for a weekday.

④ Always reserve your car in advance if you are headed to Vieques or Culebra. There are limited rentals available.

⑤ Plan your trip carefully. It's almost impossible to travel between Vieques and Culebra on a weekend.

ON THE CALENDAR

Puerto Rico's top seasonal events are listed below, and any one of them could provide the stuff of lasting memories. Contact local tourism authorities for exact dates and for further information.

ONGOING Feb.– early Mar.	The weeks preceding Lent have special significance for Catholicism and other religions, and Puerto Rico celebrates its **Carnival** with vigor. The flamboyant celebrations, held island-wide but with particular energy in Ponce, are complete with float parades, folk music, local foods, Carnival Queen pageants, and music competitions.
Late Aug.– early Sept.	Anglers of all stripes try their hand at snagging blue marlin and other game fish in the largest fishing competition in Puerto Rico, the **International Billfish Tournament,** which is hosted by the Club Náutico de San Juan. The strongest tackle might prevail—marlins can weigh as much as 900 pounds.
WINTER Dec.	The Puerto Rico National Folkloric Ballet performs its highly anticipated **Annual Criollísimo Show** regularly during the month. The dance blends modern ballet with Puerto Rican and Caribbean music and themes. Look to the Teatro Tapia in Old San Juan or the Centro de Bellas Artes Luis A. Ferré in Santurce for schedules.
Early Dec.	For 10 days in early December, **Humacao's Fiesta Patronale** celebrates the Virgin of the Immaculate Conception; the festival coincides with the city's sprucing up for Christmas. If you've got a hankering for loud engines and sea spray, visit the exciting **Puerto Rico International Offshore Cup** speed-boat races held every year in Fajardo, where local and international teams compete for prize money and prestige.
Mid-Dec.	Cataño's Casa Bacardí Visitor Center hosts the **Bacardí Artisan's Fair.** With local crafts, children's activities, folk bands, and food and drink kiosks, it's arguably the largest event of its kind in the Caribbean. Fortaleza Street in Old San Juan is closed to traffic for the annual "South of Fortaleza" **SoFo Culinary Week,** when more than 20 restaurants set their chairs, tables, and bars outside on the street.
Late Dec.	The annual **Festival de los Máscaras** honors the mask-making traditions of the northwestern town of Hatillo, where colorful masks used in religious processions have been crafted for centuries. **Navidades,** or Christmas, features costumed nativity processions, music concerts, and other festivities island-wide during the week leading to one of the busiest holidays of the year.

Jan.	The annual season of the **Puerto Rico Symphony Orchestra** begins with classical and pop performances by the island's finest orchestra. Concerts are held in San Juan.
Jan. 5–6	In Isabela, the **Fiesta de Reyes Isabelinos** (Three Kings Day) is a two-day extravaganza that includes dramatizations of the pilgrimage to find the baby Jesus. The holiday is also celebrated in many other towns around the island.
Late Jan.	The annual **Las Fiestas de la Calle San Sebastián** (San Sebastián Street Festival), named after the street in Old San Juan where the festival originated, features several nights of live music in the plazas as well as food festivals and *cabezudos* parades, where folk legends are caricatured in oversize masks.
Late Jan.– early Feb.	Each year the Puerto Rico film industry picks talent to honor in the **Puerto Rico International Film Festival**. International stars such as Benicio Del Toro and Chita Rivera attest to the power of Puerto Rican influence in the arts, and the San Juan film festival showcases island-made films and works from around the world.
Early Feb.	Coamo's **San Blas de Illescas Half Marathon** has been running, literally, since 1957. The race, in honor of the town's patron saint and part of its fiesta patronale, covers 21 km (13 mi) in the hills of the central town; it's so popular that competitors come from the world over, and the streets are lined with some 200,000 spectators.
Mid-Feb.	Ponce's **Danza Week** of cultural activities celebrates the *danza*, a colonial-era dance similar to the waltz.
Late Feb.	The mountain towns of Maricao and Yauco, centers of the island's coffee-growing region, host the annual **Festival de Café** (Coffee Harvest Festival), honoring both crops and farmers. There's folk music, crafts displays, and booths selling typical foods of the region.
SPRING Mar.	The two-day **Dulce Sueño Paso Fino Fair**, showcasing the island's famous Paso Fino horses, is held in the town of Guayama. Paso Finos are bred and trained to walk with a distinctive, smooth gait, and the horses and their trainers are held in high regard.
	Luquillo celebrates its patron saint at the **Fiestas Patronales de San José**, held each year on March 19. The festivities include traditional dances, colorful parades, and religious processions.
Apr.	Fajardo's **Festival de Chiringas** (Kite Festival) features demonstrations and flying competitions, as well as food and drink booths.

ON THE CALENDAR

	The annual Regata de Veleros Copa Kelly (Kelly Cup Sailboat Regatta) takes place off the coast of Fajardo.
Late Apr.–May	Isabela's Festival de Mundillo (Bobbin Lace Festival) showcases delicate, woven lace with demonstrations and exhibits.
May	Bayamón's Chicharrón Festival celebrates the island's famous puffy, pork-rind fritter. The city has become known for this treat thanks to the many *chicharronero* carts that line Route 2 on the way into town.
	The Fajardo Festival de Bomba y Plena turns the spotlight on Puerto Rico's lively Afro-influenced music and dance.
SUMMER June	In San Juan, the Fiesta de San Juan Bautista (San Juan Bautista Festival) honors the city's patron saint with a week of parades, music, dance, and, ultimately, a traditional backward walk into the ocean to bring good luck in the ensuing year.
June	The annual Heineken JazzFest attracts some 15,000 aficionados to San Juan for four days of outdoor concerts by the likes of David Sánchez, George Benson, Nestor Torres, and Spyro Gyra.
Early June	The annual Casals Festival in San Juan honors the late, great cellist Pablo Casals, who lived in Old San Juan. The 10 days of classical-music performances feature the Puerto Rico Symphony Orchestra as well as soloists from the island and around the world.
Late June–July	Gardenias, lilies, begonias, and thousands of tropical plants are showcased at Aibonito's annual Fiesta de Flores (Flower Festival).
July	Loíza's Fiesta de Santiago Apóstal (St. James Festival), held in July, honors Puerto Rico's African traditions and the apostle St. James with a carnival of street parades, music, and dancing.
Early July	Río Grande celebrates its Carnival, between the first and second week of July with music competitions, parades, and feasts.
Mid-July	The Barranquitas Fería de Artesanía (Barranquitas Artisans' Fair) offers spots to more than 200 local artisans to display their pottery, wood carvings, leather bags and belts, basketry, and other handiwork.
	Around July 16, such coastal towns as Naguabo, Ceiba, and Humacao conduct religious processions honoring the Virgen del Carmen. Offerings of flowers from the *flamboyán* tree are made to this virgin, the patron saint of the fishermen, and festivities continue into the evening.

FALL	
Oct.	Arecibo, on the north coast, holds the Ceti Festival, named after a tiny, sardinelike fish found in the area and considered a culinary delicacy.
Early Oct.	Naguabo's Fiestas Patronales de Nuestra Virgen del Rosario honors Our Lady of the Rosary the first 10 days of October.
Late Oct.	The northern town of Corozal hosts the Festival del Platano (Plantain Festival), which highlights this versatile staple of Puerto Rican cuisine.
Mid-Nov.	The Festival of Puerto Rican Music, held in San Juan and other locations, celebrates the vibrancy of the island's folk music, highlighted by a contest featuring the *cuatro*, a traditional guitar with five double strings.
Late Nov.	Luquillo hosts the three-day Festival de Platos Típicos (Festival of Typical Dishes), highlighting food and drink prepared with coconut.

San Juan

WORD OF MOUTH

"There is so much to do in Old San Juan. Especially if you like to eat and shop. There is so much history there and it is such a great place. It is a beautiful city. I am sure you will have a fantastic time."

—MIM04

"The area surrounding [Santurce Plaza del Mercado] has some cheap and good restaurants and it's also a great spot for 'happy hour' nightlife from about 6 to midnight on Thursday and Friday nights. It's a very casual atmosphere and because it starts early, locals often even take their kids."

—PRnative

Revised and
Updated by
Mark Sullivan

SAN JUAN IS PARADISE'S BABY IN AN URBAN COMFORTER. Puerto Rico's sprawling capital is bordered to the north by the Atlantic and to the east and west by bays and lagoons. More than a third of the island's 4 million citizens are proud to call themselves *sanjuaneros*. They go about their business surrounded by the antique and the modern, the commercial and the residential, the man-made and the natural.

By 1508 the explorer Juan Ponce de León had established a colony in an area now known as Caparra, southeast of present-day San Juan. He later moved the settlement north to a more hospitable peninsular location. In 1521, after he became the first colonial governor, Ponce de León switched the name of the island—which was called San Juan Bautista in honor of St. John the Baptist—with that of the settlement of Puerto Rico (Rich Port). The capital of paradise was born.

Defended by the imposing Fuerte San Felipe del Morro (El Morro), Puerto Rico's administrative and population center helped to keep the island firmly in Spain's hands until 1898, when it came under U.S. control after the Spanish-American War. Centuries of Spanish rule left an indelible imprint on the city, particularly in the walled area now known as Old San Juan. The area, with its cobblestone streets lined with brightly painted, colonial-era structures, has been designated a UNESCO World Heritage Site.

Old San Juan is a monument to the past, but the rest of the city is firmly in the here and now. It draws migrants from elsewhere on the island to jobs in its businesses and industries. It captivates both residents and visitors with its vibrant lifestyle as well as its balmy beaches, pulsing nightclubs, and mesmerizing museums. Wrap yourself up in even one small patch of the urban comforter, and you may never want to leave this baby.

EXPLORING SAN JUAN

San Juan's metro area stretches for 12 mi along Puerto Rico's north coast, and defining the city is rather like assembling a puzzle. Neighborhoods are irregular and sometimes overlapping—not easily pieced together—and the areas most visited by tourists run along the coast.

Farthest west is Old San Juan, the showplace of the island's rich history. On this peninsula you will find the city's finest museums and shops, as well as excellent dining and lodging options. To the east is Puerta de Tierra, a narrow strip of land sandwiched between the ocean and the bay. There are a couple of famous hotels and two noteworthy parks, the Parque de Tercer Milenio and the Parque Muñoz Rivera. Beyond Puerta de Tierra is Condado, a strip of shoreline crowded by resort hotels and apartment buildings. Here you'll find designer fashions in the boutiques and on the people strolling down the main drag of Avenida Ashford. Ocean Park, to the east, is a mostly residential neighborhood; the handful of inns and restaurants here are among the city's best. Beyond Ocean Park is Isla Verde, which looks a lot like Condado.

There are a few other neighborhoods you might explore. South of Condado and Ocean Park lies Santurce, a business district with a growing

TOP 5 PICKS FOR SAN JUAN

- Getting lost among the cobblestone streets of Old San Juan, a UNESCO World Heritage Site.
- Climbing the battlements of Fuerte San Felipe del Morro, the 16th-century fort that dominates the waterfront.
- Window shopping along Condado's Avenida Ashford, where you'll find most of the city's designer boutiques.

- Catching a few rays at Balneario de Carolina, the award-winning beach at the eastern tip of Isla Verde.
- Dining at one of the other stellar restaurants along the southern end of Calle La Fortaleza, a strip so trendy that locals call it "SoFo."

artistic community thanks to the Museo de Arte de Puerto Rico and the Museo de Arte Contemporaneo. Hato Rey is a busy financial district, where you'll find the large Plaza las Américas Mall. The mostly residential Río Piedras area is home of the Universidad de Puerto Rico.

When to Tour San Juan

The high season is roughly mid-December through mid-April. Winter hotel rates are a bit higher than in the off-season, and hotels tend to be packed, though rarely entirely full. A winter visit may allow you to participate in several colorful annual events on the San Juan social calendar. The January San Sebastián Street Festival, held in Old San Juan, consists of several nights of live music in the plazas, food festivals, and *cabezudos* (parades) in which folk legends are caricatured using oversize masks. A near-winter festival, the mid-November Festival of Puerto Rican Music, is held both in San Juan venues and out on the island. The festival celebrates Puerto Rico's traditional *plena* and *bomba* folk music with competitions and concerts.

A less expensive time to visit San Juan is during the "shoulder" seasons of fall and spring, when the weather is still fantastic and the tourist crush is less intense. Weather in San Juan is moderate and tropical year-round, with an average temperature of about 82°F (26°C). And although it's true that much of the summer encompasses the hurricane season, San Juan is still an attractive destination during those months—many accommodations charge the lowest rates of the year, restaurant reservations are easier to come by, and the streets are free of tourists.

Old San Juan

Old San Juan is compelling. Its 16th-century cobblestone streets, ornate Spanish town houses with wrought-iron balconies, busy plazas, and museums are all repositories of the island's history. Founded in 1521 by the Spanish explorer Juan Ponce de León, Old San Juan sits on a peninsula separated from the "new" parts of the city by a couple of miles and a couple of centuries. Ironically, it's youthful and vibrant. It has a cul-

Exploring
Old San Juan

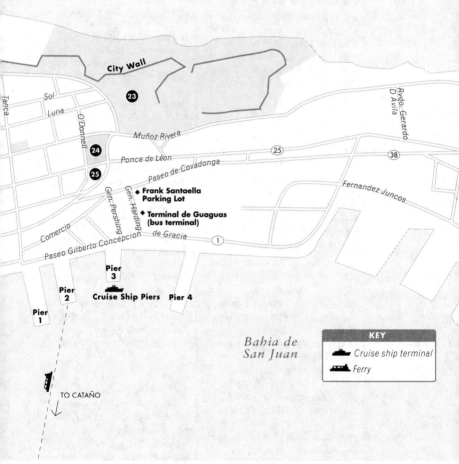

ATLANTIC OCEAN

City Wall

23

Tanca
Sol
Luna
O'Donnell
Muñoz Rivera
24
Ponce de León
25
Paseo de Covadonga
Gen. Pershing
Gen. Harding

♦ **Frank Santaella Parking Lot**

♦ **Terminal de Guaguas (bus terminal)**

Comercio
Paseo Gilberto Concepción
de Gracia
(1)

(25)

(38)

Rvdo. Gerardo D'Ávila

Fernández Juncos

Pier 3

Pier 2
Cruise Ship Piers   **Pier 4**

Pier 1

TO CATAÑO

Bahía de San Juan

KEY
🚢 Cruise ship terminal
⛴ Ferry

A GOOD WALK

Not far from the cruise ship docks is Plaza de la Dársena, a tree-shaded square surrounded by horse-drawn carriages waiting for passengers. Here you'll find **La Casita ❶** ⌐, a colonial-style structure that houses a tourist information center. Pick up a map of the city, then head west along the **Paseo de la Princesa ❷**, a wide promenade that stretches to the Bahía de San Juan. You'll pass the Antigua Cárcel de la Princesa, a prison dating from the colonial era, as you walk toward the water. On your right will be the massive walls that protected the city from invaders, including the British and the Dutch. There were once five entrances to the city, each heavily guarded against attack. You get a sense of how difficult it was to storm the barricades when you approach the portal called the **Puerta de San Juan ❸**.

Passing through the Puerta de San Juan, you find yourself inside the city walls. To the north you'll find a small square, the **Plazuela de la Rogativa ❹**. The statue here of a priest and three women commemorates the historic moment when British attackers were frightened off by torches of a religious procession, or *rogativa*, which they mistook for Spanish reinforcements. A block east from the Puerta de San Juan is another small square, called the Plaza de la Catedral. True to its name, the square faces the **Catedral de San Juan Bautista ❺**. On the northern edge of the square is a former nunnery, now converted into a luxury hotel called El Convento. The central courtyard is a great place to stop for a cool drink. On the west

side of Plaza de la Catedral is the child-friendly **Museo del Niño ❻**, which has three floors of interactive exhibits.

Head two blocks south on Calle Cristo, then one block west on Calle Fortaleza. Directly ahead of you is **La Fortaleza ❼**, the imposing former bastion now used as the governor's residence. Backtrack to Calle Cristo and head south. On the east side of the street is the **Centro Nacional de Artes Populares y Artesanías ❽**, which displays arts and crafts from around the island. Next door is the **Casa del Libro ❾**, with exhibits on books and bookbinding. At the end of the block is the **Capilla del Cristo ❿**, an ornate 18th-century chapel. The wrought-iron gates are rarely unlocked, but you can gaze through the bars at the ornate altar. To the right of the chapel is yet another small square, the **Parque de las Palomas ⓫**. This one is a roost for many of the city's pigeons. A block and a half east of here, along Calle Tetuán, is the **Casa de Ramón Power y Giralt ⓬**, the restored home of an 18th-century naval hero and politician.

Follow Calle San José north for a few blocks to the **Plaza de Armas ⓭**, the main square bordered by calles San José, San Francisco, and Cruz. On the west side of the plaza, the regal edifice known as La Intendencia once served as the Spanish Treasury. Today it houses Puerto Rico's State Department. On the north side of the plaza is the **Alcaldía ⓮**, the former city hall built between 1604 and 1789.

Continue following Calle San José until you reach Calle San Sebastián. A block-long street almost directly ahead of you leads to the massive **Museo de Arte y Historia de San Juan** ⓯, once a bustling marketplace and now an art and history museum. A block west on Calle San Sebastián is Plaza San José, a cobblestone square surrounded by colonial-era structures. The most prominent is the **Iglesia de San José** ⓰, one of the oldest churches in the Western Hemisphere. On the plaza's eastern edge are two museums: the two-story **Museo Pablo Casals** ⓱, which celebrates the life and art of the famous cellist, and the **Museo de Nuestra Raíz Africana** ⓲, which investigates African influences on Puerto Rico's culture. West of the church is the **Convento de los Dominicos** ⓳, now home to the bookshop of the Instituto de Cultura Puertorriqueña. A short walk west on Calle San Sebastián will bring you to the **Casa Blanca** ⓴, constructed in 1521 as a home for the founder of the city, Juan Ponce de León. It was rebuilt in 1523 after a hurricane destroyed the original.

West on Calle Norzagaray, you'll pass the large Plaza de Quinto Centenario, a tribute to the quincentennial of Columbus's voyages. (You can't miss the odd obelisk, embedded with shards of pottery.) On its west side is the Cuartel de Ballajá, a three-story structure that once served as a military barracks. Today the second floor is home to the **Museo de las Américas** ㉑ and its rotating exhibits of Latin American art. From here you can already see Old San Juan's star attraction, **Fuerte San Felipe del Morro** ㉒. The fort,

better known as El Morro, was built between 1540 and 1783.

East on Calle Norzagaray is Old San Juan's second fort. **Fuerte San Cristóbal** ㉓, built in the 18th century, is every bit as interesting as El Morro, but it attracts a fraction of the tourists. Near its base is the **Plaza de Colón** ㉔, bordered by Calle San Francisco and Calle O'Donnell and adorned with a large statue of Christopher Columbus. On the south side of the plaza, across Calle Fortaleza on Calle Recinto Sur, stands the **Teatro Tapia** ㉕, which has been hosting performances since 1832.

ture unto itself, reflecting the sensibilities of the stylish professionals, the bohemian art crowd, and the skateboarding teenagers who populate its streets. You'll find more streetfront cafés and restaurants, more contemporary art galleries, more musicians playing in plazas, than anywhere else in San Juan.

At the northwest end of Old San Juan, Calle Norzagaray leads to El Morro, the old city's defense bastion. On the north side of Calle Norzagaray you'll note a small neighborhood at the foot of an embankment, bordering the ocean—this is La Perla, a rough neighborhood that you would do best to avoid. The west end of the old city faces San Juan Bay, and it's here that the sandstone walls of the original city are most in evidence. On Old San Juan's south side you'll find the commercial and cruise-ship piers that jut into San Juan Harbor.

Numbers in the text correspond to numbers in the margin and on the Old San Juan map.

TIMING &   Old San Juan is a small neighborhood, approximately seven city blocks
PRECAUTIONS   square. In strictly geographical terms, it's easily traversed in a day. But to truly appreciate the numerous museums, galleries, and cafés requires two or three days—and the walk described above is designed with that in mind. If you're limited to a day, you'll need to pick and choose sights according to your interests. It can be done—it's just not quite so rewarding.

Don't consider driving in Old San Juan unless you have a penchant for sitting in traffic jams for much of the waking day. Old San Juan is a walking city, with narrow, one-way streets, narrower alleys, little parking, and sights and shops packed together in an area hardly larger than ½ square mi. Some of the streets are steep and paved with cobblestones, so wear comfortable shoes as well as a hat and sunscreen—and drink plenty of water. Old San Juan is generally a safe area, but keep in mind that pickpockets visit the same places as tourists. Keep money and credit cards out of back pockets and avoid carrying open handbags. Street hustlers are few and far between, but you will find the occasional, mostly harmless, indigent asking for money.

Free trolleys swing through Old San Juan all day, every day—they depart from the main bus terminal area across from Pier 4 and take two routes through the Old City. One route heads north to Calle Norzagaray then west to El Morro (the trolley doesn't go into El Morro, but drops you off at the long footpath leading to the fort), then south along Calle Cristo to Fortaleza, San Justo, and back along Calle Gilberto Concepción de Gracia (also called Calle la Marina) to the piers. Another takes you to the Plaza de Armas, south on Calle San José, then back to the piers. Both make regular stops (at signs marked PARADA) on their routes. When you're finished touring, taxis can be found in several spots: in front of Pier 2, on the Plaza de Armas, or on Calle O'Donnell near the Plaza de Colón.

What to See

⓮ Alcaldía. San Juan's city hall was built between 1604 and 1789. In 1841, extensive alterations were made so that it would resemble the city hall in Madrid, with arcades, towers, balconies, and an inner courtyard.

IF YOU LIKE

ARCHITECTURE

San Juan has been under construction for nearly 500 years. The Old City's colonial Spanish row houses—brick with plaster fronts painted in pastel blues, oranges, and yellows—line narrow streets and alleys paved with *adoquines* (blue-gray stones originally used as ballast in Spanish ships). Several churches, including the Catedral de San Juan Bautista, were built in the ornate Spanish Gothic style of the 16th century. The massive, white-marble El Capitolio, home of Puerto Rico's legislature, was completed in 1929. The gleaming high-rise resorts along the beaches in Condado and Isla Verde and the glistening steel-and-glass towers in the business and financial district of Hato Rey belong to the end of the 20th century.

BEACHES

Just because you're staying in the city doesn't mean you'll have to forgo time on the *playa* (beach). San Juan's beaches are among the island's best, and Condado, Isla Verde, and Ocean Park—to name just a few sandy stretches—are always abuzz. The government maintains 13 *balnearios* (public beaches), including two in the San Juan metro area. They're gated and have dressing rooms, lifeguards, parking, and in some cases picnic tables, playgrounds, and camping facilities. Admission is free; hours are generally daily from 9 to 5 in summer and Tuesday through Sunday from 9 to 5 during the rest of the year.

MUSIC

Music is a source of Puerto Rican pride, and it seems that, increasingly, everyone wants to live that *vida loca* (crazy life) espoused by Puerto Rico's own Ricky Martin. The brash Latin sound is best characterized by the music-dance form salsa, which shares not only its name with the word "sauce," but also its zesty, hot flavor. This fusion of West African percussion, jazz (especially swing and Big Band), and other Latin beats (mambo, merengue, flamenco, cha-cha, rumba) is sexy and primal. Dancing to it is a chance to let go of inhibitions.

NIGHTLIFE

Almost a big city, San Juan boasts a wide variety of restaurants and bars for people of all palates and party habits. Old San Juan and Condado, in particular, are big nighttime destinations. Many of the newer establishments have set their tables on terraces, on the beach, on indoor patios, or simply streetside to take advantage of the late-night atmosphere. Many clubs and discos open until the wee hours of the morning. Casinos are also a big attraction, mostly for visitors. Locals tend to test their luck after a wedding reception in a big hotel, unless they're regulars at the slot machines.

Renovations have refreshed the facade of the building and some interior rooms, but the architecture remains true to its colonial style. A municipal tourist information center and an art gallery with rotating exhibits are on the first floor ⊠ *153 Calle San Francisco, Plaza de Armas, Old San Juan* ☎ *787/724–7171* ✆ *Free* ⊘ *Weekdays 8–4.*

⑩ Capilla del Cristo. According to legend, in 1753 a young horseman named Baltazar Montañez, carried away during festivities in honor of San Juan Bautista (St. John the Baptist), raced down Calle Cristo and plunged over its steep precipice. A witness to the tragedy promised to build a chapel if the young man's life could be saved. Historical records maintain the man died, but legend contends that he lived. (Another version of the story has it that the horse miraculously stopped before plunging over the cliff.) Regardless, this chapel was built, and inside is a small silver altar dedicated to the Christ of Miracles. ⊠ *End of Calle Cristo, Old San Juan* ☎ *No phone* ✆ *Free.*

⑳ Casa Blanca. The original structure on this site was a frame house built in 1521 as a home for Ponce de León. But he died in Cuba, never having lived in the home, which was virtually destroyed by a hurricane in 1523. Afterward, his son-in-law had the present masonry home built. His descendants occupied the house for 250 years. From the end of the Spanish-American War in 1898 to 1966 it housed the U.S. Army commander in Puerto Rico. A museum devoted to archaeology is on the second floor. Select rooms, with period furniture, are open for viewing as well. The surrounding garden, cooled by fountains, is a tranquil spot for a restorative pause. ⊠ *1 Calle San Sebastián, Old San Juan* ☎ *787/725–1454* ⊕ *www.icp.gobierno.pr* ✆ *$2* ⊘ *Tues.–Sat. 8:30–4:20.*

⑨ Casa del Libro. On a pleasant side street, this 18th-century house contains a museum dedicated to the artistry of the printed word. The 6,000-piece collection includes some 200 rare volumes dating back more than 500 years, as well as what appears to be legal writing on a fragment of clay from 2,000 years ago. Also on hand are several antique printing presses, one constructed in 1812 in France and later brought to Puerto Rico. There are interesting temporary exhibits as well. ⊠ *255 Calle Cristo, Old San Juan* ☎ *787/723–0354* ⊕ *www.lacasadellibro.org* ✆ *$2 donation suggested* ⊘ *Tues.–Sat. 11–4:30.*

☝ ⑫ Casa de Ramón Power y Giralt. The restored home of 18th-century naval hero Don Ramón Power y Giralt is now the headquarters of the Conservation Trust of Puerto Rico. On-site are several displays highlighting the physical, cultural, and historical importance of land and properties on the island under the trust's aegis. You'll find a display of musical instruments that you can play, a bird diorama with recorded bird songs, an active beehive, and a seven-minute movie discussing the trust's efforts. Displays are in Spanish; the movie is in English or Spanish. A gift shop sells toys and Puerto Rican candies. ⊠ *155 Calle Tetuán, Old San Juan* ☎ *787/722–5834* ✆ *Free* ⊘ *Tues.–Sat. 10–4.*

❶ La Casita. With a name that means "Little House," La Casita was built in the 1930s to handle traffic at the nearby port. Today the beautiful building, with yellow stucco walls and a barrel-tile roof, serves as an information center run by the Puerto Rico Tourism Company. The friendly staff will give you all the maps and brochures you can carry. ⊠ *Plaza de la Dársena, Old San Juan* ☎ *787/722–1709* ⊕ *www. gotopuertorico.com* ☉ *Sat.–Wed. 8:30–8, Thurs. and Fri. 8:30–5:30.*

❺ Catedral de San Juan Bautista. The Catholic shrine of Puerto Rico had humble beginnings in the early 1520s as a thatch-roof, wooden structure. Hurricane winds tore off the thatch and destroyed the church. It was reconstructed in 1540, when it was given a graceful circular staircase and vaulted Gothic ceilings. Most of the work on the present cathedral, however, was done in the 19th century. The remains of Ponce de León are in a marble tomb near the transept. The trompe-l'oeil work on the inside of the dome is breathtaking. Unfortunately, many of the other frescos suffer from water damage. ⊠ *151 Calle Cristo, Old San Juan* ☎ *787/722–0861* ⊕ *www.catedralsanjuan.com* ⊠ *$1 donation suggested* ☉ *Mon.–Sat. 8–5, Sun. 8–2:30.*

❽ Centro Nacional de Artes Populares y Artesanías. Run by the Institute of Puerto Rican Culture, the Popular Arts & Crafts Center is in a colonial building next to the Casa del Libro and is a superb repository of island crafts, some of which are for sale. ⊠ *253 Calle Cristo, Old San Juan* ☎ *787/722–0621* ⊠ *Free* ☉ *Mon.–Sat. 9–5.*

⓳ Convento de los Dominicos. Built by Dominican friars in 1523, this convent often served as a shelter during Carib Indian attacks and, more recently, as headquarters for the Antilles command of the U.S. Army. Now home to some offices of the Institute of Puerto Rican Culture, the beautifully restored building contains religious manuscripts, artifacts, and art. The institute also maintains a book and music shop on the premises. Classical concerts are held here occasionally. ⊠ *98 Calle Norzagaray, Old San Juan* ☎ *787/721–6866* ⊠ *Free* ☉ *Mon.–Sat. 9–5.*

❼ La Fortaleza. Sitting on a hill overlooking the harbor, La Fortaleza was built as a fortress in 1533. Not a very good fortress, mind you. It was attacked numerous times and taken twice, by the British in 1598 and by the Dutch in 1625. When the city's other fortifications were finished, La Fortaleza was transformed into a palace. Numerous changes to the original primitive structure over the past four centuries have resulted in the present collection of marble and mahogany, medieval towers, and stained-glass galleries. The Western Hemisphere's oldest executive mansion in continuous use, it is still the official residence of the island's governor. Guided tours of the extensive gardens and the circular dungeon are conducted on the hour in English, on the half-hour in Spanish; both include a short video presentation. Call ahead, as sometimes tours are canceled because of official functions. The tours begin near the main gate in a yellow building called the Real Audiencia. ⊠ *Calle Recinto Oeste, Old San Juan* ☎ *787/721–7000 Ext. 2211* ⊕ *www.fortaleza. gobierno.pr* ⊠ *Free* ☉ *Weekdays 9–3:30.*

NEED A BREAK? On your hike up hilly Calle Cristo, stop at Ben & Jerry's (⊠ 61 Calle Cristo, Old San Juan ☎ 787/977–6882) at the corner of Calle Sol. You can savor Vermont ice cream under a palm tree or enjoy fresh-fruit smoothies next to a Green Mountain cow—depending on how you look at it. Olympic gymnast Michelle Campi and her mother, Celi Williams, have made this ice-cream parlor one of the friendliest hangouts in Old San Juan.

㉓ Fuerte San Cristóbal. This stone fortress, built between 1634 and 1785, guarded the city from land attacks. Even larger than El Morro, San Cristóbal was known in the 17th and 18th centuries as the Gibraltar of the West Indies. Five free-standing structures are connected by tunnels, and restored units include an 18th-century barracks. You're free to explore the gun turrets, officers' quarters, and passageways. Along with El Morro, San Cristóbal is a National Historic Site administered by the U.S. Park Service; it's a UN World Heritage Site as well. Rangers conduct tours in Spanish and English. ✉ *Calle Norzagaray, Old San Juan* ☎ *787/729–6960* ⊕ *www.nps.gov/saju* 🎫 *$3; $5 includes admission to El Morro* ☉ *Daily 9–5.*

Fodor'sChoice
★

㉒ Fuerte San Felipe del Morro. On a rocky promontory at the northwestern tip of the Old City is El Morro (which translates as "promontory"), a fortress built by the Spaniards between 1540 and 1783. Rising 140 feet above the sea, the massive six-level fortress covers enough territory to accommodate a 9-hole golf course. It is a labyrinth of dungeons, ramps, barracks, turrets, towers, and tunnels. Built to protect the port, El Morro has a commanding view of the harbor. You're free to wander throughout. The cannon emplacement walls are thick as a child's arm is long, and the dank secret passageways are a wonder of engineering. The fort's small but enlightening museum displays ancient Spanish guns and other armaments, military uniforms, and blueprints for Spanish forts in the Americas. There's also a gift shop. The fort is a National Historic Site administered by the U.S. Park Service; it's a UN World Heritage Site as well. Tours and a video are available in English. ✉ *Calle Norzagaray, Old San Juan* ☎ *787/729–6960* ⊕ *www.nps.gov/saju* 🎫 *$3; $5 includes admission to Fuerte San Cristóbal* ☉ *Daily 9–5.*

⓰ Iglesia de San José. With its vaulted ceilings, this church is a splendid example of 16th-century Spanish Gothic architecture. It was built under the supervision of Dominican friars in 1532, making it one of the oldest churches in the Western Hemisphere. The body of Ponce de León, the Spanish explorer who came to the New World seeking the Fountain of Youth, was buried here for almost three centuries before being moved to the Catedral de San Juan Bautista in 1913. At this writing, much-needed renovations were underway, meaning that the church was closed through much of 2006. ✉ *Calle San Sebastián, Plaza de San José, Old San Juan* ☎ *787/725–7501.*

⓯ Museo de Arte y Historia de San Juan. A bustling marketplace in 1855, this handsome building is now the modern San Juan Museum of Art and History. You'll find exhibits of Puerto Rican art and audiovisual shows that present the island's history. Concerts and other cultural events take place in the huge interior courtyard. ✉ *150 Calle Norzagaray, at Calle MacArthur, Old San Juan* ☎ *787/724–1875* 🎫 *Free* ☉ *Tues.–Sun. 10–4.*

CLOSE UP

Peaceful Music

1

CELLIST PABLO CASALS was one of the 20th century's most influential musicians. Born in Catalonia in 1876, he studied in Spain and Belgium, settled for a time in Paris, then returned to Barcelona. Tours in Europe, the United States, and South America brought him artistic and financial success and opportunities to collaborate with other prominent musicians.

By the advent of the Spanish Civil War, he was an internationally famous musician, teacher, and conductor. He was also an outspoken supporter of a democratic Spain. Forced into exile by Franco's regime, Casals arrived in Puerto Rico, his mother's birthplace, in 1956. Here the 81-year-old maestro continued to work and teach. He established the Casals Festival of Classical Music, making it a home for sublime orchestral and chamber works. During two weeks each June, the Puerto Rico Symphony Orchestra is joined by musicians from all over the world.

In Catalan, Casal's first name is "Pau," which appropriately enough means "peace." He and his friend Albert Schweitzer appealed to the world powers to stop the arms race, and he made what many experts say is his greatest work—an oratorio titled *The Manger*—his personal message of peace. Casals died in Puerto Rico in 1973, but his many legacies live on. His favorite instruments, his recordings, and some of his many awards are preserved at the Museo Pablo Casals.

–Karen English

---

❷❶ **Museo de las Américas.** One of the finest collections of its type in Puerto Rico, the Museum of the Americas is on the second floor of the imposing former military barracks, Cuartel de Ballajá. Most exhibits rotate, but the focus is on the popular and folk art of Latin America. The permanent exhibit, "Las Artes Populares en las Américas," has religious figures, musical instruments, basketwork, costumes, farming implements, and other artifacts of the Americas. The old military barracks, big and boxy in a neoclassical style and painted green and peach, was built between 1854 and 1864, and its immense inner courtyard is used for concerts and private events such as weddings. With a little notice, the staff can take you on a guided tour. ✉ *Calle Norzagaray and Calle del Morro, Old San Juan* ☎ *787/724–5052* ⊕ *www.museolasamericas. org* 🎟 *Free* ☉ *Tues.–Sun. 10–4.*

☾ ❻ **Museo del Niño.** This three-floor, hands-on "museum" is pure fun for kids. There are games to play, clothes for dress-up, a mock plaza with market, and even a barbershop where children can play (no real scissors here). One of the newer exhibits is an immense food-groups pyramid, where children can climb to place magnets representing different foods. Older children will appreciate the top-floor garden where bugs and plants are on display, and the little ones can pretend to go shopping or to work at a construction site. For toddlers, there's a playground.

Note that the when it reaches capacity, the museum stops selling tickets. ⊠ *150 Calle Cristo* ☎ *787/722–3791* ⊕ *www.museodelninopr. org* 🔊 *$5, $7 for children* ⊗ *Tues.–Fri. 9–5, weekends 11:30–5:30.*

⑱ Museo de Nuestra Raíz Africana. The Institute of Puerto Rican Culture created this museum to help Puerto Ricans understand African influences in island culture. On display over two floors are African musical instruments, documents relating to the slave trade, and a list of African words that have made it into popular Puerto Rican culture. ⊠ *101 Calle San Sebastián, Plaza de San José, Old San Juan* ☎ *787/724–4294* ⊕ *www.icp.gobierno.pr* 🔊 *Free* ⊗ *Tues.–Sat. 8:30–4:20.*

⑰ Museo Pablo Casals. The small, two-story museum contains memorabilia of the famed cellist, who made his home in Puerto Rico from 1956 until his death in 1973. Manuscripts, photographs, and his favorite cellos are on display, in addition to recordings and videotapes (shown on request) of Casals Festival concerts, which he instituted in 1957. The festival is held annually in June. ⊠ *101 Calle San Sebastián, Plaza de San José, Old San Juan* ☎ *787/723–9185* 🔊 *$1* ⊗ *Tues.–Sat. 9:30–5:30.*

⊙ ⑪ Parque de las Palomas. Never have birds had it so good. The small, shaded park bordering Old San Juan's Capilla del Cristo has a large stone wall with pigeonholes cut into it. Hundreds of *palomas* (pigeons) roost here, and the park is full of cooing local children chasing the well-fed birds. There's a small kiosk where you can buy refreshments and bags of seed to feed the birds. Stop to enjoy the wide views over the bay.

❷ Paseo de la Princesa. This street down at the port is spruced up with flowers, trees, benches, street lamps, and a striking fountain depicting the various ethnic groups of Puerto Rico. Take a seat and watch the boats zip across the water. At the west end of the paseo, beyond the fountain, is the beginning of a shoreline path that hugs Old San Juan's walls and leads to the city gate at Calle San Juan.

⑬ Plaza de Armas. The old city's original main square was once used as military drilling grounds. Bordered by calles San Francisco, Rafael Codero, San José, and Cruz, it has a fountain with 19th-century statues representing the four seasons, as well as a bandstand and a small café. This is one of the most popular meeting places in Old San Juan, so you're likely to encounter everything from local bands to artists sketching caricatures to street preachers imploring the wicked to repent.

NEED A BREAK? At **Café 4 Estaciones,** on the Plaza de Armas in Old San Juan, tables and chairs sit under a canvas canopy surrounded by potted plants. It's the perfect spot to put down your shopping bags and rest your tired feet. Grab a café con leche (coffee with hot milk), an espresso, or cold drink, and watch the children chase the pigeons.

㉔ Plaza de Colón. A statue of Christopher Columbus stands atop a high pedestal in this bustling Old San Juan square. Originally called St. James Square, it was renamed in honor of Columbus on the 400th anniversary of his arrival in Puerto Rico. Bronze plaques on the statue's base

GREAT ITINERARIES

IF YOU HAVE 1 DAY

Many people find themselves with a single day—or even less—to explore San Juan. There should be no question about your destination—head to Old San Juan. Ramble through the cobblestone streets and duck into the many shops, but save plenty of time for exploring the turrets, towers, and dungeons of **Fuerte San Felipe del Morro ㉒**, the original fortress on a rocky promontory at the old city's northwestern tip.

IF YOU HAVE 3 DAYS

It's only fitting that you spend the first day on a *playa* (beach). Choose from the city's finest at Condado, Ocean Park, or Isla Verde, and park yourself in a rented chair with a good book, a cold drink, and plenty of sunscreen. In the evening, make sure you enjoy the warm weather by dining alfresco. On the second day take a walking tour of Old San Juan. What to see? **Fuerte San Felipe del Morro ㉒** is at the top of the list, but it can often be crowded. You might want to explore the equally enthralling **Fuerte San Cristóbal ㉓**, which has underground tunnels and hidden passages. The city's original fortress, **La Fortaleza ❼**, wasn't

much protection from marauding pirates, but it does a great job at sheltering the governor. And **Casa Blanca ⑳**, a home built for Juan Ponce de León, is a wonderful way to explore how the Spanish lived in the colonial days. On your third day, hop the ferry across the bay to Cataño for a tour of the **Casa Bacardí Visitor Center ㉜**. Return in time for some shopping in the high-end shops along Calle Cristo, then dinner in one of the trendy eateries on Calle Fortaleza.

IF YOU HAVE 5 DAYS

Follow the itinerary above for your first three days in San Juan. On Day 4 head for the Santurce district. You can immerse yourself in island art at the **Museo de Arte Contemporáneo de Puerto Rico ㉘** and the **Museo de Arte de Puerto Rico ㉙**. Afterward, wander through the produce at the Plaza del Mercado in Santurce, with a fresh papaya or soursop shake in hand, and have your palm read. Be sure to note the giant bronze sculptures of avocados by artist by Annex Burgos. On the morning of Day 5, hit the beach once more, then head to Avenida Ashford in Condado for an afternoon of shopping in its ritzy boutiques.

relate various episodes in the life of the great explorer. On the north side of the plaza is a terminal for buses to and from San Juan.

❹ **Plazuela de la Rogativa.** According to legend, the British, while laying siege to the city in 1797, mistook the flaming torches of a *rogativa*—religious procession—for Spanish reinforcements, and beat a hasty retreat. In this little plaza statues of a bishop and three women commemorate the legend. The monument was created in 1971 by the artist Lindsay Daen to mark the Old City's 450th anniversary. ✉ *Caleta de las Monjas, Old San Juan.*

③ Puerta de San Juan. Dating back to 1520, this was one of the five original entrances to the city. The massive gate, painted a brilliant shade of
red, gave access from the port. It resembles a tunnel because it passes
through La Muralla, the 20-foot-thick city walls. ⊠ *Paseo de la Princesa,
Old San Juan.*

㉕ Teatro Tapia. Named after the Puerto Rican playwright Alejandro Tapia
y Rivera, this municipal theater was built in 1832 and remodeled in 1949
and again in 1987. It showcases ballets, plays, and operettas. Stop by
the box office to find out what's showing. ⊠ *Plaza de Colón, Old San
Juan* ☎ *787/721–0169.*

Greater San Juan

Modern San Juan is a study in congested highways and cement-block
housing complexes, as well as the resorts of Condado and Isla Verde.
Sightseeing in the modern city requires more effort than it does in Old
San Juan—the sights are scattered in the suburbs, accessible by taxi, bus,
or a rental car, but not on foot.

Avenidas Muñoz Rivera, Ponce de León, and Fernández Juncos are the
main thoroughfares that cross Puerta de Tierra, just east of Old San Juan,
to the neighborhoods of Condado, Ocean Park, and Isla Verde. Puente
Dos Hermanos, the "Bridge of the Two Brothers," connects Puerta de
Tierra with Condado. Avenida Ashford, which splits off into Avenida
Magdalena for a few blocks, travels through Condado to Ocean Park.
Calle Loíza connects Ocean Park with Isla Verde. These streets can be
choked with traffic, so if you are traveling more than a few blocks, consider taking the speedier Route 26.

Due south of the Laguna del Condado is Miramar, home to a few notable hotels and restaurants. Although it has a slightly seedy feel, it is
clearly on its way up. South of Condado and Ocean Park is Santurce,
a mostly commercial district where you'll find the Museo de Arte de Puerto
Rico and the Museo de Arte Contemporaneo. Hato Rey, south of Santurce, is a busy financial district, where you'll find the large Plaza las
Américas Mall. Even farther south is residential Río Piedras, home of
the Universidad de Puerto Rico.

*Numbers in the text correspond to numbers in the margin and on the
Greater San Juan map.*

**A GOOD
TOUR**

East of Old San Juan on Avenida Ponce de León you'll find **El Capitolio** ㉖ ▶,
Puerto Rico's magnificent capitol building. At the east end of Puerta de
Tierra is the Caribe Hilton, where you'll find the small bastion **Fuerte
San Gerónimo** ㉗. This little fort once guarded an entrance to the Bahía
de San Juan. Take Avenida Ashford east, branching off onto Avenida
Magdalena and then Calle Luiza. At the corner of Avenida Ponce de León
is the **Museo de Arte Contemporáneo de Puerto Rico** ㉘, with a fine collection of contemporary Puerto Rican art. Head east on Avenida Ponce de
León, then north on Avenida José de Diego to reach the **Museo de Arte
de Puerto Rico** ㉙, a former hospital that has been transformed into the
island's most ambitious art museum.

From the museum, it's a straight ride south on Avenida Ponce de León (Route 25) to the Río Piedras district, where you'll find the Universidad de Puerto Rico and its **Museo de Historia, Antropología y Arte** ㉚. Less than 1 mi to the west, at the junction of routes 1 and 847, is the 75-acre **Jardín Botánico** ㉛.

TIMING   Depending on what mode of transportation you choose, you can see these sights in a day; if you linger in the museums, exploring the Greater San Juan area might require two days. Buses are the least expensive but most time-consuming way to travel. Taxis are more convenient and you won't get lost—consider hiring a taxi by the hour and covering your selected sights in a couple of hours. Taxis charge $30 per hour for city tours, but the rate can be negotiable for long stretches of time. If you choose to rent a car, get a good map. San Juan's roads are well marked, but one-way streets pop up out of nowhere, and traffic jams at rush hour are frequent.

What to See

㉖ **El Capitolio.** The white-marble Capitol, a fine example of Italian Renaissance–style, dates from 1929. The grand rotunda, which can be seen from all over San Juan, was completed in the late 1990s. Fronted by eight Corinthian columns, it's a very dignified home for the commonwealth's constitution. Although the Senate and the House of Representatives have offices in the more modern buildings on either side, the Capitol is where the legislators meet. You can also watch the legislature in action—note that the action is in Spanish—when it is in session, most often Monday and Tuesday. Guided tours, which take 45 minutes and include visits to the rotunda and other parts of the building, are by appointment only. ⊠ *Av. Ponce de León, Puerta de Tierra* ☎ *787/977–4929* ⊕ *www. gotopuertorico.com* ⊡ *Free* ☉ *Weekdays 9–5, Sat. 9–1.*

㉗ **Fuerte San Gerónimo.** At the eastern tip of Puerta de Tierra, this tiny fort is perched on a hilltop like an afterthought. Added to San Juan's fortifications in the 18th century, it barely survived the British attack of 1797. Restored in 1983 by the Institute of Puerto Rican Culture, it's now open to the public. To find it, go to the entrance of the Caribe Hilton. ⊠ *Calle Rosales, Puerta de Tierra* ☎ *787/724–5477.*

㉛   The Universidad de Puerto Rico's main attraction is the **Jardín Botánico** (Botanical Garden), a 75-acre forest of more than 200 species of tropical and subtropical vegetation. Gravel footpaths lead to a graceful lotus lagoon, a bamboo promenade, an orchid garden with some 30,000 plants, and a palm garden. Signs are in Spanish and English. Trail maps are available at the entrance gate, and groups of 10 or more can arrange guided tours ($25). ⊠ *Intersection of Rtes. 1 and 847 at entrance to Barrio Venezuela, Río Piedras* ☎ *787/767–1710* ⊕ *www.upr.clu.edu* ⊡ *Free* ☉ *Daily 9–4:30.*

㉘ **Museo de Arte Contemporáneo de Puerto Rico.** This Georgian-style structure, once a public school, displays a dynamic range of works by both established and up-and-coming Puerto Rican artists. Many of the works on display have strong political messages, including pointed commentaries on the island's status as a commonwealth. Only a small part of

Fodor'sChoice
★

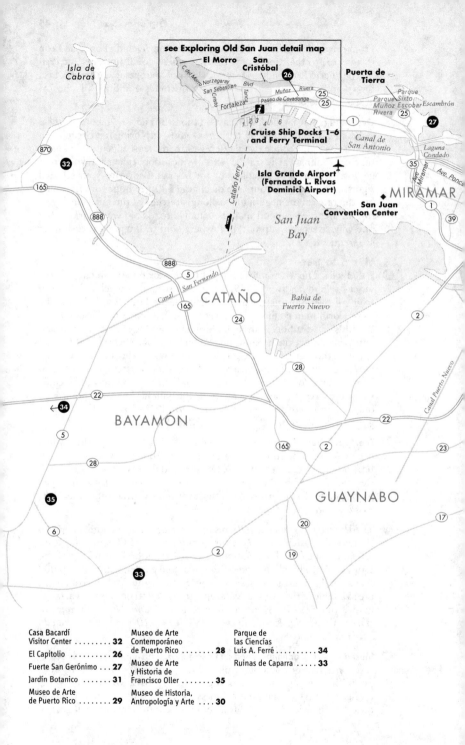

see **Exploring Old San Juan** detail map

El Morro   **San Cristóbal**

26

C del Morro
Norzagaray
San Sebastian
Blvd
Muñoz   Rivera
Fortaleza
Paseo de Covadonga
1 2 3 4 5 6

Puerta de Tierra

Parque Sixto Escambrón
Parque Muñoz Escobar Rivera

25
25
25

27

Cruise Ship Docks 1–6 and Ferry Terminal

Canal de San Antonio

Laguna Condado

Isla Grande Airport (Fernando L. Rivas Dominici Airport)

35

◆ MIRAMAR

San Juan Convention Center

1

39

San Juan Bay

Cataño Ferry

Isla de Cabras

870

32

165

888

888

5   San Fernando

Canal
165

CATAÑO

24

Bahía de Puerto Nuevo

2

28

Canal Puerto Nuevo

22

22

← 34

BAYAMÓN

5

28

35

6

165   2

2

23

GUAYNABO

20

17

19

2

33

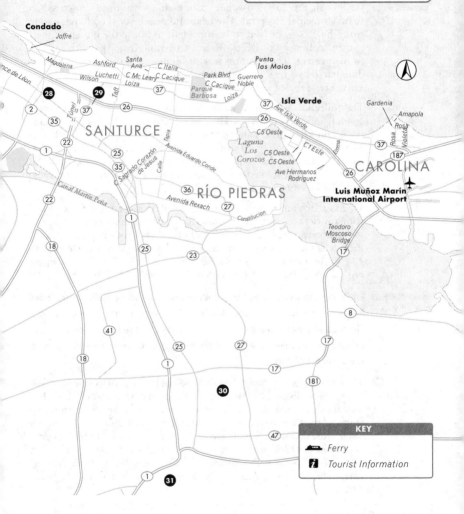

Exploring
Greater San Juan

ATLANTIC OCEAN

Condado
Joffre

Magdalena
Ashford
Santa Ana
C Italia
Park Blvd
Punta las Maias

Wilson
Luchetti
C Mc Lean
C Cacique
Guerrero Noble
Loiza
C Cacique

Taft
Parque Barbosa
Loiza

28
29

2
35
37
26
37
Isla Verde
Gardenia
Amapola

22
1
Tunel
SANTURCE
26
Ave Isla Verde
Rosa
Rosa
Violeta

C5 Oeste
37

35
25
Avenida Eduardo Conde
Laguna Los Corozos
C5 Oeste
C5 Oeste
C1 Este
Irama

187

1
C Sagrado Corazón de Jesús
Calle Tapia
Ave Hermanos Rodriguez
CAROLINA

Canal Martin Peña
36
RÍO PIEDRAS
26

22
1
Avenida Rexach
27
Constitucion
Luis Muñoz Marín
International Airport

18
25
Teodoro Moscoso Bridge

23
17

41
8

18
25
27
17

1
17
181

30

47

KEY	
🛳	*Ferry*
🛈	*Tourist Information*

1
31

the permanent collection is on display at any time, but it might be any-thing from an exhibit of ceramics to a screening of videos. ⊠ *Av. Ponce de León at Av. R. H. Todd, Santurce* ☎ *787/977–4030* ⊕ *www. museocontemporaneopr.org* ⊡ *Free* ⊘ *Tues.–Sat. 10–4, Sun. 1–4.*

㉙ **Museo de Arte de Puerto Rico.** One of the biggest museums in the
Fodor'sChoice Caribbean, this 130,000-square-foot building was once known as San
★ Juan Municipal Hospital. The beautiful neoclassical building, dating from the 1920s, proved to be too small to house the museum's per-manent collection of Puerto Rican art dating from the 17th century to the present. The solution was to build a new east wing, which is dominated by a five-story-tall stained-glass window, the work of local artist Eric Tabales.

The collection starts with works from the colonial era, most of them commissioned for churches. Here you'll find works by José Campeche, the island's first great painter. His *Immaculate Conception,* finished in 1794, is a masterpiece. Also well represented is Francisco Oller y Ces-tero, who was the first to move beyond religious subjects to paint local scenes. His influence is still felt today. A gallery on the top floor is filled with works by artists inspired by Oller.

There's much more to the museum, including a beautiful garden filled with a variety of native flora and a 400-seat theater that's worth seeing for its remarkable lace curtain. And one of the city's best restaurants, Pikayo, is tucked away in the corner of the museum's massive atrium. ⊠ *299 Av. José De Diego, Santurce* ☎ *787/977–6277* ⊕ *www.mapr. org* ⊡ *$6* ⊘ *Tues. and Thurs.–Sat. 10–5, Wed. 10–8, Sun. 11–6.*

NEED A BREAK? While in Santurce, drop by **Plaza del Mercado,** a produce market surrounded by restaurants where you can have fresh fish for lunch at reasonable prices. The area also has many *botánicas,* small shops that sell herbs, candles, and religious items. There may even be an in-house card- or palm-reader ready to show you your future.

㉚ The Universidad de Puerto Rico's **Museo de Historia, Antropología y Arte** (Museum of History, Anthropology and Art) has archaeological and his-torical exhibits that deal with the Native American influence on the is-land and the Caribbean, the colonial era, and the history of slavery. Art displays are occasionally mounted; the museum's prize exhibit is the paint-ing *El Velorio* (*The Wake*), by the 19th-century artist Francisco Oller. ⊠ *Av. Ponce de León, Río Piedras* ☎ *787/764–0000 Ext. 5852* ⊕ *www. uprrp.edu* ⊡ *Free* ⊘ *Mon.–Wed. and Fri. 9–4:30, Thurs. 9–9, week-ends 9–3.*

San Juan Environs

The suburbs of Cataño, Bayamón, and Guaynabo, west and south of San Juan, are separate municipalities but in many ways indistinguish-able from the city itself. Cataño, bordered by the Bahía de San Juan in the north, is an industrial suburb, perhaps most noted for its distillery belonging to Bacardí. Bayamón can be reached within 15 to 30 min-

Art Invasion

CLOSE UP

1

PUBLIC ART IS TRANSFORMING the Puerto Rican capital: here a monolithic metal dove; there avocados so big you can stretch out on them. The stained-glass blades of a windmill spin above an oceanfront drive. A bright red jack towers over children at play in a park. These are just some of the 25 works by local artists that the city commissioned from 1996 to 2000, when Governor Sila Marí Calderón was its mayor. Part of a $3 million urban-art project, the pieces range from realistic to abstract, and many were installed as part of larger renovations of parks, plazas, and markets.

Often the works seem perfectly at home in their environments. *Platanal*, by Imel Sierra Cabreras, has translucent panels that run across the ceiling of the restored Plaza del Mercado in Santurce. The avocados in *My Favorite Fruit* by Annex Burgos seem to spill from the entrance of this marketplace and across its front plaza. Although the large jack by María Elena Perales is a bit surreal, it's an appropriate addition to a playground in Parque Central Municipo de San Juan.

Some pieces attempt to soften or enliven their surroundings. Carmen Inés Blondet, whose *Fire Dance* is a collection of 28- to 35-foot spirals, created what seems an abstract forest in the midst of the concrete jungle. The iron spirals are interspersed with benches across a small plaza beneath an expressway. Crabs were once a common sight in Santurce (hence the name of the baseball team, the Santurce Crabbers), so Adelino González's benches for the area are bronze crabs. *Windmills of San Juan*, by Eric Tables, is a whimsical tribute to the coast and its ocean breezes. The steel tower, with its rotating wheel of color, is on a restored oceanside drive in Ocean Park.

The works haven't been without controversy. Many residents found *Paloma*, the metallic dove that towers over a busy Condado intersection, ugly; others went so far as to assert that it was the cause of traffic jams. Mayor Jorge Santini even threatened to remove it during his campaign. But it appears to be here to stay. To soften the piece, a fountain was added to its base and it's now especially beautiful at night when the water is illuminated.

As a whole, however, the statues have made San Juan more interesting. And public art has spread around the island. In January 2002 Governor Calderón unveiled plans for the Puerto Rico Public Art Project. Its budget of $15 million has funded about 100 new works. In San Juan these include stations of the urban train, the Luis Muñoz Marín International Airport, and several government buildings and city parks. The committee also envisions installing works at nature reserves, along highways, and in school playgrounds across the island. Soon, perhaps, that new bus stop, lifeguard station, or street-vendor stand you see will truly be a work of art.

–John Marino

utes from central San Juan; if you come by car, stop by the attractive central park bordered by historic buildings. Guaynabo is a mix of residential and industrial areas and is worth visiting for its historical importance—Juan Ponce de León established the island's first settlement here in Caparra, and you can visit the ruins of the original fortification.

The Casa Bacardí Visitor Center is an easy trip from Old San Juan—you simply take a ferry across the harbor. The other sites are a challenge to reach, as you must navigate some of the region's most traffic-clogged streets. Do yourself a favor and take a taxi or book a tour.

What to See

32 **Casa Bacardí Visitor Center.** Exiled from Cuba, the Bacardí family built a small distillery here in the 1950s. Today it's one of the world's largest, with the capacity to produce 100,000 gallons of spirits a day and 221 million cases a year. You can hop on a little tram to take a 45-minute tour of the bottling plant, distillery, and museum. Yes, you'll be offered a sample. If you don't want to drive, you can reach the factory by taking the ferry from Pier 2 for 50¢ each way and then a *publico* (public van service) from the ferry pier to the factory for about $2 or $3 per person. ⊠ *Rte. 888, Km 2.6, Cataño* ☎ *787/788–1500 or 787/788–8400* ⊕ *www.casabacardi.org* ▣ *Free* ☉ *Mon.–Sat. 8:30–5:30, Sun. 10–5. Tours every 15–30 min.*

33 **Ruinas de Caparra.** In 1508 Ponce de León established the island's first settlement here. The Caparra Ruins—a few crumbling walls—are what remains of an ancient fort. The small **Museo de la Conquista y Colonización de Puerto Rico** (Museum of the Conquest and Colonization of Puerto Rico) contains historical documents, exhibits, and excavated artifacts, though you can see the museum's contents in less time than it takes to say the name. Both the ruins and the museum are maintained by the Puerto Rican government's museums and parks division. ⊠ *Rte. 2, Km 6.6, Guaynabo* ☎ *787/781–4795* ⊕ *www.icp. gobierno.pr* ▣ *Free* ☉ *Tues.–Sat. 8:30–4:20.*

35 **Museo de Arte Francisco Oller.** In Bayamón's central park you'll find the 18th-century Catholic church of Santa Cruz and the former city hall, which now houses the Francisco Oller Art and History Museum. Works by local artists are displayed in the neoclassical building. Oller (1833–1917) was one of the most accomplished artists of his time, and has works on display at the Museo de Arte and the Museo de Historia, Antropolgía y Arte at the

SAINTS ON PARADE

Each of Puerto Rico's 78 municipalities has a patron saint, and each one celebrates an annual festival near the saint's birthday, sometimes lasting a week or more. These festivals are a great opportunity to hear live music and buy local arts and crafts. San Juan celebrates its patron-saint feast in the *noche de San Juan* on June 23, when locals take to the beach. The event culminates at midnight, when crowds plunge into the Atlantic to flip over backwards three times, a cleansing ritual expected to bring good fortune.

University of Puerto Rico. ✉ *17 Calle Maceo, at Calle Degetau, Bayamón* ☎ *787/787–8620* 🎫 *Free* ☉ *Tues.–Sat. 9–4.*

Ⓒ ㉞ **Parque de las Ciencias Luis A. Ferré.** The 42-acre Luis A. Ferré Science Park contains a collection of intriguing activities and displays. The Transportation Museum has antique cars and the island's oldest bicycle. In the Rocket Plaza, children can experience a flight simulator, and in the planetarium the solar system is projected on the ceiling. Also onsite are a small zoo and a natural-science exhibit. It's a long drive from central San Juan, though. ✉ *Rte. 167, Bayamón* ☎ *787/740–6878* 🎫 *$5* ☉ *Wed.–Fri. 9–4, weekends 10–6.*

WHERE TO EAT

In cosmopolitan San Juan, European, Asian, and Middle Eastern eateries vie for your attention with family-owned restaurants specializing in seafood or *comida criolla* (creole cooking). U.S. chains such as McDonald's and Subway compete with chains like Pollo Tropical, which specialize in local cuisine. Although each of the city's large hotels has two or more fine restaurants, the best dining is often in stand-alone establishments—don't be shy about venturing to such places.

Dress codes vary greatly, though a restaurant's price category is a good indicator of its formality. For less expensive places, anything but beachwear is fine. Ritzier spots will expect collared shirts for men (jacket and tie requirements are rare) and chic attire for women. When in doubt, do as the Puerto Ricans often do and dress up.

For breakfast outside of your hotel, cafés are your best bet. Although it's rare for such establishments to close between breakfast and lunch, it's slightly more common for restaurants to close between lunch and dinner. Although some places don't accept reservations, it's always a good idea to make them for dinner whenever possible. This is especially true during the busy season from November through April and on weekends at any time of the year.

WHAT IT COSTS In U.S. dollars				
	$$$$	**$$$**	**$$**	**$**	**¢**
AT DINNER	over $30	$20–$30	$12–$20	$8–$12	under $8

Prices are per person for a main course at dinner.

Old San Juan

Cafés

$$ ✗ **Café Berlin.** A handful of tables spill out onto the sidewalk at this unpretentious place overlooking Plaza Colón. There's something on the menu for everyone, from turkey breast in a mustard-curry sauce to salmon in a citrus sauce. There are even several good vegetarian dishes, including tofu in a mushroom sauce. Inside is a small bar, one of the few places in Puerto Rico that serves draft beer. ✉ *407 Calle San Francisco, Old San Juan* ☎ *787/722–5205* 🖃 *AE, MC, V.*

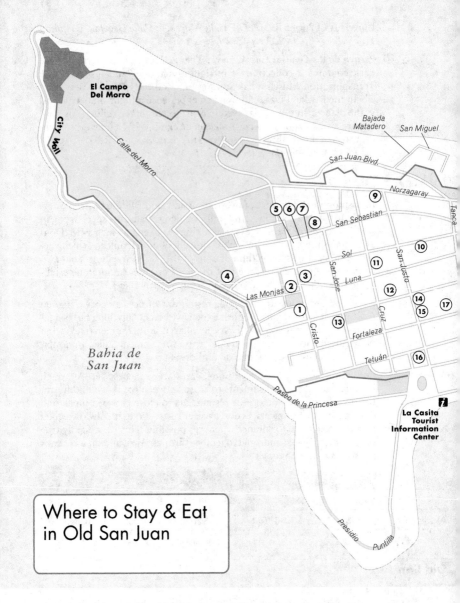

Where to Stay & Eat in Old San Juan

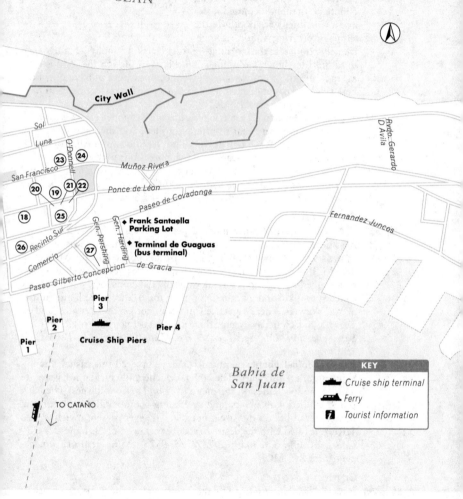

ATLANTIC OCEAN

440 yards
400 meters

City Wall

Sol
Luna
O'Donnell
23 24
San Francisco
Muñoz Rivera
20 19 21 22
Ponce de Léon
Paseo de Covadonga
18 25
Gen. Pershing
Gen. Harding
♦ Frank Santaella
  Parking Lot
26 Recinto Sur
♦ Terminal de Guaguas
  (bus terminal)
27
Comercio
Fernandez Juncos
Paseo Gilberto Concepcion
de Gracia

Rvdo. Gerardo
D'Avila

Pier
3
Pier
2
Cruise Ship Piers
Pier 4
Pier
1

TO CATAÑO

Bahia de
San Juan

KEY
⛴ Cruise ship terminal
⛴ Ferry
ℹ Tourist information

Hotels

Caleta Guesthouse **4**

El Convento Hotel **2**

Gallery Inn **9**

Hotel Milano **17**

Howard Johnson
Plaza de Armas **17**

Sheraton Old San Juan
Hotel & Casino **27**

$–$$ ✕ **La Bombonera.** You can't miss the gorgeous stained glass on the facade of this local landmark, which was established in 1903. In the window you'll see piles of freshly baked pastries. Inside there's a long counter with salmon-colored stools and a wall lined with booths of the same interesting shade. It's extremely popular in the morning—particularly on Sunday—but it's open until 8:30 for lunch and dinner. All this even though the food is only average and the grumpy waiters give the appearance of having worked here since the day it opened. ⊠ *259 Calle San Francisco, Old San Juan* ☎ *787/722–0658* ▭ *AE, MC, V.*

> **CAUTION**
>
> Sanjuaneros generally eat dinner late; if you arrive at a restaurant before 7 PM, you may be the only diners.

$–$$ ✕ **Cafeteria Mallorca.** The specialty at this old-fashioned eatery is the *mallorca*, a sweet pastry that's buttered, grilled, and then sprinkled with powdered sugar. Wash one down with a terrific cup of *café con leche*. For something more substantial, try the breakfast mallorca, which has ham and cheese. The waitstaff—all dressed in crisp green uniforms and caps—are friendly and efficient. ⊠ *300 Calle San Francisco, Old San Juan* ☎ *787/724–4607* ▭ *MC, V* ⊘ *Closed Sun.*

Caribbean

$$–$$$ ✕ **Casa Borinquen.** A portrait of independence leader Pedro Albizu Campos adorns the building's facade, a holdover from the days when a group of artists turned the crumbling walls of this house into the Museo sin Techo ("Roofless Museum"). Today it does have a roof, as well as a tropical-themed dining room serving radically delicious local cuisine. Look for the pumpkin and macadamia-nut ravioli or the grilled lamb on sugarcane skewers. There's an excellent wine shop on the premises, and on Tuesday and Thursday evening there's a free tasting upstairs. ⊠ *109 Calle San Sebastián, Old San Juan* ☎ *787/725–0888* ▭ *AE, D, MC, V* ⊘ *Closed Mon.*

$–$$ ✕ **La Fonda del Jibarito.** Sanjuaneros have favored this casual, family-run restaurant for years. The conch ceviche and chicken fricassee are among the specialties on the menu of *comida criollo* dishes. The back porch is filled with plants, and the dining room is filled with fanciful depictions of life on the street outside. The ever-present owner, Pedro J. Ruiz, is filled with the desire to ensure that everyone is happy. ⊠ *280 Calle Sol, Old San Juan* ☎ *787/725–8375* ⌂ *Reservations not accepted* ▭ *AE, MC, V.*

Contemporary

★ **$$–$$$$** ✕ **Carli Café Concierto.** As you might guess from the name, the music is as much of a draw of the food at Carli Café Concierto. The genial owner and host, Carli Muñoz, once toured with the Beach Boys (note the gold album on the wall). Many evenings he plays the gorgeous grand piano, often accompanied by singers and musicians who happen to drop in. In the Banco Popular building that dominates the skyline, this intimate bistro has black-marble tables scattered around the room. Have a seat indoors or on the outdoor patio, and dine on such Mediterranean-Caribbean specialties as seared loin of lamb or ravioli in a light pesto sauce. ⊠ *Plazoleta Rafael Carrión, Calle Recinto Sur and Calle San Justo, Old San Juan* ☎ *787/725–4927* ☰ *AE, MC, V* ⊗ *Closed Sun.*

$$–$$$ ✕ **Amadeus.** Facing Plaza San José, this bright and airy restaurant often throws open the doors and lets its tables spill into the square. If you want a little more privacy, there's also an interior courtyard and an intimate dining room with whitewashed walls, linen tablecloths, and lazily turning ceiling fans. Expect nouvelle Caribbean appetizers such as dumplings with guava-rum sauce or plantain mousse with shrimp, and entrées such as ravioli with a goat-cheese and pork with mango and sugarcane. ⊠ *106 Calle San Sebastián, Old San Juan* ☎ *787/722–8635* ☰ *AE, MC, V* ⊗ *Closed Sun., no lunch Mon.*

$$–$$$ ✕ **Barú.** A well-traveled menu has earned Barú a solid reputation among sanjuaneros, so it's often crowded. The dishes, all served in medium-sized portions so you can order several and share, range from Middle Eastern to Asian to Caribbean. Favorites include oysters in a soy-citrus sauce, risotto with green asparagus, and carpaccio made from beef, tuna, or salmon. More substantial fare includes filet mignon with horseradish mashed potatoes and pork ribs with a ginger-tamarind glaze. The dining room, in a beautifully renovated colonial house, is dark and mysterious. ⊠ *150 Calle San Sebastián, Old San Juan* ☎ *787/977–7107* ☰ *AE, MC, V* ⊗ *Closed Mon. No lunch.*

$$–$$$ ✕ **Parrot Club.** Loud and lively, this place is intent on making sure everyone is having a good time. You're likely to strike up a conversation with the bartender as you enjoy a passion-fruit cocktail or with the couple at the next table in the covered courtyard. Something about the atmosphere—ear-splitting salsa music and murals of swaying palm trees—makes connecting easy. The menu has contemporary variations of Caribbean classics. You might start with mouthwatering crabcakes or tamarind-barbecued ribs, followed by blackened tuna in a dark rum sauce or seared sea bass with lobster, leek, and scallop confit. ⊠ *363 Calle Fortaleza, Old San Juan* ☎ *787/725–7370* ⚠ *Reservations not accepted* ☰ *AE, DC, MC, V.*

Eclectic

$–$$$ ✕ **El Patio de Sam.** A great selection of beers—26, to exact, including the locally brewed Medalla—make this a popular late-night spot. Just as appealing is the dimly lighted courtyard that gives the place its name. The menu consists mostly of steaks and seafood, but there are plenty of opportunities to sample Puerto Rican fare. Save room for the flan, which melts in your mouth. There's entertainment (usually a guitarist singing old standards) every night but Sunday. ⊠ *102 Calle San Sebastián, Old San Juan* ☎ *787/723–1149* ☰ *AE, D, DC, MC, V.*

★ $$ ✕ **La Ostra Cosa.** This restaurant's succulent prawns, grilled and served with garlic butter, are supposed to be aphrodisiacs. Well, everything on the menu is rated for its love-inducing qualities. (Look out for those

MORNING COFFEE

If you want a good cup of morning coffee, check out one of the ubiquitous Subway sandwich shops; outlets in Puerto Rico make excellent café con leche.

On the Menu

Adobo. A seasoning made of salt, onion powder, garlic powder, and ground black pepper, usually rubbed on meats before they are roasted.

Aji-li-mojili. A dressing combining garlic and sweet, seeded chili peppers, flavored further with vinegar, lime juice, salt, and olive oil; it is traditionally served with lechón asado.

Alcapurrias. Banana croquettes stuffed with beef or pork, which are very popular as a fast food.

Amarillos. Fried ripe, yellow-plantain slices, a common side dish.

Arepas. Fried corn or bread cakes.

Asopao. A gumbo made with fish or chicken, flavored with spices such as garlic, paprika, and oregano as well as salt pork, cured ham, green peppers, chili peppers, onions, tomatoes, chorizo, and pimentos.

Batido. A tropical fruit-and-milk shake; basically, a smoothie.

Bacalaítos. Deep-fried codfish fritters, which are often served as an appetizer for lunch or dinner.

Chimichurri. An herb sauce of finely chopped cilantro or parsley with garlic, lemon, and oil that is usually served with grilled meats.

Chinas. In Puerto Rico *naranjas* (oranges) are called chinas, so you'll see "jugo de china" on many breakfast menus.

Empanadillas. Turnovers, bigger than *pastelillos*, filled with beef, crabmeat, conch, or even lobster.

Jueyes. Land crab, which is often boiled or served in a stew.

Lechón Asado. A slow-roasted, garlic-studded whole pig, marinated in sour orange juice and coloring made from achiote, the inedible fruit of a small Caribbean shrub, whose seeds are sometimes ground as a spice; it's traditionally served with *aji-li-mojili*.

Mofongo. A mix of plantains mashed with garlic, olive oil, and salt in a *pilón*, the traditional mortar and pestle used in the Puerto Rican kitchen.

Mojo or Mojito Isleño. A sauce made of olives and olive oil, onions, pimientos, capers, tomato sauce, vinegar, and a flavoring of garlic and bay leaves that is usually served with fried fish (not to be confused with Cuban rum drink, *mojito*).

Pasteles. Corn or yucca wrapped in a plantain leaf with various fillings.

Pastelillos. Deep-fried cheese and meat turnovers, which are a popular fast-food snack.

Picadillo. Spicy ground meat, which is used for stuffing or eaten with rice.

Pique. A condiment consisting of hot peppers soaked in vinegar, sometimes with garlic or other spices added.

Pionono. A slice of ripe plantain wrap filled with picadillo, breaded and fried.

Sofrito. A seasoned base made with pureed tomatoes, sautéed onions, bell peppers, tomatoes, sweet red chili peppers, herbs and spices, cilantro (coriander), recao, and garlic, and colored with achiote (annato seeds); it's used in rice, soups, and stews, giving them a bright yellow coloring.

Tembleque. A coconut custard, which is a popular dessert; when served, it's usually sprinkled with cinnamon or nutmeg.

Tostones. Crushed fried green plantains, usually served as an appetizer.

labeled "Ay, ay, ay!") There are some seats indoors, but opt for a seat in the walled courtyard. With brilliant purple bougainvillea tumbling down and moonlight streaming through the trees, it's one of the city's prettiest alfresco dining spots. The gregarious owner, Alberto Nazario, brother of pop star Ednita Nazario, genuinely enjoys seeing his guests satisfied. He'll sometimes take out a guitar and sing old folk songs. Don't be surprised if the locals sing along. ✉ *154 Calle Cristo, Old San Juan* ☎ *787/722–2672* ▭ *AE, MC, V.*

> **WORD OF MOUTH**
>
> "One of the most romantic restaurants I've been to is [La] Ostra Cosa in Old San Juan on Calle Cristo. It is wonderful seafood in a lush, outdoor courtyard. The menu lists the 'aphrodisiac value' of each item."   —mom929.

French

$$$–$$$$ ✗ **La Chaumière.** With black-and-white floor tiles, wood-beamed ceiling, and floral-print curtains, this two-story restaurant evokes provincial France. It has been under the same management since 1969, and with all that experience the service is smooth. Daily specials augment a menu of stellar French classics, including breast of duck with a cassis glaze and veal with a mustard cream sauce. If you want to go all out, there's the huge chateaubriand for two. ✉ *367 Calle Tetuan, Old San Juan* ☎ *787/722–3330* ▭ *AE, DC, MC, V* ☉ *Closed Sun. No lunch.*

Indian

$–$$ ✗ **Tantra.** This little gem sits square in the middle of Old San Juan's up-and-coming restaurant row, known locally as SoFo (South Fortaleza Street). The menu, which combines Indian and Caribbean flavors, has traditional dishes such as tandoori chicken and inventive surprises like beef tenderloin in a casava purée. The jewel-tone interior invites you to linger, and many patrons do so for an after-dinner puff on an Asian water pipe. ✉ *356 Calle La Fortaleza, Old San Juan* ☎ *787/977–8141* ▭ *AE, MC, V.*

Italian

★ **$$$–$$$$** ✗ **Il Perugino.** This colonial-era house has been transformed into something out of ancient Rome. But did those Romans ever feast on appetizers like foie gras on a bed of white onions or marinated salmon with chives? As good as these are, the main courses are even better. The ravioli stuffed with chicken liver, spinach, and black truffles are a wonder, as is the pork filet with thyme and blueberries. The extensive wine cellar, housed in the former cistern, is sure to contain the perfect complement to your meal. Everything here is discreet, from the entrance (just an awning over a doorway) to the service. ✉ *105 Calle Cristo, Old San Juan* ☎ *787/722–5481* ▭ *MC, V.*

$$–$$$ ✗ **Sofia.** Ignore the tongue-in-cheek recordings of "That's Amore." Everything else in this red-walled trattoria is the real deal, from the gleaming vegetables on the antipasto table to the interesting vintages on the small but well-chosen wine list. Start with the squid stuffed with sweet sausage, then move onto the linguine with clams and pancetta or the cannelloni filled with roasted duck and topped with marscapone cheese. The plates of pasta are huge, so you might want to consider a half-order (which is more the size of a three-quarter order). Save room for—what else?—a tasty tiramisu. ✉ *355 Calle San Francisco, Old San Juan* ☎ *787/721–0396* ▤ *AE, MC, V.*

Latin

$$–$$$ ✕ **La Mallorquina.** Dating from 1848, La Mallorquina is thought to be the island's oldest restaurant. The menu is heavy on such basic Puerto Rican and Spanish fare as *asopao* (a stew with rice and seafood) and paella, but the atmosphere is what really recommends the place. Friendly, nattily attired staffers zip between tables agains peach-colored walls and beneath the whir of ceiling fans. ✉ *207 Calle San Justo, Old San Juan* ☎ *787/722–3261* ▤ *AE, MC, V* ☾ *Closed Sun.*

$–$$ ✕ **Spanglish.** On a quiet side street, this café has a laid-back vibe that has people coming back again and again. The food, from old family recipes, includes Puerto Rican favorites like garbanzo-bean stew flavored with ham and sausage and veal tips simmered in wine. The creamy flan has also developed quite a following. There's a small bar in back where you can sample the trademark drink, a fruity rum punch. ✉ *105 Calle Cruz, Old San Juan* ☎ *787/722–2424* ▤ *MC, V.*

Mexican

$–$$ ✕ **Lupi's.** Dining in Old San Juan doesn't have to mean fighting for a table. This Mexican restaurant is the best of the string of laid-back eateries along Calle Recinto Sur. Plates of steaming hot tacos, burritos, and other reasonably authentic fare arrive at your table within minutes of placing your order. And if you want to watch the big game—whatever that might happen to be—it will doubtless be playing in the television over the bar. ✉ *313 Calle Recinto Sur, Old San Juan* ☎ *787/722–1874* ▤ *AE, MC, V.*

Pan-Asian

★ **$$$–$$$$** ✕ **Kudetá.** The name is an inside joke—it's pronounced like *coup d'e-tat*, the French term for "revolution." A bit of an exaggeration, perhaps, but the kitchen has scored more than a few victories with dishes that blend Caribbean main dishes with Asian cooking methods. That's why the steak is covered with a wasabi demiglace and the oysters are submerged is tasty green curry. The minimalist dining room is also a triumph, especially the sage-colored banquettes covered with aubergine-and-gold pillows. The black-clad staff couldn't be friendlier, and they are happy to help you negotiate the menu. ✉ *314 Calle La Fortaleza, Old San Juan* ☎ *787/977–5023* ▤ *AE, MC, V.*

$$–$$$ ✕ **Dragonfly.** It's not hard to find this little restaurant—it's the one with crowds milling about on the sidewalk. If you can stand the wait—as you undoubtedly will, since reservations aren't accepted—then you'll get to sample chef Roberto Trevino's Latin-Asian cuisine. (For the best chance of avoiding a line, come when it opens at 6 PM.) The *platos* (plates) are meant to be shared, so order several for your tables. Favorites include pork-and-plantain dumplings with an orange dipping sauce, smoked-salmon pizza with wasabi salsa, and lamb spareribs with a tamarind glaze. The dining room, all done up in Chinese red, resembles an opium den. ✉ *364 Calle La Fortaleza, Old San Juan* ☎ *787/977–3886* ⌂ *Reservations not accepted* ▤ *AE, MC, V* ☾ *Closed Sun. No lunch.*

Seafood

$$–$$$$
FodorsChoice
★

✕ **Aguaviva.** The name means "jellyfish," which explains why this ultracool, ultramodern place has lighting fixtures shaped like that sea creature. Elegantly groomed oysters and clams float on cracked ice along the raw bar. The extensive menu is alive with inventive ceviches, some with tomato or roasted red peppers and olives, and fresh takes on classics like paella. For something more filling, try dorado served with a shrimp salsa, or tuna accompanied by seafood enchiladas. You could also empty out your wallet for one of the *torres del mar,* or towers of the sea. This gravity-defying dish has comes hot or cold and includes oysters, mussels, shrimp—you name it. Oh, and don't pass up the lobster mashed potatoes. Those alone are worth the trip—and the wait. ⊠ *364 Calle La Fortaleza, Old San Juan* ☎ *787/722–0665* ⌕ *Reservations not accepted* 🗎 *AE, D, MC, V.*

Spanish

$$$
FodorsChoice
★

✕ **El Picoteo.** You could make a meal of the small dishes that dominate the menu at this tapas restaurant. You won't go wrong ordering the sweet sausage in brandy or the turnovers stuffed with lobsters and passing them around the table. If you're not into sharing, there are five different kinds of paella that arrive on huge plates. There's a long, lively bar inside; one dining area overlooks a pleasant courtyard, whereas the other takes in the action along Calle Cristo. Even if you have dinner plans elsewhere, consider stopping here for a nightcap. ⊠ *El Convento Hotel, 100 Calle Cristo, Old San Juan* ☎ *787/723–9621* 🗎 *AE, D, DC, MC, V.*

Steak

$$$–$$$$

✕ **Fogata.** This dining room seems to be blushing—the walls and the gauzy curtains are the same shade of crimson. It has nothing to be ashamed of, as it serves some delicious grilled meats. After you select an entrée—say, skewered shrimp or double-cut veal chops—you can cover it with toppings ranging from a rum-peppercorn glaze to spiced butter. If you can't decide, the mixed grill has a bit of everything. The view of the Bahía de San Juan usually includes an ocean liner or two. ⊠ *Sheraton Old San Juan Hotel & Casino, 100 Calle Brumbaugh, Old San Juan* ☎ *787/289–1944* 🗎 *AE, MC, V.*

Puerta de Tierra

Italian

$$$
FodorsChoice
★

✕ **Crú.** If you thought carpaccio was only made with beef, then you're in for a wonderful surprise. At Crú, one of San Juan's best new restaurants, a special carpaccio menu includes old standards like beef with truffle oil and Parmesan cheese, as well as new concoctions like halibut with fresh mango and cuttlefish with caramelized onions. It's all laid out for you on a bed of ice so you can choose whatever strikes your fancy. Main dishes include penne with porcini mushrooms and filet of lamb with eggplant. The dining room, like the rest of the Normandie Hotel, has some wonderful art–deco flourishes. ⊠ *Normandie Hotel, 499 Av. Muñoz Rivera, Puerta de Tierra* ☎ *787/729–2929* 🗎 *AE, MC, V.*

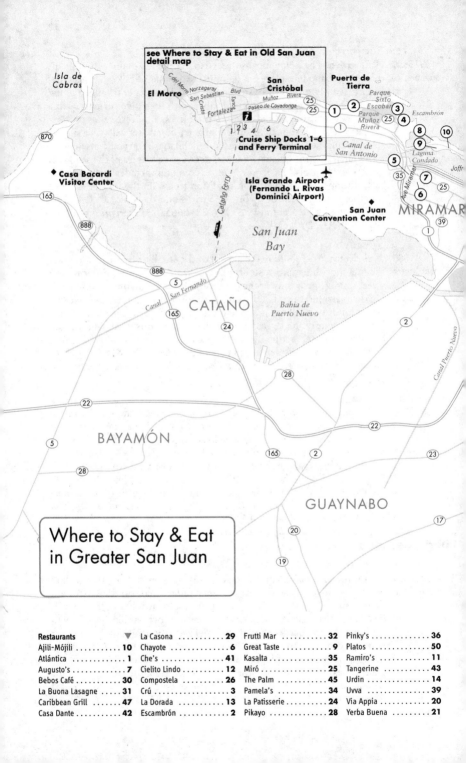

see **Where to Stay & Eat in Old San Juan** detail map

Isla de Cabras

870

El Morro

C del Morro
Norzagaray
San Cristo
San Sebastian
Fortaleza
Paseo de Covadonga

San Cristóbal

Muñoz Rivera

Puerta de Tierra

Parque Sixto Escobar
Parque Muñoz Rivera

Escambrón

Canal de San Antonio

Laguna Condado

MIRAMAR

Joffr

Casa Bacardí Visitor Center

165

888

Cataño Ferry

Isla Grande Airport (Fernando L. Rivas Dominici Airport)

San Juan Convention Center

San Juan Bay

888

5

San Fernando

Canal

165

CATAÑO

24

Bahia de Puerto Nuevo

28

22

BAYAMÓN

5

28

165

2

22

23

GUAYNABO

20

19

17

Canal Puerto Nuevo

Where to Stay & Eat in Greater San Juan

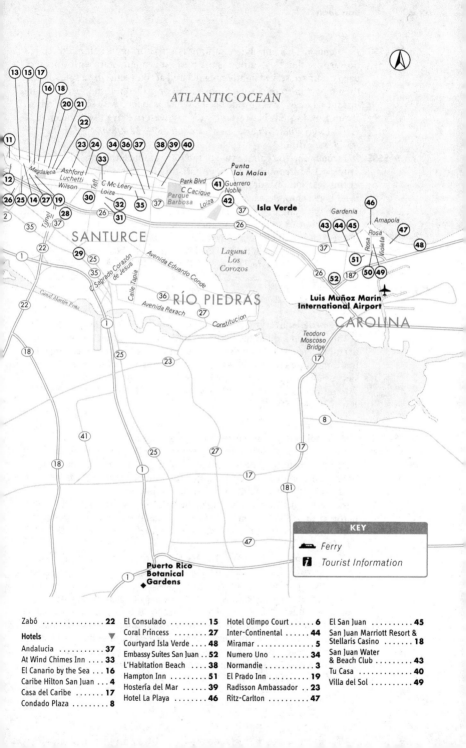

ATLANTIC OCEAN

Punta
las Maías

Park Blvd
C Mc Leary   Guerrero
Loiza   Noble
Parque
Barbosa   Loiza

SANTURCE

Isla Verde

Gardenia   Amapola

Rosa
Violeta

Laguna
Los
Corozos

RÍO PIEDRAS

Avenida Eduardo Conde

Calle Tapia

Avenida Rexach

Constitucion

Luis Muñoz Marín
International Airport

CAROLINA

Teodoro
Moscoso
Bridge

Puerto Rico
Botanical
Gardens

KEY

🛳 Ferry

🛈 Tourist Information

Seafood

$$–$$$$ ✕ **Atlántica.** This popular restaurant is across from its namesake, so it's no surprise that the seafood is the freshest around. Start with a plate of fried calamari, served lightly breaded and accompanied by a spicy sauce, then move on to the broiled lobster tail or grilled red snapper in a garlic sauce. Locals swear by the paella, which is loaded with scallops, clams, shrimp, and squid. The restaurant is just west of Playa Escambrón. ⊠ 7 *Calle Lugo Viñas, Puerta de Tierra* ☎ 787/722–0890 ⊟ AE, MC, V ◷ Closed Mon.

$–$$$$ ✕ **Escambrón.** You can see two of the forts of Old San Juan—Fuerte San Filipe del Morro and Fuerte San Cristóbal—from the covered terrace of this seafood restaurant. The beach itself is only a few feet away. The food here is more creative than you'd expect, with dishes ranging from shrimp with cilantro and roasted garlic butter to lobster grilled with a rum and butter sauce. Not in the mood for seafood? There are plenty of meat dishes, including skirt steak and pork chops. The restaurant is walking distance from the Caribe Hilton and the Normandie. ⊠ *Playa Escambrón, Puerta de Tierra* ☎ 787/724–3344 ⊟ AE, MC, V.

Condado

Cafés

$–$$ ✕ **La Patisserie.** Everything—from the pastries to the pastas—is delicious at this café on a quiet block in Condado. For breakfast there are wonderful omelets stuffed with fresh vegetables and imported cheeses. For lunch there are sandwiches—from pastrami to king crab—served on croissants, baguettes, or any other type of bread. For dinner try the grilled salmon or the chicken in white wine. ⊠ *1504 Av. Ashford, Condado* ☎ 787/728–5508 ⊟ AE, MC, V.

Caribbean

$$–$$$$
Fodor'sChoice
★ ✕ **Ajili-Mójili.** Set in a plantation-style house, this elegant dining room sits on the edge of Condado Bay. Traditional Puerto Rican food is prepared with a flourish. Sample the fried cheese and *bolitas de yautia y queso* (cheese and yam dumplings), then move on to the *gallinita rellena* (stuffed cornish game hen). The plantain-crusted shrimp in a white-wine herb sauce is delicious, as is the paella overflowing with shrimp, octopus, mussels, chicken, and spicy sausage. Prices, however, are pretty high despite the quality. ⊠ *1006 Av. Ashford, Condado* ☎ 787/725–9195 ⊟ AE, DC, MC, V.

$$–$$$ ✕ **Yerba Buena.** Tables on the terrace are hard to come by at this restaurant, one of the most popular in Condado. That's fine, because the glassed-in dining room is even more comfortable and has exactly the same view. Cuban classics such as *ropa vieja* (meat cooked so slowly that it becomes tender shreds) seamlessly blend local dishes with imaginative presentation. The shrimp has a coconut-and-ginger sauce, the halibut filet one of mango and orange liqueur. The restaurant claims to use the "original" recipe for its *mojito*, Cuba's tasty rum, lime, and mint drink. Live Latin jazz is played many nights. ⊠ *1350 Av. Ashford, Condado* ☎ 787/721–5700 ⊟ AE, MC, V ◷ Closed Mon.

Chinese

$–$$$ ✕ **Great Taste.** Chinese restaurants can be found everywhere in San Juan, but this one is worth a special trip. Don't be disappointed by the dining room, which has little personality. Every bit of creativity goes into the food. As you might guess, it's heavy on the seafood, with dishes like fish with ginger and scallion or fried shrimp with crispy minced garlic. There are plenty of meat dishes as well, including shredded duck with spicy bean sauce. (If you can't find it on the menu, look under the heading for chicken.) There's a dim sum menu with nearly 40 different choices, and a sushi bar with enough selections to put other places to shame. Make sure to take a look at the beautiful view over the Laguna del Condado. ✉ *1018 Av. Ashford, Condado* ☎ *787/721–8111* ▭ *AE, D, DC, MC, V.*

Contemporary

$$$$ ✕ **Pikayo.** Chef Wilo Benet is clearly the star here—a plasma television lets diners watch everything that's going on in his kitchen. The Puerto Rico native artfully fuses Caribbean cuisine with influences from around the world. Veal is served in a swirl of sweet-pea couscous, for example, and beef medallions are covered with crumbled blue cheese and a red-wine reduction. The regularly changing menu is a feast for the eye as well as the palate, and might include perfectly shaped tostones stuffed with oven-dried tomatoes, or mofongo topped with saffron shrimp. A changing selection of paintings wraps around the minimalist dining room—the restaurant is, after all, inside a museum. It's in Santurce, just south of Condado. ✉ *Museo de Arte de Puerto Rico, 299 Av. José de Diego, Santurce* ☎ *787/721–6194* ▭ *AE, MC, V* ⊘ *Closed Sun. and Mon.*

★ **$$$–$$$$** ✕ **Chayote.** Slightly off the beaten path, this chic eatery is definitely an "in" spot. The chef gives haute international dishes tropical panache. Starters include chayote stuffed with prosciutto and corn tamales with shrimp in a coconut sauce. Half the entrées are seafood dishes, including pan-seared tuna with a ginger sauce and red snapper served over spinach. The ginger flan is a must for dessert. The sophisticated dining room is hung with works by local artists. It's in Miramar, just a few blocks from Condado. ✉ *Hotel Olimpo Court, 603 Av. Miramar, Miramar* ☎ *787/722–9385* ▭ *AE, MC, V* ⊘ *Closed Sun. and Mon. No lunch Sat.*

$$–$$$ ✕ **Zabó.** In a restored plantation house surrounded by a quiet garden, this inventive restaurant seems as if it's out on the island somewhere rather than just off bustling Avenida Ashford. Make sure to order several of the tasty appetizers—such as breaded calamari in a tomato-basil sauce—so you can share them with your dinner companions. Of the notable main courses, try the veal chops stuffed with provolone and pancetta, or the miso-marinated salmon served over lemony basmati rice. ✉ *14 Calle Candida, Condado* ☎ *787/725–9494* ▭ *AE, D, DC, MC, V* ⊘ *Closed Sun. and Mon. No lunch Tues.–Thurs. and Sat.*

Continental

$$$–$$$$ ✕ **Augusto's.** Austrian-born chef Augusto Schreiner, a graduate of the Salzburg Culinary School, regularly wins awards for his classic European cuisine. The menu changes seasonally; some of the dishes commonly served are veal chops with roasted root vegetables and duck breast with bok choy. The angular lines of the dining room are softened by large bouquets of flowers. ⊠ *Courtyard Miramar, 801 Av. Ponce de León, Miramar* ☎ *787/725–7700* ▤ *AE, MC, V* ☉ *Closed Sun. and Mon. No lunch Sat.*

Italian

$–$$ ✕ **Via Appia.** The food at this no-frills café is just as authentic and as tasty—from the pizza to the veal and peppers to house red wine—as its higher-priced *paisanos*. The outdoor-seating area looks out on Condado's busy Ashford Avenue, which is usually filled with people coming from and going to the beach. The wine bar next door has a bit more ambience. ⊠ *1350 Av. Ashford, Condado* ☎ *787/725–8711* ▤ *AE, MC, V.*

Latin

$–$$ ✕ **Bebos Café.** At this longtime favorite huge platters of delicious comida criolla are constantly streaming out of the kitchen. The friendly service and low prices are why the place is always packed. The menu includes everything from grilled flank steak to seafood-stuffed mofongo to barbecued ribs. The selection of good local desserts includes flan and dense, moist *tres leches* cake. Breakfast is also popular. ⊠ *1600 Calle Loíza, Condado* ☎ *787/268–5087* ▤ *AE, MC, V.*

$–$$ ✕ **Cielito Lindo.** You know the moment you walk in the door that this is the real deal. The first clue is the smell of grilled meat coming from the kitchen. The juicy flank steaks are indeed standouts, but so are the burritos and enchiladas. There's also a wide selection of margaritas, each one iced to perfection and served with a lime wedge. The decor—paper streamers hanging from the ceiling—will remind you of eateries in small towns all over Mexico. ⊠ *1108 Av. Magdalena, Condado* ☎ *787/723–5597* ▤ *AE, MC, V.*

Seafood

$–$$$ ✕ **La Dorada.** This fine seafood establishment in the middle of Condado's restaurant row is surprisingly affordable. The grilled seafood platter is the specialty, but there are plenty of other excellent dishes, including mahimahi in caper sauce and codfish in green sauce. The friendly staff makes you feel genuinely welcome. ⊠ *1105 Av. Magdalena, Condado* ☎ *787/722–9583* ▤ *AE, D, MC, V.*

Spanish

$$$–$$$$ ✕ **La Casona.** Business executives come here for power lunches, but La Casona is also a nice spot for a romantic dinner. The restored Spanish colonial residence has well-appointed rooms and blooming gardens. The menu is based solidly in Spain, but has many creative flourishes—start with the duck pâté or smoked salmon and move on to the duck breast in a raspberry sauce or the rack of lamb, which is first baked and then sautéed with brandy and fruit. It's in Santurce, just south of Condado. ⊠ *609 Calle San Jorge, Santurce* ☎ *787/727–2717* ▤ *AE, D, DC, MC, V* ☉ *Closed Sun.*

$$$–$$$$ ✕ **Compostela.** A 10,000-bottle wine cellar is just one of the draws of this Spanish restaurant. The chef is often honored in local competitions for specialties such as lobster with basil butter, medallions of lamb with raspberries, and duck with orange and ginger sauce. The paella is the best in town. The dining room is elegant, with crisp linens and gleaming silverware. ⊠ *106 Av. Condado, Condado* ☎ *787/724–6088* ☐ *AE, DC, MC, V* ☺ *Closed Sun. No lunch Sat.*

$$$–$$$$ ✕ **Ramiro's.** The smell of chef Jesus Ramiro's imaginative Castilian cooking fills this sea-green dining room. Ramiro is also known for his artistic presentation: flower-shaped peppers filled with fish mousse, a mix of seafood caught under a vegetable net, roast duckling with sugarcane honey, and, if you can stand more, a kiwi dessert sculpted to resemble twin palms. ⊠ *1106 Av. Magdalena, Condado* ☎ *787/721–9049* ☐ *AE, DC, MC, V.*

$$–$$$ ✕ **Miró.** Like its namesake, the painter Joan Miró, this small restaurant draws its inspiration from the Catalan region of Spain, where the cuisine is heavy on seafood and hearty tapas. Prints by the artist hang on the walls, lending the dining room a colorful feel. Start off with braised chorizo and peppers, or steamed clams with garlic. Main courses include delicious lamb chops, as well as grilled tuna with anchovy and caper butter or codfish in a red-pepper and eggplant sauce. ⊠ *74 Av. Condado, Condado* ☎ *787/723–9593* ☐ *AE, MC, V.*

$$–$$$ ✕ **Urdin.** The name of this restaurant comes from the Basque word for "blue," which also happens to be the dining room's dominant color. The menu here is mostly Spanish dishes, but Caribbean touches abound. The soup and seafood appetizers are particularly good, and a highly recommended entrée is *chillo urdin de lujo* (red snapper sautéed with clams, mussels, and shrimp in a tomato, herb, and wine sauce). ⊠ *1105 Av. Magdalena, Condado* ☎ *787/724–0420* ☐ *AE, MC, V.*

Ocean Park

Cafés

★ **$–$$**   ✕ **Kasalta.** Those who think coffee can never be too strong should make a beeline to Kasalta, which has an amazing inky black brew that will knock your socks off. Make your selection from the display cases full of luscious pastries and other tempting treats. Walk up to the counter and order a sandwich, such as the savory Cubano, or such items as the meltingly tender octopus salad. ⊠ *1966 Calle McLeary, Ocean Park* ☎ *787/727–7340* ☐ *AE, MC, V.*

¢–$ ✕ **Frutti Mar.** This bright luncheonette off bustling Loíza Street has great vegetarian fare, baked goods, and fruit frappés. There are tasty garden burgers, and eggplant, hummus, and tofu sandwiches and platters. The Saturday special, vegetarian *sancocho* is a hearty blend of tubers and vegetables, slow-cooked in a sweet-herb sofrito. The natural carrot muffins, pistachio coffee cake, and Arabian desserts will have you carrying paper bags out of the place. It's open only until 6 PM. ⊠ *101 Diez de Andino, Ocean Park* ☎ *787/722–4103* ☐ *No credit cards* ☺ *Closed Sun. No dinner.*

¢–$ ✕ **Pinky's.** This tiny café near the beach is known for its gourmet wraps and sandwiches, as well as its freshly squeezed juices and fruity frappés. The pink sub is a blend of turkey, salami, and mozzarella, topped with black olives, chopped tomatoes, and basil. The surfer wrap is a mix of grilled turkey and mozzarella topped with pesto mayonnaise. Don't see what you want? You are free to make up your own. Seating is limited, but takeout is available. Or place your order from the beach, where speedy delivery people tend to your hunger pangs. ⊠ *51 Calle María Moczo, Ocean Park* ☎ *787/727–3347* ▭ *MC, V* ⊘ *Closed Mon. No dinner.*

Caribbean

$$–$$$ ✕ **Casa Dante.** If you're curious about mofongo—sweet plantains mashed into a paste and filled with just about anything imaginable—this is where locals will send you. This self-proclaimed "casa del mofongo" adds chicken or any combination of seafood to an excellent version. You can even order it as a side alongside grilled churrasco or sautéed red snapper. The restaurant sits in Ocean Park, on the border of Isla Verde, and does delivery as well. ⊠ *39 Av. Isla Verde, Punta Las Marías* ☎ *787/ 726-7310* ▭ *MC, V* ⊘ *Closed Mon.*

★ **$$–$$$** ✕ **Pamela's.** For the ultimate tropical dining experience, make a beeline here, the only city restaurant that offers outdoor seating on the sand, just steps away from the ocean, though it's also possible to dine indoors in air-conditioned comfort. The contemporary Caribbean menu is as memorable as the alfresco setting; daily specials might include blackened salmon glazed with a Mandarin honey sauce or Jamaican jerk shrimp and coconut corn arepas with guava coulis. ⊠ *Numero Uno Guesthouse, 1 Calle Santa Ana, Ocean Park* ☎ *787/726–5010* ▭ *AE, D, MC, V.*

Italian

$–$$ ✕ **La Buona Lasagne.** Don't let the elegance fool you. The prices are truly reasonable at this restaurant far from the well-trodden areas and in a restored art-deco structure with tile floors, large picture windows, and pastel walls. The menu includes about 30 pasta dishes, all freshly made with top-quality ingredients. The basic meat lasagne is just as good as the more elaborate penne with smoked salmon and a cream sauce. ⊠ *104 Calle Diez de Andino, Ocean Park* ☎ *787/721-7488* ▭ *AE, MC, V* ⊘ *Closed Sun. No dinner Mon.–Wed.*

Latin

$$–$$$$ ✕ **Che's.** On the eastern edge of Ocean Beach, this Argentine-style steak house is worth the trip. Haven't tried churrasco, the marinated skirt steak that locals love? This is the place to do it. Other specialties of the kitchen include grilled sweetbreads. The hamburgers are huge, and the french fries are fresh. The wine list, which tends toward Chilean and Argentine vintages, is also a winner. It's in Ocean Park, just before you get to Isla Verde. ⊠ *35 Calle Caoba, Punta Las Marías* ☎ *787/726- 7202* ▭ *AE, D, DC, MC, V.*

Mediterranean

$$–$$$$ ✕ **Uvva.** You might feel you're in the South Pacific or Bali when you take a seat at one of the bamboo tables at this romantic restaurant, especially when you see the oiled teak beams across the ceiling and the shutters that swing up to catch the breeze. The menu has a bit of a split personality—the appetizers lean toward Caribbean favorites, whereas the entrées are mostly Mediterranean staples. It all comes together with such dishes as seared tuna with a ginger and cilantro vinaigrette or sesame-crusted salmon served on a bed of Asian vegetables. There are always several vegetarian options on the menu. ⊠ *Hostería del Mar, 1 Calle Tapia, Ocean Park* ☎ *787/727–0631* ▤ *AE, D, DC, MC, V.*

Isla Verde

Caribbean

$$$–$$$$ ✕ **Caribbean Grill.** Seafood is the specialty of this restaurant, one of the most popular in the Ritz-Carlton. Fresh fruit makes an appearance in many dishes, adding a distinct flavor. Start off with shrimp ceviche with a tangerine-cilantro sauce, then move on to the jerk spiced tuna steak or the red snapper baked in a banana leaf. Don't expect stuffed parrots and other paraphernalia; The elegant dining room is reminiscent of a plantation house. You can also dine outdoors on the terrace. ⊠ *Ritz-Carlton San Juan Hotel, Spa & Casino, Av. Las Gobernadores (Rte. 187), Isla Verde* ☎ *787/253–1700* ▤ *AE, D, DC, MC, V* ☺ *No dinner Sun.*

$$–$$$$ ✕ **Platos.** In the heart of Isla Verde, this restaurant attracts a young, hip crowd. The menu is something old, something new. Puerto Rican favorites are jazzed up, so that the skirt steak is served with pumpkin risotto and the grilled pork is covered with a guava glaze. The bar is a great place for a beer in the afternoon or for cocktails before heading to the clubs. ⊠ *2 Calle Rosa, Isla Verde* ☎ *787/791–7474* ▤ *AE, MC, V.*

Contemporary

$$–$$$$ ✕ **Tangerine.** The dining room spills onto a terrace fronting the ocean, whose the steady breezes are as much a part of the dreamy scene as the muted-orange lighting and cream walls. This place is all about sensual pleasures, so it's no surprise that the descriptions of many of the dishes sound a bit risqué. (A plate with three types of marinated fish is named, quite simply, "Threesome.") Appetizers such as roasted pumpkin soup with lemongrass foam and crispy wild mushroom dumplings are seductive but overpriced. Artful entrées include chicken breast stuffed with eggplant puree and a pan-seared sea bass with sea-urchin butter sauce. ⊠ *San Juan Water & Beach Club, 2 Calle Tartak, Isla Verde* ☎ *787/728–3666* ▤ *AE, MC, V.*

Continental

$$–$$$$ ✕ **The Palm.** The same great steaks and seafood are served here as at this popular chain's other locations, including the original in New York City. When you leave, you half expect to look up at the Brooklyn Bridge. Caricatures of local and international celebrities stare down at you from the walls. The dark wood of the bar and the other furnishings let you know that you're in for some serious dining. The 10-ounce filet mignon is relatively petite, at least when compared to the rib eye that weights in at 24 ounces. Then there's the lobster, which starts at 3 pounds and goes higher. ⊠ *El San Juan Hotel & Casino, 6063 Av. Isla Verde, Isla Verde* ☎ *787/791–1000* ▤ *AE, D, DC, MC, V.*

WHERE TO STAY

San Juan prides itself on its clean, comfortable, plentiful accommodations, and hoteliers, by and large, aim to please. Big hotels and resorts, several with casinos, and a few smaller establishments line the sandy strands along Condado and Isla Verde. Between these two neighborhoods, the Ocean Park area has homey inns, as do the districts of Miramar and Santurce, although the latter two areas aren't directly on the beach. Old San Juan has only a few noteworthy hotels, one of which has a casino.

> **CAUTION**
>
> The small, government-sponsored inns called *paradores* are primarily *en la isla* (out on the island) rather than in San Juan.

Staying in a self-catering apartment or condo has advantages over a resort, especially for families. You can cook when and what you want, and you can enjoy considerable autonomy. Several companies represent such properties in San Juan. When booking, be sure ask about maid service, swimming pools, and any other amenities that are important to you.

Prices

The city's rooms aren't inexpensive: for a high-end beach-resort room, expect to pay at least $200 to $300 for a double in high season—roughly mid-November through mid-April. For smaller inns and hotels, doubles start at $100 to $150. As a rule, if your room is less than $50 in high season, then the quality of the hotel might be questionable. Although most hotels operate on the European plan (EP, no meals included), a few larger establishments offer other meal plans and/or all-inclusive packages; there's only one true all-inclusive hotel in Puerto Rico, and it's not in San Juan.

	WHAT IT COSTS In U.S. dollars				
	$$$$	$$$	$$	$	¢
FOR 2 PEOPLE	over $350	$250–$350	$150–$250	$80–$150	under $80

Prices are for a double room in high season, excluding 9% tax (11% for hotels with casinos, 7% for paradores) and typical 5%–12% service charge.

Apartment Rentals

Puerto Rico Vacation Apartments (⌧ Calle Marbella del Caribe Oeste S-5, Isla Verde, 00979 ☎ 787/727–1591 or 800/266–3639 🖷 787/268–3604 ⊕ www.sanjuanvacations.com) represents some 200 properties in Condado and Isla Verde.

Old San Juan

$$$$ 🖹 **El Convento.** Carmelite nuns once inhabited this 350-year-old convent, Fodor'sChoice but they never had high-tech gadgets like in-room broadband connections or plasma TVs. The accommodations here beautifully combine the old and the new. All the guest rooms have hand-hewn wood furniture, shuttered windows, and mahogany-beamed ceilings, but some have a little extra. Room 508 has two views of the bay, while Rooms 216, 217, and 218 have private walled patios. Guests gather for the complimentary wine and hors d'oeuvres that are served before dinner. The streetside Café Bohemio, the second-floor El Picoteo, and the courtyard Café del Níspero are all good dining choices. ⌧ *100 Calle Cristo, Old San*

*Juan ✆ Box 1048, 00902 ☎ 787/723–9020 or 800/468–2779 🖷 787/
723–9260 ⊕ www.elconvento.com ⟿ 63 rooms, 5 suites ♿ 3 restaurants, in-room safes, cable TV, in-room DVD players, in-room broadband, Wi-Fi, pool, gym, 2 bars, library, shop, dry cleaning, laundry service,
concierge, Internet room, business services, meeting room, parking
(fee), no-smoking rooms ▭ AE, D, DC, MC, V ⦿ EP.*

★ **$$–$$$** 🏨 **Gallery Inn.** You can shop from your bed at this 200-year-old man-
sion, as owner Jan D'Esopo has filled the rooms with her own artworks.
And not just the rooms, either; the hallways, the staircases, and even
the roof are lined with her fascinating bronze sculptures. Even if you
aren't a guest, D'Esopo is pleased to show you around and may even
offer you a glass of wine. (Just make sure that Campeche, one of her
many birds, doesn't try to sneak a sip.) No two rooms are alike, but all
have four-poster beds, hand-woven tapestries, and quirky antiques filling every nook and cranny. There are views of the coastline from several of the rooms, as well as from the spectacular rooftop terrace. The
first-floor Galería San Juan displays artwork by D'Esopo and others.
There's no restaurant, but meals for groups can be prepared upon request. ✉ 204–206 Calle Norzagaray, Old San Juan, 00901 ☎ 787/722–
1808 🖷 787/724–7360 ⊕ www.thegalleryinn.com ⟿ 13 rooms, 10 suites
♿ Dining room, some refrigerators, hot tub, piano, no-smoking rooms;
no a/c in some rooms, no room TVs ▭ AE, DC, MC, V ⦿ CP.

$$–$$$ 🏨 **Sheraton Old San Juan Hotel.** This hotel's triangular shape subtly
echoes the cruise ships docked nearby. Rooms facing the water have dazzling views of these behemoths as they sail in and out of the harbor. Others have views over the rooftops of Old San Juan. The rooms have been
plushly renovated and have nice touches like custom-designed beds. On
the top floor you'll find a sunny patio with a pool and whirlpool bath,
as well as a spacious gym with the latest equipment; the concierge level
provides hassle-free check-ins, Continental breakfasts, and evening hors
d'oeuvres. ✉ 100 Calle Brumbaugh, Old San Juan, 00901 ☎ 787/
721–5100 or 866/376–7577 🖷 787/289–1910 ⊕ www.
sheratonoldsanjuan.com ⟿ 200 rooms, 40 suites ♿ Restaurant, room
service, in-room safes, some minibars, cable TV with movies, in-room
broadband, Wi-Fi, pool, gym, hot tub, bar, casino, dry cleaning, laundry service, concierge floor, business services, Internet room, meeting
rooms, travel services, parking (fee), car rental, no-smoking rooms
▭ AE, D, DC, MC, V ⦿ EP.

$ 🏨 **Hotel Milano.** This affordable hotel is near the best and worst of Old
San Juan. On the plus side, it's on a lively street lined with restaurants
and bars. On the bad side, the street can be noisy. For less clamor, opt
for a room at the back. Rooms in
the five-story building won't win
any prizes, but they are clean and
comfortable. The open-air restaurant on the top floor has expansive
views of the barrel-tile rooftops.
The friendly staff goes above and
beyond the call of duty, arranging
for your laundry to be washed or

> **WORD OF MOUTH**
>
> "[Hotel Milano is] very clean and
> convenient although parking is
> easiest at the garage about two
> blocks away."   –bggirl.

confirming that your flight is departing on time. ⊠ *307 Calle Fortaleza, Old San Juan, 00901* ☏ *787/729–9050 or 877/729–9050* 🖷 *787/722–3379* ⊕ *www.hotelmilanopr.com* ⟿ *30 rooms* ⚭ *Restaurant, mini-bars, cable TV, bar, laundry service, no-smoking rooms* ▭ *AE, MC, V* ⊚⏐ *CP.*

$ 🏨 **Howard Johnson Plaza de Armas.** On Old San Juan's main square, this hotel couldn't have a more convenient location. All of the most popular sites are within easy walking distance. Some of the building's best architectural details, such as the tile floors, have been preserved. The best rooms are in the front, where shuttered doorways lead to balconies overlooking the Plaza de Armas. Inner rooms are a bit cramped and have very small windows. The interior courtyard has a hip little bar. ⊠ *202 Calle San José, Old San Juan, 00901* ☏ *787/722–9191* 🖷 *787/725–3091* ⊕ *www.hojo.com* ⟿ *51 rooms* ⚭ *Some refrigerators, cable TV, W-Fi, bar, shop* ▭ *AE, D, DC, MC, V* ⊚⏐ *CP.*

¢–$ 🏨 **The Caleta.** In an area overlooking the Bahía de San Juan, short-term studio rentals give you a sense of what it would be like to live in Old San Juan. Narrow stairs and hallways lead to the studios, each of which has its own character and can accommodate up to four people. Some have balconies overlooking the street. Returning guests often request the Sunshine Studio, with its warm light and outstanding views. Although the hotel usually requires a minimum stay, you can sometimes arrange daily rates. ⊠ *151 Clara Lair St., Old San Juan, 00901* ☏ *787/725–5347* 🖷 *787/977–5642* ⊕ *www.thecaleta.com* ⟿ *8 studios* ⚭ *Fans, kitchenettes, cable TV, dry cleaning, laundry facilities; no a/c in some rooms, no smoking* ▭ *AE, MC, V* ⊚⏐ *EP.*

Puerta de Tierra

◷ $$$–$$$$ 🏨 **Caribe Hilton San Juan.** How many hotels can claim to have their own fort? Fuerte San Gerónimo, which once guarded the entrance to San Juan Bay, is on the grounds of this sprawling resort, which also has a private beach, a luxurious spa, and one of the best-developed kids' programs on the island. (There's even an hour of free babysitting, so you can have a grown-up meal at Morton's or one of the other on-site restaurants.) Unfortunately, the guest rooms are a little past their prime, and the open-air lobby is crowded, noisy, and free of any charm whatsoever. The staff can seem disorganized at times. ⊠ *Calle Los Rosales, Puerta de Tierra, 00901* ☏ *787/721–0303 or 877/464–4586* 🖷 *787/725–8849* ⊕ *www. hiltoncaribbean.com* ⟿ *602 rooms, 44 suites* ⚭ *9 restaurants, room service, in-room safes, minibars, cable TV with movies and video games, in-room broadband, Wi-Fi, 3 tennis courts, pool, wading pool, health club, hair salon, outdoor hot tub, spa, beach, bar, video game room, shops, children's programs (ages 4–12), babysitting, dry cleaning, laundry service, concierge, business services, meeting rooms, parking (fee), no-smoking floors* ▭ *AE, D, DC, MC, V* ⊚⏐ *EP.*

$$$ 🏨 **Normandie Hotel.** One of the Caribbean's finest examples of art-deco
Fodor'sChoice architecture, this ship-shaped hotel hosted high-society types back in the
★ 1930s. After a stem-to-stern renovation, it's ready to sail again. Egyptian motifs in the grand ballroom and other period details have been meticulously restored. Guest rooms, many of them as big as suites, are

decorated in sensuous shades of cream and oatmeal. Business travelers will appreciate the huge desks outfitted with broadband access. Those in search of relaxation need look no further than the sparkling pool or the compact spa with its massage area overlooking the ocean. N Bar, on the second floor, has quickly become a see-and-be-seen place for the city's trendy crowd. ⊠ *499 Av. Muñoz Rivera, Puerta de Tierra, 00901* ☎ *787/729–2929* 🖷 *787/729–3083* ⊕ *www.normandiepr.com* ⌑ *58 rooms, 117 suites* 👌 *2 restaurants, in-room safes, minibars, cable TV, in-room broadband, Wi-Fi, pool, gym, massage, spa, beach, 2 bars, shop, babysitting, dry cleaning, laundry service, business services, convention center, Internet room, meeting rooms, car rental, parking (fee), no-smoking rooms* ▤ *AE, MC, V* ⧆ *EP.*

Condado

🐚 **$$$–$$$$**   🏨 **San Juan Marriott Resort & Stellaris Casino.** The shape and color of a cardboard box, this hotel doesn't add much to the skyline of Condado. There's nothing about the hotel that even hints that you are in the Caribbean. The hanger-like lobby is no more distinctive, and it reverberates with the exceptionally loud music from the lounge and the ringing of slot machines from the adjoining casino. It's only when you get to the rooms that there's a bit of flair—tropical fabrics and bright colors lighten the mood considerably. And of course there's the view of the ocean you have from most of the balconies. The high points are undoubtedly the pair of pools, which add a bit of whimsy with their gushing fountains and swirling mural. Restaurants include the Tuscany, known for its fine northern Italian cuisine. ⊠ *1309 Av. Ashford, Condado, 00907* ☎ *787/722–7000 or 800/465–5005* 🖷 *787/722–6800* ⊕ *www.marriott. com* ⌑ *512 rooms, 17 suites* 👌 *4 restaurants, room service, in-room safes, minibars, cable TV with movies and video games, in-room broadband, Wi-Fi, 2 tennis courts, pool, health club, hair salon, hot tub, beach, bar, 2 lounges, casino, children's programs (ages 4–12), dry cleaning, laundry service, concierge floor, business services, meeting rooms, travel services, parking (fee), no-smoking rooms* ▤ *AE, D, DC, MC, V* ⧆ *EP.*

🐚 **$$–$$$**   🏨 **Condado Plaza Hotel & Casino.** The Atlantic Ocean and the Laguna del Condado border this high-rise (once a Wyndham), whose two wings—fittingly named Ocean and Lagoon—are connected by a covered walkway. Standard rooms have nice touches like walk-in closets and dressing areas. A stay on the Plaza Club floor entitles you to 24-hour concierge service, use of a private lounge, as well as complimentary Continental breakfast and refreshments all day. Find your own place in the sun on the beach or beside one of four pools. Dining options include the poolside Tony Roma's. ⊠ *999 Av. Ashford, Condado, 00902* ☎ *787/721–1000 or 800/468–8588* 🖷 *787/722–7955* ⊕ *www. condadoplaza.com* ⌑ *570 rooms, 62 suites* 👌 *7 restaurants, room service, in-room safes, some in-room hot tubs, minibars, cable TV, in-room VCRs, in-room broadband, Wi-Fi, 2 tennis courts, 3 pools, wading pool, health club, 3 hot tubs, beach, dock, boating, 2 bars, 2 lounges, casino, children's programs (ages 4–12), dry cleaning, laundry service, concierge, concierge floor, business services, airport shuttle, parking (fee), no-smoking rooms* ▤ *AE, D, DC, MC, V* ⧆ *EP.*

$$–$$$ ⊞ **Radisson Ambassador Plaza Hotel & Casino.** It's not on the ocean, but this resort hotel is half a block away. You can be strolling along the sandy beach in less than five minutes. Even closer is the rooftop pool, which has a view over the rooftops of Condado. The casino's energy seems to spill out into—if not overrun—the small lobby. The rest of the hotel has the same frenetic feel. The rooms are a bit old-fashioned, with heavy draperies and fussy furnishings. The second-floor restaurant, La Scala, serves northern Italian cuisine; you will also find dozens of restaurants on the street just outside the front door. ⊠ *1369 Av. Ashford, Condado, 00907* ☎ *787/721–7300 or 800/333–3333* 📠 *787/723–6151* ⊕ *www. radisson.com* 🛏 *146 rooms, 87 suites* ⚹ *2 restaurants, room service, in-room safes, minibars, cable TV with movies, in-room VCRs, in-room broadband, pool, gym, hair salon, hot tubs, 2 bars, casino, dry cleaning, laundry facilities, laundry service, concierge, business services, meeting rooms, travel services, parking (fee), no-smoking floors* ⊟ *AE, D, DC, MC, V* ⦶ *EP.*

$ ⊞ **At Wind Chimes Inn.** Hidden behind a whitewashed wall covered with bougainvillea, this Spanish-style villa has the feel of an exclusive retreat. So much about the place invites you to relax: the patios shaded by royal palms, the terra-cotta-tiled terraces, and the small pool with a built-in whirlpool spa. And there's the soft, ever-present jingling of wind chimes, reminding you that the beach is just a block away. The spacious guest rooms have a tropical feel. The Boat Bar, open only to guests, serves a light menu from 7 AM to 11 PM. ⊠ *1750 Av. McLeary, Condado, 00911* ☎ *787/727–4153 or 800/946–3244* 📠 *787/728–0671* ⊕ *www. atwindchimesinn.com* 🛏 *17 rooms, 5 suites* ⚹ *Some kitchenettes, cable TV, pool, bar, Internet, parking (fee), no-smoking rooms* ⊟ *AE, D, MC, V* ⦶ *EP.*

$ ⊞ **El Canario by the Sea.** You can't see the ocean from this three-story hotel, as it's wedged between blocky condo complexes. Walk out the front door, however, and you can be on the beach in less than a minute. Rooms are comfortable, although they won't win any prizes for their decor. Continental breakfast is served on a pretty brick patio. If this place is booked, the company has two more properties in Condado. ⊠ *4 Av. Condado, Condado, 00907* ☎ *787/722–8640 or 800/533–2649* 📠 *787/ 725–4921* ⊕ *www.canariohotels.com* 🛏 *25 rooms* ⚹ *In-room safes, cable TV, no-smoking rooms* ⊟ *AE, DC, MC, V* ⦶ *CP.*

$ ⊞ **El Consulado.** One of the loveliest buildings in Condado, this small hotel once served as the Spanish consulate. Today the colonial-style structure, complete with stucco walls and a barrel-tile roof, is more about affairs of the heart than affairs of state. The comfortable guest quarters have dark-wood furnishings that subtly evoke a bygone era. Continental breakfast is served on a flower-filled brick patio beside the hotel, and numerous restaurants are within walking distance. ⊠ *1110 Av. Ashford, Condado, 00907* ☎ *787/289–9191* 📠 *787/723–8665* ⊕ *www.farohotels. net* 🛏 *29 rooms* ⚹ *Some refrigerators, cable TV, Wi-Fi* ⊟ *AE, D, DC, MC, V* ⦶ *CP.*

$ ⊞ **Coral Princess.** This art–deco building—one of the few left in Condado—has personality to spare. The ample guest rooms subtly reflect the hotel's heritage with crisp lines and simple furnishings. The hotel is

1

a block from the neighborhood's main drag, so you don't have to fight the crowds every time you walk out the front door. The beach is five minutes away, but you can always take advantage of the swimming pool on the palm-shaded terrace or the hot tub on the rooftop. ☒ *1159 Av. Magdalena, Condado, 00911* ☏ *787/977–7700* 🖷 *787/722–5032* ⊕ *www.coralpr.com* ↩ *25 rooms, 1 apartment* ♿ *Some kitchenettes, cable TV, in-room broadband, pool, hot tub, bar* ⊟ *AE, D, DC, MC, V* ⑩ *CP.*

♨ **$** 🏨 **El Prado Inn.** The multilingual staff at this quiet inn is as capable of satisfying your business and leisure needs as a large hotel. Like a secret garden, this 1930s art deco–style former mansion sits across a park two blocks south of the Condado beach (a three-minute walk) and four blocks north of the Plaza del Mercado. It's close to all the action, yet placidly removed from it. Each room is individually decorated with furniture and fabrics from Southeast Asia and Morocco. This inn welcomes about 50% American and 50% international repeat guests who have found themselves a sort of home base. ☒ *1350 Calle Lucchetti, Condado, 00907* ☏ *787/728–5925* 🖷 *787/725–6978* ⊕ *www.elpradoinn.net* ↩ *22 rooms* ♿ *Fans, in-room safes, some kitchens, some refrigerators, cable TV, pool, free parking* ⊟ *AE, MC, V* ⑩ *CP.*

$ 🏨 **Miramar.** This gleaming high-rise sits in the middle of Miramar, an up-and-coming neighborhood halfway between Condado and Old San Juan. It's a good location if you want to be close to the historic district but don't want the hassle of driving through the narrow streets. There's no beach, but some of the city's best are a short drive away. All the generously sized rooms have kitchenettes. Many of those on the upper floors have nice views of Condado Bay. ☒ *606 Av. Ponce de León, Miramar, 00907* ☏ *787/977–1000* 🖷 *787/723–1180* ⊕ *www.miramarhotelpr.com* ↩ *50 rooms* ♿ *Restaurant, kitchenettes, refrigerators, bar* ⊟ *AE, MC, V* ⑩ *CP.*

¢–$ 🏨 **Casa del Caribe.** Tucked discreetly off Ashford Avenue, this guesthouse is one of the most affordable hotels in Condado. Rooms decorated with works by local artists are simple, but comfortable. The wraparound verandah, surrounded by an overgrown garden, is the perfect place for a siesta. The hospitable staff will help you arrange island tours. Monthly rates are available. ☒ *57 Calle Caribe, Condado, 00907* ☏ *787/722–7139 or 877/722–7139* 🖷 *787/723–2575* ⊕ *www.casadelcaribe.net* ↩ *12 rooms, 1 suite* ♿ *Some kitchenettes, cable TV, parking (fee), some pets allowed (fee), no-smoking rooms* ⊟ *AE, D, MC, V* ⑩ *CP.*

¢ 🏨 **Hotel Olimpo Court.** Personal attention is key at this quiet, family-run hotel. It's something that owner Alexandra Rodríguez learned from her grandmother, and it has rewarded her with many repeat guests. Daily, weekly, and monthly rates are available for the single and double rooms, all of which are impeccably clean. Some have kitchenettes and small private balconies. The on-site restaurant, Chayote, is one of the city's best and most creative. The hotel is in Miramar, very close to Condado. ☒ *603 Miramar Av., Miramar, 00907* ☏ *787/724–0600* 🖷 *787/977–0655* ↩ *45 rooms* ♿ *Restaurant, kitchenettes, cable TV, free parking, no-smoking floors* ⊟ *AE, MC, V* ⑩ *EP.*

Ocean Park

★ **$–$$** ☷ **Hostería del Mar.** This small hotel manages to charm you before you even walk in the door. You'll probably pause, as most people do, to admire the pond filled with iridescent goldfish before continuing into the wood-paneled lobby. The decor might be described as South Seas meets South Beach. The spacious guest rooms continue the tropical theme, aided by colorful fabrics and rattan furnishings. Many rooms have views of the beach, which is only a few feet away. Make sure to enjoy the kitchen's creative cuisine, either in the dining room or at a table on the sand. The staff is courteous and helpful. ✉ *1 Calle Tapia, Ocean Park, 00911* ☎ *787/ 727–3302 or 877/727–3302* 🖷 *787/268–0772* ⊕ *www.hosteriadelmarpr. com* ⇔ *8 rooms, 5 suites* ↻ *Restaurant, some kitchenettes, cable TV, beach, bar, free parking; no smoking* ⊟ *AE, D, DC, MC, V* ❄ *EP.*

$–$$ ☷ **Numero Uno.** The name refers to the address, but Numero Uno is also how this small hotel rates with its guests. It's not unusual to hear people trading stories about how many times they've returned to this relaxing retreat. Behind a whitewashed wall is a patio where you can catch some rays beside the pool, dine in the restaurant, or enjoy a cocktail at the bar. A few steps away, a sandy beach beckons; guests are provided with beach chairs and umbrellas. Rooms are decorated in sophisticated shades of cream and taupe; several have ocean views. ✉ *1 Calle Santa Ana, Ocean Park, 00911* ☎ *787/726–5010* 🖷 *787/727–5482* ⊕ *www. numero1guesthouse.com* ⇔ *11 rooms, 2 apartments* ↻ *Restaurant, fans, some kitchenettes, refrigerators, cable TV, in-room broadband, pool, beach, bar* ⊟ *AE, MC, V* ❄ *CP.*

$–$$ ☷ **Tu Casa.** This white-adobe lodging sits in the middle of a residential area a couple of blocks from the beach. Proprietor Nancy Hernández has tastefully decorated each of the rooms—some have canopy beds covered with yards of fabric, others have wrought-iron beds piled high with fluffy comforters. Many have private balconies or access to a terrace with a sweeping view of the ocean. Common spaces, including a pool and bar area and plant-shaded patios, make it easy to unwind. ✉ *2071 Calle Cacique, Ocean Park, 00911* ☎ *787/727–5100* 🖷 *787/982–3349* ⊕ *www.tucasaguest.com* ⇔ *20 rooms* ↻ *Restaurant, kitchenettes, microwaves, refrigerators, cable TV, pool, beach, bar, no-smoking rooms* ⊟ *AE, MC, V* ❄ *CP.*

★ **$** ☷ **Andalucia.** In a Spanish-style house, this charming little inn lives up to its name with details like hand-painted tiles and ceramic pots filled with greenery. In the central courtyard there's a kidney-shaped hot tub big enough for you and four or five of your closest friends. Bamboo headboards and other nice touches give the rooms a tropical feel. Hosts Esteban Haigler and Emeo Cheung give you the warmest welcome imaginable, making you feel that their home is yours. One of the prettiest beaches in the city is a five-minute walk away. ✉ *2011 Calle McLeary, Ocean Beach, 00911* ☎ *787/232–5478* 🖷 *787/728–7838* ⊕ *www.andalucia-puertorico.com* ⇔ *8 rooms* ↻ *Cable TV, some kitchenettes, refrigerators, hot tub, massage, Internet room* ❄ *EP.*

$ ☷ **L'Habitation Beach Guesthouse.** Don't let the name fool you—this oceanfront inn may have a French name, but its laid-back vibe is pure

Caribbean. The primarily gay clientele is extremely loyal, coming back year after year. Those unlucky enough to find it fully booked often drop by anyway to recline on the sandy beach or sip a cocktail on the palm-shaded patio. (The margaritas here will knock your sandals off.) Rooms are simple and comfortable; Numbers 8 and 9 are the largest and have ocean views. ⊠ *1957 Calle Italia, Ocean Park, 00911* ☎ *787/727–2499* 🖷 *787/727–2599* ⊕ *www.habitationbeach.com* 🖙 *10 rooms* ᕍ *Snack bar, fans, cable TV, beach, bar, coin laundry, free parking* ▤ *AE, D, MC, V* ¶◎¶ *CP.*

Isla Verda

$$$$ 🖭 **El San Juan Hotel & Casino.** The glamour of an earlier era pervades this hotel—or putting it another way, it is time to get rid of the mahogany paneling, marble floors, and centuries-old tapestries that make the lobby so depressing. Luckily, the new owners of this property are investing $35 million in renovations. The rooms have a much more modern feel, with creamy walls and unfussy furnishings. All have high-tech amenities such as Internet access and CD players. Take dinner at the Ranch, a rooftop country-western bar and grill. ⊠ *6063 Av. Isla Verde, Isla Verde, 00902* ☎ *787/791–1000 or 800/468–2818* 🖷 *787/791–0390* ⊕ *www. thesanjuanhotel.com* 🖙 *332 rooms, 57 suites* ᕍ *8 restaurants, room service, in-room safes, minibars, cable TV, in-room VCRs, in-room broadband, 3 tennis courts, 2 pools, wading pool, health club, 5 hot tubs, beach, 14 bars, casino, nightclub, shops, children's programs (ages 5–17), dry cleaning, laundry service, concierge, business services, meeting rooms, travel services, parking (fee), no-smoking rooms* ▤ *AE, DC, MC, V* ¶◎¶ *EP.*

☾ **$$$$**　🖭 **Ritz-Carlton San Juan Hotel, Spa & Casino.** The elegance of marble floors
Fodor's Choice　and gushing fountains won't undermine the feeling that this is a true
★　beach getaway. The hotel's sandy stretch is lovely, as is the cruciform pool, which is lined by statues of the hotel's signature lion. Works by Latin American artists adorn the lobby lounge and the hallways leading to the well-equipped business center. Rooms have a mix of traditional wooden furnishings and wicker pieces upholstered in soft fabrics. A full-service spa begs to pamper you with aloe body wraps and *parcha* (passion-fruit juice) massages. Though most room windows are sealed shut to muffle airport noise, many suites open onto terraces. Tastefully so, the casino has its own separate entrance. ⊠ *6961 Av. Los Gobernadores, Isla Verde, 00979* ☎ *787/253–1700 or 800/241–3333* 🖷 *787/ 253–1777* ⊕ *www.ritzcarlton.com* 🖙 *403 rooms, 11 suites* ᕍ *3 restaurants, room service, minibars, cable TV, in-room broadband, Wi-Fi, 2 tennis courts, pool, fitness classes, gym, hair salon, hot tub, massage, sauna, spa, 3 bars, casino, nightclub, babysitting, children's programs (ages 4–12), dry cleaning, laundry service, concierge, concierge floor, business services, meeting rooms, parking (fee), no-smoking floor* ▤ *AE, D, DC, MC, V* ¶◎¶ *EP.*

$$$ 🖭 **Embassy Suites San Juan Hotel & Casino.** Overshadowing neighbors with more prestigious names, the coral-colored Embassy Suites is one of the prettiest hotels in Isla Verde. The glass elevators that whisk you up to your room overlook the plant-filled atrium that includes a pond and waterfall. Outside is a lagoon-style pool and an adjacent bar. The suites are not luxurious, but they are spacious enough for a family. The location—just 1 mi from the airport—makes the hotel popular with people traveling for business. The one drawback is that while the beach is nearby, you have to cross some busy streets to get to it. ⊠ *8000 Calle Tartak, Isla Verde, 00979* ☎ *787/791–0505 or 888/791–0505* ≜ *787/791–7776* ⊕ *www.embassysuitessanjuan.com* ⇦ *299 suites* ♿ *2 restaurants, room service, in-room safes, minibars, microwaves, refrigerators, cable TV with video games, in-room data ports, Wi-Fi, pool, health club, hot tub, bar, shop, dry cleaning, coin laundry, laundry service, meeting rooms, travel services, parking (fee), no-smoking floors* ⊟ *AE, D, DC, MC, V* ⍝ *BP.*

$$–$$$ ⊞ **Courtyard by Marriott Isla Verde Beach Resort.** This 12-story hotel tries to be all things to all people—and succeeds to a great degree. Harried business executives appreciate its location near the airport and high-tech offerings like high-speed Internet connections. Families prefer the many dining options and the fact that the city's best beach is just outside. The place is buzzing during the day, especially around the three swimming pools. At night the action centers on the lobby bar, where live salsa music often has people dancing. (If you don't know how, you can take lessons.) The best part is the price: it's undoubtedly one of the best values in San Juan. ⊠ *7012 Boca de Cangrejos, Isla Verde, 00979* ☎ *787/791–0404 or 800/791–2553* ≜ *787/791–1460* ⊕ *www.sjcourtyard.com* ⇦ *260 rooms, 33 suites* ♿ *3 restaurants, room service, in-room safes, refrigerators, cable TV, in-room VCRs, in-room broadband, Wi-Fi, 3 pools, gym, hot tub, beach, bar, lounge, casino, shop, dry cleaning, coin laundry, laundry service, playground, Internet room, business services, meeting rooms, parking (fee)* ⊟ *AE, D, DC, MC, V* ⍝ *BP.*

$$–$$$ ⊞ **Inter-Continental San Juan Resort & Casino.** Despite the name, this 16-story hotel in the heart of Isla Verde is downright dowdy. The curvy balconies give the facade an old-fashioned feel, and the low-ceilinged lobby does not invite you to linger. But the spacious rooms have pleasant views of the ocean or the city; suites overlook the palm-shaded pool area. The jangling casino is just off the lobby, and on-site restaurants include the poolside Restaurant Ciao Mediterraneo, Ruth's Chris Steak House, and the Grand Market Café. ⊠ *5961 Av. Isla Verde, Isla Verde, 00979* ☎ *787/791–6100 or 800/443–2009* ≜ *787/253–2510* ⊕ *www.ichotelsgroup.com* ⇦ *380 rooms, 22 suites* ♿ *6 restaurants, room service, in-room safes, some in-room hot tubs, minibars, cable TV with movies and video games, in-room data ports, pool, gym, hair salon, hot tub, spa, beach, boating, 3 bars, casino, nightclub, shops, dry cleaning, laundry facilities, laundry service, concierge, business services, meeting rooms, car rental, travel services, no-smoking rooms* ⊟ *AE, D, MC, V* ⍝ *EP.*

★ $$–$$$ ⊞ **San Juan Water & Beach Club.** There's water everywhere at this boutique hotel, from the droplets that decorate the reception desk to the deluge that runs down the glass walls of the elevators. Guest rooms, all of which are decorated in a minimalist style, have an under-the-sea feel because of the soft glow of blue neon. Four rooms are equipped with telescopes for stargazing or people-watching along the beach. No matter which room you choose, you'll have a view of the ocean. The lobby's Liquid lounge is a popular stop along the party trail for hipsters. Wet, the rooftop bar, lets you recline on white leather sofas as you take in the view of the skyline. ⊠ *2 Calle Tartak, Isla Verde, 00979* ☎ *787/ 728-3666 or 888/265-6699* 🖷 *787/728-3610* ⊕ *www. waterandbeachclubhotel.com* ⇨ *84 rooms* ⌂ *Restaurant, room service, in-room safes, minibars, cable TV, in-room VCRs, in-room data ports, pool, gym, hot tub, massage, beach, 2 bars, dry cleaning, laundry service, concierge, Internet, meeting rooms, parking (fee), no-smoking floors* ⊟ *AE, D, DC, MC, V* ℽ◎ℾ *EP.*

$$ 🏨 **Hampton Inn & San Juan Resort.** If you can live without being directly on the beach, you can get a room here for much less than at many of its competitors just across the road. The palm-shaded pool is so pleasant that you might not even make it to the beach. The guest rooms are standard issue, but they are decorated in tropical colors and count coffeemakers and irons among their amenities. Free coffee and tea are available in the lobby around the clock. The Guacamayo Pool Bar & Grill has a basic menu of hamburgers, fries, and the like. ⊠ *6530 Av. Isla Verde, Isla Verde, 00979* ☎ *787/791-8777 or 800/426-7866* 🖷 *787/791-8757* ⊕ *www.hamptoninn.com* ⇨ *147 rooms, 54 suites* ⌂ *Restaurant, in-room safes, some microwaves, refrigerators, cable TV, in-room data ports, Wi-Fi, pool, gym, bar, laundry facilities, business services, meeting rooms, car rental, parking (fee), no-smoking floors* ⊟ *AE, MC, V* ℽ◎ℾ *CP.*

$ 🏨 **Hotel La Playa.** Almost hidden on a quiet side street, the family-owned Hotel La Playa sits above the glistening green waters of Isla Verde. There's nothing fancy here, just 15 rooms in a motel-style building. What is exceptional is the oceanfront location, which comes without an oceanfront price tag. A plant-filled courtyard leads to a small bar where you can enjoy the cool breezes off the water. The restaurant, on a deck over the water, is famous for its hamburgers. ⊠ *6 Calle Amapola, Isla Verde, 00979* ☎ *787/791–1115 or 800/791–9626* 🖷 *787/791–4650* ⊕ *www. hotellaplaya.com* ⇨ *15 rooms* ⌂ *Restaurant, cable TV, beach, bar, free parking* ⊟ *AE, MC, V* ℽ◎ℾ *CP.*

$ 🏨 **Villa del Sol.** With stucco walls and a barrel-tile roof, this little hotel resembles the manor house of a hacienda. Swaying palm trees line the entrance, which takes you to an interior courtyard. Enjoy the sun from one of the chaise longues surrounding the pool or on the second-story terrace. The cheerful rooms are more spacious than you'd expect in a budget hotel. The only thing you're giving up by staying here is the beachfront, but the ocean is only a block away. ⊠ *4 Calle Rosa, Isla Verde, 00979* ☎ *787/791–2600* 🖷 *787/791–5666* ⊕ *www.villadelsolpr.com* ⇨ *24 rooms* ⌂ *Restaurant, cable TV, refrigerator, pool, bar, meeting room, car rental, free parking* ⊟ *AE, D, MC, V* ℽ◎ℾ *EP.*

NIGHTLIFE & THE ARTS

Several publications will tell you what's happening in San Juan. *Qué Pasa*, the official visitor's guide, has current listings of events in the city and out on the island. For more up-to-the-minute information, pick up a copy of the English-language the *San Juan Star,* the island's oldest daily; the weekend section, which appears each Thursday, is especially useful. *Bienvenidos* and *Places,* both published by the Puerto Rico Hotel & Tourism Association, are also helpful. The English-language *San Juan City Magazine* has extensive calendars as well as restaurant reviews and cultural articles. The English-language radio station WOSO 1040 AM also provides valuable information for visitors.

There are also publications for Spanish-speaking visitors, including the "Wikén" section of the Spanish-language newspaper *El Nuevo Día;* the paper also gives a weekly rundown of events on its Web site: ⊕ www. endi.com. *Noctámbulo* is a Spanish-language pocket-size music and nightlife guide aimed at island youth that has extensive listings and is distributed in area clubs, bars, and restaurants.

Nightlife

From Thursday through Sunday, it's as if there's a celebration going on nearly everywhere in San Juan. Be sure you dress to party, particularly on Friday and Saturday nights; Puerto Ricans have flair, and both men and women love getting dressed up to go out. Bars are usually casual, but if you have on jeans, sneakers, and a T-shirt, you may be refused entry at nightclubs and discos.

Well-dressed visitors and locals alike often mingle in the lobby bars of large hotels, many of which have bands in the evening. Some hotels also have clubs with shows and/or dancing; admission starts at $10. Casino rules have been relaxed in recent years, injecting life into what was once a conservative hotel gaming scene, but you still won't be allowed in with tank-tops or shorts. There are more games as well as such gambling perks as free drinks and live music.

In Old San Juan, Calle San Sebastián is lined with bars and restaurants. Salsa music blaring from jukeboxes in cut-rate pool halls competes with mellow Latin jazz in top-flight night spots. The young and the beautiful often socialize in Plaza San José. Late January sees the Fiestas de la Calle San Sebastián, one of the Caribbean's best street parties.

Young professionals as well as a slightly older bohemian crowd fill Santurce, San Juan's historical downtown area, until the wee hours. The revitalized Plaza del Mercado (off Calle Canals, between Ponce de León and Baldorioty de Castro) has structures—many painted in bright colors—dating from the 1930s or earlier. On weekend nights the area's streets are closed to vehicular traffic. You can wander around with drinks, which are served in plastic cups, and sway to music that pours from countless open-air establishments and the marketplace's front plaza.

Bars

El Batey. This wildly popular hole-in-the-wall bar won't win any prizes for its decor. Grab a marker to add your own message to the graffiti-covered walls, or add your business card to the hundreds that cover the lighting fixtures. The ceiling may leak, but the jukebox has the best selection of oldies in town. Join locals in a game of pool. ⊠ *101 Calle Cristo, Old San Juan* ☎ *787/725–1787.*

The Piña Colada Wars

THIS MIXTURE OF PINEAPPLE JUICE, coconut cream, and liberal amounts of rum, always garnished with a wedge of pineapple and a maraschino cherry, was invented by Ramón Marrero at the Caribe Hilton in 1954 or by Ramón Portas Mingot at the Barranchina Bar in 1963, depending on whom you believe. Was it Marrero, a young bartender who is said to have spent three months on a concoction that would appeal to patrons at the Beachcomber's Bar? (His secret? Using only fresh pineapple juice.) Or was it Mingot, an elderly bartender who was satisfying the whims of patrons at the bar in Old San Juan? (He said his were so frothy because he froze the pineapple juice and coconut cream mixture instead of simply adding crushed ice.)

The two venues have fought over bragging rights for decades. The Caribe Hilton issues press release after press release reminding people that the drink was born in its seaside bar. (If what its public relations department says is true, the drink celebrated its 50th anniversary in 2004.) The Barranchina Bar put up a plaque that tells passersby that it is the true birthplace of the beverage. The Caribe Hilton seems to have the edge. Coco López, the company that makes the coconut cream most often used in the drink, honored Monchito in 1978. In gratitude for his contributions to the "bartending arts," they presented him with a color television set. But the origins of the piña colada—which means "strained pineapple"—remains as unclear as the cocktail itself. You may have to sample several before you make up your own mind.

–Mark Sullivan

Borinquen Brewing Company. Behind glass at the back, sleek metal vats hold this microbrewery's lagers and stouts. The taps sprouting from the wooden bar are a rarity in Puerto Rico, where draft beer is virtually nonexistent. The music is good, and there's often sports on TV. The island art on the walls reaffirms that you're in the Caribbean and not a mainland suburb. ☒ *4800 Av. Isla Verde, Isla Verde* ☎ *787/268–1900* ☉ *Closed Mon.*

Coaches. This typical sports pub is well outfitted with televisions if your travel plans coincide with that game you just can't miss. Local Ivy League graduates often congregate here to watch big sporting events showcasing their alma maters. The annual Harvard–Yale football game can get ugly. The restaurant-bar also becomes a venue for live rock, Latin pop, and reggae bands at night, especially on weekends. Food offerings include U.S.-style burgers, chicken, steaks, and salads, as well as some Mexican food and local goodies. ☒ *137 Av. Roosevelt, Hato Rey* ☎ *787/758–3598.*

Karma. Music of all kinds, from *rock en español* to hip-hop to Latin rhythms, is played this popular, spacious bar-lounge in the heart of Santurce, and there's often a lively crowd. A menu of Spanish and Puerto Rican tapas is available when hunger strikes. ☒ *1402 Av. Ponce de León, Santurce* ☎ *787/721–5925.*

Liquid. In the lobby of the San Juan Water & Beach Club Hotel, glass walls filled with undulating water surround fashionable patrons seated on stools that seem carved from gigantic, pale seashells. If the wild drinks and pounding music are too much, head upstairs to Wet, a less frenetic and more welcoming space on the penthouse floor, where you can relax at the bar or on a leather banquette. ⊠ *San Juan Water & Beach Club, 2 Calle Tartak, Isla Verde* ☎ *787/725–4664.*

Casinos

By law, all casinos are in hotels, and the government keeps a close eye on them. They're allowed to operate from noon to 4 AM, but within those parameters individual casinos set their own hours. In addition to slot machines, typical games include blackjack, roulette, craps, Caribbean stud poker (a five-card stud game), and *pai gow* poker (a combination of American poker and the ancient Chinese game of pai gow, which employs cards and dice). That said, an easing of gaming regulations has set a more relaxed tone and made such perks as free drinks and live music more common. The range of available games has also greatly expanded. The minimum age is 18.

Condado Plaza Hotel & Casino. With its tentlike chandeliers and whirring slots, the Condado Plaza casino is popular with locals. A band performs at one on-site bar, and the TV is tuned in to sports at another. ⊠ *999 Av. Ashford, Condado* ☎ *787/721–1000.*

Inter-Continental San Juan Resort & Casino. You may feel as if you're in Las Vegas here, perhaps because this property was once a Sands. A torch singer warms up the crowd at a lounge-bar just outside the gaming room. Inside, a garish chandelier dripping with strands of orange lights runs the length of a mirrored ceiling. ⊠ *5961 Av. Isla Verde, Isla Verde* ☎ *787/791–6100.*

Ritz-Carlton San Juan Hotel, Spa & Casino. With its golden columns, turquoise and bronze walls, and muted lighting, the Ritz casino is refined by day or night. There's lots of activity, yet everything is hushed. ⊠ *Av. Las Gobernadores, Isla Verde* ☎ *787/253–1700.*

El San Juan Hotel & Casino. Slow-turning ceiling fans hang from a carved-wood ceiling, and neither the clangs of the slots nor the sounds of the salsa band disrupt the semblance of old world. The polish continues in the adjacent lobby, with its huge chandeliers and polished mahogany paneling. ⊠ *6063 Av. Isla Verde, Isla Verde* ☎ *787/791–1000.*

San Juan Marriott Resort & Stellaris Casino. The crowd is casual, and the decor is tropical and bubbly at this spacious gaming room. A huge bar, where Latin musicians usually perform, and an adjacent café are right outside. ⊠ *1309 Av. Ashford, Condado* ☎ *787/722–7000.*

Sheraton Old San Juan Hotel & Casino. It's hard to escape this ground-floor casino, the only place to gamble in Old San Juan. You can see it from the hotel's main stairway, from the balcony above,

> **CAUTION**
>
> Dress for the larger casinos in San Juan tends to be on the formal side, and the atmosphere is refined. Tank tops or shorts are usually not acceptable attire.

and from the lobby lounge. Light bounces off the Bahía de San Juan and pours through its many windows; passengers bound off their cruise ships and pour through its many glass doors. ⊠ *101 Calle Brumbaugh, Old San Juan* ☎ *787/721–5100.*

Dance Clubs

Babylon. A long line of well-heeled patrons usually runs out the door of the club at the El San Juan Hotel & Casino. Those with the staying power to make it inside step into a pop-art style disco with pulsating music and beautiful people. Those who tire of waiting often head to El Chico Lounge, a small room with live entertainment right off the hotel lobby. It's open Thursday to Saturday. ⊠ *6063 Av. Isla Verde, Isla Verde* ☎ *787/791–1000.*

Candela. This lounge–art gallery housed in an historic building hosts some of the most innovative local DJs on the island and often invites star spinners from New York or London. This is the island's best showcase for experimental dance music. The festive, late-night haunt is open Tuesday through Saturday from 8 PM onward, and the conversation can be as stimulating as the dance floor. ⊠ *110 San Sebastián, Old San Juan* ☎ *787/977–4305.*

> ### RAGGAETÓN
>
> If you go out to San Juan's popular dance clubs, you're likely to hear this hip-hop–influenced mix of Jamaican reggae and dancehall styles along with some Latin rhythms. The music has a strong electronic drum-machine beat, and the lyrics will be in Spanish. Many believe that the music began in Puerto Rico, but its popularity has spread much further.

Club Lazer. This multilevel club has spots for quiet conversation, spaces for dancing to loud music, and a landscaped roof deck overlooking San Juan. The crowd is different every night; Saturday is ladies' night. ⊠ *251 Calle Cruz, Old San Juan* ☎ *787/725–7581.*

Martini's. An older, dressy crowd frequents this dance club—a one-time conference room—in the Inter-Continental hotel. It's known for its Las Vegas–style reviews; acts have included celebrity impersonators and flamenco music and dance troupes. Record parties and fashion shows are also held here from time to time. ⊠ *Inter-Continental San Juan Resort & Casino, 5961 Av. Isla Verde, Isla Verde* ☎ *787/791–6100 Ext. 356.*

The Noise. A young crowd frequents this Old San Juan dance club to listen to hip-hop, reggae, and underground music. There are often long lines out the door from Thursday through Saturday nights, which are the only nights it operates. ⊠ *203 Calle Tanca, Old San Juan* ☎ *787/724–3426.*

Pool Palace. No, there's no swimming pool here. The name refers to the 15 pool tables that are the centerpiece of this cavernous club. If a game of eight ball isn't your thing, there's also a dance floor the size of an airplace hanger and a lounge area with clusters of cozy leather sofas. ⊠ *330 Calle Recinto Sur, Old San Juan* ☎ *787/725–8487.*

Rebar. The Pier 10 nightclub is a venue for some of the top acts in tropical and jazz music, but on Friday and Saturday nights from 10 PM onwards, it becomes Rebar, a South Beach–inspired disco complete with a beautiful crowd, danceable disco music, and lots of colorful drinks. ⊠ *Pier 10, Av. Fernández Juncos, Puerta de Tierra* ☎ *787/729–9722.*

Teatro Puerto Rico. This cavernous club with an upstairs lounge hosts a variety of DJs spinning trance-like rhythms. There's also often live music and other performances. A popular local drag queen performs Sunday nights. It's closed on Monday and Tuesday. ⊠ *1420 Av. Ponce de León, Santurce* ☎ *787/723–3416.*

Gay & Lesbian Bars & Clubs

With its sophisticated nightlife, San Juan has become a popular destination for gay and lesbian tourists. The Condado, perhaps the heart of gay San Juan, is a favorite destination for happy hour. It hosts an annual gay-pride march each June, full of music and dancing, that rivals those in similar cities around the world. Santurce, just south of Condado, is full of bars and clubs that cater to men and women of all ages. Most are located on or near Avenida Ponce de Leon.

Puerto Rico Breeze (⊕ www.puertoricobreeze.com) is a monthly newspaper covering Puerto Rico's gay and lesbian community. It's chock full of listings, articles, and advertisements on dining options, entertainment, and lodging alternatives.

Atlantic Beach. The oceanfront-deck bar of this hotel is famed in the gay community for its early-evening happy hours. But the pulsating tropical music, the wide selection of exotic drinks, and the ever-pleasant ocean breeze make it a hit regardless of sexual orientation. Good food is also served on deck. ⊠ *1 Calle Vendig, Condado* ☎ *787/721–6100.*

Cups. This women-oriented bar in the middle of Santurce has been a mainstay of San Juan's nightlife since 1980. Karaoke on Thursday is especially popular. It's open Wednesday to Saturday. ⊠ *1708 Calle San Mateo, Santurce* ☎ *787/268–3570.*

Eros. A balcony bar overlooks all the drama on the dance floor at this popular club. Most of the time DJs spin music ranging from house and hip hop to salsa and reggaetón, but there are occasional nights that send you back to the 1970s and '80s with disco nights. It's open Wednesday to Sunday. ⊠ *1257 Av. Ponce de León, Santurce* ☎ *787/722–1131.*

Junior's. Open every evening, this neighborhood bar attracts nearly equal numbers of men and women. The jukebox plays a constant stream of salsa, which often draws crowds to the dance floor. It has some of the cheapest drinks in town. ⊠ *613 Calle Condado, Santurce* ☎ *787/723–9477.*

Nuestro Ambiente. This bar stays open long after all the others have closed their doors. It is popular with both men and women. ⊠ *1412 Av. Ponce de León, Santurce* ☎ *787/724–9083.*

Starz. The new kid on the block, this cavernous club has dancing on Friday and Saturday nights, as well as a popular after-the-beach party on Sunday evening. ⊠ *365 Av. de Diego, at Av. Ponce de León, Santurce* ☎ *787/721–8645.*

Latin Music

Café Bohemio. When the kitchen closes around 11 PM, this little restaurant shows exactly how bohemian it can be. The music lasts until 2 AM;

Thursday is the best night, with Latin jazz and crowds of pretty people who spill out onto a terrace. ✉ *El Convento Hotel, 100 Calle Cristo, Old San Juan* ☎ *787/723–9200.*

El Balcón del Zumbador. A little off the beaten path, this venue has the city's best Afro-Caribbean music. Performers have included salsa great Roberto Roena, master percussionist Cachete Maldonado, and the legendary Cuban group Los Van Van. ✉ *2330 Av. Borinquen, at Calle Barbosa, Santurce* ☎ *787/726–3082.*

Hijos de Borinquen. Famed artist Rafael Tufiño, who stops in once in a while and has a stool with his name on it, immortalized this beloved bar in one of his paintings. The audience often sings along with the Puerto Rican ballads; some people even play maracas, cowbells, or bongos. The pitch is fevered during Andrés Jiménez's revolutionary anthem "Despierta Borinquen." It's closed Monday. ✉ *151 Calle San José, at Calle San Sebastián, Old San Juan* ☎ *787/723–8126.*

Nuyorican Café. There's something interesting happening here nearly every night, be it an early evening play, poetry reading, or talent show or a band playing Latin jazz, Cuban son, or Puerto Rican salsa later on. During breaks between performances the youthful, creative set converses in an alley outside the front door. It's closed on Monday. ✉ *312 Callejón de la Capellia, Old San Juan* ☎ *787/977–1276.*

Rumba. The air-conditioning blasts, the music thumps, and the crowd pretends not to notice how hip the place has become. With a large dance and stage area and smokin' Afro-Cuban bands, it's one of the best parties in town. ✉ *152 Calle San Sebastián, Old San Juan* ☎ *787/725–4407.*

Night Bites

San Juan is a cosmopolitan city by Caribbean standards, welcoming to all kinds of visitors, with many places open late—if not all night, at least for a good portion of it. The establishments listed here are generally open until at least midnight during the week and 2 AM on weekends. But many are open much later. Old San Juan's Brick House, for example, proudly proclaims that its kitchen never closes until 3 AM.

Brick House Bar & Grill. This friendly bar and sidewalk café on Old San Juan's bustling Plaza Somohano is adjacent to the Teatro Tapia. You can get tasty burgers until 3 AM, as well as plenty of good conversation. If you eat elsewhere, chances are you will see your server here, once his or her shift ends. ✉ *359 Calle Tetuán, Old San Juan* ☎ *787/724–3359.*

Buren. A funky, tropical-color bistro with a charming interior patio, this place across the street from El Convento Hotel serves good pizza and pasta, as well as Caribbean- and Mediterranean-inspired dishes. The house wines by the glass are all good, and there's often a jazz or flamenco musician performing live. ✉ *103 Calle Cristo, Old San Juan* ☎ *787/977–5023.*

Dunbar's. The crowd may be full of young professionals, but everyone is casual at this beachside bar. There's good food, sports on TV, a pool room, and live music Thursday through Saturday. ✉ *1954 Calle Mc-Cleary, Ocean Park* ☎ *787/728–2920.*

El Hamburger. This no-frills barbecue shack serves up the best burger in San Juan, with sides of crunchy french fries and onion rings. The wood-

and-zinc structure sits on a bluff overlooking the Atlantic. Usually open until midnight, it's open until 3 AM on Friday and Saturday nights. ⊠ *402 Av. Muñoz Rivera, Puerta de Tierra* 🕾 *787/721–4269.*

Hard Rock Café. Are you really surprised to find that there's a Hard Rock in Old San Juan? These days, they're almost as common as McDonald's. This one attracts a surprising number of locals. ⊠ *253 Recinto Sur, Old San Juan* 🕾 *787/724–7625.*

Krugger's. Old San Juan bar-hoppers head to this fried-food emporium and adjacent bar when the late-night munchies hit. Codfish fritters, beef turnovers, crab and plantain rolls, and more are served until the wee hours. ⊠ *52 Calle San José, Old San Juan* 🕾 *787/723–2474* ☉ *Closed Mon.*

Makarios. Italy meets the Middle East, brick-oven pizza meets hummus, and crostinis meet falafel on a big outdoor-seating area that spills onto a plaza. The first indoor level is a sleek, modern bar with a small dining area, where there's a pizza and snack menu and Western music. Upstairs is more serious Middle Eastern cuisine, hypnotic rhythms, and a skillful bellydancer. ⊠*356 Calle Tetuán, Old San Juan* 🕾*787/723–8653.*

El Patio de Sam. The clientele swears that this Old San Juan institution serves the island's best burgers. Potted plants and strategically placed canopies make the outdoor patio a fine place to eat in any weather. ⊠ *102 Calle San Sebastián, Old San Juan* 🕾 *787/723–1149.*

Restaurant Don Tello. Photos of famous and not-so famous diners line the walls of this well-kept restaurant. You can head to the dining room for a sit-down meal or feast on the barbecued chicken, *pinchos* (pork kabobs), and *bacalaítos* (salt-cod fritters) that are served curbside. On Monday stop by for *sancocho*, a beef broth loaded vegetables that is reputed to cure hangovers. ⊠ *180 Calle Dos Hermanos, Santurce* 🕾 *787/724–5752.*

Señor Frog's. Latin America's answer to Hard Rock Café, Señor Frog's attracts the cruise-ship crowd. The menu is a nod toward Mexico, with south-of-the-border favorites like nachos and quesadillas. ⊠ *Paseo Portuario, Old San Juan* 🕾 *787/977–4142.*

The Arts

San Juan is the epicenter of Puerto Rico's lively arts scene, and on most nights there's likely to be a ballet, a play, or an art opening somewhere in town. If you're in town on the first Tuesday of the month, take advantage of Old San Juan's **Noches de Galerias** (🕾 787/723–6286). Galleries and select museums open their doors after hours for viewings that are accompanied by refreshments and music. Afterward, people head to bars and music clubs, and the area remains festive until well past midnight. The event is so popular that finding a parking space is difficult; it's best to take a cab.

Island Culture

LeLoLai. This year-round festival celebrates Puerto Rico's Indian, Spanish, and African heritage. Performances showcasing island music and folklore take place each week in different hotels around the island. It's sponsored by the Puerto Rico Tourism Company. 🕾 *787/721–2400.*

Performing Arts

San Juan is arguably one of the most important cultural centers of the Caribbean, both for home-grown culture and the healthy influx of visiting artists that the local population supports. The city hosts the Puerto Rico Symphony Orchestra, the world-renowned Pablo Casals classical-music festival in winter, and an annual series of opera concerts. Many hit plays in New York and other large markets get produced locally, and there are often three or four other local theatrical productions taking place on any given weekend, many of them downright adventurous.

MAJOR EVENTS **The Casals Festival** (☎ 787/723–9185 ⊕ www.festcasalspr.gobierno.pr) has been bringing some of the most important figures in classical music to San Juan ever since Pablo Casals, the famous cellist, conductor, and composer, started the festival in 1957. Casals went on to direct it until his death in 1973. It has continued to serve as a vibrant stage for top-notch classical performers since then. Most of the shows take place at the Centro de Bellas Artes Luis A Ferré, but there are also performances at the University of Puerto Rico and other venues. The festival takes place from mid-February through mid-March. Tickets are available at the box office of the Centro de Bellas Artes Luis A Ferré.

San Juan is a great place to hear jazz, particularly Latin jazz, and the annual **Puerto Rico Heineken Jazzfest** (☎ 866/994–0001 ⊕ www.prheinekenjazz.com), which takes place in June, is one of the best opportunities for it. Each year's festival is dedicated to a particular musician. Honorees have included Chick Corea, Mongo Santamaria, and Tito Puente. Although the festival was born at the Tito Puente Amphiteatro, it has since moved to the Puerta de Tierra oceanside park and sports facility right outside Old San Juan. With the Atlantic surf crashing outside the park and the stars overhead, it's a stimulating atmosphere in which to soak up fine jazz music.

TICKETS Two major outlets sell tickets for events throughout Puerto Rico. **Ticket Center** (✉ Plaza Las Américas, 525 Av. Franklin Delano Roosevelt, Hato Rey ☎ 787/792–5000 ⊕ www.ticketcenterpr.com) can get you seats to most large-scale events. **Ticketpop** (✉ Banco Popular, 1500 Av. Ponce de León, Santurce ☎ 787/294–0001 ⊕ www.ticketpop.com) also sells tickets to popular events.

PERFORMANCE VENUES **Anfiteatro Tito Puente** (Tito Puerte Amphitheater). Surrounded by lagoons and trees, the open-air theater is a great spot to hear hot Latin jazz, reggae, and Spanish pop music. It's named after the late, great musician who is widely credited with bringing salsa to the rest of the world. Shows usually take place Thursday through Sunday nights. ✉ *Parque Luis Muñoz Marín, Hato Rey* ☎ 787/751–3353.

Centro de Bellas Artes Luis A. Ferré (Luis A. Ferré Center for the Performing Arts). With three different theaters holding up to 1,800 people, this is the largest venue of its kind in the Caribbean. There's something going on nearly every night, from pop or jazz concerts to plays, operas, and ballets. It's also the home of the San Juan Symphony Orchestra. ✉ *Av. José de Diego and Av. Ponce de León, Santurce* ☎ 787/725–7334.

Coliseo Roberto Clemente. The arena has become an important island venue for concerts in addition to its status as a sports facility. Rap, reggae, salsa, jazz, and pop musicians all play this venue, which holds 10,000 people. Recent concerts have included Ricky Martin and the Rolling Stones. ⊠ *Av. Roosevelt at Plaza las Américas, Hato Rey* ☎ *787/754–7422.*

Estadio Hiram Bithorn (Hiram Bithorn Stadium). Particularly big acts often use this outdoor stadium adjacent to the Roberto Clemente Coliseum, which hosts baseball games and large concerts. There's seating capacity for 18,000, more when the infield is used for fans. ⊠ *Av. Roosevelt at Plaza las Américas, Hato Rey* ☎ *787/765–5000.*

> ## UNCONVENTIONAL DESIGN
>
> Undulating waves of glass and steel form the facade of the new Puerto Rico Convention Center, a futuristic meeting place that opened in San Juan in 2006. Locals tout the statistics, such as the fact that the facility's 580,000 square feet make it the largest meeting space in the Caribbean. But it's the eye-catching design—the architects call it "techno-tropic"—that has drawn raves. Located on what was once a naval base in a newly-christened neighborhood—conveniently the "Convention District"—it is convenient to Miramar, Condado, and Old San Juan.

Teatro Tapia. Named for Puerto Rican playwright Alejandro Tapia, the theater hosts traveling and locally produced theatrical and musical productions. Matinee performances with family entertainment are also held here, especially around the holidays. ⊠ *Plaza Colón, Old San Juan* ☎ *787/721–0169.*

GROUPS **Orquesta Sinfónica de Puerto Rico** (Puerto Rico Symphony Orchestra). The island's orchestra is one of the most prominent in the Americas. Its 76 members perform a full 48-week season that includes classical-music concerts, operas, ballets, and popular-music performances. The orchestra plays most shows at Centro de Bellas Artes Luis A Ferré, but it also gives outdoor concerts at museums and university campuses around the island, and has an educational outreach program in island schools. Pablo Casals served as the impetus to this group, helping to create it in 1956. ☎ *787/721–7727* ⊕ *www.sinfonicapr.gobierno.pr.*

SPORTS & THE OUTDOORS

Many of San Juan's most enjoyable outdoor activities take place in and around the water. With miles of beach stretching across Isla Verde, Ocean Park, and Condado, there's a full range of water sports, including sailing, kayaking, windsurfing, kiteboarding, Jet Skiing, deep-sea fishing, scuba diving, and snorkeling.

Options for land-based activities include tennis and walking or jogging at local parks. With a bit of effort—meaning a short drive out of the city—you'll find a world of championship golf courses and rain-forest trails. Baseball is big in Puerto Rico, and the players are world-class; many are recruited from local teams to play in the U.S. major leagues.

The season runs from October through February. Games are played in San Juan as well as other venues around the island.

Beaches

★ **Balneario de Carolina.** A government-maintained beach, this balneario east of Isla Verde is so close to the airport that the leaves rustle when planes take off. The long stretch of sand, which runs parallel to Avenida Los Gobernadores, is shaded by palms and almond trees. There's plenty of room to spread out, and lots of amenities: lifeguards, restrooms, changing facilities, picnic tables, and barbecue grills. The gates are open daily from 8 to 6, and parking is $2. ⊠ *Av. Los Gobernadores, Isla Verde.*

★ **Balneario de Escambrón.** In Puerta de Tierra, this government-run beach is just off Avenida Muñoz Rivera. This patch of honey-colored sand has shade provided by coconut palms and surf that's generally gentle. There are also lifeguards, bathhouses, bathrooms, and restaurants. The park is open daily from 7 to 7, and parking is $3. ⊠ *Off Av. Muñoz Riviera, west of the Normandie Hotel, Puerto de Tierra.*

Playa del Condado. East of Old San Juan and west of Ocean Park, this long, wide beach is overshadowed by an unbroken string of hotels and apartment buildings. Beach bars, water-sports outfitters, and chair-rental places abound (expect to pay $3 or $4 for a chair). You can access the beach from several roads off Avenida Ashford, including Calle Cervantes and Calle Candina. The protected water at the small stretch of beach west of the Condado Plaza hotel is particularly calm and popular with families; surf elsewhere in Condado can be a bit strong. The stretch of sand near Calle Vendig (behind the Atlantic Beach Hotel) is especially popular with the gay community. If you're driving, on-street parking is your only option. ⊠ *Off Av. Asford, Condado.*

Playa de Isla Verde. The most popular beach within the city limits, Isla Verde is hidden from view by high-rise hotels and sprawling condo developments. There are plenty of places to rent beach chairs and water-sports equipment or grab a bite to eat. Unfortunately, there's not much street parking, so you might want to pay to park at a hotel. ⊠ *Off Av. Isla Verde, Isla Verde.*

NEED A BREAK?
★ ☺
Of Condado's many beach bars, one of the best is the terrace at **Piu Bello Gelato** (⊠ 1302 Av. Ashford, Condado ☎ 787/977-2121), across the street from the Marriott. It serves sandwiches, salads, and—best of all—homemade gelato in tropical flavors like mango and passion fruit. There's also Wi-Fi service.

Playa de Ocean Park. The residential neighborhood east of Condado and west of Isla Verde is home to this 1½-km-long (1-mi-long) stretch of golden sand. The waters are often choppy but still swimmable—take care, however, as there aren't any lifeguards. Windsurfers say the conditions here are nearly perfect. The beach is popular with young people, particularly on weekends, as well as gay men. Parking is a bit difficult, as many of the streets are restricted to residents. ⊠ *Ocean Park.*

Waving a Blue Flag

WITH 365 DIFFERENT BEACHES in Puerto Rico, choosing where to spread out your towel might seem like a daunting task. The decision is easier now that four have been designated with a Blue Flag. Chosen by the Foundation for Environmental Education, a nonprofit agency, Blue Flag beaches have to meet 27 criteria, focusing on water quality, the presence of a trained staff, and the availability of facilities such as water fountains and restrooms.

It's no wonder that Playa Flamenco, on the island of Culebra, made the cut. After all, it's rated one of the world's best beaches. More surprisingly, two of the beaches are in San Juan: Balneario Escambrón, in Puerta de Tierra, and Balneario Carolina, in Isla Verde. The fourth is Luquillo's Balneario Monserrate. This means that three of Puerto Rico's finest beaches are within an hour's drive of the capital.

–Mark Sullivan

Baseball

Does the name Roberto Clemente ring a bell? The late, great star of the Pittsburgh Pirates, who died in a 1972 plane crash delivering supplies to Nicaraguan earthquake victims, was born near San Juan and got his start in the Puerto Rican pro leagues. Many other Puerto Rican stars have played in the U.S. major leagues, including the brothers Roberto Alomar and Sandy Alomar Jr.; their father, Sandy Alomar; and Hall of Fame inductees Tony Perez and Orlando Cepeda. Baseball games in the San Juan area are played at **Estadio Hiram Bithorn** (✉ Hato Rey ☎ 787/725–2110), named for the first Puerto Rican to play in the major leagues. It's home to the Cangrejeros de Santurce, which means the Santurce Crabbers. (No, that last part was not a joke.)

Biking

Most streets don't have bike lanes, and auto traffic makes bike travel somewhat risky; further, all the fumes can be hard to take. That said, recreational bikers are increasingly donning their safety gear and wheeling through the streets, albeit with great care.

As a visitor, your best bet is to look into a bike tour offered by an outfitter. One popular 45-minute trip travels from Old San Juan's cobblestone streets to Condado. It passes El Capitolio and runs through either Parque del Tercer Milenio (ocean side) or Parque Luis Muñoz Rivera, taking you past the Caribe Hilton Hotel and over Puente Dos Hermanos (Dos Hermanos Bridge) onto Avenida Ashford. The truly ambitious can continue east to Ocean Park, Isla Verde, and right on out of town to the eastern community of Piñones and its beachside bike path.

At **Hot Dog Cycling** (✉ 5916 Av. Isla Verde, Isla Verde ☎ 787/982–5344 ⊕ www.hotdogcycling.com), Raul del Río and his son Omar rent mountain bikes for $30 a day. They also organize group excursions to El Yunque and other places out on the island.

Diving & Snorkeling

The waters off San Juan aren't the best places to scuba dive, but several outfitters conduct short excursions to where tropical fish, coral, and sea horses are visible at depths of 30 to 60 feet. Escorted half-day dives range from $45 to $95 for one or two tanks, including all equipment; in general, double those prices for night dives. Packages that include lunch and other extras start at $100; those that include accommodations are also available.

Snorkeling excursions, which include transportation, equipment rental, and sometimes lunch, start at $50. Equipment rents at beaches for about $10. Avoid unsupervised areas, as rough waters and strong undertows make some places dangerous.

Eco Action Tours (☎ 787/791–7509 ⊕ www.ecoactiontours.com) offers diving trips for all skill levels. **Mundo Submarino** (✉ Laguna Garden Shopping Center, 108 Av. Laguna, Isla Verde ☎ 787/791–5764) sells and rents snorkeling and diving equipment. **Ocean Sports** (✉ 1035 Av. Ashford, Condado ☎ 787/723–8513 ✉ 77 Av. Isla Verde, Condado ☎ 787/268–2329 ⊕ www.osdivers.com) offers certified scuba dives; airtank fill-ups; and equipment repairs, sales, and rentals. It also rents surfboards by the day.

Fishing

Puerto Rico's waters are home to large game fish such as snook, wahoo, dorado, tuna, and barracuda; as many as 30 world records for catches have been set off the island's shores. Prices for fishing expeditions vary, but they tend to include all your bait and tackle, as well as refreshments, and start at $500 (for a boat with as many as six people) for a half-day trip to $1,000 for a full day. Other boats charge by the person, starting at $150 for a full day.

Half-day and full-day excursions can be arranged through **Mike Benítez Sport Fishing** (✉ Club Náutico de San Juan, Miramar ☎ 787/723–2292) From the 45-foot *Sea Born* you can fish for sailfish, white marlin, and blue marlin.

Golf

Puerto Rico is the birthplace of golf legend and raconteur Chi Chi Rodriguez—and he had to hone his craft somewhere. The island has more than a dozen courses, including some of championship caliber. Several make good day trips from San Juan. Be sure to call ahead for details on reserving tee times; hours vary and several hotel courses allow only guests to play or give preference to them. Greens fees start at $25 and go as high as $190.

Three golf clubs are within fairly easy striking distance of San Juan. The four 18-hole golf courses at the **Puerto Rico Golf at Hyatt** all got a face-lift in 2005, and are just west of San Juan. For more information, *see* Golf *under* Dorado *in* Chapter 5, Rincón & the Porta del Sol.

There are more options to the east of the city. **Palmas del Mar Country Club** has two good golf courses. For more information *see* Golf *under* Humacao *in* Chapter 2, El Yunque

> ## A GOLF GREAT
>
> Juan "Chi Chi" Rodriguez, who was born in Rio Piedras, was the first Puerto Rican golfer to be inducted into the World Golf Hall of Fame.

& the Northeast. The spectacular **Westin Río Mar Country Club** has a clubhouse with a pro shop and two restaurants set between two 18-hole courses. For more information *see* Golf *under* Río Grande *in* Chapter 2, El Yunque & the Northeast.

Hiking

El Yunque, the Caribbean National Forest, is within easy striking distance of San Juan, being about an hour's drive east. The park, which is officially known as the Bosque Nacional del Caribe, has more than a dozen hiking trails.

Eco Action Tours (☎ 787/791–7509 ⊕ www.ecoactiontours.com) organizes a variety of hikes and excursions throughout the island, including El Yunque.

Horse Racing

Try your luck with the exactas and quinielas at **Hípodromo El Comandante** (✉ Rte. 3, Km 15.3, Canóvanas ☎ 787/641–6060 ⊕ www.comandantepr.com), a large Thoroughbred racetrack about 20 minutes east of San Juan. On race days the dining rooms open at 12:30 PM. Post time is at 2:30 on Wednesday and Friday through Monday. There's an air-conditioned clubhouse and restaurant, as well as a bar where there's dancing to the music of a rumba band on Friday after the last race. Parking and admission to the grandstand are free; clubhouse admission is $3.

Kayaking

The Laguna del Condado is popular for kayaking, especially on weekends. You can simply paddle around it or head out under the Puente Dos Hermanos to the San Gerónimo fort right behind the Caribe Hilton and across from the Wyndham Condado Plaza. Kayaks rent for $25 to $35 an hour.

Las Tortugas Adventures (✉ Cond. La Puntilla, 4 Calle La Puntilla, Apt. D1-12, Old San Juan ☎ 787/725–5169 ⊕ www.kayak-pr.com) organizes group-kayaking trips to the Reserva Natural Las Cabezas de San Juan and the Bahía Mosquito in eastern Puerto Rico.

Spas

Eden Spa. The treatments at this small spa sounds good enough to eat—fresh fruit and sugar body wraps, for example, or the lemongrass and mint pedicure. Many of the therapies use botanicals found on the island, which is why the scent of passion fruit and pineapple is in the air. The seven-room facility is across from the cruise-ship port, so cruise-ship passengers drop by for pampering. The spa is closed Sunday. ✉ *331 Calle Recinto Sur, Old San Juan* ☎ *787/721–6400.*

Surfing

★ Although the west-coast beaches around Rincón are considered *the* places to surf in Puerto Rico, San Juan was actually the place where the sport got its start on the island. In 1958 legendary surfers Gary Hoyt and José Rodríguez Reyes began surfing at the beach in front of Bus Stop 2½, facing El Capitolio. Although this spot is known for its big waves, the conditions must be nearly perfect to surf here. Today many surfers head to Puerta de Tierra and a spot known as La Ocho (in front of Bus Stop 8 behind the Dumas Restaurant). Another, called the Pressure Point, is behind the Caribe Hilton Hotel.

In Condado you can surf La Punta, a reef break behind the Presbyterian Hospital, with either surf or boogie boards. In Isla Verde, white water on the horizon means that the waves are good at the beach break near the Ritz-Carlton known as Pine Grove. East of the city, in Piñones, the Caballo has deep-to-shallow-water shelf waves that require a big-wave board known as a "gun." The surf culture frowns upon aficionados who divulge the best spots to outsiders. If you're lucky, though, maybe you'll make a few friends who'll let you in on where to find the best waves.

At Ocean Park beach, famous surfer Carlos Cabrero, proprietor of **Tres Palmas Surf Shop** (✉ 1911 Av. McLeary, Ocean Park ☎ 787/728–3377), rents boards (daily rates are $25 for boogey, $30 short boards, $35 for foam boards, and $40 for long boards), repairs equipment, and sells all sorts of hip beach and surfing gear.

Tennis

If you'd like to use the tennis courts at a property where you aren't a guest, call in advance for information about reservations and fees. The four lighted courts of the **Isla Verde Tennis Club** (✉ Calles Ema and Delta Rodríguez, Isla Verde ☎ 787/727–6490) are open for nonmember use at $4 per hour, daily from 8 AM to 10 PM. The **Parque Central de San Juan** (✉ Calle Cerra, exit on Rte. 2, Santurce ☎ 787/722–1646) has 17 lighted courts. Fees are $3 per hour from 8 AM to 6 PM and $4 per hour from 6 PM to 10 PM.

Windsurfing & Kite Surfing

★ The waves can be strong and the surf choppy, but the constant wind makes for good sailing, windsurfing, or kiteboarding (maneuvering a surfboard using a parachutelike kite), particularly in Ocean Park and Punta Las Marías (between Ocean Park and Isla Verde). In general, you can rent a Windsurfer for about $25 an hour (including a lesson).

Real Kiteboarding (✉ 2430 Calle Loíza, Punta Las Marías ☎ 787/728–8716 ⊕ www.realkiteboarding.com) is a full-service kiteboarding center that offers lessons. You'll get the best windsurfing advice and equipment from Jaime Torres at **Velauno** (⌧2430 Calle Loíza, Punta Las Marías ☎ 787/728–8716 ⊕ www.velauno.com), the second-largest full-service windsurfing center in any U.S. territory. It has rentals, repair services, and classes. It also sells new and used gear and serves as clearinghouse for information on windsurfing events throughout the island.

SHOPPING

In Old San Juan, Calle Fortaleza and Calle San Francisco have everything from T-shirt emporiums to jewelry stores to shops that specialize in made-to-order Panama hats. Running perpendicular to those streets is Calle Cristo, lined with factory-outlet stores, including Coach, Gant, Guess, and Ralph Lauren. On weekends, artisans sell their wares at stalls around the Paseo de la Princesa.

With many stores selling luxury items and designer fashions, the shopping spirit in Condado is reminiscent of that in Miami. Avenida Condado is a good bet for souvenirs and curios as well as art and upscale jewelry or togs. Avenida Ashford is considered the heart of San Juan's fashion district. There's also a growing fashion scene in the business district of Hato Rey. Thanks to Puerto Rico's vibrant art scene, more and more galleries and studios are opening, and many are doing so in neighborhoods outside the old city walls. If you prefer shopping in air-conditioned comfort, there are plenty of malls in and just outside San Juan.

Markets & Malls

Look for vendors selling crafts from around the island at the **Artesanía Puertorriqueña** (⌧ Plaza de la Dársena, Old San Juan ☎ 787/722–1709). It's convenient for cruise-ship passengers, as it's across from Pier 1. Several vendors also sell handbags, hats, and other items along nearby Calle San Justo.

For a mundane, albeit complete shopping experience, head to **Plaza Las Américas** (⌧ 525 Av. Franklin Delano Roosevelt, Hato Rey ☎ 787/767–5202), which has 200 shops, including the world's largest JCPenney store, the Gap, Sears Roebuck, Macy's, Godiva, and Armani Exchange, as well as restaurants and movie theaters.

About 10 minutes east of San Juan you'll find **Plaza Carolina** (⌧ Av. Fragosa, Carolina ☎ 787/768–0514). Get there via Route 26. **Plaza del Sol** (⌧ 725 West Main Av., Bayamón ☎ 787/778–8724) includes Old Navy and Banana Republic. It's about 30 minutes west of San Juan. Off Avenida John F. Kennedy, about 15 minutes south of San Juan, **Plaza San Patricio** (⌧ Av. San Patricio Av. at Av. Franklin Delano Roosevelt, Guaynabo ☎ 787/792–1255) has a Boston Shoe and a Footaction USA, as well as restaurants and movie theaters.

Factory Outlets

With no sales tax, Old San Juan has turned into an open-air duty-free shop for people pouring off the cruise ships. With only a few hours in port, they pass by more interesting shops and head directly for the factory outlets on and around Calle Cristo. The prices aren't particularly good, but nobody seems to mind. Designer bags can be had at **Coach** (✉ 158 Calle Cristo ☎ 787/722–6830). There's clothing for men and women at **Gant** (✉ Calle Cristo and Calle Fortaleza ☎ 787/724–4326). The staff is eager to please. **Guess** (✉ 213 Calle Cristo) stocks clothing that appeals to a slightly younger crowd. Taking up several storefronts, ★ **Ralph Lauren** (✉ Calle Cristo and Calle Fortaleza ☎ 787/722–2136) has perhaps the best deals around. Stop here toward the end of your trip, as there are plenty of items such as pea coats and scarves that you won't be wearing until you get home.

It's not in Old San Juan, but **Belz Factory Outlet World** (✉ Rte. 3, Km 18.4 ☎ 787/256–7040) has more than 75 factory outlet stores, including Nike, Guess, Mikasa, Gap, Levi's, Liz Claiborne, and Tommy Hilfiger. It's in Canóvanas, about 20 minutes east of San Juan.

Specialty Shops

Art

Atlas Art (✉ 208 Calle Cristo, Old San Juan ☎ 787/723–9987) carries contemporary paintings and prints as well as sculptures in glass and bronze. The gorgeous **Galería Botelli** (✉ 208 Calle Cristo ☎ 787/723–9987) displays the works of the late Angel Botelli, who as far back as 1943 was hailed as the "Caribbean Gauguin." His work, which often uses the bright colors of the tropics, usually depicts island scenes. His work hangs in the Museo de Arts de Puerto Rico. There are works on display here by other prominent local artists as well. Among those who ★ have displayed their works at **Galería Petrus** (✉ 726 Hoare St., Miramar ☎ 787/289–0505 ⊕ www.petrusgallery.com) are Dafne Elvira, whose surreal oils and acrylics tease and seduce (witness a woman emerging from a banana peel); Marta Pérez, another surrealist, whose bewitching paintings examine such themes as how life on a coffee plantation might have been; and Elizam Escobar, a former political prisoner whose oil paintings convey the often-intense realities of human experience. Petrus also sells the architectonic designs of Imel Sierra (who created the sculpture *Paloma* in Condado), which combine wood and metal elements.

★ Half a block from the Museo de Arte de Puerto Rico, **Galería Raíces** (✉ 314 Av. José de Diego, Santurce ☎ 787/723–8909) is dedicated to showing work by such emerging Puerto Rican artists as Nayda Collazo Llorens, whose cerebral and sensitive multimedia installations examine connections and patterns in games, codes, and human memory. Raíces also displays the work of sculptors Annex Burgos and Julio Suárez. **Galería San Juan** (✉ 204–206 Calle Norzagaray, Old San Juan ☎ 787/722–1808) shows sensuous sculptures of faces and bodies by artist

ART FOR ART'S SAKE

Many galleries stay open during Old San Juan's Noches de Galerias, held from 6 to 9 on the first Tuesday of the month September to December and February to May.

Jan D'Esopo. The gallery—really a part of the guesthouse she runs—is a work of art in itself. The place is a bit hard to find, so look for the busts over the front door.

Galería Tamara (✉ 210 Av. Chardón, Suite 104-A, Hato Rey ☎ 787/764–6465) has abstract oil studies by Wilfredo Chiesa and oil paintings of placid home scenes by Carmelo Sobrino. **Galería Viota** (✉ 739 Av. San Patricio, Las Lomas ☎ 787/782–1752) features paintings and silkscreens by master Augusto Marín and large-format abstract expressionist works by the Paris-based Ricardo Ramírez.

Books

★ A Condado classic, **Bell, Book & Candle** (✉ 102 Av. José de Diego, Condado ☎ 787/728–5000) caters to the local English-speaking community. If you forgot to bring a book with you to Condado Beach, pick up a paperback at **Bookworm** (✉ 1129 Av. Ashford, Condado ☎ 787/722–3344). **By the Book** (✉ 1300 Av. Ashford, Condado ☎ 787/724–4272) has a great selection of English-language magazines.

Borders (✉ Plaza Las Américas, 525 Av. Franklin Delano Roosevelt, Hato Rey ☎ 787/777–0916), part of the U.S. superstore chain, fills 28,000 square feet in the city's biggest mall. **Librería Thekes** (✉ Plaza Las Américas, 525 Av. Franklin Delano Roosevelt, Hato Rey ☎ 787/765–1539) sells contemporary fiction, magazines, and travel books in English and Spanish.

★ Among the city's finest bookshops is **Cronopios** (✉ 255 Calle San José, Old San Juan ☎ 787/724–1815), which carries a full range of fiction and nonfiction in both English and Spanish, as well as music CDs.

There are many small bookstores near the Universidad de Puerto Rico campus in Río Piedras. A local favorite is **Librería La Tertulia** (✉ Calle Amalia Marín and Calle González, Río Piedras ☎ 787/765–1148). Although it specializes in books printed in Spanish, it also has English-language titles.

Cigars

The **Cigar House** (✉ 255 Calle Fortaleza, Old San Juan ☎ 787/723–5223) has a small, eclectic selection of local and imported cigars. **Club Jibarito** (✉ 202 Calle Cristo, Old San Juan ☎ 787/724–7797), with its large walk-in humidor, is *the* place for local and imported cigars, as well as such smoking paraphernalia as designer lighters, personal humidors, pipes, and pipe tobacco. Also on hand are silk ties, cuff links, and designer pens from Alfred Dunhill.

Clothing

ACCESSORIES **Louis Vuitton** (✉ 1054 Av. Ashford, Condado ☎ 787/722–2543) carries designer luggage and leather items, as well as scarves and business accessories. Aficionados of the famous Panama hat, made from delicately hand-woven straw, should stop at **Olé** (✉ 105 Calle Fortaleza, Old San Juan ☎ 787/724–2445). The shop sells top-of-the-line hats for as much as $1,000. There are plenty for women, as well.

MEN'S CLOTHING After many years of catering to a primarily local clientele, **Clubman** (✉ 1351 Av. Ashford, Condado ☎ 787/722–1867) is still the classic choice

Design Lions

1

PUERTO RICO'S YOUNG fashion designers have opened many a boutique and atelier in metropolitan San Juan during the last few years. Their styles may differ, but these young lions all share an island heritage—complete with a tradition of true craftsmanship—and a level of sophistication acquired after studying and traveling abroad. The result is a fascinating assortment of original, exclusive, high-quality designs.

With all the warmth and sun, it goes without saying that Puerto Rico's designers are most inspired when it comes to creations for the spring and summer seasons. Lacy, flowing creations and lightweight, if not sheer, fabrics dominate designs for women. For men the trend is toward updated linen classics in tropical whites and creams. Whatever you find will be one of a kind, with stylish—if not playful or downright sexy—lines. Some of these designers have their own shops in San Juan.

Which designers should you check out? Lisa Cappalli, a graduate of New York City's Parsons School of Design, favors lace, as lace-making is a tradition in her family. David Antonio uses upbeat colors—bold reds and vibrant oranges—in his updated classics. Harry Robles is a bit more established than his peers; he specializes in gowns for women, and his draping designs are often dramatic and always elegant. Each of these young designers has a shop in San Juan.

To see their collections, consider visiting during San Juan Fashion Week, which takes place each year in March and September. The events are full of shows and cocktail parties, all organized by the Puerto Rico Fashion Designers Group under the leadership of island-fashion icons Nono Maldonado and Mirtha Rubio.

–Isabel Abislaimán

for gentlemen's clothing. **Lord Jim** (⊠ 250 Calle San Francisco, Old San Juan ☎ 787/722–3589) has a fantastic selection of leather goods, including shoes you won't find anywhere else. **Monsieur** (⊠ 1126 Av. Ashford, Condado ☎ 787/722–0918) has stylish casual clothing for men. In his shop called **Otto** (⊠ 69 Av. Condado, Condado ☎ 787/722–4609), local designer Otto Bauzá stocks his own line of casual wear for younger men. **Pedro Serranor** (⊠ 1110 Av. Ashford, Condado ☎ 787/722–0662) designs eye-catching swimwear for men.

MEN'S & WOMEN'S CLOTHING ★

Prolific designer **David Antonio** (⊠ 69 Av. Condado, Condado ☎ 787/725–0600) runs a shop that's small but full of surprises. His joyful creations range from updated versions of the men's classic *guayabera* shirt to fluid chiffon and silk tunics and dresses for women. **Nono Maldonado** (⊠ 1051 Av. Ashford, Condado ☎ 787/721–0456) is well-known for his high-end, elegant linen designs for men and women. He should know a thing or two about style—he worked for many years as the fashion editor of *Esquire*. **Verovero** (⊠ 1302 Av. Ashford, Condado ☎ 787/725–2332) stocks women's shoes that look as if they were designed by engineers.

WOMEN'S
CLOTHING **E'Leonor** (✉ 1310 Av. Ashford, Condado ☎ 787/725–3208) is a well-established store for bridal apparel, evening gowns, and cocktail dresses as well as more casual attire. Look for designs by Vera Wang and St. John. **Harry Robles** (✉ 1752 Calle Loíza, Ocean Park ☎ 787/727–3885) sells his elegant gowns in this shop. **Lisa Cappalli** (✉ 151 Av. José de Diego, Condado ☎☎ 787/724–6575) sells her lacey and sensuous designs in this boutique. **Mademoiselle** (✉ 1504 Av. Ashford, Condado ☎ 787/728–7440) sells only European apparel, including NewMan, Gerard Darel, and Ungaro Fever. The window displays at **Nativa** (✉ 55 Calle Cervantes, Condado ☎ 787/724–1396) are almost as daring as the clothes its sells. **Pasarela** (✉ 1302 Av. Ashford, Condado ☎ 787/724–5444), which means "cat walk" in Spanish, seems a fitting name for a boutique offering designs by the likes of Nicole Miller, Luca Luca, La Perla, and Renato Nucci.

Furniture & Antiques

★ For almost two decades, Robert and Sharon Bartos of **El Alcázar** (✉ 103 Calle San José, Old San Juan ☎ 787/723–1229) have been selling antiques and objets d'art from all over the world. **Casas y Cosas** (✉ Calle Cruz at Calle Luna, Old San Juan ☎ 787/721–6290) has some lovely old furnishing dating back to the late 19th century. At **DMR Gallery** (✉ 204 Calle Luna, Old San Juan ☎ 787/722–4181) artist Nick Quijano sells classic Spanish-colonial furniture and his own designs in a variety of Latin American woods. Near the Museo de Arte de Puerto Rico, **Trapiche** (✉ 316 Av. José de Diego, Condado ☎ 787/724–1469) purveys a fine selection of furniture and home accessories from Puerto Rico and the Dominican Republic.

Gifts

Exotic *mariposas* cover the walls of **Butterfly People** (✉ 257 Calle de la Cruz, Old San Juan ☎ 787/732–2432). It's a lovely place, with clear plastic cases holding everywhere from a pair of common butterflies to dozens of rarer specimens. Only the YOU BREAK IT, YOU BOUGHT IT signs detract from the colorful display. You can find a world of unique spices and sauces from around the Caribbean, kitchen items, and cookbooks at **Spicy Caribbee** (✉ 154 Calle Cristo, Old San Juan ☎ 787/625–4690).

Handicrafts

★ **Artefacto** (✉ 99 Calle Cristo, Old San Juan ☎ 787/386–6164) is the cleverest shop in San Juan. At first the items on display look like traditional crafts, but look again and you notice that everything is a little offbeat. A little wooden shrine, for example, might be sheltering an image of Marilyn Monroe. **Arte & Máscaras** (✉ 222 Calle San José, Old San Juan ☎ 787/724–9020) has walls covered with festival masks made all over Puerto Rico. At the **Convento de los Dominicos** (✉ 98 Calle Norzagaray, Old San Juan ☎ 787/721–6866)—the convent on the north side of the old city that houses the offices of the Instituto de Cultura Puertorriqueña—you'll find baskets, masks, the famous ten-string *cuatro* guitars, *santos* (carved statues of the saints), books and tapes, and reproductions of Taíno artifacts.

The **Haitian Gallery** (✉ Calle Fortaleza and Calle O'Donnell, Old San Juan ☎ 787/725–0986) carries Puerto Rican crafts as well as folksy, often
★ inexpensive, paintings from around the Caribbean. **Mi Pequeño San Juan**

(✉ 107 Calle Cristo, Old San Juan ☎ 787/977–1636) specializes in tiny versions of the doorways of San Juan. These ceramics, all done by hand right in the shop, are a wonderful souvenir of your stay. You might even find the hotel where you stayed reproduced in plaster. For one-of-a-kind santos, art, and festival masks, head for **Puerto Rican Arts & Crafts** (✉ 204 Calle Fortaleza, Old San Juan ☎ 787/725–5596).

Jewelry

In the Banco Popular building, the family-run **Abislaimán Joyeros** (✉ Plaza Don Rafael, 206 Calle Tetuán, Old San Juan ☎ 787/724–3890) sells fine jewelry designs by Sal Prashnik and Jose Hess, as well as watches by Baume & Mercier. **Aetna Gold** (✉ 111 Calle Gilberto Concepción de Gracia, Old San Juan ☎ 787/721–4756), adjacent to the Sheraton Old San Juan Hotel, sells exquisite gold jewelry designed in Greece. For a wide array of watches and jewelry, visit the two floors of **Bared** (✉ 154 Calle Fortaleza, Old San Juan ☎ 787/722–2172), with a charmingly old-fashioned ambience.

Diamonds and gold galore are found at **Joseph Manchini** (✉ 101 Calle Fortaleza, Old San Juan ☎ 787/722–7698). **Joyería Cátala** (✉ Plaza de Armas, Old San Juan ☎ 787/722–3231) is distinguished for its large selection of pearls. **Joyería Riviera** (✉ 257 Fortaleza St., Old San Juan ☎ 787/725–4000) sells fine jewelry by David Yurman and Rolex watches.

N. Barquet Joyeros (✉ 201 Calle Fortaleza, Old San Juan ☎ 787/721–3366), one of the bigger stores in Old San Juan, has Fabergé jewelry, pearls, and gold as well as crystal and watches. **Portofino** (✉ 250 Calle San Francisco, Old San Juan ☎ 787/723–5113) has an especially good selection of watches. **Rheinhold Jewelers** (✉ Plaza Las Américas, 525 Av. Franklin Delano Roosevelt, Hato Rey ☎ 787/767–7837 ✉ Wyndham El San Juan Hotel, 6063 Av. Isla Verde, Isla Verde ☎ 787/791–2521) sells exclusive designs by Stephen Dueck and Tiffany's.

SAN JUAN ESSENTIALS

To research prices, get advice from other travelers, and book travel arrangements, visit www.fodors.com.

Transportation

BY AIR

San Juan's busy Aeropuerto Internacional Luis Muñoz Marín is the Caribbean hub of American Airlines, which flies nonstop from Baltimore, Boston, Chicago, Dallas, Fort Lauderdale, Miami, Newark, New York–JFK, Orlando, Philadelphia, Tampa, and Washington, D.C.–Dulles. Continental Airlines flies nonstop from Houston and Newark. Delta flies nonstop from Atlanta, Orlando, and New York–JFK. JetBlue flies nonstop from New York–JFK. Spirit Air flies nonstop from Fort Lauderdale and Orlando. United flies nonstop from Chicago, New York–JFK, Philadelphia, and Washington, D.C.–Dulles. US Airways flies nonstop from Baltimore, Boston, Charlotte, Chicago, Philadelphia, and Washington, D.C.–Dulles. International carriers serving San Juan include Air Canada from Toronto, Air France from Paris, Iberia from Madrid, and British Airways from London.

It used to be that travelers arriving at San Juan's international airport had to transfer to nearby Aeropuerto Fernando L. Rivas Dominici (close to Old San Juan and Condado) to take a flight to Vieques or Culebra. This is no longer the case, as all the carriers servicing the islands now also have flights from the internacional airport. Air Flamenco, Isla Nena Air Service, and Vieques Air Link offer daily flights from both airports in San Juan to Vieques and Culebra. American Eagle and Cape Air fly between the international airport and Vieques.

Puerto Rico is also a good spot from which to hop to other Caribbean islands. American Eagle serves many islands in the Caribbean from San Juan; Cape Air connects San Juan to St. Thomas and St. Croix. Seaborne Airlines has seaplanes departing from San Juan Piers 6 and 7 to St. Thomas and St. Croix.

✈ **International Airlines Air Canada** ☎ 888/247-2262 ⊕ www.aircanada.com. **Air France** ☎ 800/237-2747 ⊕ www.airfrance.com. **American Airlines/American Eagle** ☎ 800/433-7300 ⊕ www.aa.com. **British Airways** ☎ 800/247-9297 ⊕ www.britishairways.com. **Continental** ☎ 800/231-0856 ⊕ www.continental.com. **Delta** ☎ 800/221-1212 ⊕ www.delta.com. **Iberia** ☎ 787/725-7000 ⊕ www.iberia.com. **Jet-Blue** ☎ 800/538-2583 ⊕ www.jetblue.com. **Spirit Air** ☎ 800/772-7117 ⊕ www.spiritair.com. **United Airlines** ☎ 800/864-8331 ⊕ www.united.com. **US Airways** ☎ 800/428-4322 ⊕ www.usairways.com.

✈ **Regional Airlines Air Flamenco** ☎ 787/724-1818 ⊕ www.airflamenco.net. **Cape Air** ☎ 800/525-0280 ⊕ www.flycapeair.com. **Isla Nena Air Service** ☎ 787/741-6362 or 877/812-5144 ⊕ www.islanena.8m.com. **Seaborne Airlines** ☎ 888/359-8687 ⊕ www.seaborneairlines.com. **Vieques Air Link** ☎ 787/722-3736 or 888/901-9247 ⊕ www.vieques-island.com/val.

AIRPORTS & TRANSFERS
The Aeropuerto Internacional Luis Muñoz Marín is in Isla Verde, 18 km (11 mi) east of downtown. San Juan's other airport, the small Aeropuerto Fernando L. Rivas Dominici (also known as the Isla Grande Airport) near the city's Miramar neighborhood, serves flights to and from destinations in Puerto Rico and throughout the Caribbean. (Although it was still operating at this writing, the airport's future was uncertain.)

Before you leave for Puerto Rico, check with your hotel about transfers: many area establishments provide transport from the airport, free or for a fee, to their guests. Otherwise, your best bets are *taxis turísticos* (tourist taxis). Uniformed officials at the airport can help you make arrangements. They will give you a slip with your exact fare written on it to hand to the driver. Rates are based on your destination. A taxi turístico to Isla Verde costs $10. It's $14 to Condado and $19 to Old San Juan. There's a 50¢ charge for each bag handled by the driver.

The Baldorioty de Castro Expressway (Route 26) runs from the airport into the city. Exits are clearly marked along the way, though you should check with your hotel to determine which one is best for you to take.

With regular traffic, the drive from the airport all the way west to Old San Juan takes about 20 minutes, but you should plan on 40 minutes. 🚇 Aeropuerto Fernando L. Rivas Dominici ☎ 787/729-8711. Aeropuerto Internacional Luis Muñoz Marín ☎ 787/791-4670.

BY BOAT & FERRY

Cruise ships pull into the city piers on Calle Gilberto Concepción de Gracia. There are often hundreds of people fighting over the handful of taxis lined up along the street. Save yourself the hassle and walk the few blocks to Old San Juan. If you are headed to other neighborhoods, take a taxi from nearby Plaza Colón.

The ferry between Old San Juan and Cataño is operated by the Autoridad de los Puertos. It costs a mere 50¢ one-way and runs daily every 15 or 30 minutes from 5:45 AM until 10 PM. The ferry, which departs from Pier 2, is the one to take if you wish to visit the Bacardí Rum Factory.

Traveling to Vieques or Culebra, Island Hi-Speed Ferry leaves from Pier 2 in Old San Juan. During high season the ferry makes one daily round-trip (leaving in the morning, returning in the afternoon). Travel time is 1 hour 45 minutes to Culebra, 2 hours 15 minutes to Vieques. Round-trip fares are $68 to Culebra, $78 to Vieques. Reservations are recommended. 🚇 The **Autoridad de los Puertos** ☎ 787/788-1155. **Island Hi-Speed Ferry** ☎ 787/724-6600 ⊕ www.islandhighspeedferry.com.

BY BUS

The Autoridad Metropolitana de Autobuses (AMA) operates buses that thread through San Juan, running in exclusive lanes on major thoroughfares and stopping at signs marked PARADA. Destinations are indicated above the windshield. Bus B-21 runs through Condado all the way to Plaza Las Américas in Hato Rey. Bus A-5 runs from San Juan through Santurce and the beach area of Isla Verde. Fares are 50¢ or 75¢, depending on the route, and are paid in exact change upon entering the bus. Most buses are air-conditioned and have wheelchair lifts and lock-downs. 🚇 **AMA** ☎ 787/767-7979.

BY CAR

Although car rentals in Puerto Rico are inexpensive (rates can start at $39 a day), we don't recommend that you rent a car if you are staying only in San Juan (at most, you might want to rent a car for a day to explore more of the island). Parking is difficult in San Juan—particularly in Old San Juan—and many hotels charge; also, traffic can be very heavy at times. With relatively reasonable taxi rates, it simply doesn't pay to rent a car unless you are going out of the city.

The main highways into San Juan are Route 26 from the east (it becomes the Baldorioty de Castro Expressway after passing the airport), Route 22 (José de Diego Expressway) from the west, and Route 52 (Luis A. Ferré Expressway) from the south.

Avenidas Ashford and McLeary run along the coastal neighborhoods of Condado and Ocean Park. The main inland thoroughfares are avenidas Fernández Juncos, Ponce de León, and Luis Muñoz Rivera, which travel from Old San Juan, through Puerta de Tierra and Santurce, and on to Hato Rey. Running north–south are avenidas Franklin Delano Roosevelt and Central (also known as Piñeiro), which intersect Muñoz Rivera and Ponce de León. Avenida Kennedy runs mostly north–south and leads to the suburbs of Bayamón and Guaynabo.

GASOLINE There aren't many gas stations in Old San Juan, but they're abundant elsewhere in the city. Some close at 11 PM or so; others are open 24 hours.

PARKING There's some on-street parking, but meters are often broken. No-parking zones are indicated with yellow paint or signs, though rarely both. Just because a spot on the street is painted white (or not at all), doesn't mean it's a parking space. Fines for parking illegally range from $15 to $250.

In Old San Juan, park at La Puntilla, at the head of Paseo de la Princesa. It's an outdoor lot with the Old City's cheapest rates (they start at 50¢ an hour). You could also try the Felisa Rincón de Gautier lot on Calle Gilberto Concepción de Gracia or the Frank Santaella lot between Paseo de Covadonga and Calle Gilberto Concepción de Gracia. Parking starts at $1.25 for the first hour. The lots open at 7 AM and close at 10 PM weekdays and as late as 2 AM on weekends.

ROAD CONDITIONS City streets (the occasional pothole aside) and some highways are in good condition, but several of the older, heavily trafficked routes aren't well maintained. People tend to ignore the law prohibiting jaywalking; watch out for pedestrians when driving in town.

RULES OF THE ROAD Speed limits are posted in miles, distances in kilometers. In general, city speed limits are 35 mph; on the highways they're 55 to 65 mph. Right turns on red lights are permitted. Seat belts are required; the fine for not using them is $50.

TRAFFIC Traffic jams are common—particularly at rush hours (7 AM to 9 AM and 3 PM to 6 PM)—throughout the metropolitan area. Several areas along main highways are undergoing repairs; be prepared for sudden slowdowns.

🚗 **Major Agencies Avis** ☎ 787/774-3556. **Hertz** ☎ 787/654-3131. **National** ☎ 787/791-1805. **Thrifty** ☎ 787/367-2277.

🚗 **Local Agencies Charlie Car Rental** ☎ 787/791-1101 ⊕ www.charliecars.com. **L&M Car Rental** ☎ 787/725-8307. **Vias** ☎ 787/791-4120.

BY TAXI

The Puerto Rico Tourism Company oversees a well-organized taxi program. Taxis turísticos, which are painted white and have the *garita* (sentry box) logo, charge set rates based on zones; they run from the airport and the cruise-ship piers to Isla Verde, Condado, Ocean Park, and Old San Juan, with rates ranging $10 to $19. Make sure to agree on a price before you get inside. City tours start at $30 per hour.

Although you can hail cabs on the street, virtually every San Juan hotel has taxis waiting outside to transport guests; if there's none available, you or a hotel staffer can call one. Major Taxi and Metro Taxi are reliable companies. Note that these radio taxis might charge an extra $1 for the pickup.

🚖 **Major Taxi** ☎ 787/723-2460. **Metro Taxi** ☎ 787/725-2870.

BY TRAIN

The Tren Urbano, an elevated light-rail system, travels throughout the metropolitan area, with stops at the University of Puerto Rico and Bayamón, but does not stop near the main tourist areas or at the airport, so you're unlikely to ride it if you're just in town for tourism. The fare is $1.50, which includes transfers to city buses. The system runs from 5:30 AM to 11 PM. It's run by the Alternativa de Transporte Integrado, better known as the ATI.

🚖 **Alternativa de Transporte Integrado** ☎ 787/723-3760 ⊕ www.ati.gobierno.pr.

Contacts & Resources

BANKS & EXCHANGE SERVICES

Banks are generally open weekdays from 9 to 5. The island's largest bank is Banco Popular de Puerto Rico, which has currency-exchange services and branches and ATMs all over the island. Other banks include Citibank, which has a branch across the street from the Radisson Ambassador Plaza in Condado and another convenient branch near the cruise-ship pier in Old San Juan.

🚖 **Banco Popular de Puerto Rico** ✉ 1060 Av. Ashford, Condado ☎ 787/725-4197 ✉ Plaza Las Américas, 525 Av. Franklin Delano Roosevelt, Hato Rey ☎ 787/753-4590 ✉ 1818 Av. Loíza, Ocean Park ☎ 787/721-5557. **Citibank** ✉ 206 Calle Tanca, Old San Juan ☎ 787/721-0108 ✉ 1358 Av. Ashford, Condado ☎ 787/721-5656.

EMERGENCIES

🚖 **General Emergencies** Ambulance, police, and fire ☎ 911.
🚖 **Hospitals Ashford Presbyterian Memorial Community Hospital** ✉ 1451 Av. Ashford, Condado ☎ 787/721-2160. **Clínica Las Américas** ✉ 400 Av. Franklin Delano Roosevelt, Hato Rey ☎ 787/765-1919.
🚖 **Pharmacies Puerto Rico Drug Company** ✉ 157 Calle San Francisco, Old San Juan ☎ 787/725-2202. **Walgreens** ✉ 1130 Av. Ashford, Condado ☎ 787/725-1510 ✉ 1963 Av. Loíza, Ocean Park ☎ 787/728-0083.

INTERNET, MAIL & SHIPPING

In San Juan, Internet cafés are few and far between. If that weren't bad enough, many hotels have yet to install high-speed Internet access in their rooms. Your best bet is to use your hotel business center.

In Condado and Isla Verde, branches of Cyber Net are open weekdays until 10 and weekends until midnight. In Isla Verde, try Internet Active, in a small shopping center across the street from the Hampton Inn. It's open daily 11 to 11.

San Juan post offices offer Express Mail next-day service to the U.S. mainland and to Puerto Rican destinations. Post offices are open weekdays from 7:30 to 4:30 and Saturday from 8 to noon.

Letters addressed to San Juan should carry the recipient's name, the street number and name or post-office box, and "San Juan, PR," plus the five-digit U.S. Postal Service Zip Code. San Juan consists of various neighborhoods, which aren't important to include on an envelope, but which may help you get around. From east to west, roughly, these include Old San Juan, Puerto da Tierra, Condado, Miramar, Ocean Park, Isla Verde, Santurce, and Hato Rey. The metropolitan area includes such suburbs as Cataño, Carolina, Guaynabo, and Bayamón.

🔂 **Internet Cafés** **Cyber Net** ⊠ 1128 Av. Ashford, Condado ☎ 787/724-4033 🖂 5980 Av. Isla Verde, Isla Verde ☎ 787/728-4195. **Internet Active** ⊠ Av. Isla Verde and Calle Rosa, Isla Verde ☎ 787/791-1916.

🔂 **Post Offices** **Old San Juan Branch** ⊠ 153 Calle Fortaleza, Old San Juan ☎ 787/723-1277. **Puerta de Tierra Branch** ⊠ 163 Av. Fernandez Juncos, Puerta de Tierra ☎ 787/722-4134.

OVERNIGHT SERVICES | Most major courier services—Federal Express, UPS, Airborne Express—do business in Puerto Rico. Your best bet is to let the staff at a store like the UPS Store help you with your shipping. The company has several branches in the metropolitan area, including Old San Juan and Condado.

🔂 **UPS Store** ⊠ 400 Calle Calaf, Old San Juan ☎ 787/250-0501 🖂 1357 Av. Ashford, Condado ☎ 787/724-8678 🖂 1507 Av. Ponce de León, Santurce ☎ 787/723-0613.

MEDIA

The English-language daily, the *San Juan Star,* covers local and international news and local events. Radio Oso, WOSO 1030 on the AM dial, provides the local English-speaking community with up-to-the minute news.

TOUR OPTIONS

In Old San Juan free trolleys can take you around, and the tourist board can provide you with a copy of *Qué Pasa,* which contains a self-guided walking tour. The Caribbean Carriage Company gives tours of Old San Juan in horse-drawn carriages. It's a bit hokey, but it gets you off your feet. Look for these buggies at Plaza de la Dársena near Pier 1; the cost is $35 to $75 per couple.

Wheelchair Getaway offers city sightseeing trips as well as wheelchair transport from airports and cruise-ship docks to San Juan hotels. Colonial Adventure at Old San Juan offers group tours of the city's historic buildings. Legends of Puerto Rico has tours of Old San Juan as well as the modern neighborhoods that few travelers ever visit.

🔂 **Caribbean Carriage Company** ☎ 787/797-8063. **Colonial Adventure at Old San Juan** ☎ 787/793-2992 or 888/774-9919. **Legends of Puerto Rico** ☎ 787/605-9060 🌐 www.legendsofpr.com. **Wheelchair Getaway** ☎ 787/883-0131 or 800/868-8028.

VISITOR INFORMATION

You'll find Puerto Rico Tourism Company information officers (identified by their caps and shirts with the tourism company patch) near the baggage-claim areas at Luis Muñoz Marín International Airport. It's open daily from 9 AM to 10 PM in high season and daily from 9 AM to 8 PM in low season.

In San Juan the tourism company's main office is at the old city jail, La Princesa, in Old San Juan. It operates a branch in a pretty yellow colonial building in Plaza de la Dársena. It's open Thursday and Friday 9 to 5:30, Saturday to Wednesday 9 to 8. Be sure to pick up a free copy of *Qué Pasa,* the official visitor guide. Information officers are posted around Old San Juan (look for them at the cruise-ship piers and at the Catedral de San Juan Bautista) during the day.

La Oficina de Turismo del Municipio de San Juan, run by the city, has offices in Old San Juan (at the Alcaldía) and in Condado (in front of the Condado Plaza Hotel on Avenida Ashford). Both are open weekdays from 8 to 4.

Oficina de Turismo del Municipio de San Juan ⊠ Alcaldía, 153 Calle San Francisco, Old San Juan ☎ 787/724-7171 ⊠ 999 Av. Ashford, Condado ☎ 787/740-9270. **Puerto Rico Tourism Company** 🖂 Box 902-3960, Old San Juan Station, San Juan 00902-3960 ☎ 787/721-2400 ⊠ Plaza de la Dársena, near Pier 1, Old San Juan ☎ 787/722-1709 ⊠ Luis Muñoz Marín International Airport ☎ 787/791-1014 or 787/791-2551 ⊕ www.gotopuertorico.com.

El Yunque &
the Northeast

WORD OF MOUTH

"We enjoyed a hike in [El Yunque] down to the waterfall. It took about 45 minutes each way. That alone gave us a nice feel for the rain forest. We rented a car, [and it] was about 45 minutes from San Juan. Your hotel can set you up with a tour if you don't feel like renting a car."

—lv2trvl

"The water [in Laguna Grande in Reserva Natural Las Cabezas de San Juan] is unlike anything else you will ever see—every time you dip your oar in, there is a glowing trail behind it. . . . There are other places in Puerto Rico to see this phenomenon, but this one is only about 60 to 90 minutes from San Juan."

—Dyan

Revised and
Updated by
Mark Sullivan

TREE FROGS, RARE PARROTS, AND WILD HORSES only start the list of northeastern Puerto Rico's offerings. The backdrops for encounters with an array of flora and fauna include the 28,000-acre El Yunque, the only tropical rain forest in the U.S. National Forest system; the seven ecosystems in the Reserva Natural Las Cabezas de San Juan; and Laguna Grande, where tiny sea creatures appear to light up the waters.

The natural beauty and varied terrain continue in the area's towns as well. Loíza, with its strong African heritage, is tucked among coconut groves. Río Grande—which once attracted immigrants from Austria, Spain, and Italy—sits on the island's only navigable river. Naguabo overlooks what were once immense cane fields as well as Cayo Santiago, where the only residents are monkeys.

You can golf, ride horses, hike marked trails, and plunge into water sports throughout the region. In many places along the coast, green hills cascade down to the ocean. On the edge of the Atlantic, Fajardo serves as a jumping-off point for diving, fishing, and catamaran excursions. Luquillo is the site of a family beach so well equipped that there are even facilities enabling wheelchair users to enter the sea.

If you wish to get away from it all with a neatly packaged trip, eastern Puerto Rico has some of the island's top resorts: the El Conquistador Resort and the Westin Río Mar. You'll also find the island's only all-inclusive resort, the Paradisus Puerto Rico. The extensive facilities and luxury services at these large, self-contained complexes make the list of regional offerings more than complete.

Exploring El Yunque & the Northeast

As the ocean bends around the northeastern coast, it laps onto beaches of soft sand and palm trees, crashes against high bluffs, and almost magically creates an amazing roster of ecosystems. Beautiful beaches at Luquillo are complemented by more rugged southeastern shores. Inland, green hills roll down toward plains that once held expanses of coconut trees, such as those still surrounding the town of Loíza, or sugarcane, as evidenced by the surviving plantations near Naguabo and Humacao. Most notable, however, is the precipitation-fed landscape: green is the dominant color here.

About the Restaurants

Some restaurants carry the tourist board's *meson gastronómico* designation. Such establishments specialize in typical island food. The eastern region has both formal restaurants, where reservations are very necessary, and casual beach-side eateries, where you can walk in unannounced in beach attire and have a fine meal of fresh fish. Bills generally don't include service charges, so a 15% tip is customary and expected. Most restaurants are open for dinner from late afternoon until at least 10 PM.

TOP 5 PICKS FOR THE NORTHEAST

- Hiking past the waterfalls of El Yunque, the only rain forest within the U.S. National Forest system.

- Taking a dip at the Balneario de Luquillo, one of the prettiest beaches in Puerto Rico.

- Sitting elbow-to-elbow with locals at one of the dozens of out-

door seafood shacks on the highway before you get to the the Balneario de Luquillo.

- Gasping at the eye-popping views from the lighthouse at Reserva Natural Las Cabezas de San Juan.

- Hitting the tree-lined fairways of the courses at Palmas del Mar.

WHAT IT COSTS In U.S. dollars				
$$$$	**$$$**	**$$**	**$**	**¢**
AT DINNER over $30	$20–$30	$12–$20	$8–$12	under $8

Prices are per person for a main course at dinner.

About the Hotels

The east coast has a wide variety of lodgings, from government-approved paradores to small lodges in the mountains to large, lavish resorts along the coast. The Westin Río Mar Beach Golf Resort & Spa is a good option, as is the El Conquistador Resort & Golden Door Spa. The island's only all-inclusive property, the massive Paradisus Puerto Rico, is less polished than it should be for the high cost.

WHAT IT COSTS In U.S. dollars				
$$$$	**$$$**	**$$**	**$**	**¢**
FOR 2 PEOPLE over $350	$250–$350	$150–$250	$80–$150	under $80

Prices are for a double room in high season, excluding 9% tax (11% for hotels with casinos, 7% for paradores) and 5%–12% service charge.

Timing

In general, the island's northeast coast—preferred by those seeking abandoned beaches and nature reserves over casinos and urban glitz—tends to be less in demand than San Juan. The exception is Easter and Christmas, when Luquillo and Fajardo become crowded with local sun lovers, merrymakers, and campers. Island festivals also draw crowds, but planning a trip around one of them will give you a true sense of the region's culture. Be sure to make reservations well in advance if you're visiting during high season, which runs from December 15 through April 15.

Numbers in the text correspond to numbers in the margin and on the Eastern Puerto Rico and El Yunque maps.

IF YOU LIKE

BEACHES

The Atlantic east coast is edged with sandy, palm-lined shores that are occasionally cut by rugged stretches. Some of these beaches are quiet, isolated escapes. Others—such as Luquillo and Seven Seas near Fajardo—are jammed with water-loving families, especially on weekends and during the Easter holidays.

GREAT FOOD

Puerto Ricans love sybaritic pleasures, and that includes fine dining—whether it be on Continental, Nueva Latina, or authentically native cuisine. In the east you'll find fine fare of all types. On the traditional side, look for the deep-fried snacks (often stuffed with meat or fish) known as *frituras*, as well as numerous dishes laced with coconut. Plantains appear as the starring ingredient in the hearty *mofongo*, a seafood-stuffed dish, or as *tostones* (fried plantain chips). Fresh fish is commonly prepared with tomatoes, onions, and garlic, or some combination of the three.

GOLF

There's something to be said for facing a rolling, palm-tree-lined fairway with the distant ocean at your back. And then there are the ducks, iguanas, and pelicans that congregate in the mangroves near some holes. That's what golf in eastern Puerto Rico is all about. The Arthur Hills–designed course at El Conquistador is one of the island's best. The Flamboyán course, a Rees-Jones creation at Palmas del Mar Country Club, consistently gets raves, as do the courses at the Westin Río Mar. An old-time favorite is the Bahía Beach Plantation course, which was developed on a former coconut plantation.

THE NORTHEASTERN COAST

Just east of San Juan, at the community of Piñones, urban chaos is replaced with the peace of winding, palm-lined roads that are interrupted at intervals by barefoot eateries and dramatic ocean views. The first major town you'll encounter is Loíza, where residents proudly claim their African heritage and where renowned mask-makers live. Farther southeast and inland is Río Grande, a community that grew by virtue of its location beside the island's only navigable river. The river rises within El Yunque, the local name for the Caribbean National Forest, a sprawling blanket of green covering a mountainous region south of Río Grande. Back on the coast, Balneario de Luquillo (Luquillo Beach) has snack kiosks, dressing rooms, showers, and facilities that enable wheelchair users to play in the ocean.

CAUTION

Leave yourself plenty of time for driving to El Yunque or any of the resorts in the northeast. Route 3, the main route east, is notorious for its bumper-to-bumper traffic.

Southeast of Luquillo sits the Reserva Natural Las Cabezas de San Juan, with its restored lighthouse and variety of ecosystems. Anchoring the island's east coast is Fajardo, a lively port city with a large marina, ferry service to the outer islands, and a string of offshore cays. Catamarans based here sail to and from great snorkeling spots, yachts stop by to refuel or stock up on supplies, and local fishing craft chug in and out as part of a day's work.

Piñones

❶ *16 km (10 mi) east of San Juan.*

Funky Piñones is little more than a collection of open-air, seaside eateries. Sand floors, barefoot patrons, and tantalizing seafood—traditionally washed down with icy beer—have made it popular with locals, especially on weekend evenings. Chilled *agua de coco* is served right from the coconut. During the day you can rent a bike and follow the marked seaside trail that meanders for 11 km (7 mi). At this writing, plans were on the table to expand the bike path all the way to Isla Verde in San Juan.

The area has grown as a nightlife designation, as fancier establishments, some with live music, have opened up. And there are raucous open-air dance halls playing mostly Dominican merengue or local rap, which is influenced by salsa and reggae. But the action begins to cook before sunset. As mid-afternoon turns into evening and people begin to leave the beach for refreshments, the air is thick with smoke from grilled fish, beef and chicken kabobs, and the kettles of oil used to fry codfish and crab fritters. When the giant orange Caribbean sun starts to fall behind the San Juan skyline salsa and merengue—not to mention reggae and Latin pop—start to blare out from the jukeboxes and sound systems of the dozens of ramshackle establishments dotting Route 187, the sector's main road. Traffic on the two-lane road into and out of the area is daunting on Friday and Saturday nights, when nights heat up the most and many places have merengue combos, Brazilian-jazz trios, or reggae bands.

One of the most pleasant ways to pass the time is the **Paseo Piñones.** This 6½-mi boardwalk passes through sand dunes and crosses lagoons and mangrove forests. All the while, a line of coconut palms shades you from the sun. You'll share the path with bikers, joggers, and in-line skaters. Food kiosks abound. ✉ *Piñones.*

Where to Eat

$$–$$$ ✕ **Soleil.** A bit more refined than some of its neighbors, this restaurant actually sits on a wooden platform positioned *above* the sand. Even nicer is the upstairs deck that lets you gaze at the ocean instead of the parking lot. The grilled steak served with *chimichurri* is as good as it gets, and juicy barbecued chicken with tamarind sauce is equally tasty. There are also a couple of bars, and bands playing Latin music set the scene on weekend nights. The staff can get overwhelmed when there's a crowd. ✉ *Rte. 187, Km 4.5* ☎ *787/253–1033* 🖃 *AE, MC, V.*

$$–$$$ ✕ **The Waterfont.** A bit farther down the beach than its rowdier rivals, this restaurant attracts a slightly older crowd of *sanjuaneros* whose primary objective is eating rather than drinking. The menu is also more

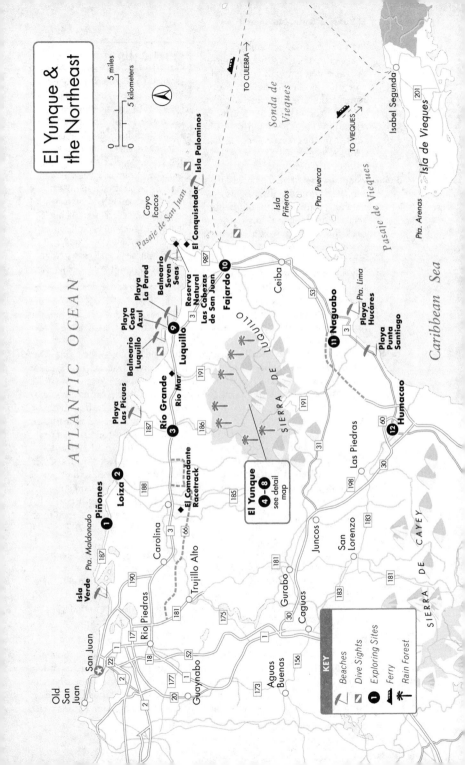

mature, offering such entrées as red snapper in a garlic sauce or lobster tails in lemon butter. If you can't decide, the sampler platter has everything from fried fritters to fresh oysters. You can choose a table in the dimly lighted dining room or outside on the covered patio. ⊠ *Rte. 187, Km 5* ☎ *787/791–5859* ⊟ *AE, MC, V.*

$–$$$ ✕ **Bamboobei.** You can't miss this funky hangout because of its eye-catching color scheme. But behind the brilliant blue building is a great deck that looks across a bike path to the beach. There's always live music on weekends—jazz on Saturday, something else on Friday. Other times you can just enjoy the rhythms floating out from the speakers. The

> **CHIMICHURRI**
>
> Whenever you get a steak in Puerto Rico, you'll also usually get a little glass jar of a green herb-filled sauce with a small, plastic spoon. This is chimichurri, the traditional accompaniment to grilled steak. The sauce, made from finely chopped cilantro or parsley, garlic, lemon, and oil, can be sprinkled liberally or sparingly over the meat to give it a little kick. You will rarely find steak sauce in Puerto Rico, except at an American chain, though you can usually get ketchup if chimichurri isn't to your liking.

menu is pretty much what you'd expect—heavy on the seafood—but it jazzes things up with lots of coconut and tropical fruit. ⊠ *Rte. 187, Km 5* ☎ *787/253–0948* ⊟ *MC, V.*

$–$$ ✕ **Pulpo Loco by the Sea.** Talk about truth in packaging—the Crazy Octopus has its palm-shaded tables planted firmly in the sand just a few yards from the ocean. As you might guess, octopus, oysters, mussels, and crab lead the lineup at this colorful seafood shack, though you can always munch on local favorites like fried codfish fritters. If your thirst is greater than your hunger, you can opt for a beer served in a plastic cup. The staff is friendly, and seems to know all the customers on a first-name basis. ⊠ *Rte. 187, Km 4.5* ☎ *787/791–8382* ⊟ *AE, MC, V.*

$–$$ ✕ **Tutti Frutti.** If you're looking for a break from all that seafood, try this brightly painted café facing the main drag, which serves some of the town's best comida criolla. The unusual name refers to the fresh-fruit smoothies that are constantly being whipped up in the blender. If you can't decide on a flavor, take a cue from the scowling pineapple positioned over the front door. The café is open late on weekends. ⊠ *Rte. 187, Km 5* ☎ *787/791–2787* ⊟ *No credit cards.*

$ ✕ **The Reef.** This place has one of the most dazzling views of San Juan, especially in the evening when the city lights are twinkling. Perched atop a coastal bluff, it's at the first left once you cross the bridge into Piñones. Grab one of the tables on the deck and order some of the simple seafood dishes like octopus or king-crab salads, served in *vasos* or *platos* (glasses or plates). ⊠ *Off Rte. 187, Km 1* ☎ *787/791–1973* ⊟ *MC, V.*

Nightlife

Nearly all the restaurants and cafés in Piñones have live music on weekends, mostly fine jazz and island rhythms, and many locals go as much for the drinks and live entertainment as for the food. Many of these beachfront dance halls are frequented by a largely Dominican clientele, and you're likely to see some smoking merengue dancing. Couples also twirl

GREAT ITINERARIES

IF YOU HAVE 1 DAY

If you have a day, or even less than a day, to visit eastern Puerto Rico, you should make a beeline to **El Yunque ❹-❽**. Route 3 is the quickest way. This rain forest, officially known as the Caribbean National Forest, has hiking trails of various lengths leading to secluded waterfalls and mountaintop towers with spectacular views. It's wonderful to explore even if you never get out of your car. If you are staying overnight, your best bet is nearby 🏨 **Río Grande ❸**.

IF YOU HAVE 3 DAYS

If you have a bit more time, you can see much more of the region. To avoid the unrelenting string of strip malls along Route 3, take Route 187 as it winds along the coast. Stop for lunch at one of the seafood shacks that line the beach as **Piñones ❶**, then check out the interesting art in the town of **Loíza ❷**. Spend the night in or near 🏨 **Río Grande ❸**, a town that makes a good base for exploring the region. On your second day, get up early to beat the crowds to **El Yunque ❹-❽**. Make sure to bring binoculars and watch for the rare Puerto Rican green parrot. On Day 3 you should head to **Luquillo ❾**, which has one of the prettiest beaches on the island. Make sure to stop for lunch in one of the *kioskos* (food stands) on Route 3 just before you reach the town.

IF YOU HAVE 5 DAYS

If you have five days, follow the itinerary above. On Day 4 head east along Route 3 to the coastal city of 🏨 **Fajardo ❿**, which has plenty of accommodations in every price range. Make sure you have called ahead to reserve a spot on a tour of Reserva Natural Las Cabezas de San Juan. If there's no moon, sign up for a late-night excursion to the reserve's bioluminscent bay. On Day 5 take a snorkeling trip to some of the nearby coral reefs. Many people who travel to Fajardo take advantage of the ferry service to the smaller islands of Vieques or Culebra.

to salsa or the grittier beats of local rap. You'll easily find several open-air establishments drawing weekend crowds for their steaming dance floors inside and smoking barbecue pits outside.

The Reef (✉ Off Rte. 187, Km 1 ☎ 787/791–1973) has a jukebox for those rare evenings when there isn't live music. You can also shoot some eight ball at one of the pool tables. **Soleil** (✉ Rte. 187, Km 4.5 ☎ 787/253–1033) has bars upstairs as well as down, so you never have to go far to order a drink. This place can get packed on weekends.

Sports & the Outdoors

Piñones is bordered by a 10-mi strip of beaches along the coast, which winds to a bluff called Vacia Talega, a once infamous lovers' lane with a wonderful view of the coast, which is lined with dense palm groves and towering sea grapes. The area has some fine surf, and several spots have become favorites of local and visiting surfers. You'll also find good fishing, snorkeling, and scuba opportunities. Away from the coast is Torrecilla Baja, one of the largest mangrove swamps on the island.

BEACHES

If you want to find solitary coastline near Piñones, you can. The water is fine; however, the surf is strong, and swimming—especially in winter—can be dangerous at some beaches. You'll find a **protected swimming area** (⊠ Route 187, Km 8) right in front of the cluster of food kiosks built by the government for resident cooks. A large barrier reef blocks the strong currents and serves as the foundation for the large bathing pools in front of a sandy beach. At the **end of Piñones** (⊠ 2 km before the bridge over the Loíza River) you'll find another protected cove that is a favorite of bathers.

> **CAUTION**
>
> Environmental concerns and a lack of infrastructure have so far held up large projects that are still planned for the area, but the pressure to build continues. For now, Piñones is the largest undeveloped coastal area near San Juan, and just a 10-minute drive from Isla Verde. Visit now, before it's spoiled by overdevelopment.

BICYCLING

The area's big outdoor attraction is a bike path that follows the swaying coconut palms on a quiet, breezy stretch, sometimes crossing over the main roadway, but mostly running parallel to it. Along most of its 7 mi, it's a wooden boardwalk for bicycles. On weekends and holidays you can rent bikes from several places along Route 187 and explore the path on your own. The going rate is $5 per hour. Many are clustered at the start of the bike trail, at the first left once you cross the bridge into Piñones. If you want a bike, head to **Dos Locos** (⊠ Rte. 187, Km 5 ☎ 787/565–2537). This little kiosk sits beside Pulpo Loco By the Sea.

DIVING & FISHING TRIPS

Locals go fishing and crabbing right off the coast, and its likely that the crab fritters you eat in any beachfront shack are local as well. Boating, deep-sea fishing, and scuba-diving trips are run out of the marina right below the bridge from Isla Verde. **Cangrejos Yacht Club** (⊠ Rte. 187, Km 1 ☎ 787/791–1015) is open Monday through Saturday from 8 to 5, on Sunday from 10 to 3. **Capt. José Campos** (☎ 787/724–2079) runs offshore deep-sea fishing trips for up to six people. He also runs fishing trips through the area's lagoon system. **Nico Guzmán** (☎ 787/383–1502) conducts four-hour deep-sea or lagoon fishing trips on small boats for two people.

KAYAKING

You can rent kayaks and paddle through the mangrove swamp that runs along the interior of Piñones; the swamp is rich in flora and fauna—both marine and bird life. **Las Tortugas Adventures** (⊠ Cond. La Puntilla, 4 Calle La Puntilla, Apt. D1–12, Old San Juan ☎ 787/725–5169 or 787/889–7734 ⊕ www.kayak-pr.com) is a reputable outfitter based in Old San Juan that leads organized kayak trips into the mangrove waterway, which is a nature reserve under the jurisdiction of the commonwealth's Department of Natural & Environmental Resources. Trip lengths vary from two to four hours, and prices range from $45 to $65 per person, depending on group size and the extent of the excursion.

Loíza

2 *15 km (9 mi) east of Piñones.*

The drive from Piñones to Loíza, a coastal town of 30,000 steeped in African heritage, is along a curving road banked by palms and other foliage. The ocean pops into view from time to time, as do pastel wooden houses—sometimes elevated on stilts—and kiosks serving coconut drinks and fried snacks. Locals stroll along the road's shoulder carrying clusters of coconuts, fruit of the area's many groves.

Loíza is known for its colorful festivals and its respect for tradition. Early on the region in which it is set was largely undeveloped because the marshy land–bred mosquitoes. It later became a haven for the descendants of slaves. Their music is recalled in the bomba dance that is popular here.

Bomba is key to the revelries at the annual Festival de Santiago Apóstol (St. James the Apostle Festival). During the celebration, which lasts for 10 days late in July, masked and costumed Loízanos combine religious processions—to a spot where a statue of the Virgin Mary is said to have been found under a tree many generations ago—with fireworks and other secular merrymaking. Each year, the family elected to "host" the festival erects an elaborate altar for the Mary statue and provides refreshments for the townspeople. Despite the festivities, St. James isn't Loíza's patron saint. St. Patrick holds that distinction, and the church is dedicated to him. Lively St. Patrick's Day festivities occur if the holiday falls on a weekend. Otherwise, residents save their energy for the bigger Santiago Apóstol fiesta.

Loíza's small downtown has been renovated and is pleasant; its citizens are proud of their town and welcome visitors. When it's not festival time, the area is worth a stop for the scenery and to see the crafts, including museum-quality festival masks made from coconut shells.

Some portions of the **Iglésia de San Patricio** (St. Patrick's Church) date from 1645, making it one of the island's oldest churches. It's home to a statue of the Virgin Mary that is worshiped during the Santiago Apóstol festivities. A side altar holds a statue of St. Patrick, the city's patron saint. If you'd like to see the interior without attending services, you can walk through the church just before or after Sunday mass. ⊠ *10 Calle Espíritu Santo, El Centro* ☎ *787/876–2229* ✆ *Free* ⊙ *Sun. mass 10* AM.

IT'S THE BOMBA

The *bomba* a dance—for which Loíza is famous—can be traced to the Kongo people of West Africa. Sometimes wearing a flouncy white dress, the woman of a dancing couple moves in a relatively fixed pattern of steps while her partner improvises to the drumbeat. A lead singer and a choir perform a call-and-response song—recounting a local story or event—while percussionists play maracas, two *fuas* (wooden sticks that are smacked against a hard surface), two *buleadores* (low-timbre, barrel-shape drums), and a *subidor* (higher-pitch drum).

The Arts

Bomba's renaissance dates from 1961, when a TV producer showed up in Loíza searching for residents who remembered the dance. In response, mask-maker Castor Ayala put together the **Ballet Folklórico Hermanos Ayala** (⊠ Artesanías Castor Ayala, Rte. 187, Km 6.6 ☎ 787/876–1130), a folk-music and dance troupe that performs around the island and elsewhere in Latin America. The group has no headquarters, but you can get its schedule at Artesanías Castor Ayala.

Shopping

Among the offerings at **Artesanías Castor Ayala** (⊠ Rte. 187, Km 6.6 ☎ 787/876–1130) are coconut-shell festival masks dubbed "Mona Lisas" because of their elongated smiles. Craftsman Raul Ayala Carrasquillo has been making these pieces for more than 40 years, following in the footsteps of his late father. These wild masks, most with tentacle-like horns, are prized by collectors. ⚠ **Buyer beware: these masks have been much-copied by other artisans, so look for the signature on the back.** His one-room shop, in a shack that was painted yellow many years ago, is one the road between Loíza and Río Grande.

At **Estúdio de Arte Samuel Lind** (⊠ Rte. 187, Km 6.6 ☎ 787/876–1494), down a short, dusty lane across the street from the Artesanías Castor Ayala, artist Samuel Lind sculpts, paints, and silk-screens images that are quintessentially Loízano. Lind's work is displayed in the two floors of his latticework studio. Of special note are his colorful folk-art posters.

Río Grande

❸ *5 km (3 mi) east of Canóvanas; 13 km (8 mi) southeast of Loíza; 35 km (21 mi) southeast of San Juan.*

This urban cluster of about 50,000 residents proudly calls itself "The City of El Yunque," as it's the closest community to the rain forest, and most of the reserve falls within its district borders. Two images of the rare green parrot, which makes its home in El Yunque, are found on the city's coat of arms; another parrot peeks out at you from the town's flag. The city is also near the posh Westin Río Mar Beach Golf Resort & Spa, known for its seaside golf courses, lovely beach, and first-class restaurants.

Río Espíritu Santo, which runs through Río Grande, begins in El Yunque's highest elevations and is the island's only navigable river. It was once used to transport lumber, sugar, and coffee from plantations. Immigrants flocked to the region to take advantage of the employment opportunities; many of today's residents can trace their families to Spain, Austria, and Italy.

The **Museo del Cartel José Hernández** is devoted to posters, a tradition on the island, and the artists who design them. The collection dates from the 1950s and includes many posters created for island festivals and art exhibits. ⊠ *37 Calle Pimentel, El Centro* ☎ *787/887–2370* 🎫 *Free* ☉ *Tues.–Sun. 9–5.*

2

Sports & the Outdoors

BEACH **Playa Las Picúas** is northeast of Río Grande, on a bay close to where Río Espíritu Santo meets the Atlantic. There are no facilities, but the water is fine. ⊠ *Northeast of Río Grande.*

HORSEBACK **Hacienda Carabali** (⊠ Rte. 992, Km 4, at Mameyes River Bridge, Bar-
RIDING rio Mameyes ☎ 787/889–5820 or 787/889–4954), a family-run operation, is a good place to jump in the saddle and ride one of Puerto Rico's
Paso Fino horses. Riding excursions ($45 an hour) include a one-hour
jaunt along Río Mameyes and the edge of El Yunque and a two-hour
ride along Balneario de Luquillo.

Where to Eat

★ $$$–$$$$ ✕ **Palio.** Northern Italian dishes such as rack of lamb with olive tape-
nade and poached salmon with spinach are the star attractions at this
award-winning restaurant. The friendly staff serves everything with a
flourish, whipping up the salads and other dishes beside your table. The
arrival of the specialty coffees, served in mugs engulfed in blue flames,
is such an showstopper that people at neighboring tables applaud. The
dining room, with its black-and-white checkerboard floor and its dark-
wood paneling, is gently curved, so it never feels cramped. ⊠ *Westin
Río Mar Beach Golf Resort & Spa, 6000 Río Mar Blvd., Río Grande*
☎ *787/888–6000* ⚑ *Reservations essential* ⊟ *AE, D, DC, MC, V*
⊘ *No lunch.*

$$–$$$ ✕ **Shimas.** The designers of this Asian-style eatery certainly had their
tongues in their cheeks. Keeping the place cool are Japanese-style fans
that wave at you from the ceiling. The sushi bar is a big draw, as are
the Chinese and Thai entrées on the cross-cultural menu. Start with the
duck spring rolls, then move on to the lobster with a sweet-and-spicy
sauce. ⊠ *Westin Río Mar Beach Golf Resort & Spa, 6000 Río Mar Blvd.,
Río Grande* ☎ *787/888–6000* ⚑ *Reservations essential* ⊟ *AE, D, DC,
MC, V* ⊘ *No lunch.*

$–$$$ ✕ **Richie's.** Perched on a mountaintop, this restaurant—a well-located
option for Westin Río Mar guests who don't want to dine on-property—
has an pair of open-air dining rooms that overlook the coastline. It's no
surprise that seafood is the specialty here—try the fried plantains filled
with shrimp, conch, octopus, or lobster for an appetizer, then move on
to grouper stuffed with crab and served in a spicy sauce. The staff is
young and eager to please. ⊠ *Río Mar Blvd., just past entrance to the
Westin Río Mar Beach Golf Resort & Spa, Río Grande* ☎ *No phone*
⊟ *AE, MC, V.*

$–$$ ✕ **Antojitos Puertorriqueñes.** The menu here couldn't be simpler—dishes
like fried pork with plantains or stewed crab with beans and rice are
your best options. The premises are just as straightforward, just a covered patio with plastic tables and chairs. But at these prices, who can
complain? ⊠ *160 Río Mar Blvd.* ☎ *787/888–7378* ⊟ *No credit cards.*

$–$$ ✕ **Villa Pesquera.** The view of the Río Espíritu may initially draw you
into this restaurant, but it's the savory seafood that will keep you coming back. Try the catch of the day—whatever it is, it's always a winner.
This is also a sweet spot for a sunset cocktail. ⊠ *Rte. 877, Km 6.6* ☎ *787/
887–0140* ⊟ *MC, V.*

Where to Stay

$$$$ ⬛ **Paradisus Puerto Rico.** Puerto Rico's first—and only—all-inclusive resort, to the east of the Westin Río Mar, is on an enviable stretch of pristine coastline. The open-air lobby, with its elegant floral displays, resembles a Japanese garden, and the swimming pool's columns call to mind ancient Greece. If it sounds like there's an identity crisis here, you're right. It's a mishmash of styles that don't come together in a coherent way. But the hotel, run by Sol Meliá, does fairly well at being all things to all people. The 500 suites, many with their own hot tubs, are spread among two-story bungalows. Many look out onto the pair of 18-hole golf courses, which still had some unfinished landscaping, even at this writing. The staff is friendly and accommodating. ✉ *Rte. 968, Km 5.8, Coco Beach 00745* ☎ *787/657–1026 or 800/336–3542* 🖷 *787/657–1055* ⊕ *www.solmelia.com* ⇌ *500 suites, 5 villas* ⚎ *6 restaurants, fans, in-room safes, some in-room hot tubs, minibars, cable TV with movies, 2 18-hole golf courses, 3 tennis courts, pool, wading pool, health club, spa, beach, dive shop, snorkeling, windsurfing, boating, waterskiing, fishing, 4 bars, casino, dance club, showroom, shops, children's programs (ages 4–12), dry cleaning, laundry service, concierge, Internet, business services, convention center, meeting room, car rental, travel services* ▭ *AE, D, MC, V* ⍉ *AI.*

★ $$$$ ⬛ **Westin Río Mar Beach Golf Resort & Spa.** On more than 500 acres, this sprawling resort is geared toward outdoor activities. Many people come to play the championship golf courses or hike in the nearby rain forest. But the biggest draw is the 2-mi-long stretch of sand just steps from the door. There's a kiosk near the swimming pools that rents sailboats and other equipment; a dive shop organizes excursions to nearby places of interest. Even the extensive programs for children are mostly outdoors. The seven-story hotel, which wraps around lush gardens, never feels overwhelming. Some rooms are on the small side but are cleverly designed to make use of all the available space. The newest addition is the Mandara Spa, which transports you to the South Pacific with its hand-carved wood furnishings from Bali. ✉ *6000 Río Mar Blvd., Río Grande 00745* ☎ *787/888–6000* 🖷 *787/888–6235* ⊕ *www.westinriomar.com* ⇌ *528 rooms, 72 suites, 59 villas* ⚎ *7 restaurants, café, in-room safes, cable TV with movies and video games, in-room VCRs, in-room broadband, Wi-Fi, 2 18-hole golf courses, 13 tennis courts, 2 pools, health club, spa, beach, dive shop, windsurfing, boating, fishing, bicycles, 4 bars, casino, dance club, game room, shop, children's programs (ages 4–12), dry cleaning, laundry service, concierge, business services, convention center, Internet room, meeting rooms, airport shuttle, car rental, no-smoking rooms* ▭ *AE, D, DC, MC, V* ⍉ *EP.*

$–$$$ ⬛ **Río Grande Plantation Eco Resort.** Walking paths pass flowers and wind around fruit trees at this peaceful resort in the foothills of El Yunque. It's on a portion of what was, in the late 1700s, a 200-acre sugarcane plantation and is often used for corporate retreats. Accommodations are primarily two-story villas, which have such amenities as hot tubs and kitchenettes. The staff members pride themselves on being attentive to their guests. ✉ *Rte. 956, Km 4, Barrio Guzman Abajo* ⍛ *Box 6526, Loíza Station, Santurce, San Juan 00914* ☎ *787/887–2779*

🖀 787/888–3239 ⊕ *www.riograndeplantation.com* 🛌 *19 villas, 4 rooms, 1 cottage* ☖ *Restaurant, kitchenettes, microwaves, refrigerators, cable TV, in-room VCRs, pool, hot tub, basketball, business services, Internet room, meeting rooms* ☰ *AE, MC, V* ﴾◎﴿ *EP.*

Nightlife

Pick a game—Caribbean stud poker, blackjack, slot machines—and then head to the Las Vegas–style casino at the **Westin Río Mar Beach Golf Resort & Spa** (✉ 6000 Río Mar Blvd., Río Grande ☎ 787/888–6000). If all that betting gives you a thirst, step into the Players Bar, which is connected to the gaming room.

Sports & the Outdoors

Activities in Río Grande region are mostly oriented around the two big resorts, the Westin Río Mar Beach Golf Resort & Spa and the newer Paradisus Puerto Rico, but only guests can use the facilities at Paradisus.

DIVING & SNORKELING The **Westin Dive Center** (✉ Westin Río Mar Beach Golf Resort & Spa, 6000 Río Mar Blvd., Río Grande ☎ 787/888–6000) offers scuba and snorkeling rentals and lessons. Large catamaran snorkeling trips leave from the resort for the calm seas and deserted islands off the cost of northeastern Puerto Rico. The cost is $75 to $145 per person, including snacks. The trips offer awesome sunbathing and snorkeling opportunities.

GOLF The 18-hole **Bahía Beach Plantation Course** (✉ Rte. 187, Km 4.2 ☎ 787/256–5600 ⊕ www.golfbahia.com) skirts the north-coast beaches. A public course, it was carved out of a long-abandoned coconut grove, and coconut palms and other native trees and tropical vegetation dominate the scene. Giant iguanas roam the premises, as hawks, waterfowl, and tropical birds fly overhead. The course also offers views of El Yunque, and most greens run either along lakes or the untamed Río Grande coastline. Greens fees range from $65 to $85, depending on day of the week and the time of day. The Bahía Cantina, an on-site bar-restaurant, offers refreshments and sustenance.

The **Berwind Country Club** (✉ Rte. 187, Km 4.7 ☎ 787/876–3056) has an 18-hole course known for its tight fairways and demanding greens. It's open for nonmembers from Tuesday through Friday, with greens fees of $65, which includes a cart and bucket of balls. On Sunday afternoons nonmembers can play if they make arrangements in advance.

Coco Beach Golf & Country Club (✉ Paradisus Puerto Rico Sol Melía All-Inclusive Resort, 100 Clubhouse Dr. ☎ 787/657–2000) has two 18-hole course designed by Tom Kite and Bruce Besse. The courses are bordered by the coastline and a view of El Yunque. When we stopped by, the grass was patchy in many places. Greens fees are $85 for hotel guests and $195 for nonguests.

★ The spectacular **Westin Río Mar Country Club** (✉ Westin Río Mar Beach Golf Resort & Spa, 6000 Río Mar Blvd., Río Grande ☎ 787/888–6000 ⊕ www.westinriomar.com) has a clubhouse with a pro shop and two restaurants between two 18-hole courses. The River Course, designed by Greg Norman, has challenging fairways that skirt the Mameyes River. The Ocean Course has slightly wider fairways than its sister; iguanas can usually be spotted sunning themselves near its fourth hole. If you're not a resort guest, be sure to reserve tee times at least 24 hours in advance. Greens fees range from $100 to $165 for hotel guests and $135 to $190 for nonguests, depending on tee time.

TENNIS   The facilities at the **Peter Burwash International Tennis Center** (✉ Westin Río Mar Beach Golf Resort & Spa, 6000 Río Mar Blvd., Río Grande ☎ 787/888–6000 ⊕ www.westinriomar.com) are the best in the area. Besides the 13 courts with spectacular views, there are lessons for everyone from novices to old pros. For meals there's the Tex-Mex cuisine of Cactus Jack's.

WATER SPORTS   You can rent sea kayaks ($25 an hour for single-person kayaks, $35 and $45 for two- and three-person models) from **Iguana Water Sports** (✉ Westin Río Mar Beach Golf Resort & Spa, 6000 Río Mar Blvd., Río Grande ☎ 787/888–6000). The helpful staff also rents everything from rafts ($10 a day) to windsurfing equipment ($25 an hour).

Shopping

Puerto Rican pottery, with some designs inspired by the Taíno Indians, fills the shelves of **Cerámicas Los Bohíos** (✉ Av. 65th Infantry, Km 21.7 ☎ 787/887–2620). The picturesque **Treehouse Studio** (✉ Unmarked rd. off Rte. 3 ☎ 787/888–8062), not far from the rain forest, sells vibrant watercolors by Monica Laird, who also gives workshops. Call for an appointment and directions.

El Yunque

Fodor'sChoice   *11 km (7 mi) southeast of Río Grande; 43 km (26 mi) southeast of San*
★   *Juan.*

More than 28,000 acres of verdant foliage and often rare wildlife make up El Yunque, the only rain forest within the U.S. National Forest system. Formally known as the Bosque Nacional del Caribe (Caribbean National Forest), El Yunque's colloquial name is believed to be derived from the Taíno word *yukiyú* (good spirit), although some people say it comes directly from *yunque,* the Spanish word for "anvil," because some of the forest's peaks have snub shapes.

Rising to more than 3,500 feet above sea level, this protected area didn't gain its "rain forest" designation for nothing: more than 100 billion gallons of precipitation fall over it annually, spawning rushing

> ### BE PREPARED
>
> When you come to El Yunque, bring binoculars, a camera with a zoom lens, bottled water, and sunscreen; wear a hat or visor, good walking shoes, and comfortable clothes. Although daytime temperatures rise as high as 80°F (27°C), wear long pants, because some plants can cause skin irritations. There are no poisonous snakes in the forest (or on the island as a whole), but bugs can be ferocious, so a strong repellent is a must. And remember: This is a rain forest, so be prepared for frequent showers.

El Yunque (Caribbean National Forest)

streams and cascades, 240 tree species, and oversized impatiens and ferns. In the evening millions of inch-long *coquís* (tree frogs) begin their calls. El Yunque is also home to the *cotorra*, Puerto Rico's endangered green parrot, as well as 67 other types of birds.

The forest's 13 hiking trails are extremely well maintained; many of them are easy to navigate and less than 1 mi long. If you prefer to see the sights from a car, as many people do, simply follow Route 191 as it winds into the mountains. Several observation points are along this often narrow road, which is the park's main thoroughfare. Las Cabezas observation point is at Km 7.8; Cascada La Coca, one of two waterfalls where you can take a refreshing dip (the other, La Mina, is to the south), lies just past Km 8.1; and the Torre Yokahú observation point sits at Km 8.9. When hurricanes and mud slides haven't caused portions of the road to be closed, you can drive straight from the entrance to Km 13, the base of Pico El Yunque, the peak that forms the centerpiece of this amazing park.

Arrive early and plan to stay the entire day. The road into El Yunque opens at 7:30 AM and closes at 6 PM. You'll be charged an admission fee if you visit El Portal, the information center that has an interesting movie and interactive exhibits, but everything else is free. There are picnic areas with sheltered tables and bathrooms, as well as several basic eateries along the way.

A lizard's tongue darts across three movie screens, a forest erupts in flames, a tiny seedling pushes up from the ground and flourishes. Before you begin exploring El Yunque, check out the high-tech, interactive displays— explaining rain forests in general and El Yunque in particular—at **El Portal**, the information center near the northern entrance. The beautifully designed facility is a good stop for families, as many of the exhibits are geared toward youngsters. Kids especially like a short film narrated by actor Jimmy Smits (whose mother is Puerto Rican) about efforts to save the endangered Puerto Rican parrot. All exhibits are in English and Spanish. This is also a good place to pick up a map of the park and talk to rangers about which trails are open. You can also stock up on water, snacks, film, and souvenirs at the small gift shop. ⊠ *Rte. 191, Km 4.3, off Rte. 3* ☎ *787/ 888–1880* ⊕ *www.fs.fed.us/r8/caribbean* 🖃 *$3* ☉ *Daily 9–5.*

> **SHORT ON TIME?**
>
> If you're only going to drive through El Yunque, you can probably skip the El Portal information center. There's only one road through the park, so you can't get lost.

❺ The first spectacular sight you're likely to see in El Yunque is **Cascada La Cola** (La Cola Falls), which plunges 85 feet down a rocky cliff. The waterfall is inches from the road, so it's visible even to those who don't want to navigate the trails. The gate to the park, which opens at 7:30 AM and closes at 6 PM, is just before the falls. ⊠ *Rte. 191, Km 8.1.*

❻ Resembling the turret of a castle, **Torre Yokahú** (Yokahú Observation Tower) rises unexpectedly from a little hill not far from the road. A peek through the windows of its circular stairway gives you a hint of the vistas awaiting you at the top: 1,000-year-old trees, exotic flowers in brilliant hues, birds in flight. Postcards and books on El Yunque are sold in the small kiosk at the tower's base. The parking lot has restrooms. ⊠ *Rte. 191, Km 8.9.*

❼ Just beyond the halfway point along the road into El Yunque, the **Centro de Información Sierra Palm** is a great place to stop for trail updates. El Yunque's steep slopes, unstable wet soil, heavy rainfall, and exuberant plant life result in the need for intensive trail maintenance; some trails must be cleared and cleaned at least twice a year. Rangers at the office here have information on closures, conditions of open trails, what flora and fauna to look for, and any activities planned that day. There are restrooms and water fountains near the parking lot. ⊠ *Rte. 191, Km 11.6.*

Palo Colorado, the red-bark tree in which the endangered cotorra nests, ❽ dominates the forest surrounding the **Centro de Información Palo Colorado**. The center—which is home to Forest Adventure Tours and its two-hour, ranger-led hikes (reservations are required)—is the gateway for several walks. The easy Baño del Oro Trail loops 2 km (1 mi) through an area dubbed the Palm Forest. The even shorter El Caimitillo Trail starts at the same place and runs for about 1 km (½ mi). Al-

CLOSE UP

202 Parrots & Counting

THE TAÍNO INDIANS CALLED IT the *iguaca*, Spanish speakers refer to it as the *cotorra*, and scientists know it as *Amazona vittata*. Whatever moniker it takes, the Puerto Rican green parrot—the only one native to the island—is one of the world's rarest birds. It nests primarily in the upper levels of El Yunque and in the nearby Sierra de Luquillo. The bird is almost entirely green, though there are touches of blue on its wings, white rings around its eyes, and a red band just above its beak. It's only about 12 inches long, and its raucous squawk doesn't match its delicate appearance. The parrots mate for life. In February (the rain forest's driest season), they build nests within tree hollows and lay three to four eggs. Both parents feed the young.

When the Spanish arrived, the parrot population was an estimated 1 million on the main island, Vieques, and Culebra. But deforestation, hurricanes, and parasites have reduced the population (parrot hunting was common until being outlawed in 1940). By 1967 there were only 19 birds; in a 1975 count the total was only 13.

But things are looking up, especially with work beginning on a $2.5-million state-of-the-art breeding facility in El Yunque. At this writing, there were an estimated 44 green parrots in the wild and another 158 in captivity. Officials are optimistic that their numbers will continue to grow. If you're very observant (and very lucky), you might just spot one.

2

though it begins as asphalt, the challenging El Yunque–Mt. Britton Trail turns to gravel as it climbs Pico El Yunque. At a higher elevation you can follow the Mt. Britton spur to an observation tower built in the 1930s. Without detours onto any of the side trails, El Yunque Trail takes about three hours round-trip and includes some mild ascents. Signs clearly mark each turnoff, so it's hard to get lost if you stay on the path. All the trails here are edged by giant ferns, bamboo, and oversized impatiens. There are restrooms and parking at the center and a picnic area nearby. ⊠ *Rte. 191, Km 11.9* ☎ *787/888–5646* ⊕ *www.fs.fed.us/r8/caribbean* ☎ *Free* ⊙ *Daily 8–5.*

Where to Eat

$$–$$$ ✕ **Las Vegas.** The atmosphere here is casual, thanks to the many hikers that drop in on their way to or from El Yunque. But the food is a cut above what you'd expect to find in such an out-of-the-way place. Look for tartare of red snapper served with fried plantains or crab turnovers with melon chutney. The roasted lamb in a wine and herb sauce makes a hearty dinner. ⊠ *Rte. 191, Km 1.3* ☎ *787/809–6586* ▭ *AE, MC, V* ⊙ *Closed Mon.–Wed.*

¢ ✕ **Muralla.** The rangers at El Yunque swear by this place, a cement-block building just past Cascada La Cola. You won't find a cheaper meal anywhere in Puerto Rico, that's for sure. The *arroz habicuela con pollo* (fried chicken with rice and beans) is a steal at less than $5. The barking dog on the roof and the unusual artwork in the open-air dining room—a

huge blob of papier mâché that may or may not be a boulder—add to
the atmosphere. Get here early, as the place closes at 5 PM. ⊠ *Rte. 191,
Km 7.4* 🕾 *No phone* ⊟ *No credit cards* ⊙ *Closed Thurs. No dinner.*

Shopping

While in El Yunque, buy a recording of the tree frog's song or a video
about the endangered green parrot, pick up a coffee-table book about
the rain forest, try on El Yunque T-shirts, and check out the books for
ecominded children at the large **Caribbean National Forest Gift Shop**
(⊠ El Portal, Rte. 191, Km 4.3 🕾 787/888–1880). Tucked among the
rain-forest gifts are other Puerto Rican items, including note cards,
maps, soaps, jams, and coffee.

**EN
ROUTE**   All along Route 3, from Canóvanas to Fajardo, roadside stands and
kiosks sell fruit and sugarcane beverages, fried snacks, and fresh
seafood. There are also artisans selling their wares, handmade hammocks, even tropical birds. For locals driving from El Yunque or Río
Grande to Luquillo, the trip would be unthinkable without a stop at
the *friquitines* (seafood kiosks) that line Route 3 west of the beach
turnoff. They're busy all day, serving passing truckers, area businesspeople, and sand-covered families en route to or from the beach in
Luquillo. Although some kiosks have larger seating areas than others, they all offer much the same fare, including cold drinks, plates of
fried fish (head and tail still attached), conch salad, and fritters (usually codfish or corn).

Luquillo

🅾 *13 km (8 mi) northeast of Río Grande; 45 km (28 mi) east of San Juan.*

Known as the "Sun Capital" of Puerto Rico, Luquillo has one of the island's best-equipped family beaches. It's also a community where fishing traditions are respected. On the east end of Balneario de Luquillo,
past the guarded swimming area, fishermen launch small boats and drop
nets in open stretches between coral reefs.

Like many other Puerto Rican towns, Luquillo has its signature festival, in this case the Festival de Platos Típicos (Festival of Typical Dishes),
a late-November culinary event that revolves around one ingredient: coconut. During the festivities, many of the community's 18,000 residents
gather at the main square to sample treats rich with coconut or coconut
milk. There's also plenty of free entertainment, including folk shows,
troubadour contests, and salsa bands.

Beaches

Fodor'sChoice   Just off Route 3, gentle, shallow waters lap the edges of palm-lined **Bal-
★   neario de Luquillo,** which is a magnet for families. It's well equipped with
dressing rooms and restrooms, lifeguards, guarded parking, food stands,
picnic areas, and even cocktail kiosks. Its most distinctive facility,
though, is the Mar Sin Barreras (Sea Without Barriers), a low-sloped
ramp leading into the water that allows wheelchair users to take a dip.
The beach is open every day but Monday from 9 to 5. Admission is $2
per car. ⊠ *Off Rte. 3.*

2

Waving palm trees and fishing boats add charm to the small **Playa Costa Azul,** although the ugly residential buildings along the water make an unattractive backdrop. The water here is good for swimming, and the crowds are thinner than elsewhere, but there are no facilities. ⊠ *Off Rte. 193, near Rte. 3.*

> **WORD OF MOUTH**
>
> ["We] also visited Luquillo Beach, a wonderful public beach within easy driving distance [of San Juan]. Well worth a visit for the nice water and postcard views."
>
> –SAnParis

Playa La Pared, literally "The Wall Beach," is a surfer haunt. Numerous local competitions are held here throughout the year, and several surfing shops are close by just in case you need a wet suit or a wax for your board. The waves here are medium-range. It's very close to Balneario de Luquillo, but has a separate entrance. ⊠ *Off Rte. 3.*

Where to Eat

$–$$ ✕ **Brass Cactus.** "Gringoland" is how one local described this Tex-Mex eatery. There are so many English-speaking tourists that management doesn't even bother to print the menu in Spanish. But the ribs and burgers melt in your mouth, and the helpings of crispy fries are generous. Nearly every dish—Southwestern or otherwise—is washed down with beer. Televisions broadcast the latest sporting events, and on the weekend bands often replace the jukebox. ⊠ *Rte. 3, Complejo Turistico Condominio* ☎ 787/889–5735 ▭ *AE, MC, V.*

$–$$ ✕ **Victor's Place.** In a small blue building on the main plaza, this local institution has been serving up Puerto Rican specialties since 1936. Traditionally prepared seafood dishes like the *asopao* (a thick soup flavored with conch, octopus, or lobster) come with large servings of beans, rice, and fried plantains. If you want something fancier, there's lobster tail rolled in bacon or Conch in a spicy sauce. The decor is nautical, with fishing nets hanging from the ceiling. ⊠ *2 Calle Jesús T. Piñero* ☎ 787/889–5705 ▭ *MC, V* ◷ *Closed Mon.*

¢–$ ✕ **Lolita's.** Burritos—15 different kinds, including the non-traditional "soy meat"—are the specialties of this casual Mexican restaurant. Combo plates let you taste a bit of everything, from tacos to enchiladas. Everything is washed down with oversized margaritas, of course. Those who eschew tequila can try the house sangria or a vintage from the unusually varied wine list. ⊠ *Rte. 3, Km 41.3, Barrio Juan Martín* ☎ 787/889–5770 or 787/889–0250 ▭ *AE, MC, V.*

¢ ✕ **La Parrilla.** There are more than 50 *kioskos,* or food stands, along the highway on the way to Luquillo Beach. They all serve basically the same thing—fried seafood. This place, true to its name, also has a grill, so there are burgers and other meat dishes in addition to the fish. There's even a comfortable patio in the rear that let's you escape the traffic noise. ⊠ *Luquillo Beach, Kiosk #2* ☎ 787/889–0590 ▭ *No credit cards.*

Where to Stay

$ ▥ **Luquillo Beach Inn.** This five-story, white-and-pink hotel is within walking distance of the public beach and caters to families—children stay free with their parents. The modest one- or two-bedroom suites have sofa beds, kitchenettes, and living rooms equipped with TVs and VCRs; the largest sleep up to six people. It's a good jumping-off point for visits to El Yunque. Transportation (about $45) can be arranged from San Juan if you don't wish to rent a car. ✉ *701 Ocean Dr., 00773* ☎ *787/ 889–1063 or 787/889–3333* 🖷 *787/889–1966* ⊕ *home.coqui.net/jcdiaz/ fotos3.html* ⤵ *20 rooms* ♿ *Fans, kitchenettes, cable TV with movies, in-room VCRs, pool, outdoor hot tub, bar, dry cleaning, laundry service, business services, free parking* ⊟ *AE, MC, V* ⊮ *EP.*

Sports & the Outdoors

DIVING   **Divers' Outlet** (✉ 38 Calle Fernández Garcia ☎ 787/889–5721 or 888/ 746–3483) is a full-service dive shop. It offers PADI certification, rents equipment, and can arrange scuba outings.

SURFING   Not far from Playa La Pared, **La Selva Surf Shop** (✉ 250 Calle Fernández Garcia ☎ 787/889–6205 ⊕ www.rainforestsafari.com/selva.html) has anything a surfer could need, including news about current conditions. The family-run shop also sells sunglasses, sandals, bathing suits, and other beach necessities.

Fajardo

🔟 *11 km (7 mi) southeast of Luquillo; 55 km (34 mi) southeast of San Juan.*

Fajardo, founded in 1772, has historical notoriety as a port where pirates stocked up on supplies. It later developed into a fishing community and an area where sugarcane flourished. (There are still cane fields on the city's fringes.) Today it's a hub for the yachts that use its marinas; the divers who head to its good offshore sites; and the day-trippers who travel by catamaran, ferry, or plane to the off-islands of Culebra and Vieques. With the most significant docking facilities on the island's eastern side, Fajardo is a bustling city of 37,000—so bustling, in fact, that its unremarkable downtown is often congested and difficult to navigate.

Puerto del Rey Marina, home to 1,100 boats, is one of the Caribbean's largest marinas. It's the place to hook up with a scuba-diving group, arrange an excursion to Vieques's bioluminescent bay, or charter a fishing boat. The marina also has several restaurants and boating-supply stores. ✉ *Rte. 3, Km 51.2* ☎ *787/860–1000.*

Villa Marina is the second-largest marina in Fajardo, and is home to charter fishing boats as well as several catamaran operators who give day tours for swimming and snorkeling to the deserted islands right off Puerto Rico's northeast coast. ✉ *Rte. 987, Km 1.3* ☎ *787/728–2450, 787/863– 5131, or 787/863–5061* ⊕ *www.villamarinapr.com.*

The 316-acre **Reserva Natural Las Cabezas de San Juan,** on a headland north of Fajardo, is owned by the nonprofit Conservation Trust of Puerto Rico. You ride in open-air trolleys and wander down boardwalks through seven ecosystems, including lagoons, mangrove swamps, and dry-forest areas. Green iguanas skitter across paths, and guides identify other endangered species. A half-hour hike down a wooden walkway brings you to the mangrove-lined **Laguna Grande,** where bioluminescent microorganisms glow at night. The restored **Fajardo lighthouse** is the final stop on the tour; its Spanish-colonial tower has been in operation since 1882, making it Puerto Rico's second-oldest lighthouse. The first floor houses ecological displays; a winding staircase leads to an observation deck. A few miles past the reserve is the fishing area known as **Las Croabas,** where seafood snacks are sold along the waterfront. The only way to see the reserve is on a mandatory guided tour; reservations are required. ⊠ *Rte. 987, Km 6* ☎ *787/722–5882 or 787/860–2560* ⊕ *www.fideicomiso.org* ⊠ *$5* ⊙ *Tours Fri.–Sun. at 2.*

Beaches

A long stretch of powdery sand near the Reserva Natural Las Cabezas de San Juan, **Balneario Seven Seas** may turn out to be the best surprise of your trip. Facilities include food kiosks, picnic tables, changing areas, restrooms, and showers. On weekends the beach attracts crowds keen on its calm, clear waters—perfect for swimming and other water sports. If you've never tried out a sea kayak, this is a good place to learn. ⊠ *Rte. 987.*

Where to Eat

$$$–$$$$ ✕ **Blossoms.** Hung with elaborate lanterns, this dining room is a fanciful version of the Far East. The first thing you'll notice is the sound of meats and vegetables sizzling on the large teppanyaki tables. The chefs here know they're on stage, and they perform with a flourish. Hunan and Szechuan specialties round out the menu. Despite the abundance of fresh fish, it's not so easy to find a sushi bar in this part of Puerto Rico. The one here, with a seemingly endless array of dishes, is excellent. ⊠ *El Conquistador Resort & Golden Door Spa, Rte. 987, Km 3.4* ☎ *787/863–1000* ⊜ *Reservations essential* ⊟ *AE, D, DC, MC, V* ⊙ *No lunch Mon.–Sat.*

> **WORD OF MOUTH**
>
> "There are several casual restaurants along the Seven Seas beach in Las Croabas, [and] most specialize in 'arepas rellenas'—fried dumplings/turnovers that are filled with seafood."   –marigross

$$$–$$$$ ✕ **Otello's.** You can dine inside, enveloped in the soft glow cast by dozens of candles, or slide outside to the terrace for a meal under the stars. This northern Italian restaurant, one of the many at the El Conquistador Resort, is among the best on the island's eastern coast. It's certainly one of the most elegant, with crisp linens and delicate crystal. Start with the minestrone soup—it's a guaranteed winner—and follow it with fettuccine tossed with grilled shrimp or one of the other pasta or dishes. ⊠ *El Conquistador Resort & Golden Door Spa, Rte. 987, Km 3.4* ☎ *787/863–1000* ⊜ *Reservations essential* ⊟ *AE, D, DC, MC, V* ⊙ *No lunch.*

$$–$$$ ✕ **A La Banda.** At Puerto del Rey Marina, this waterfront eatery has tables in a dining room with nautical details or on a terrace overlooking the boats bobbing on the waves. Steaks and poultry figure on the menu, but the kitchen truly excels at seafood dishes, including fresh lobster. ⊠ *Rte. 3, Km 51.4* ☎ *787/860–9162* ⊟ *MC, V.*

$$–$$$ ✕ **Anchor's Inn.** Seafood is the specialty at this restaurant perched high on a bluff overlooking the ocean. This is a great place to sample specialties such as *chillo entero* (fried whole red snapper). The convenient location, down the road from El Conquistador Resort, lures travelers who have had enough hotel food. ✉ *Rte. 987, Km 2.7* ☎ *787/863–7200* ⚑ *Reservations not accepted* ▭ *AE, MC, V* ⊘ *Closed Tues.*

$–$$ ✕ **Rosa's Sea Food.** Despite its name, this family-run restaurant at Marina Puerto Real is also a good spot for beef and chicken. But if you want to see what people from all around the island are raving about, stick with the seafood. The specialty here is pieces of lobster, simmered with onions, tomatoes, and red peppers. The grilled and sautéed fresh fish, from tuna to red snapper, is also a winner. You can't miss the restaurant, as it's inside a two-story house painted a vivid shade of pink. ✉ *536 Calle Tablado* ☎ *787/863–0213* ⚑ *Reservations not accepted* ▭ *AE, MC, V* ⊘ *Closed Wed.*

Where to Stay

$$$–$$$$
Fodor'sChoice
★

▢ **El Conquistador Resort & Golden Door Spa.** The name means "The Conqueror," and this sprawling complex has claimed the northeastern tip of the island for itself. Perched on a bluff overlooking the ocean, it certainly is one of Puerto Rico's loveliest destination resorts. Arranged in five "villages," The whitewashed buildings have a colonial-era feel. Cobblestone streets and fountain-filled plazas convey a sense of cohesiveness. The resort's beach is on Palomino Island, just offshore; a free shuttle boat takes you there in about 15 minutes. A branch of the Japanese-influenced Golden Door Spa is widely considered among the Caribbean's best spas. The staff prides itself on its attentive service. ✉ *1000 Av. El Conquistador, Box 70001, 00738* ☎ *787/863–1000 or 800/468–0389* 🖷 *787/863–6500* ⊕ *www.elconresort.com* ⊳ *750 rooms, 17 suites, 155 villas* ⚴ *17 restaurants, in-room safes, minibars, cable TV with movies and video games, in-room VCRs, in-room broadband, Wi-Fi, 18-hole golf course, 4 tennis courts, 8 pools, hot tub, health club, hair salon, spa, beach, dive shop, snorkeling, windsurfing, boating, jet skiing, marina, 5 bars, casino, nightclub, shop, children's programs (ages 4–12), dry cleaning, laundry service, business services, convention center, meeting rooms, airport shuttle, parking (fee), car rental, no-smoking rooms* ▭ *AE, D, DC, MC, V* ⦿ *EP.*

> ### WORD OF MOUTH
>
> "El Conquistador is my favorite hotel in Puerto Rico. It's almost unnecessary to leave the hotel because there are so many things to see and do."　　–pinkfloyd18

$ ▢ **Fajardo Inn.** The whitewashed buildings that make up this hilltop resort have lovely views of the Atlantic Ocean and El Yunque. A bit closer are the lush gardens, part of the hotel's efforts to begin reforestation on this part of the island. All rooms have simple furnishings and white-tile floors; some have balconies that let you enjoy the sunrise. Two restaurants, Starfish and Blue Iguana, are so good that they attract locals. The closest beach is the public Balneario Seven Seas, about a five-minute drive away. ✉ *Rte. 195, 52 Parcelas, Beltran Sector, 00740* ☎ *787/860–*

2

6000 or 888/860–6006 🖷 *787/860–5063* ⊕ *www.fajardoinn.com* 🛏 *54 rooms* ⚲ *2 restaurants, some kitchenettes, some refrigerators, cable TV, pool, sports bar, meeting room, free parking; no smoking* ▭ *AE, MC, V* ⫶◯⫶ *EP.*

¢   ▣ **La Familia.** From the white wooden guesthouse—the property's centerpiece—the view is right out to the ocean. It's a convenient spot to land for the night since it's close to the Seven Seas public beach and several seafront seafood restaurants. On the list of government-approved paradores, it's the best place in town to stay if you're not at the El Conquistador. The restaurant serves decent breakfasts and light lunches. ✉ *Rte. 987, Km 4.1, Las Croabas 00648* 🕾 *787/863–1193* 🖷 *787/860–5354* 🛏 *35 rooms* ⚲ *Restaurant, cable TV, pool, bar, shop, meeting rooms, free parking* ▭ *AE, DC, MC, V* ⫶◯⫶ *EP.*

Nightlife

Although most of the evening action takes place in the El Conquistador Resort's lounges, there are a few neighborhood bars where locals drink beer. You can play slots, blackjack, roulette, and video poker at **El Conquistador Casino** (✉ El Conquistador Resort & Golden Door Spa, 1000 Av. El Conquistador 🕾 787/863–1000), a typical hotel gambling facility within the resort's lavish grounds.

Sports & the Outdoors

GOLF   The 18-hole Arthur Hills–designed course at **El Conquistador Resort &**
★   **Golden Door Spa** (✉ 1000 Av. El Conquistador 🕾 787/863–6784) is famous for its 200-foot changes in elevation. From the highest spot, on the 15th hole, you have great views of the surrounding mountains. The trade winds make every shot challenging. Greens fees for resort guests range from $100 to $165 and are even higher for nonguests.

DAY SAILS   Several reputable catamaran and yacht operators in Fajardo make excursions to the reefs and sparkling blue waters surrounding a handful of small islets just off the coast. Many of the trips include transportation from San Juan and transportation to and from San Juan–area hotels. Whether or not you're staying in Fajardo, the day-trips on the water will show you classic Caribbean scenes of coral reefs rife with sea life, breathtakingly clear water, and palm-fringed, deserted beaches. The day sails, with stops for snorkeling, include swimming breaks at deserted beaches and picnic lunches. Most of the craft are outfitted for comfort, with quality stereo systems and full-service bars. There are many competent operators offering a nearly identical experience, so your selection will probably be based on price and which operators serve your San Juan hotel, or which operate out of the marina in Fajardo that you are visiting. Prices range from $55 to $95; price is affected by whether you join up with a trip in San Juan or in Fajardo and by what is included in the price. Ask whether extras, such as picnic lunches and a full-service bar, are included. They are quickly becoming standard features.

At **East Winds Excursions** (✉ Puerto del Rey Marina, Rte. 3, Km 51.4 🕾 787/863–3434 or 877/937–4386 ⊕ www.eastwindcats.com) catamarans ranging in size from 45 feet to 65 feet take you offshore for snorkeling. Two of the catamarans are powered, and this cuts down tremendously on the amount of travel time to outlying islands. Trips includes stops at isolated beaches and a lunch buffet. All craft are outfitted with swimming decks, freshwater showers, and full-service bars. Prices include lunch. These vessels are some of the plushest day sails in the area.

Erin Go Braugh (⊠ Puerto del Rey Marina, Rte. 3, Km 51.4 ☎ 787/860–4401 or 787/409–2511 ⊕ www.egbc.net) is a sailing yacht based in Fajardo that takes a tour of the glistening waters and islands offshore. It is known for its barbecue picnic lunches. Snorkel and fishing equipment are also provided. Longer charters are available for groups.

The *Spread Eagle II* (⊠ Puerto del Rey Marina, Rte. 3, Km 51.4 ☎ 787/887–8821 or 888/523–4511 ⊕ www.snorkelpr.com) is a 51-foot catamaran that heads out to isolated beaches on the islands off Fajardo. The trip includes an all-you-can-eat buffet and unlimited piña coladas. To top it off, you get a free snorkel to bring home. There are also sunset and moonlight cruises.

At Villa Marina, the *Traveler* (⊠ Villa Marina, Rte. 987, Km 1.3 ☎ 787/863–2821 ⊕ www.puertoricosnorkel.com) is a 54-foot catamaran that takes you to pristine coral reefs for an afternoon of snorkeling. Of course there's the usual lunch buffet and plenty of rum punch.

DIVING The waters off eastern Puerto Rico are probably the best suited for scuba diving and snorkeling and compare favorably to other Caribbean diving destinations. Most operators will take you on dives up to 65 feet down, where visibility averages 40 feet to 60 feet and the water is still warm. The east has bountiful coral reefs, with a good variety of hard and soft coral, as well as a large variety of marine life. Fine snorkeling and diving spots can be found immediately offshore from Fajardo, and there are many small, uninhabited islets from which to dive just off the coast. Experienced divers will find more than enough variety to fulfill themselves, and those just starting out will find eastern Puerto Rico a perfect place, with easy dives that offer a taste of the real beauty of life underwater.

La Casa del Mar Dive Center (⊠ El Conquistador Resort & Golden Door Spa, 1000 Av. El Conquistador ☎ 787/863–1000 Ext. 7919 or 787/860–3483) focuses its scuba and snorkeling activity on the islets of Palominos, Lobos, and Diablo. There are also boating charters and trips to the Vieques's bioluminescent bay. A two-tank morning dive costs from $99 to $124 depending on your equipment needs; single-tank afternoon dives are $69 to $94. An afternoon of snorkeling costs $50 per person. You can also take a full-day trip to Culebra, which costs $125 to $150 for divers and $85 for snorkelers, including lunch.

At **Sea Ventures Pro Dive Center** (⊠ Puerto del Rey Marina, Rte. 3, Km 51.4 ☎ 787/863–3483 ⊕ www.divepuertorico.com) you can get PADI certified, arrange dive trips to 20 offshore sites, or organize boating and sailing excursions. A two-tank dive for certified divers, including equipment, is $99.

KAYAKING Several tour operators, including some based in San Juan, offer nighttime kayaking tours in the bioluminescent bay at the Reserva Natural Las Cabezas de San Juan, just north of Fajardo.

Eco Action Tours (☎ 787/791–7509 or 787/640–7385 ⊕ www.ecoactiontours.com) provides transportation and gives tours of the Fajardo shimmering bay by kayak every night, with pickup service in Fajardo area and San Juan hotels. The outfit also offers sailing tours to Culebra, daylong snorkeling trips, and Jet Ski rentals.

Las Tortugas Adventures (☎ 787/725–5169 or 787/889–7734 ⊕ www.kayak-pr.com) provides transportation from San Juan for a one-day kayaking trip in the Reserva Natural Las Cabezas de San Juan. Rates include transportation from San Juan, but it's possible to join up with the group from Fajardo.

Shopping

Maria Elba Torres runs the **Galería Arrecife** (⊠ El Conquistador Resort & Golden Door Spa, 1000 Av. El Conquistador ☎787/863–3972), which shows only works by artists living in the Caribbean. Look for ceramics by Rafael de Olmo and jewelry made from fish scales. Chocolate-loving Laurie Humphrey had trouble finding a supplier for her sweet tooth, so she opened the **Paradise Store** (⊠Rte. 194, Km 0.4 ☎787/863–8182). Lindt and other gourmet chocolates jam the shop, which also sells flowers and such gift items as Puerto Rican–made soaps.

THE EASTERN COAST

From Fajardo, a good way to explore the southeast is to travel along the old coastal road, Route 3, as it weaves on and off the shoreline and passes through small towns. The route takes a while to travel but offers terrific beach and mountain scenery.

Naguabo

🕕 *18 km (11 mi) southwest of Fajardo.*

In this fast-growing municipality's downtown, pastel buildings give the main plaza the look of a child's nursery: a golden-yellow church on one side faces a bright-yellow city hall, and a pink-and-blue amphitheater anchors one corner. It's a good spot for people-watching until the heat drives you to the beach.

> **WORD OF MOUTH**
>
> "The rainforest is fabulous, especially the lesser-known south side of El Yunque, up the mountain from the town of Naguabo."
> –tripster.

Offshore, Cayo Santiago—also known as Monkey Island—is the site of some of the world's most important rhesus monkey research. A small colony of monkeys was introduced to the island in the late 1930s, and since then scientists have been studying their habits and health, especially as they pertain to the study of diabetes and arthritis. You can't land at Cayo Santiago, but Captain Frank Lopez sails a small tour boat—*La Paseadora Naguabeña*—around it.

Beach

Playa Húcares is *the* place to be. Casual outdoor eateries and funky shops vie with the water for your attention. Two Victorian-style houses anchor one end of the waterfront promenade; a dock with excursion boats anchors the other. ⊠ *Off Rte. 3, south of Naguabo.*

Where to Stay & Eat

¢–$ ╳ **Chumar.** As at the other food kiosks along Playa Húcares, you order at the counter and then grab a seat at one of the plastic tables that line the sidewalk. It's right on the ocean, so you are almost guaranteed that the fish will be fresh. Paper plates and plastic cutlery accompany the down-home seafood. ⊠ *Rte. 3, Km 66* ☎ *787/874–0107* ▤ *MC, V.*

$ ▥ **Casa Cubuy Ecolodge.** El Yunque's southern edge is the setting for this hotel. If you're up for a hike, trails from the lodge lead to a waterfall. If you'd rather relax, hammocks await you on the tiled veranda. Guest rooms are simple—no phones or TVs—but comfortable, with tile floors, rattan furniture, white bedspreads, plenty of windows, and balconies. You must climb many stairs to reach the upper rooms; if this is a problem, request a room on the lower level. The proprietor, who believes that healthful eating translates into healthful living, serves breakfasts that are both tasty and wholesome. Light picnic lunches can also be ordered in the morning to take with you on hikes.

> **WORD OF MOUTH**
>
> "Casa Cubuy is located in the nearby rainforest. Wonderful rooms, views, hiking & breakfasts. You could see 3 waterfalls from our room. Just remember to take along some food or snacks. If they don't have 6 people request dinner, you are on your own & it is a long ride back into town."
> –SAnParis.

⊠ *Rte. 191, Km 22, Barrio Río Blanco, 00744* ☎ *787/874–6221* ⊕ *www.casacubuy.com* ↝ *8 rooms* ♻ *Fans, hiking; no a/c, no room TVs, no smoking* ▤ *AE, MC, V* ♜ *BP.*

Sports & the Outdoors

Captain Frank Lopez will sail you around Cayo Santiago aboard *La Paseadora* (⊠ Playa Húcares dock, Rte. 3, Km 66.6 ☎ 787/850–7881). Lopez, a charming, well-informed guide, gears the outings to the group. In an hour or 90 minutes, you can motor around the island and watch the monkeys. You can also make arrangements in advance for snorkeling stops or for the captain to drop you off at another islet and pick you up later.

Humacao

🔟 *15 km (9 mi) southwest of Naguabo; 55 km (34 mi) southeast of San Juan.*

Humacao is known for the sprawling resort called Palmas del Mar and its two world-class golf courses, the Flamboyán and the Palm, which draw golfers from all over the world. Although it's not thought of as a tourist destination, Humacao does have some interesting neocolonial buildings along its crowded downtown streets.

2

The former residence of sugar baron Antonio Roig Torruellas, **Museo Casa Roig** was built in 1919. Czech architect Antonio Nechodoma designed the facade, unusual for its wide eaves, mosaic work, and stained-glass windows with geometric patterns. This was Puerto Rico's first 20th-century building to go on the register of National Historic Places. The Roig family lived in the home until 1956; it was then abandoned before being turned over to the University of Puerto Rico in 1977. It's currently a museum and cultural center, with historical photos, furniture, and rotating exhibits of works by contemporary island artists. ⊠ *66 Calle Antonio López* ☎ *787/852–8380* ⊕ *www.uprh.edu/~museocr* 🖃 *Free* ⊙ *Wed.–Fri. and Sun. 10–4.*

Plaza de Humacao, downtown's broad square, is anchored by the pale pink Catedral Dulce Nombre de Jesús (Sweet Name of Jesus Cathedral), which dates from 1869. It has a castlelike facade, and even when its grille door is locked, you can peek through to see the sleek altar, polished floors, and stained-glass windows dominated by blues. Across the plaza, four fountains splash under the shade of old trees. People pass through feeding the pigeons, children race down the promenade, and retirees congregate on benches to chat. Look for the little monument with the globe on top; it's a tribute to city sons who died in wars. ⊠ *Av. Font Martel at Calle Ulises Martinez.*

As you travel from Naguabo to Humacao, there are stretches of beach and swaths of undeveloped land, including the swamps, lagoons, and forested areas of the **Refugio de Vida Silvestre de Humacao.** This nature reserve has an information office, restrooms, and camp sites. ⊠ *Rte. 3, Km 74.3* ☎ *787/852–4440* 🖃 *Free* ⊙ *Weekdays 7:30–4:30.*

Beach

Right beside the Refugio de Vida Silvestre de Humacao, **Playa Punta Santiago** is a long strand with closely planted palm trees that are perfect for stringing up hammocks. The beach, one of 12 government-operated public beaches, has changing facilities with showers and restrooms, food kiosks, and lifeguard stations. Parking is $3. ⊠ *Rte. 3, northeast of Humacao.*

Where to Eat

$$$–$$$$
Fodor'sChoice
★

✕ **Chez Daniel.** When the stars are out, there could hardly be a more romantic setting than this restaurant in the Anchor's Village Marina. The casual atmosphere belies the elegance of Daniel Vasse's culinary creations. His French country–style dishes are some of the best on the island. The Catalan-style *bouillinade,* full of fresh fish and bursting with the flavor of a white garlic sauce, is exceptional. Pair it with a bottle from the extensive wine cellar. Sunday brunch, with its seemingly endless seafood bar, draws people from all over the island. ⊠ *Anchor's Village Marina, Rte. 906, Km 86.4* ☎ *787/850–3838* ⚐ *Reservations essential* ☱ *AE, MC, V* ⊙ *Closed Tues. No lunch Mon.–Thurs.*

Where to Stay

$$
🏨 **Four Points by Sheraton Palmas del Mar Resort.** The only hotel in Palmas del Mar, this hotel sits amid acres and acres of condo developments.

It's surprisingly modest in scale, given its opulent surroundings. Rooms have a luxurious feel, with lovely wood furnishings and rich fabrics. None has a view of the ocean, but they all have balconies overlooking the pool or the lush grounds. Since you have access to the facilities at Palmas del Mar, you can stroll around the marina or hit the links at the two championship golf courses. ⊠ *170 Candelero Dr., 00792* 🕾 *787/850–6000* 🖷 *787/850–6001* ⊕ *www.starwoodhotels.com* ⇨ *107 rooms ⚴ 1 restaurant, room service, in-room safes, minibars, cable TV with movies, in-room broadband, Wi-Fi, 2 18-hole golf courses, 20 tennis courts, pool, health club, beach, dive shop, dock, snorkeling, windsurfing, fishing, horseback riding, 2 bars, casino, shop, business services, Internet room, meeting rooms, airport shuttle ⊟ AE, D, DC, MC, V* ❡❂❡ *EP.*

$ 🖃 **Palmas de Lucía.** Lights shaped like palm trees illuminate the pool area at this family-run hotel. Don't worry—there are plenty of the real thing on the pretty stretch of beach just outside. The rooms are larger than you'd expect for the price, and have spotless kitchenettes. The hotel is in Yabucoa, several miles south of Humacao. ⊠ *Rte. 901 at Rte. 9911, Yabucoa 00767* 🕾 *787/893–4423* 🖷 *787/893–0291* ⊕ *www.palmasdelucia.com* ⇨ *34 rooms ⚴ Restaurant, cable TV, microwaves, refrigerators, laundry service, game room ⊟ AE, MC, V* ❡❂❡ *EP.*

Nightlife

The casino at the **Four Points by Sheraton Palmas del Mar Resort** (⊠ 170 Candelero Dr. 🕾 787/850–6000) offers everything from blackjack to slot machines. The action is liveliest on weekends.

Sports & the Outdoors

FISHING **Shiraz Charters** (⊠ Palmas del Mar Country Club, Rte. 906 🕾 644–5786 ⊕ www.charternet.com/fishers/shiraz) specializes in deep-sea fishing charters in search of tuna. Eight-hour trips start at about $150 per person, including equipment and snacks.

GOLF **Palmas del Mar Country Club** (⊠ Rte. 906 🕾 787/285–2256 ⊕ www.
★ palmascountryclub.com) has two good golf courses: the Rees Jones–designed Flamboyán course, named for the nearly six dozen flamboyant trees that pepper its fairway, winds around a lake, over a river, and to the sea before turning toward sand dunes and wetlands. It's been rated one of the top five in the world. The older, Gary Player–designed Palm course has a challenging par 5 that scoots around wetlands. Greens fees are $70 to $100.

EL YUNQUE & THE NORTHEAST ESSENTIALS

To research prices, get advice from other travelers, and book travel arrangements, visit www.fodors.com.

Transportation

BY AIR

Air Flamenco, Isla Nena Air Service, and Vieques Air Link offer several daily flights between Fajardo and San Juan, as well as between Fajardo and Vieques and Culebra. Trips to any of these destination are between 10 and 15 minutes; the cost ranges from \$40 to \$100 round-trip.

🛩 **Air Flamenco** ☎ 787/724-1818 ⊕ www.airflamenco.net. **Isla Nena Air Service** ☎ 787/741-6362 or 877/812-5144 ⊕ www.islanena.8m.com. **Vieques Air Link** ☎ 787/741-8331 or 888/901-9247 ⊕ www.vieques-island.com/val.

AIRPORTS Fajardo is served by the one-room Aeropuerto Diego Jiménez Torres, which is just southwest of the city on Route 976. The landing field at Aeropuerto Regional de Humacao is used mostly by private planes.

🛩 **Aeropuerto Diego Jiménez Torres** ☎ 787/860-3110. **Aeropuerto Regional de Humacao** ☎ 787/852-8188.

BY BUS

Públicos travel between San Juan and Fajardo, stopping en route at the ferry terminal. The full journey can take up to two hours, depending on where you board and where you are dropped off. However, the fare is a huge bargain at \$5 (pay the driver as you board). To get to Fajardo, you simply flag públicos down anywhere along Route 3.

Within cities and towns, local buses pick up and discharge at marked stops and cost 35¢ to 50¢. You enter and pay (the exact fair is required) at the front of the bus and exit at the front or the back.

BY CAR

Unless you are planning to hop directly onto a ferry to Vieques or Culebra, you should consider renting a car in eastern Puerto Rico. Even the destination resorts are fairly isolated, and you may appreciate the mobility if you want to get out and have a meal away from the resort, if not to explore El Yunque or some of the great beaches on your own. Rates generally start about \$35 a day, but it's sometimes possible to rent directly from your lodging, so ask about packages that include lodging and a car rental.

From San Juan the east coast is accessible via Route 3, or Route 187 if you want to visit Loíza. At Fajardo the road intersects with Route 53, a fast toll road that continues down the coast. Route 3, however, also continues along the coast and provides a more scenic, if slower, trip.

EMERGENCY SERVICES Rental-car agencies usually give customers emergency road-service numbers to call. There's no AAA service on Puerto Rico.

GASOLINE Gas stations are found along major roads and within cities and towns. Gasoline is sold in liters, not gallons. Although few eastern stations have round-the-clock hours, many are open until midnight and most are open seven days a week. Note that gas is rarely self-service; an attendant usually pumps it.

PARKING Although parking can be a nightmare (a pricey one at that) in San Juan, it's no problem out on the island except during festivals. Some mid-size cities have metered on-street parking as well as lots; in smaller communities street parking is the norm, and it's generally free. Most of the bigger resorts charge for parking.

ROAD CONDITIONS The main roads are in good shape, but many highway exit and other signs have been blown down by hurricanes, and may or may not have been replaced. When it rains, be alert for flash flooding, even on the major highways.

🔒 Agencies **Avis** ✉ El Conquistador Resort & Golden Door Spa, 1000 Av. El Conquistador, Fajardo ☎ 787/863-2735 ✉ 170 Candelero Dr., Humacao ☎ 787/285-1376 ✉ Westin Río Mar Beach Golf Resort & Spa, 6000 Río Mar Blvd., Río Grande ☎ 787/888-6638 ⊕ www.avis.com. **L & M** ✉ Rte. 3 Marginal, Km 43.8, Fajardo ☎ 787/860-6868 ⊕ www.lmcarrental.com. **Leaseway of Puerto Rico** ✉ Rte. 3, Km 44.4, Fajardo ☎ 787/860-5000.

BY FERRY

The Puerto Rico Ports Authority runs passenger ferries from Fajardo to Culebra and Vieques. Service is from the ferry terminal in Fajardo, about a 90-minute drive from San Juan. A municipal parking lot next to the ferry costs $5 a day—handy if you are going to one of the islands just for the day.

If you are thinking of taking your rental car from the main island over to Vieques, there is a cargo ferry that travels from Fajardo, and it does take cars. It only operates during the week, and the schedule is laughably erratic. Reservations must be made well in advance with a cash deposit; even then you might be bumped at the last minute if there is no room. To top it all off, rental agencies discourage taking their cars to Vieques, as the gravel roads are better negotiated with SUVs. Locals don't take their cars over to Vieques, and neither should you. It's a much better option to rent a car on Vieques.

The Fajardo–Vieques ferry departs from Vieques weekdays at 6:30 AM, 11 AM, 3 PM, and 6:30 PM, returning at 9:30 AM, 1 PM, 4:30 PM, and 8 PM. On weekends ferries depart from Vieques at 6:30 AM, 1 PM, and 4:30 PM, returning at 9 AM, 3 PM, and 6 PM. Tickets for the 45-minute journey are $2 each way. The Fajardo–Culebra ferry leaves Culebra daily at 6:30 AM, 1 PM, and 5 PM, returning at 9 AM, 5 PM, and 7 PM. The 90-minute trip is $2.25. Ferry schedules change with alarming frequency. Call to confirm before you plan your trip.

🔒 **Fajardo ferry terminal** (Fajardo Port Authority) ☎ 787/863-4560.

BY TAXI

You can flag cabs down on the street, but it's faster and safer to have your hotel call one for you. Either way, make sure the driver is clear on whether he or she will charge a flat rate or use a meter to determine the fare. In most places the cabs are metered. Instead of renting a car, some people opt to take a taxi to Fajardo. The cost from the San Juan area should be about $80 for up to five people.

🔒 **Fajardo Taxi Service** ☎ 787/860-1112. **Humacao Taxi** ☎ 787/852-6880.

Contacts & Resources

BANKS & EXCHANGE SERVICES

Banks and ATMs (or ATHs, as they're known here) are plentiful. Banks are usually open weekdays from 9 to 5; very few open on Saturday, and those that do are open only until noon.

🔒 **Banco Popular** ✉ Rte. 3, Km 42.4, Fajardo ☎ 787/860-1570. **Banco Roig** ✉ 55 Calle Antonio Lopez, Humacao ☎ 787/852-8601.

2

EMERGENCIES

⚑ Emergency Numbers General ☏ 911. **Medical Clinics** ☏ 787/876-2042, 787/876-2429 in Loíza, 787/823-2550, 787/887-2020 in Río Grande, 787/889-2620, 787/889-2020 in Luquillo, 787/863-2550, 787/863-2020 in Fajardo, 787/874-7440, 787/874-2020 in Naguabo.

⚑ Hospitals Hospital Dr. Dominguez ✉ 300 Font Martelo, Humacao ☏ 787/852-0505. **Hospital Gubern** ✉ 110 Antonio Barcelo, Fajardo ☏ 787/863-0669. **Hospital San Pablo del Este** ✉ Av. General Valero, Km 2.4, Fajardo ☏ 787/863-0505. **Ryder Memorial Hospital** ✉ Salida Humacao-Las Piedras, Humacao ☏ 787/852-0768.

⚑ Pharmacies Walgreens ✉ Fajardo Plaza, Fajardo ☏ 787/860-1060 ✉ Oriental Plaza, Humacao ☏ 787/852-1868.

INTERNET, MAIL & SHIPPING

Puerto Rico is part of the U.S. postal system, and most communities of any size have multiple branches of the post office. Some aren't open on Saturday, however. Big hotels and resorts also have postal drop boxes.

There are very few Internet cafés in this part of the country, but all of the larger hotels have in-room Internet access.

⚑ Post Offices Fajardo main post office ✉ 102 Calle Garrido Morales E, Fajardo ☏ 787/863-0802. **Naguabo main post office** ✉ 100 Rte. 31, Naguabo ☏ 787/874-3115.

OVERNIGHT SERVICES Puerto Rico has express overnight mail delivery through the U.S. Postal Service as well as Federal Express, which usually operates through office supply stores or other commercial outlets. (Note that FedEx doesn't offer Saturday pickup on the island.)

⚑ Office Max ✉ Rte. 3, Fajardo ☏ 800/463-3339. **Post Net** ✉ Rte. 3, Río Grande ☏ 800/463-3339 ✉ 118 Av. Ortiz Estela, Humacao ☏ 800/463-3339.

SAFETY

Although crime isn't as high in the island's eastern areas as it is in San Juan, use prudence. Avoid bringing valuables with you to the beach; if you must do so, be sure not to leave them in view in your car. It's best to keep your car locked while driving, and avoid out-of-the-way beaches after sunset.

VISITOR INFORMATION

The island's tourism offices are hit and miss when it comes to helpful material. The cities usually offer information through offices connected to city hall, and most are open only during business hours on weekdays.

⚑ Fajardo Tourism Office ✉ 6 Av. Muñz Rivera, Fajardo ☏ 787/863-1400 ⊕ www.fajardopr.org. **Luquillo Tourism Office** ✉ 154 Calle 14 de Julio, Luquillo ☏ 787/889-2851. **Naguabo Tourism Office** ✉ Rte. 3, Km 66.6, Playa Húcares, Naguabo ☏ 787/874-0389. **Río Grande Office of Tourism and Culture** ✉ Calle San José, Plaza de Recreo, Río Grande ☏ 787/887-2370.

Vieques & Culebra

WORD OF MOUTH

"[Vieques] is a beautiful island that hasn't been overdeveloped, and the beaches haven't been taken over by Hyatts and Hiltons. Thank goodness!! BYOE—bring your own everything."
—BeachGirl247

"Most of the islands have pretty shades of blue and green. But I was in Culebra, and the water there sparkled like I never saw water sparkle before. It was like looking at diamomds!!!!!"
—noonema

Revised and
Updated by
Mark Sullivan

ALTHOUGH THEY ARE JUST A FEW MILES off the coast of Puerto Rico, the islands of Vieques and Culebra feel like another world. While the rest of the mainland rings with the adrenaline rush of Latin America, this pair of palm-ringed islands have the laid-back vibe of the Caribbean. Not surprising, as St. Thomas and St. Croix are clearly visible from from the eastern edges of Culebra.

Vieques and Culebra are alike in many ways. Neither has much traffic—in fact, you won't find a single traffic light on either island. High-rise hotels haven't cast a shadow on the beautiful beaches. And there are no casinos, fast-food chains, strip malls, or most other trappings of modern life. "Barefoot" is often part of the dress code at the casual restaurants, and the hum you hear in your room is more likely than not coming from a ceiling fan rather than an air-conditioner.

But each island has its own personality. Vieques is the biggest of the siblings, so it gets the most attention. The island, 21 mi long and 4 mi wide, has two small communities. Isabel Segunda, the town on the northern shore where the ferry docks, is a knot of one-way streets. It's not pretty, but it has a couple of interesting sights, including a hilltop fortress. On the southern shore is the town of Esperanza, little more that a string of low-cost restaurants and hotels along a waterfront promenade. Nearby is the world-famous Bahía Mosquito, a bioluminescent bay that twinkles like the night sky. The bulk of the island is a national park, the Vieques National Wildlife Refuge. Within the park you'll find dozens of beaches with names like Red, Green, and Blue, as well as many more that have no official name.

At 7 mi long and 4 mi wide, Culebra is much smaller. There's only one community, the tiny town of Dewey. People come to Culebra to see Playa Flamenco, consistently rated as one of the two or three best beaches in the world, as well as many lesser-known but equally beautiful beaches. The island is mostly unspoiled, a quality which brings many people back year after year.

Getting to the islands is much easier than in years past. Both are accessible from Fajardo—either on 90-minute ferry trips or 10-minute puddle-jumper flights. There are also flights from either of San Juan's airports that take between 20 and 30 minutes. The flights are scenic, skirting the main island's northern coast before heading out over the azure waters of the Caribbean.

Exploring Vieques & Culebra

It's nearly impossible to see either island without renting a car. Sure, you could stay at one of the small hotels along the waterfront in Vieques, eating at the handful of restaurants within walking distance, but you'd miss out on most of what the island has to offer. Scooters are another option for getting around, especially on tiny Culebra, but they aren't a good idea if you are headed to the beach. Roads are dusty, paved with loose gravel, and riddled with huge potholes.

TOP 5 PICKS FOR VIEQUES & CULEBRA

- Swimming after dark in Bahía Mosquito, the astounding biolu-minscent bay on Vieques.
- Catching some rays on Culebra's Playa Flamenco, consistently ranked as one of the world's best beaches.
- Hiking to the deserted lighthouse on one of the islands that make

up the Refugio Nacional de Vida Silvestre de Culebra.
- Watching the sunset from the cantilevered deck at Al's Mar Azul, the best happy hour spot on Vieques.
- Discovering Playa Media Luna, or one of the dozens of other deserted beaches that fringe Vieques.

About the Restaurants

Most of the restaurants on Vieques and Culebra are extremely casual, meaning that the dress code doesn't get much stricter than NO SHOES, NO SHIRT, NO SERVICE. Because even the most formal restaurants on the islands are on covered terraces on in open-air dining rooms, there's not a single establishment where you'll be frowned on for wearing shorts. Pack a couple of nice shirts and you'll be set.

Caribbean cuisine—meaning lots of fresh fish and local produce—is the norm here. Even if a restaurant focuses on a different type of food, you can be sure that mangos, papayas, and other tropical fruits will make an appearance. Bills often include a service charge; if it isn't included, a 15% tip is customary. Most restaurants are open for dinner from about 6 PM until at least 10 PM.

WHAT IT COSTS In U.S. dollars				
	$$$$	$$$	$$	$	¢
AT DINNER	over $30	$20–$30	$12–$20	$8–$12	under $8

Prices are per person for a main course at dinner.

About the Hotels

Vieques has a wide variety of lodgings, from surf shacks across from the beach to boutique hotels high up on secluded hillsides. There's something here for everyone. Looking for tropical splendor? Try Hacienda Tamarindo or the Inn on the Blue Horizon. Interesting architecture? There's Hix Island House or Bravo Beach Resort. An intimate inn where you'll meet all of your fellow travelers? Head to Casa de Amistad or Trade Winds.

Culebra has fewer options. Dewey, the island's only town, has a hand-

> **CAUTION**
>
> If you plan to rent a car on Vieques or Culebra, make sure you reserve it in advance, especially when visiting during high season. The rental agencies have a limited number of vehicles, and when they are gone, you're out of luck.

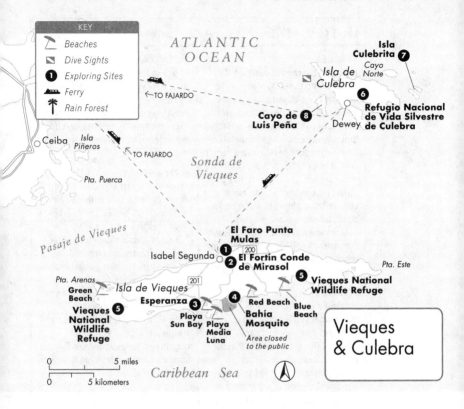

ful of small inns that are easy on the wallet. Scattered around the island are a couple of more luxurious lodgings. There's nothing here that remotely resembles a chain hotel, and that's how the locals like it.

WHAT IT COSTS In U.S. dollars				
$$$$	$$$	$$	$	¢
FOR 2 PEOPLE over $350	$250–$350	$150–$250	$80–$150	under $80

Prices are for a double room in high season, excluding 9% tax (11% for hotels with casinos, 7% for paradores) and 5%–12% service charge.

Timing

High season runs from December 15 through April 15. The crowds are the most unbearable at Christmas and Easter, when Vieques and Culebra are packed with families enjoying the sun and sand. Be sure to make reservations well in advance if you're visiting during the holidays. The shoulder season, when prices are a bit lower, is a good option. Remember, however, that some restaurants and hotels are only open during the high season. The only time you might want to avoid is late August through late October, when most hurricanes roll through the area.

IF YOU LIKE

BEACHES

Beautiful beaches abound on Vieques and Culebra. Many of the best stretches of sand on Vieques—Red Beach, Blue Beach, and Green Beach, to name a few—are on land that was once part of a naval base. This means that development hasn't reared its ugly head. It also means there are few, if any, amenities at most of these beaches, so make sure to bring plenty of water and a picnic lunch. The beaches on Culebra are just as unspoiled. Playa Flamenco, on the island's northern coast, is considered one of the best in the world.

SEAFOOD

Hopefully you like seafood, since that's what you'll get at almost every eatery on Vieques and Culebra. The good news is that the fish is as fresh as you'll find anywhere, since that red snapper was probably splashing around in the Caribbean that very morning. Unlike some other parts of Puerto Rico, here you can order it in any number of ways. Chefs are experimenting with European and Asian cooking techniques, so you may find your fish smoked or even in a sushi roll.

WATER SPORTS

Some of the best snorkeling and diving can be found in the waters surrounding Vieques and Culebra. You can sign up for a half-day or full-day excursion to nearby coral reefs, which are teeming with colorful fish. It's also possible to grab a mask and snorkel, then simply wade out for a few yards to see what you can see. Playa Esperanza, on the southern coast of Vieques, is a good place for beginners. More experienced snorkelers will prefer Blue Beach or Green Beach.

Numbers in the text correspond to numbers in the margin and on the Vieques and Culebra maps.

VIEQUES

13 km (8 mi) southeast of Fajardo.

Looking for a place to play Robinson Crusoe? Then head to Vieques, where you can wander along almost any stretch of sand and never see another soul. You can while away the hours underneath the coconut palms, wade in the warm water, or grab a mask and snorkel and explore the coral reefs that ring the island.

For many years the island was known mostly for the conflict between angry islanders and aloof federal officials. Over the course of six decades, the U.S. Navy used two-thirds of Vieques, mostly on the island's eastern and western tips, as a bombing range. Residents complained that their mighty neighbor stifled economic development and harmed the environment. After an April 1999 bombing accident took the life of one resident, waves of protests that brought the maneuvers to a standstill

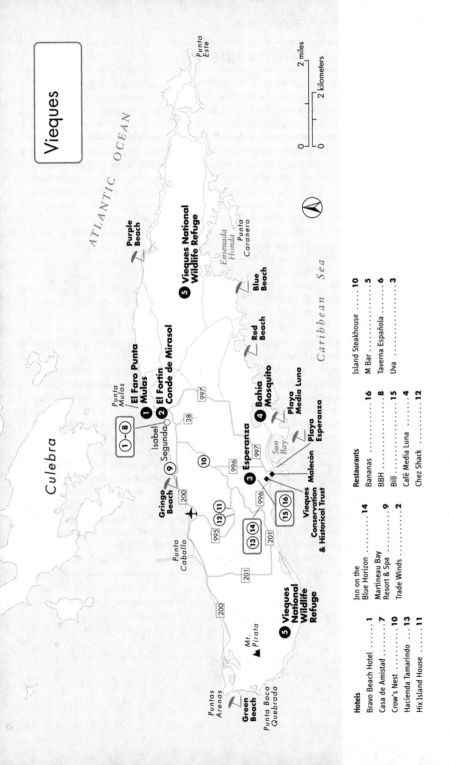

Vieques

ATLANTIC OCEAN

Caribbean Sea

Culebra

Punta Mulas
1 El Faro Punta Mulas
2 El Fortín Conde de Mirasol

Isabel Segunda

5 Vieques National Wildlife Refuge
Purple Beach

Blue Beach

Red Beach

4 Bahía Mosquito
Playa Media Luna

3 Esperanza
Sun Bay
Malecón · Playa Esperanza
Vieques Conservation & Historical Trust

Gringo Beach

5 Vieques National Wildlife Refuge

Mt. Pirata

Puntas Arenas
Green Beach
Punta Boca Quebrada

Punta Caballo

Punta Este

Ensenada Honda
Punta Caranero

0 · 2 miles
0 · 2 kilometers

Hotels

GREAT ITINERARIES

IF YOU HAVE 1 DAY

If you are headed to one of the islands for an overnight excursion, your best best is **Vieques.** Get here by plane, either from San Juan or Fajardo, to maximize your time on the island. Spend the day exploring the beaches, especially the half-moon-shaped Sun Bay. In the evening you can dine at one of the oceanfront restaurants in Esperanza, then head off for an excursion to **Bahía Mosquito ❹**, a bay filled with glow-in-the-dark dinoflagellates. Dive in and the outline of your body will be outlined with an eerie blue phosphorescence. Spend the night in Esperanza or Isabel Segunda.

IF YOU HAVE 3 DAYS

If you have a few days, you can see most of Vieques. Start your first day in Isabel Segunda, where you can take a few snapshots of **El Faro Punta Mulas ❶** then explore the hilltop fortress called **El Fortín Conde de Mirasol ❷**. Head off for an afternoon by the ocean, perhaps at Green Beach or one of the delightfully deserted beaches on the northern part of the island. Enjoy the sunset from Al's Mar Azul, a favorite hangout for expats, or from the deck of a catamaran. In the cool of the evening, have dinner in one of the chic eateries in Isabel Segunda. On your second day, go for a hike in the **Vieques National Wildlife Refuge ❺**, at either end of the island, a swath of wilderness that was once a naval base. Head for lunch at Sun Bay, a popular beach that has its own snack bar, or pack a picnic and head off to Playa Media Luna or one of the little-known gems on the southern coast. After dinner, make sure to book a tour of **Bahía Mosquito ❹**.

IF YOU HAVE 5 DAYS

If you have a few more days, you can see both Vieques and Culebra. After following the itinerary above, head to Culebra on your fourth day. (There is a ferry that runs between the two islands, as well as numerous private boats that will be happy to shuttle you back and forth.) Your destination should be Playa Flamenco, a U-shaped beach bordered by an unbroken string of palm trees. The mountains beyond make a striking backdrop. Dine that evening in one of the eateries in or around the only town, the diminutive Dewey. On your last day, try snorkeling in **Refugio Nacional de Vida Silvestre de Culebra ❻**, the island's lovely nature preserve. One of the best places is **Isla Culebrita ❼**, an islet dominated by a deserted lighthouse.

and political pressure from the island's government, the military reluctantly agreed to leave on May 1, 2003.

Ironically, the military's presence helped to keep the island pristine by limiting the land available for rambling resorts. Today, most of the military's holdings have been turned into the Vieques National Wildlife Refuge. The western end of the island has the most public access. Here you'll find Monte Pirata, the island's highest peak. (At 987 feet, it isn't much of a mountain, but it looks impressive.) More and more of the eastern part of the island is being opened every year. The park is your gateway to some of the island's best beaches, including Green Beach in the west and Red and Blue beaches in the east.

Exploring Vieques

Just because Vieques is sleepy doesn't mean there's nothing to do besides hit the beach. There are two communities—Isabel Segunda and Esperanza—where you can dine at an open-air eatery, stock up on supplies, or book a trip to the astonishing Bahía Mosquito, perhaps the world's most luminous bioluminescent bay.

Isabel Segunda
29 km (18 mi) southeast of Fajardo by ferry.

Since it's the transportation hub of Vieques, you won't be able to avoid Isabel Segunda. The ferry drops off passengers at the town's dock, and propeller planes deposit passengers at the tiny airport to the west. If you want to rent a car, or gas up the one you already have, you need to make a trip to Isabel Segunda.

But Isabel Segunda (or Isabel II, as it's often labeled on maps) has some charms that are not immediately apparent. There's a lovely lighthouse on the coast just east of the ferry dock, and on the hill above town you'll find the last fort the Spanish constructed in the New World. Some of the best bars and restaurants are found here, as well as lodgings ranging from funky to fancy.

❶ El Faro Punta Mulas, a Spanish-built lighthouse beside the ferry dock in Isabel Segunda, dates from 1895. It was built to guide vessels into the harbor, which is surrounded by a chain of dangerous reefs. It's said that the red light can be seen from as far away as St. Croix and St. Thomas. In 1992 the elegant structure was carefully restored and transformed into a maritime museum that traces much of the island's history, including the visit by South American liberation leader Simón Bolívar. Sadly, the museum had been closed for more than a year when this book was updated, and there were no plans to reopen it. The lighthouse itself is worth a look, however. ⊠ *At end of Rte. 200* ☎ *787/741–0060.*

❷ On a hilltop overlooking Isabel Segunda is **El Fortín Conde de Mirasol** (Count of Mirasol Fort), the last military structure begun by the Spanish in the New World. It was erected on Vieques's northern coast in 1840 at the order of Count Mirasol, then governor of Puerto Rico. It took more than a decade to complete, which meant Mirasol had to repeatedly ask for more money. (Queen Isabel, on being petitioned yet again, asked Mirasol whether the walls were made of gold.) The fort helped solidify Spanish control of the area, keeping British, French, Dutch, and Danish colonists away and dissuading pirates from attacking Isabel Segunda. After sitting empty for several decades, it was transformed into a museum in 1991. The museum has an impressive collection of artifacts from the Taíno Indians and other cultures that thrived on this and nearby islands before the arrival of the Spanish. There are also exhibits on the island's years as a sugar plantation and its occupation by the U.S. Navy.

Vieques Libre

FOR NEARLY SIX DECADES, the U.S. Navy had a stranglehold on Vieques. It controlled the island's eastern and western ends and exerted enormous influence over the destiny of the civilian area sandwiched in between. Though long protested, the bombing continued. When an off-target bomb killed a civilian on Navy land in April 1999, opposition began to transform the island's placid beaches into political hotbeds. As a result of the protests that followed, the Navy finally withdrew from its Atlantic Fleet training grounds in May 2002.

Protesters camping out on the bombing range kept it shut down from 1999 to 2000. Hundreds of Puerto Rican residents were arrested for trespassing on Navy land during war games. They were joined by celebrity protesters from the United States, including environmental lawyer Robert F. Kennedy Jr. (who gave his baby daughter the middle name "Vieques"), the wife of Reverend Jesse Jackson, and Reverend Al Sharpton, all of whom were arrested for trespassing on the bombing range. For much of 2000 and 2001, protests were so commonplace that there were semipermanent encampments of opponents. Songs with such titles as "Paz Pa' Vieques" ("Peace for Vieques") began to surface, as did bumper stickers and T-shirts with protest slogans. Latin pop celebrities such as singer–songwriter Robie Draco Rosa (who wrote Ricky Martin

hits like "Livin' la Vida Loca"), actor Edward James Olmos, singer Millie Corejter, Puerto Rican rock band Fiel a la Vega, protest-singer Zoraida Santiago, local actors, painters, doctors, and lawyers, added to the fanfare when they joined the activities.

President Bill Clinton finally agreed that residents could vote on whether to continue to host the Navy. A nonbinding referendum held in 2001 found that 68% of the island's voters wanted the military to leave immediately. Although some members of Congress argued that the Navy should stay indefinitely–their cries grew louder after September 11, 2001, when even local protesters called for a moratorium on civil disobedience–the administration agreed to withdraw the troops. In 2003, the naval base was officially closed.

The Navy's departure has undoubtedly spurred development on Vieques–one need only look at the additions to the tiny airport and plans for a modern ferry terminal. Amenities such as a golf course running along the northern coast are also in the works. But locals are working to make sure that the island retains its laid-back character. By the end of 2005, much of the former military base had already been transformed into the Vieques National Wildlife Refuge. This move should preserve most of the island in its unspoiled state.

⊠ 471 Calle Magnolia, Isabel Segunda ☎ 787/741–1717 ⊕ www. enchanted-isle.com/elfortin ⌨ $2 ⊙ Wed.–Sun. 10–4.

Esperanza

❸ *10 km (6 mi) south of Isabel Segunda*

The only time there's a traffic jam in Esperanza is when one of the wild horses frequently seen on the nearby beaches wanders into the road. This community, once a down-at-heel fishing village, is now a string of budget bars, restaurants, and hotels. All of them overlook Playa Esperanza, a shallow stretch of sand made all the more picturesque by the presence of a tiny islet called Cayo Afuera. In the evening, there's not a better way to enjoy the sunset than a stroll along Esperanza's **Malecón**, a waterfront walkway running the length of the beach.

♻ The **Vieques Conservation & Historical Trust** was established to help save Bahía Mosquito, one of the last remaining bioluminescent bays in the world. The small museum, located on the main drag in Esperanza, has interesting information about the bay, as well as the island's flora and fauna. A little pool lets kids get acquainted with starfish, sea urchins, and other denizens of the not-so-deep. There's also a tiny gift shop where the profits are funneled back into the foundation. *⊠ 138 Calle Flamboyán, Esperanza ☎ 787/741–8850 ⊕ www.vcht.com ⌨ Free ⊙ Tues.–Sun. 11–4.*

Elsewhere on Vieques

Isabel Segunda and Esperanza are just a tiny portion of Vieques. Most of the island—more than two-thirds of it, in fact—was commandeered by the military until 2003. It's now a nature preserve that draws thousands of visitors each year.

❹ East of Esperanza, **Bahía Mosquito** (Mosquito Bay) is also known as Bioluminescent Bay or Phosphorescent Bay. It's one of the world's best spots to have a glow-in-the-dark experience with undersea dinoflagellates. Tour operators offer kayak trips or excursions on nonpolluting boats to see the bay's tiny microorganisms that appear to light up when their water is agitated. Dive into the bay and you'll emerge covered in sparkling water. Look behind your boat, and you'll see a twinkling wake. Even the fish that jump from the water will bear an eerie glow. The high concentration of dinoflagellates sets the bay apart from the other spots (including others in Puerto Rico) that are home to these tiny organisms. The bay is at its best when there's little or no moonlight; rainy nights are beautiful, too, because the raindrops splashing in the water produce ricochet sparkles. Some of the best excursions to the bay are offered by Sharon Grasso of Island Adventures. *⊠ Reach via unpaved roads off Rte. 997.*

❺ A portion of the west and the entire eastern end of the island is being administered as the **Vieques National Wildlife Refuge,** comprising 18,000 acres—about 14,900 acres on the eastern end and 3,100 acres on the west—making it the biggest protected natural reserve in Puerto Rico. Most of eastern Vieques is being administered by the U.S. Fish & Wildlife Service as a nature reserve, except for the 900-acre bombing range on the

FodorśChoice
★

Underwater Fireworks

ON MOST MOONLESS NIGHTS strings of kayaks float along the surface of Bahía Mosquito. The people have come here, to this otherwise unremarkable bay on the island of Vieques, to witness one of nature's most eye-popping events. As a paddle skims the top of the water, thousands of points of light appear just below the surface. Behind each kayak is a blue-green glow that slowly fades. Those who trail their fingers in the water can see the outline of every digit.

This glow is produced by dinoflagellates, single-celled organisms that are found everywhere. But the species found in the Caribbean, called Pyrodinium bahamense, happens to glow when the surrounding water is disturbed in any way. The concentration of dinoflagellates in Bahía Mosquito is an astounding 720,000 per gallon—more than anywhere else on earth. This accounts for the nightly display of underwater fireworks.

Bahía Mosquito—which means, of course, Mosquito Bay—is not the only bioluminescent bay in Puerto Rico. There are a handful of others, including Fajardo's Laguna Grande and La Parguera's Bahía de Fosforescente. But they can't compare to the glittering waters of Bahía Mosquito. That's why travelers flock here from all around Puerto Rico.

The conditions at Bahía Mosquito are perfect for growing dinoflagellates. A mangrove forest surrounding the bay constantly drops leaves and branches into the water. As bacteria eat the decaying matter, they produce prodigious amounts of vitamin B12—an essential part of the dinoflagellate diet. The lagoon's mouth, resembling the neck of a bottle, keeps the nutrients from being swept out to sea. The narrow mouth also keeps the brackish water in and the salty water out. These tiny creatures, like the rest of us, are healthier when they don't have so much salt in their diet.

Other bioluminescent bays around the world have lost their luster, mostly because of pollution. Light pollution is one of the main causes, as the dinoflagellates can't compete with the glare of headlights or the glow of streetlamps. (Even the moon makes the glow difficult to discern.) On Vieques, conservation-minded citizens constantly remind their neighbors to make sure their outdoor lights are shaded so they point downward. They have also fought development near the bay, including a new road and a sports complex that would have destroyed the bay almost overnight.

Water pollution is another problem, including industrial waste, sewage drainage, and agricultural runoff. Ironically, spillage from the gas- and diesel-powered boats that take tourists to see the spectacle is often the culprit. The smoke-belching boats that depart for La Parguera's Bahía de Fosforescente every night are slowly putting themselves out of business. The display in La Parguera, once as dazzling as the one in Vieques, is dismal.

On Vieques these boats are banned from Bahía Mosquito. Instead, there are kayaks and electric-powered pontoon boats that barely cause a ripple on the surface. But there are plenty of waves when the passengers dive into the inky black water, leaving behind them a trail of light that reminds many people of the tail of a comet.

3

far eastern end, which will be permanently closed off, a consequence of its contamination by the ordnance shot over its 60-year existence. But most of the rest of eastern Vieques is pristine nature, astonishingly beautiful and well-forested, with a hilly center region overlooking powder-white sandy beaches and a coral-ringed coastline; it served mainly as a buffer zone between the military maneuvers and civilian population. The vast majority of this acreage remains off-limits to visitors as a search for unexploded munitions and contaminants is carried out. Cleanup plans, which the Puerto Rico government hopes will allow much more public access to the island, were still being drawn up at this writing. ⬠ *Box 1527, 00765* ☎ *787/741–2138* ⊕ *southeast.fws.gov/vieques.*

Beaches

Many of the beaches around the island have oddly similar names: Red Beach, Blue Beach, and Green Beach. The U.S. Navy, lacking any imagination, simply assigned them random colors. Some beaches are known by one name by tourists, another by locals. Islanders know Sun Bay as Sombé.

> ### WORD OF MOUTH
>
> "What's great about the beaches in Vieques is that there's nothing—and nobody—on most of them. Our children love exploring and checking out different beaches."   –ccc.

Blue Beach. Beyond Red Beach, you'll find a handful of covered cabanas here. There can be strong surf in some spots, making swimming here difficult at times. ⊠ *Off Rte. 997, east of Red Beach.*

Green Beach. On the western edge of the island is this beach, which is reached via a dirt road. Miles of coral reef just off shore attract snorkelers and divers. From the shore you can catch a glimpse of El Yunque on the mainland. ⊠ *At the western end of Rte. 200.*

Playa Esperanza. The most accessible beach is across from the town of the same name. People staying in any of the inexpensive accommodations in Esperanza can simply walk across the road. There are some good opportunities for snorkeling, especially around Cayo Afuera, an uninhabited islet. Manatees are occasionally spotted here, as well as barracudas and nurse sharks. If you're looking for swimming or sunbathing, there are much better beaches nearby. ⊠ *Esperanza Malecón, Esperanza.*

★ **Playa Media Luna.** An unpaved road east of Playa Sun Bay leads to a pretty little beach that's ideal for families because the water is calm and shallow. This is a good spot to try your hand at snorkeling. Take note, though, that there are no facilities. ⊠ *Off Rte. 997, east of Playa Sun Bay.*

Red Beach. Located on former U.S. Navy land on the eastern end of Vieques, this beautiful beach is reached via a well-maintained dirt road. It's open daily from sunrise to sunset. The water is crystal-clear, and its location in Bahía Corcho means that the waves are usually not so strong. ⊠ *Off Rte. 997, east of Playa Media Luna.*

★ **Sun Bay.** Of Vieques's more than three dozen beaches, this one east of Esperanza is easily the most popular. Its 1-mi-long white sands skirt a crescent-shaped bay. You'll find food kiosks, picnic tables, and changing facilities. On weekdays, when the crowds are thin, you might also find wild horses grazing among the palm trees. Parking is $3, but there's often nobody at the gate to take your money. ⊠ *Rte. 997, east of Esperanza.*

> **WORD OF MOUTH**
>
> "Do not miss Sun Bay. I thought it was the prettiest beach there. I absolutely loved it. The Jeep was key. We are sooooo glad we rented a Jeep. It was a necessity."   −lv2trvl.

Where to Eat

$$$–$$$$
Fodor'sChoice
★ ✕ **Uva.** On Vieques, Carlos Alzogaray has single-handedly changed how people approach seafood. The chef at this "Caribbean-fusion" eatery serves mahimahi, as does everyone else, but he turns it into ceviche with a lemon-passionfruit sauce. His tuna steak is marinated in a soy-ginger sauce and served over soba noodles. Even his lobster is completely rethought, appearing as a carpaccio with avocado ragout. Meat dishes include a huge rib-eye with lobster mashed potatoes. And there's a great wine list, as you might guess from the pillars covered with thousands of corks. For lunch, you can pick up wraps and other items at the less expensive Uva Next Door. ⊠ *359 Calle Antonio Mellado, at Calle Luis Muñoz Rivera, Isabel Segunda* ☎ *787/741–2050* ⌂ *Reservations essential* ☰ *AE, MC, V* ☉ *Closed Tues.*

$$–$$$$ ✕ **Island Steakhouse.** When islanders go out to dinner, they often end up at this spot far away from the beach. But its location on a rather secluded hilltop doesn't mean fewer crowds. This is especially true each Friday, when the chef throws the regular menu out the window and cooks up "novo Latino" fare and it's hard to secure a table. On a normal night, get one of the sizzling steaks, which range in size from "petite" to "hearty." The rib-eye, one of the most popular items, weighs in at 20 ounces. There's also seafood, of course. The lobster basted with spiced rum is especially fine. The second-floor terrace might remind you of a tree house, as it looks directly into the branches. The restaurant is on Route 201, between Isabel Segunda and Esperanza. ⊠ *Crow's Nest, Rte. 201, Km 1.6* ☎ *787/741–0011* ⌂ *Reservations essential* ☰ *AE, MC, V* ☉ *Closed Mon.–Thurs. No lunch.*

$$–$$$ ✕ **Café Media Luna.** Tucked into a beautifully restored building in Isabel Segunda, this eatery has been a favorite for many years. Its popularity might be due to the convenient downtown location, or the intimate tables on the balconies that surround the second-floor dining room. More likely, however, it's the creativity of the cooks. (You can watch all the action, as the kitchen is in full view.) Try the cornish hen in a sweet-spicy coconut sauce or the seared yellowfin tuna served with vegetable tempura. Not so hungry? Then share one of the tasty pizzas. Half a dozen are on offer at any given time. ⊠ *351 Calle Antonio Mellado, Isabel Segunda, Vieques* ☎ *787/741–2594* ⌂ *Reservations essential* ☰ *AE, MC, V* ☉ *Closed Mon. and Tues. No lunch.*

$$–$$$ ✕ **Chez Shack.** This restaurant is not a shack—but it's close. It's in a delightfully ramshackle building on a one-lane road winding through the hills. The dining room is inches from the pavement, but it's unlikely a single car will pass by while you're enjoying your meal. Chicken, beef, and seafood are grilled to tender perfection. The restaurant is justi-

fiably famous for its weekly barbecue night with a steel band, but there's usually some good jazz or island rhythms on the sound system. The restaurant is on Route 995, off Route 201. ⊠ *Rte. 995, Km 1.8* 📷 *787/741–2175* 🍴 *Reservations essential* 🖿 *AE, MC, V.*

$$–$$$ ✕ **M Bar.** In the center of Isabel Segunda, this bar and grill is definitely for meat lovers. The chef will throw just about anything on the grill, from assorted sausages to pork chops to rib-eye steaks. (Locals swear the latter are the best on the island.) There's also grilled seafood, including half and whole lobsters. Add one of the lip-smacking glazes, such as honey-soy sauce, garlic butter, or tamarind barbecue sauce. This eatery is in the same building as the immensely popular Uva. ⊠ *359 Calle Antonio Mellado, at Calle Luis Muñoz Rivera, Isabel Segunda* 📷 *787/741–4000* 🍴 *Reservations essential* 🖿 *AE, MC, V* ☉ *Closed Mon.*

$–$$$ ✕ **Bilí.** Next door to Bananas, this place deserves more than the overflow from its more established neighbor. It has the same view, a fresher decor, and more authentic food. For lunch, order a tasty sandwich such as skirt steak with mango, peppers, blue cheese, and caramelized onions that is accompanied by cassava fries. For more substantial fare, there's fried chicken with a guava glaze or angel-hair pasta with crab meat stewed in coconut milk and tomatoes. In the evening you can stop by for a beer and not have to shout to be heard. ⊠ *144 Calle Flamboyán, Esperanza* 📷 *787/741–1382* 🖿 *AE, MC, V.*

$$ ✕ **Taverna Española.** Right on the main square in Isabel Segunda, this family-run restaurant may not look much like Spain, but it certainly tastes like it. The menu is heavy on the seafood, including a respectable paella. There are plenty of other dishes as well, including grilled shrimp and octopus simmered in garlic sauce. You won't see many tourists here, but it's packed with locals on the weekend. ⊠ *Calle Carlos Lebrón and Calle Santa Rosa, Isabel Segunda* 📷 *787/741–1175* 🖿 *AE, MC, V.*

$–$$ ✕ **Bananas.** If you're looking for authentic island cuisine, this ain't it. This longtime favorite, across from the waterfront in Esperanza, is geared almost entirely to gringos. That doesn't mean the grub isn't good, though. Find a spot at one of the curvy concrete tables and order the red-snapper sandwich (popular at lunchtime), or go all out for baby-back ribs or jerk chicken. The salads are excellent, including the *caribeño* (fresh greens with curried chicken) and the *festival* (greens with grilled chicken, blue cheese, and cranberries). At night Bananas is the hot spot on this side of the island. ⊠ *142 Calle Flamboyán, Esperanza* 📷 *787/741–8700* 🖿 *AE, MC, V.*

$–$$ ✕ **BBH.** In this stylish dining room there's not a bad seat in the house. Choose one of the comfortable couches near the door, a stool at the bar, or a banquette overlooking the swimming pool. A few choice tables are outside on the covered terrace. Just as good is the wide array of small dishes created by chef Christopher Ellis. Not content to stay in Spain, his tapas travel the globe. Some, like the chipolte barbecued pork, are clearly from Mexico. The mussels, in red coconut-curry broth, have an Asian flair. If there is a wait for a table, your server will suggest you enjoy a cocktail at the Palms, which is just around the corner. ⌧ *North Shore Rd., Isabel Segunda* 🕾 *787/741–1128* 🍽 *Reservations essential* 🗖 *AE, D, MC, V.*

Where to Stay

Private Villa Rentals

One good way to visit Vieques is to rent one of the beautiful vacation homes that have been built in the hilly interior or along the coasts. These are concentrated in three major areas: Bravos de Boston, Esperanza, and Pilón. Several local real-estate agents deal in short-term rentals of at least a week. A list of properties is available from gay-friendly **Rainbow Realty** (🕾 787/741–4312 ⊕ www.enchanted-isle.com/rainbow). There are some high-end properties available through **Vieques Villa Rental** (🕾 787/721–0505 ⊕ www.viequesvillarental.com).

Hotels & Guesthouses

$$$–$$$$ 🏨 **Martineau Bay Resort & Spa.** The first large-scale resort on Vieques is having growing pains. It's in the process of being transformed from a family-friendly Wyndham into a chic W Hotel, a process that should be finished by the end of 2006. In the meantime, it has very little personality. Not that it isn't beautiful—the plantation-style villas do sit on lushly landscaped grounds. Rooms are spacious—at least 600 square feet—and many have spectacular views of the northern coast, which is better known for its sunsets than the quality of its beaches. The restaurants are more than adequate, but there are much better options a short drive away. The resort is on Route 200, not far from the airport. ⌧ *Rte 200, Km 3.2, Box 9368, 00765* 🕾 *787/741–4100 or 800/658–7762* 🖷 *787/741–4171* ⊕ *www.martineaubayresort.com* 🛏 *138 rooms, 20 suites* 🍴 *2 restaurants, room service, fans, some in-room hot tubs, cable TV, in-room data ports, 2 tennis courts, pool, gym, spa, snorkeling, boating, bar, Internet room, business services, meeting rooms, convention center, car rental* 🗖 *AE, D, DC, MC, V* 🍽 *EP.*

$$–$$$$ 🏨 **Inn on the Blue Horizon.** This inn, consisting of six Mediterranean-style villas, was the tiny island's first taste of luxury. It's still one of the most sought-after accommodations, mostly because of its breathtaking setting on a bluff overlooking the ocean. The entire place is often booked months in advance by weddings and other big groups. Everything is geared toward upping the romance quotient, from the inti-

mate guest rooms to the open-air bar, where the staff will make any cocktail you can name—or create a new one and name it after you. Sadly, the popular Blue Macaw restaurant closed for good in 2005. ⊠ *Rte. 996, Km 4.2, Esperanza, Vieques* ⌖ *Box 1556, Vieques 00765* ☎ *787/741–3318* 🖷 *787/741–0522* ⊕ *www.innonthebluehorizon.com* ⇟ *10 rooms* ⌂ *Restaurant, fans, pool, massage, beach, bicycles, bar, library; no room phones, no room TVs, no kids under 14* ▭ *AE, MC, V* ⦿ *BP.*

$$–$$$
Fodor'sChoice
★
🏠 **Hix Island House.** Constructed entirely of concrete—wait, keep reading! This award-winning hotel, set on 13 secluded acres, is one of the most striking in Puerto Rico. The idea, according to architect John Hix, was to design a place that echoed the gray granite boulders strewn around Vieques. He was successful, as his three buildings blend beautifully into the environment. A minimalist aesthetic runs through the rooms, which avoid the blockiness of most concrete buildings through the use of sinewy lines and sexy curves. Sunny terraces, unglazed windows, and showers that are open to the stars (yet still very private) make sure nature is never far away. And the resort's embrace of the environment goes beyond form into function, with the use of recycled water and even solar-power systems. Even the swimming pool is ecofriendly, avoiding the use of excess chemicals. The hotel is on Route 995, off Route 201. ⊠ *Rte. 995, Km 1.5, Box 1556, 00765* ☎ *787/741–2302* 🖷 *787/741–2797* ⊕ *www.hixislandhouse.com* ⇟ *13 rooms* ⌂ *Fans, kitchenettes, refrigerators, pool, fitness classes, massage, shop; no a/c, no room phones, no room TVs* ▭ *AE, MC, V* ⦿ *CP.*

$$
Fodor'sChoice
★
🏠 **Bravo Beach Hotel.** If this boutique hotel were plopped down into the middle of South Beach, no one would raise an eyebrow. What was once a private residence has been expanded to include four different buildings, all with views of nearby Culebra from their balconies. The guest rooms have a minimalist flair, brightened by splashes of red and yellow. High-tech offerings include a Sony Playstation in every room. If you're traveling with an entourage, the two-bedroom villa has plenty of space to entertain. One of the pools is the setting for the Palms, a chic lounge; the other is the backdrop for the not-to-be-missed tapas

> **WORD OF MOUTH**
>
> "The concierge [at Bravo Beach Hotel] was very helpful with making dinner reservations, and arranging a kayak trip to the bioluminiescent bay, which is not to be missed."   –trekker.

bar. The hotel is on a pretty stretch of beach, several blocks north of the ferry dock in Isabel Segunda. ⊠ *North Shore Rd., Isabel Segunda, Vieques 00765* ☎ *787/741–1128* 🖷 *787/741–3908* ⊕ *www. bravobeachhotel.com* ⇟ *9 rooms, 1 villa* ⌂ *Restaurant, minibars, cable TV with movies and games, Wi-Fi, 2 pools, bar; no room phones, no kids under 14* ▭ *AE, D, MC, V* ⦿ *BP.*

$$
🏠 **Crow's Nest.** This butter-yellow guesthouse sits on a hilltop, so there are stunning views of the ocean in the distance. If you want to go to the beach, those in and around Esperanza and Isabel Segunda are within a few minutes' drive. In the meantime, you can relax in the swimming pool. The large rooms have balconies that overlook the lovely gardens. Island

Steakhouse, housed on a second-floor terrace, is one of the most popular restaurants on Vieques. Less expensive is El Jardín, a Caribbean eatery on the patio. The hotel is on Route 201, between Isabel Segunda and Esperanza. ⊠ *Rte. 201, Km 1.6, 00765* ☎ *787/741–0033 or 888/484–3783* 🖶 *787/741–1294* ⊕ *www.crowsnestvieques.com* ⤴ *15 rooms, 2 suites* ⟁ *2 restaurants, fans, some kitchenettes, microwaves, refrigerators, cable TV, in-room data ports, pool; no children under 12* ⊟ *AE, MC, V* ⦿ *BP.*

$$ 🏨 **Hacienda Tamarindo.** The century-old tamarind tree rising through the center of the main building gives this place its name. The plantation-style house, with its barrel-tile roof and wood-shuttered windows, is one of the most beautiful on the island. It's easy to find a spot all to yourself, whether it's on a shady terrace or beside the spectacular pool. The guest rooms were individually decorated by Linda Vail, who runs the place along with her husband Burr. "Caribbean chic" might be the best way to describe her effortless way of combining well-chosen antiques, elegant wicker furniture, and vintage travel posters. The nicest room might be Number One, which is in a separate building and has a private terrace overlooking the ocean. The beach is nearby, but you'll need a car to get there. ⊠ *Rte. 996, Km 4.5, Esperanza, Vieques* ⟐ *Box 1569, Vieques 00765* ☎ *787/741–8525* 🖶 *787/741–3215* ⊕ *www. haciendatamarindo.com* ⤴ *16 rooms* ⟁ *Fans, cable TV, Wi-Fi, pool; no room phones, no room TVs, no kids under 15* ⊟ *AE, MC, V* ⦿ *BP.*

FodorśChoice
★

¢–$ 🏨 **Casa de Amistad.** A groovy vibe permeates this small guesthouse not far from the ferry dock in Isabel Segunda. Citrus colors and wicker furnishings give the place a tropical feel. It's hard not to feel at home here, especially when you can use the common kitchen to pack a picnic lunch or borrow an umbrella for your trip to the beach. The rooftop terrace is a great place to chill out. There's a gift shop on the premises that sells original art by the owners. ⊠ *27 Calle Benito Castano, Isabel Segunda 00765* ☎ *787/741–3758* 🖶 *787/741–4782* ⊕ *www.casadeamistad. com* ⤴ *7 rooms* ⟁ *Fans, pool, shop, Internet room* ⊟ *MC, V* ⦿ *EP.*

¢ 🏨 **Trade Winds.** The best of a string of inexpensive guesthouses along the main road in Esperanza, Trade Winds has an unbeatable location across from the waterfront promenade. Any number of eateries can be found a short stroll away. Rooms are basic but more than adequate if you plan on spending most of your time at the beach. They share several terraces, all overlooking the ocean. ⊠ *142 Calle Flamboyán, Esperanza* ⟐ *Box 1012, 00770* ☎ *787/741–8666* 🖶 *787/741–2964* ⊕ *www.enchanted-isle.com/tradewinds* ⤴ *11 rooms* ⟁ *Restaurant, fans, refrigerators, bar, shop* ⊟ *AE, MC, V* ⦿ *EP.*

Nightlife

Not far from the ferry terminal, **Al's Mar Azul** (⊠ Calle Plinio Peterson, Isabela Segunda ☎ 787/741–3400) is where everyone gathers to watch the sunset. The main virtue of this open-air bar is a deck overlooking the ocean. You'll find dart boards, pool tables, and a juke box.

Bananas (⊠ 142 Calle Flamboyán, Esperanza ☎ 787/741–8700) is the place for burgers and beer—not necessarily in that order. There's sometimes live music and dancing.

La Nasa (✉ Calle Flamboyán, Esperanza ☎ No phone) is the only establishment on the waterfront side of the street in Esperanza. This simple wooden shack, decorated with strings of Christmas lights the entire year, serves up cheap and very cold beer and rum drinks. Locals congregate on plastic chairs out front or stare off into the placid Caribbean from an open-air back room.

The Palms (✉ North Shore Rd., Isabel Segunda ☎ 787/741–1128) is the most stylish bar on the north side of the island. Sip creative cocktails under the eponymous trees as you admire the crystalline pool.

Sports & the Outdoors

Biking

The friendly folks at **La Dulce Vida** (☎ 787/741–0495 ⊕ www.bikevieques. com) can set you up with mountain bikes and all the equipment you need for $25 to $35 a day. They'll even bring the bikes to wherever you happen to be staying. Customized tours of the island—which range from easy rides on country roads to muddy treks into the hills—are $30 to $65 per hour. But you need to book the tours far in advance.

Boating & Kayaking

Any number of companies offer trips to Bahía Mosquito, the most famous of the island's bioluminescent bays. Most are trips in single-person kayaks, which can be a challenge if you don't have experience or if you aren't in the best shape. A better option for most people is a boat. Make sure it's an electric-powered model, as the gas-powered ones are bad for the environment.

Aqua Frenzy Kayaks (✉ At dock area below Calle Flamboyán, Esperanza ☎ 787/741–0913) rents kayaks and arranges kayak tours of Bahía Mosquito and other areas. Reservations are required for the excursion to glowing Bahía Mosquito; the excursion costs $30. Make reservations at least 24 hours in advance.

Blue Caribe Kayaks (✉ 149 Calle Flamboyán, Esperanza ☎ 787/741–2522 ⊕ www.enchanted-isle.com/bluecaribe) offers kayak trips to Bahía Mosquito for about $30, as well as trips to deserted parts of the coast and to nearby islets. You can also rent a kayak and set off on your own.

★ **Island Adventures** (✉ Rte. 996, Esperanza ☎ 787/741–0720 ⊕ www. biobay.com) is run by former schoolteacher Sharon Grasso, who will take you to Bahía Mosquito aboard nonpolluting, electrically powered pontoon boats. The best part is leaping into the water, where the outline of your body will be softly illuminated. The cost is about $30 per person.

> **WORD OF MOUTH**
>
> "We did the Bio Bay tour with Island Adventures . . .. Island adventures has bathrooms where you can change when you get back. The pontoon boat is best as if it's a moonlit night you can swim under the pontoons for full effect."
> –HowardC.

Marauder Sailing Charters (☎ 787/435–4858) operates the *Marauder,* a 34-foot sailing yacht anchored off Esperanza. It sails around the southern coast, allowing a close-up look of the pristine nature of most of the island. There's a mid-day stop at a secluded spot for swimming, snorkeling, and sun bathing, followed by a gourmet lunch. The yacht has a good sound system and open bar. A minimum of two people and a maximum of six people can book a trip, which runs from 10 AM to 3 PM. The cost is $95 per person. A two-hour sunset sail costs $45 per person.

Diving & Snorkeling
Nan-Sea Charters (☎ 787/741–3224), run by affable "Chipper the Skipper," promises to take you snorkeling at a beach so remote that it doesn't have a name. The cost is $60 per person for groups up to six people.

Blue Caribe Kayaks (✉ 149 Calle Flamboyán, Esperanza ☎ 787/741–2522 ⊕ www.enchanted-isle.com/bluecaribe) will rent you snorkels, masks, and fins for $12 a day. The efficient staff can also arrange snorkeling trips to nearby islets.

Fishing
Caribbean Flyfishing Company (☎ 787/741–1337) and Captain Franco Gonzales will take you on any type of fishing trip that you have in mind, from short trips to the shallows to longer journeys to the open ocean.

Jet Skiing
In a shack near the beach, **Extreme Water Sports** (✉ Calle Flamboyán, Esperanza ☎ 787/741–1337) rents out the latest equipment to ride the waves. Jet Skis are $60 for a half-hour, $100 for an hour. The company also rents scooters for $55 a day

Shopping

Most residents do their shopping on the mainland, so there are very few shops on Vieques. You'll find mostly clothing shops that lean toward beach attire, as well as a few art galleries.

Casa Vieja Gallery (✉ Rte. 201, Esperanza ☎ 787/741–3078) is where several local artists show and sell their work.

Diva's Closet (✉ 134 Calle Flamboyán, Esperanza ☎ 787/741–7595), which is next door to Kim's Cabin, carries an array of women's clothes. Here you'll find everything you need for the beach or for brunch.

Kim's Cabin (✉ 136 Calle Flamboyán, Esperanza ☎ 787/741–0520), which has been in business on Vieques since the early 1990s, is a local institution. There's jewelry in the front room and two other rooms with clothing for men and women.

★ **Siddhia Hutchinson Fine Art Studio & Gallery** (✉ 15 Calle 3, Isabel Segunda ☎ 787/741–8780) is north of the ferry dock. The artist has lived on Vieques since the early 1990s, creating pastel watercolor prints of Caribbean scenes, as well as limited-edition ceramic dinnerware. The gallery is open Monday through Saturday, 10 AM to 4 PM. **Taína Pottery Workshop** (☎ 787/741–1556) is a local female artisans collective that makes beautiful ceramics, pottery, and other artwork. Visits to the studio are by appointment only.

CULEBRA

28 km (17 mi) east of Fajardo by ferry

Culebra is known around the world for its curvaceous coastline. Playa Flamenco, the tiny island's most famous stretch of sand, is considered one of the two or three best beaches in the world. If Playa Flamenco gets too crowded, as it often does around Easter or Christmas, there are many other beaches that will be nearly deserted. And if you crave complete privacy, hire a motorboat to take you to one of the nearby islets such as Isla Culebrita or Cayo Luis Peña. It won't be difficult to find a little cove that you will have all to yourself.

There's archaeological evidence that Taíno and Carib peoples lived on Culebra long before the arrival of the Spanish in the late 15th century. The Spanish didn't bother laying claim to it until 1886; its dearth of fresh water made it an unattractive location for a settlement. The U.S. Navy, however, thought it was a very valuable piece of real estate. It used this island, as well as nearby Vieques, for target practice beginning in the early 20th century. Despite their smaller numbers, the residents of Culebra were more successful in their efforts to oust the military. The troops left Culebra in 1975.

Exploring Culebra

Almost everything about Culebra is diminutive. The island's only community, named in honor of U.S. Admiral George Dewey, is set along a single street leading from the ferry dock. You can explore all the shops along Calle Pedro Márquez in a half-hour. The one-room airport is a mile or so to the north. Except for one sprawling resort, there are no hotels with more than a dozen rooms.

6 Commissioned by President Theodore Roosevelt in 1909, **Refugio Nacional de Vida Silvestre de Culebra** is one of the nation's oldest wildlife refuges. Some 1,500 acres of the island make up a protected area. It's a lure for hikers and bird-watchers: Culebra teems with seabirds, from laughing gulls and roseate terns to red-billed tropic birds and sooty terns. Maps of trails in the refuge are hard to come by, but you can stop by the U.S. Fish & Wildlife Service office east of the airport to find out about trail conditions and determine whether you're headed to an area that requires a permit. The office also can tell you whether the leatherback turtles are nesting. From mid-April to mid-July, volunteers help to monitor and tag these creatures, which nest on nearby beaches, especially Playa Resaca and Playa Brava. If you'd like to volunteer, you must agree to help out for at least three nights. ⊠ *Rte. 250, north of Dewey* ☎ *787/742–0115* ⊕ *southeast.fws.gov* ✉ *Free* ☉ *Daily dawn to dusk.*

7 Part of the Refugio Nacional de Vida Silvestre de Culebra, **Isla Culebrita** is clearly visible from the northeast corner of Culebra. This islet is a favorite destination for sunbathers who want to escape the crowds at Playa Flamenco. On the northern shore there are several tide pools; snuggling into one of them is like taking a warm bath. Snorkelers and divers love the fact that they can reach the reef from the shore. You can also hike

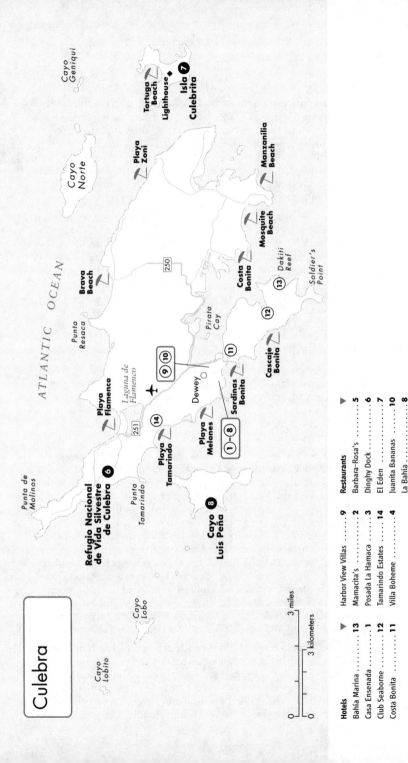

Culebra

Cayo Lobo

Cayo Lobito

Punta de Molinos

ATLANTIC OCEAN

Cayo Norte

Cayo Geniqui

Tortuga Beach

Lighthouse ♦

Isla ❼ Culebrita

Playa Zoni

Brava Beach

Punta Resaca

Laguna de Flamenco

Playa Flamenco

Refugio Nacional de Vida Silvestre de Culebra ❻

250

251

⑭

Dewey

⑨ ⑩

Sardinas Bonita

Punta Tamarindo

Playa Tamarindo

Playa Melones

① – ⑧

Cayo Luis Peña ❽

⑪

Pirata Cay

⑫

Cascaje Bonita

Costa Bonita

⑬

Dakiti Reef

Mosquite Beach

Manzanilia Beach

Soldier's Point

0 ——— 3 miles

0 ——— 3 kilometers

Hotels ▶

Bahía Marina **13**
Casa Ensenada **1**
Club Seaborne **12**
Costa Bonita **11**

Harbor View Villas **9**
Mamacita's **2**
Posada La Hamaca **3**
Tamarindo Estates **14**
Villa Boheme **4**

Restaurants ▶

Barbara-Rosa's **5**
Dinghy Dock **6**
El Eden **7**
Juanita Bananas **10**
La Bahía **8**

around the island and visit the ruins of an old lighthouse. To get there, take a dive boat or hire a water taxi.

8 A kayak is a great way to reach **Cayo Luis Peña,** an islet just off the western edge of Culebra. There are a handful of protected beaches where you can soak up the sun and not run into a single soul. Cayo Luis Peña is also part of the Refugio Nacional de Vida Silvestre de Culebra.

Beaches

FodorsChoice ★ **Playa Flamenco.** On the island's north coast is an amazingly lovely stretch of white sand. This beach, with its almost perfect half-moon shape, is consistently ranked as one of the two or three best in the world. Once you see it, you'll know why. Mountains rise up on all sides, making it feel miles away from civiliza-

tion. It's only when the propeller planes fly low over the beach that you remember that the airport in just over the ridge. During the week Playa Flamenco is pleasantly uncrowded; on the weekend, though, it fills up fast with day-trippers. This is the only beach on Culebra with amenities such as restrooms, showers, and kiosks selling simple fare. ⊠ *Rte. 251, west of the airport.*

Playa Melones. Just west of Dewey, this beach is a favorite spot for snorkelers. The reef that runs around the rocky point is easy to reach from shore. To get here, head uphill on the unmarked road behind the church. ⊠ *Off Rte. 251, west of Dewey.*

Playa Tamarindo. North of Playa Melones, this beach is another good destination for snorkelers. It's a little hard to find, which means you'll probably have the place to yourself. To find it, head west on Route 251. When you see the signs pointing toward Tamarindo Estates, take a left. ⊠ *Off Rte. 251, north of Playa Melones.*

Playa Zoni. On the island's northeastern end, this beach is far more isolated than Playa Flamenco, and it's just as beautiful. From the shore you can catch a glimpse of Isla Culebrita, not to mention St. Thomas and St. Croix. ⊠ *At the end of Rte. 250, 11 km (7 mi) northeast of Dewey.*

Where to Eat

$–$$$ ✕ **Dinghy Dock.** Culebra's version of heavy traffic—the arrival and departure of the water taxi—takes place around the dock that gives this restaurant its name. The menu leans toward grilled meats, from pork chops to sirloin steaks. Daily specials often concentrate on the restaurant's forte: creole-style seafood, including swordfish and yellowtail. The adjacent bar is usually packed with expats. It can get noisy, so don't expect a quiet dinner for two. ⊠ *Calle Fulladoza, Dewey* ☎ *787/742–0581* ☒ *MC, V.*

★ **$–$$$** ✕ **Juanita Bananas.** Trees overflowing with bananas, papayas, and passion fruit line the walkway that leads to one of Culebra's best eateries. Chef Jennifer Daubon, whose parents also ran a restaurant on the island, focuses on the freshest local produce, which is why about an acre of land on the surrounding hillside is used for growing vegetables and herbs. The menu changes with the seasons, but look for dishes like lobster limonjili, which is medallions of lobster in a fresh lime and garlic sauce. The dining room, with its low lights and soft music, is the most romantic in Culebra. ⊠ *Calle Melones, Km 1* ☎ *787/742–3855* ◬ *Reservations essential* ☒ *MC, V.*

★ **$–$$** ✕ **La Bahía.** She's been in the kitchen for more than 25 years, which explains why Margarita Suárez never gets flustered, no matter how many people pack into her little restaurant. Her specialty is seafood, and dishes like conch simmered with onions and garlic are simple and satisfying. Don't be surprised if she offers you a taste of whatever else she's cooking. Make sure to try her mofongo—it's not available anywhere else on the island. The restaurant is a little hard to find; from Calle de Escudero, turn onto the road that runs past the new school. Take the first left and continue uphill until you see the restaurant on your left. ⊠ *Off Calle Escudero, Dewey* ☎ *787/484–1243* ☒ *MC, V* ☉ *Closed Mon.–Wed.*

★ **¢–$** ✕ **Barbara-Rosa's.** Her husband is on hand to chat with the customers, but Barbara Petersen does everything else: takes your order, cooks it up, and serves it with a flourish. You won't find better food anywhere on the island, and that includes the places that charge twice as much. Locals swear by her tender, flaky fish and chips. (The secret, Barbara's husband happily points out, is using red snapper.) Finish with key lime pie or peach and pineapple cobbler. ⊠ *Calle Escudero, Dewey* ☎ *787/ 742–3271* ☒ *MC, V* ☉ *Closed Sun. and Mon.*

¢ ✕ **El Eden.** Looking for something to pop in your picnic basket? This deli on the edge of town makes scrumptious salads and sandwiches that are big enough for two. There's also the island's best selection of wine and beer. To get here, cross the bridge on Calle Escudero, then take a quick right and a quick left. ⊠ *Off Calle Escudero, Dewey* ☎ *787/742– 0509* ☒ *MC, V.*

Where to Stay

Villa Rentals

Lovely vacation homes are available all over the island. **All Vacation Reservations** (⊠ Calle Pedro Marquez, Dewey ☎ 787/742–3112 ⊕ www. allvacationreservations.com) has a complete list of all the homes available for rental, ranging from studios to three-bedroom houses.

Hotels & Guesthouses

$$ ✕⌂ **Bahía Marina.** If you're looking for space to spread out, these one-bedroom apartments are for you. Each sleeps four, thanks to the fold-out couch in the living room. Full kitchens are equipped with everything you need to make dinner for the family. Step outside onto your private deck or head out to the swimming pool, and you have unobstructed views of the hills surrounding Fulladoza Bay. The second-floor restaurant ($$–$$$) takes full advantage of the island's fresh seafood. ⊠ *Calle Fulladoza, Km 1.5* ⌕ *Box 807, 00646* ☎ *787/742–0535* 🖷 *787/742–0536* ⊕ *www.bahiamarina.net* ⤴ *16 apartments* ⌂ *Restaurant, room service, kitchens, microwaves, refrigerators, cable TV, Wi-Fi, pool, dock, bar* ⊟ *AE, MC, V* ⦿ *CP.*

$$ ✕⊡ **Club Seaborne.** The prettiest place to stay in Culebra, this cluster of plantation-style cottages sits on a hilltop overlooking Fulladoza Bay. The place feels completely isolated, but it is only a mile or so from the center of town. Opt for one of the rooms surrounding the pool or one of the spacious villas. The largest sleeps five, making it a favorite of families. Specializing in seafood, the terrace restaurant ($$–$$$) is one of the best on the island. The friendly staff are happy to help you set up snorkeling and diving trips or arrange transportation to the beach. ⊠ *Calle Fulladoza, Km 1.5* ⌕ *Box 357, 00775* ☎ *787/742–3169* 🖷 *787/742–3176* ⊕ *www.clubseabourne.com* ⤴ *3 rooms, 8 villas, 1 cottage* ⌂ *Restaurant, some kitchens, cable TV, pool, bar, library* ⊟ *AE, MC, V* ⦿ *CP.*

$ ✕⊡ **Mamacita's.** PLEASE DON'T FEED THE IGUANAS reads a sign hanging on the terrace of this longtime favorite. Set beneath lazily turning ceiling fans, the disarmingly charming restaurant ($–$$$) overlooks a canal filled with fishing boats. The menu, which is scribbled on a chalk-

> ## WORD OF MOUTH
>
> "[H]ave a blast over at Mamacita's—friendly service, great food, good people."   –RJTravels.

board, includes dishes like pork tenderloin with pineapple or salmon with a cilantro sauce. The bar gets crowded during happy hour, which starts early in these parts. If you like it so much you don't want to leave, there are guest rooms upstairs with tropical furnishings. The best have balconies overlooking the canal. ⊠ *66 Calle Castelar, Dewey 00775* ☎ *787/742–0090* 🖷 *787/742–0301* ⊕ *www.mamacitaspr.com* ⤴ *10 rooms, 1 suite* ⌂ *Restaurant, fans, some kitchenettes, some microwaves, some refrigerators, cable TV, dock, bar* ⊟ *AE, MC, V* ⦿ *EP.*

$$$–$$$$ ⊡ **Costa Bonita.** The closest that the island has to a resort, Costa Bonita is made up of plantation-style buildings huddled together at the edge of the water. The rooms and suites are more than comfortable, with golds and greens that lend them a tropical feel. All have kitchenettes and balconies overlooking the water. The best part of the hotel, however, is the free-form pool dotted here and there with palm trees. Of course there's a swim-up bar. The hotel is on Ensenada Honda, east of the airport. ⊠ *Ensenada Honda* ⌕ *Box 147, 00775* ☎ *787/742–3000* 🖷 *787/742–3003* ⊕ *www.costabonitaresort.com* ⤴ *82 rooms, 82 suites* ⌂ *3 restaurants, kitchenettes, microwaves, refrigerators, cable TV, in-room DVDs, Wi-Fi, pool, hot tub, beach, laundry facilities, bar, shop* ⊟ *AE, MC, V* ⦿ *EP.*

$$ ⊡ **Tamarindo Estates.** On a 60-acre estate on the western coast of Culebra, this string of one- and two-bedroom beach cottages is on a long, sandy beach. Most of the cottages are a bit farther inland, affording great

views of the coastline from their covered verandas. Each has a full kitchen. There's a shared beach house with showers and other amenities, including a pool with an oceanfront deck. The waters of nearby Luis Peña Channel are perfect for snorkeling, and it's about a 10-minute drive to Flamenco Beach. ⊠ *Off Rte. 251* ⌂ *Box 313, 00775* ☎ *787/ 742–3343* ⎙ *787/742–3342* ⊕ *www.tamarindoestates.com* ↩ *16 cottages* ♿ *Fans, kitchens, cable TV, in-room VCRs, pool, beach, car rental* ⊟ *MC, V* ⊚ *EP.*

$–$$ ⊡ **Casa Ensenada.** You'll feel like you're staying in a friend's house when you arrive at this inn on the edge of town. It doesn't look like much from the street, but the palm-shaded patio in the back looks out on the sailboats cruising around Ensenada Bay. If you can't wait to join them, you can rent a boat from the dock. Otherwise, just relax with a cocktail in one of the chaise longues. There are three rooms in the main house, each with a full kitchen stocked with all the utensils you need to make dinner. If you book for six nights, you get the seventh free. ⊠ *142 Calle Escudero, Dewey 00775* ☎ *787/742–3559* ⊕ *www.casaensenada.com* ↩ *3 rooms* ♿ *Cable TV, in-room VCRs, kitchens, boating, dock* ⊟ *MC, V* ⊚ *EP.*

$–$$ ⊡ **Harbor View Villas.** Built within 6 acres of tropical foliage, this longtime favorite overlooks the shimmering Bahía de Sardinas. French doors open up to a cantilevered deck with splendid views of the countryside. Each villa has a spacious master bedroom with a private terrace; some have a second bedroom as well. Smaller suites are also available. On the road to Melones Beach, the hotel is very close to the town of Dewey. ⊠ *Calle Melones, Km 1, 00775* ☎ *787/742–3855 or 800/440–0070* ⎙ *787/742–3171* ⊕ *www.harbourviewvillas.com* ↩ *3 villas, 3 suites* ♿ *Restaurant, fans, kitchens, refrigerators; no a/c in some rooms, no room TVs* ⊟ *No credit cards* ⊚ *EP.*

$ ⊡ **Posada La Hamaca.** The shady terrace behind this little lodging sits on a mangrove-lined canal where owner Al Custer docks his motorboat. The guest rooms—as simple as they come—have louvered windows with the same view. The inn sits on the edge of Dewey, putting you within walking distance of restaurants, shops, and grocery stores. Ginny Tawalski, who commandeers the front desk, used to run a dive shop, so she will let you know the best places to scuba or snorkel. She sends you off to the beach with a little cooler filled with ice. ⊠ *68 Calle Castelar, Dewey 00775* ☎ *787/742–3516* ⎙ *787/742–0181* ⊕ *www.posada.com* ↩ *10 rooms, 1 apartment* ♿ *Fans, some kitchenettes, dock; no room phones* ⊟ *MC, V* ⊚ *EP.*

$ ⊡ **Villa Boheme.** This guesthouse's shady terrace, with several hammocks hanging between the palm trees, is a great place to hang out. You may not feel the need to do anything more strenuous than reach for your margarita, but if you do, there are some kayaks that you can rent to explore Ensenada Bay. Rooms are simple, but they all have views of the water; all share a communal kitchen, but some have kitchens of their own. This Spanish-style lodging, painted a particularly pretty shade of apricot, is one of the most distinctive on the island. ⊠ *Calle Fulladoza, Dewey 00775* ☎ *787/742–3508* ⊕ *www.villaboheme.com* ↩ *12 rooms* ♿ *Cable TV, in-room VCRs, some kitchenettes, some refrigerators, boating, dock* ⊟ *AE, MC, V* ⊚ *EP.*

Nightlife

Dinghy Dock (✉ Calle Fulladoza, Dewey ☎ 787/742–0581) is the spot where the island's expat community begins piling into the bar around sunset. It can be a raucous scene, especially when there's a band. The party continues into the wee hours, even during the week.

El Batey (✉ Calle Escudero ☎ 787/742–3828) is popular on the weekends, when locals dance to salsa music. It's in a cement-block building halfway between the airport and the town.

Happy Landings (✉ Rte. 250 and Rte. 251 ☎ 787/742–0135), at the end of the airport's runway, might just as accurately have been called Happy Hour. The open-air bar is popular with locals.

Sports & the Outdoors

Biking

Since there's very little traffic, biking is a good way to explore the island. You can rent bikes for $20 a day at **Culebra Bike Shop** (✉ Calle Fulladoza, Dewey ☎ 787/742–2209). The shop is next door to the Dinghy Dock.

Boating & Kayaking

At **Culebra Boat Rentals** (✉ 142 Calle Escudero, Dewey ☎ 787/742–3559 ⊕ www.culebraboatrental.com) affable Butch Pendergast will rent you anything from a two-person sailboat ($100 a day) to a six-person motorboat ($215 a day). The rates go down quite a bit if you rent for more than one day.

Run by Captain Luís Grundler, **Culebra Water Taxi** (✉ 66 Calle Castelar, Dewey ☎ 787/360–9807) has kayak and snorkeling trips to Dakity Bay that cost $45 per person, including lunch.

The glass-bottom boat at **Tanamá** (☎ 787/501–0011) lets you explore the undersea world without even getting wet.

Diving & Snorkeling

Travelers have told us that dives with **Aquatic Adventures** (☎ 787/742–0605 ⊕ www.culebradiveshop.com) are spectacular. Captain Taz Hamrick knows these waters well; he takes small groups to the best dive sites. One-tank dives are $50; two-tank dives are $85. He also leads snorkeling expeditions.

Run by Monica and Walter Rieder, **Culebra Divers** (✉ 4 Calle Pedro Marquez, Dewey ☎ 787/742–0803 ⊕ www.culebradivers.com) caters to people who are new to scuba diving. You travel to dive sites on one of the company's pair of 26-foot cabin cruisers. One-tank dives

> ### WORD OF MOUTH
>
> "Culebra is not for someone looking to be pampered, or someone who wants a golf vacation or shopping vacation. But if you want quiet and solitude and beauty (this, especially underwater!), this might be for you. I have very fond memories of this island."   –cj.

are $60, and two-tank dives are $95. You can also rent a mask and snorkel to explore on your own. The office is in downtown Dewey, across from the ferry terminal.

Shopping

Culebra is smaller than Vieques but has much better shopping. Dewey has several shops on its main drag that sell trendy jewelry, fashionable clothing, and a range of souvenirs from tacky to terrific.

La Cava (⊠ 138 Calle Escudio, Dewey ☎ 787/742–0566) stocks a little bit of everything. Forgot your snorkel? Left your bathing suit at home? This is a good place to find a replacement.

★ In a wooden shack painted vivid shades of yellow and red, **Fango** (⊠ Calle Castelar s/n, Dewey ☎ 787/556–9308) is the island's best place for gifts. Jorge Acevedo paints scenes of island life, while Hannah Staiger designs sophisticated jewelry. The shop is no bigger than a walk-in closet, but you could easily spend an hour or more browsing among their one-of-a-kind works.

On Island (⊠ 4 Calle Pedro Marquez, Dewey ☎ 787/742–0439) has a selection of black prints of the island's flora and fauna. There is also a nice display of handmade jewelry.

Paradise (⊠ 6 Calle Salisbury, Dewey ☎ 787/742–3565) is a good spot for souvenirs ranging from wrought-iron iguanas to hand-carved seagulls to plush baby turtles.

VIEQUES & CULEBRA ESSENTIALS

To research prices, get advice from other travelers, and book travel arrangements, visit www.fodors.com.

Transportation

BY AIR

It used to be that travelers arriving at San Juan's Aeropuerto Internacional Luis Muñoz Marín had to transfer to nearby Aeropuerto Fernando L. Rivas Dominici to take a flight to Vieques or Culebra. This is no longer the case, as all carriers servicing the islands now have flights from Aeropuerto Internacional Luis Muñoz Marín.

Air Flamenco, Isla Nena Air Service, and Vieques Air Link offer daily flights from both airports in San Juan to Vieques and Culebra. Cape Air flies between the international airport and Vieques. Trips from either airport in San Juan last between 20 and 30 minutes, whereas those from Fajardo last about 10 minutes. Fares vary quite a bit, but are between $120 and $150 from San Juan and between $40 and $50 from Fajardo. These companies use small propeller planes that hold a maximum of nine passengers.

The big news in 2005 was that American Eagle had begun one daily flight between San Juan and Vieques. This means that travelers flying on American won't have to deal with their checked bags in San Juan. The

64-seat plane—seven times larger than those used by the competition—will be the only plane en route to Vieques that has a flight attendant.

🔶 **Air Flamenco** ☎ 787/724-1818 ⊕ www.airflamenco.net. **American Eagle** ☎ 800/433-7300 ⊕ www.aa.com. **Cape Air** ☎ 800/525-0280 ⊕ www.flycapeair.com. **Isla Nena Air Service** ☎ 787/741-6362 or 877/812-5144 ⊕ www.islanena.8m.com. **Vieques Air Link** ☎ 787/741-8331 or 888/901-9247 ⊕ www.vieques-island.com/val.

AIRPORTS Most international travelers fly to Vieques and Culebra from San Juan's Aeropuerto Internacional Luis Muñoz Marín (SJU) or San Juan's Aeropuerto Fernando L. Rivas Dominici (SIG; also known as Aeropuerto Isla Grande). A smaller number fly from Fajardo's Aeropuerto Diego Jiménez Torres (FAJ), which is just southwest of the city on Route 976.

Aeropuerto Antonio Rivera Rodríguez (VQS), on Vieques's northwest coast, is a 10-minute cab ride from Isabel Segunda or a 15-minute taxi ride from Esperanza. The airlines have offices on the top floor of the octagonal main terminal, and the single gate is on the lower level. There are no amenities to speak of, although there's an open-air eatery across the road. At this writing, American Eagle had broken ground on an addition to the main terminal that will have a separate gate for its flights. The new addition will also have car-rental agency.

Culebra's Aeropuerto Benjamin Rivera Noriega (CPX) is at the intersection of Route 250 and Route 251. The one-room facility has two car-rental agencies and a scooter-rental kiosk. There's a small café inside the terminal, and several others are across the road. The airport is about three minutes from downtown Dewey.

🔶 **Aeropuerto Antonio Rivera Rodríguez** ✉ Vieques ☎ 787/741-0515. **Aeropuerto Benjamin Rivera Noriega** ✉ Culebra ☎ 787/742-0022.

BY BUS

There is no public bus system around Puerto Rico. If you are planning to take a ferry to Vieques or Culebra, you can take a *público* (a privately operated, shared minivan) from San Juan to Fajardo. The two-hour journey costs about $6, depending on where you board and where you are dropped off; if you take this very inexpensive mode of transportation, expect things to be a bit crowded. There are no central terminals: you simply flag públicos down anywhere along the route.

Vieques and Culebra are served by their own inexpensive públicos, whose drivers often speak English. Just flag them down along their routes. Rates vary depending on your destination, but are usually under $5.

BY CAR

Think about getting around on Vieques or Culebra without a car? Think again. If you plan on staying in a town, there's no need for a car. If you want to do anything else—say, go to the beach—you need a way to get there. And don't think about taking that car you rented in San Juan to the off-islands. The main roads are in great shape, but the secondary roads are so riddled with potholes that an SUV is a must.

On Vieques and Culebra you'll find local agencies, including several that specialize in SUVs. Rates are between $40 to $80 a day, depending on the age of the car. It's sometimes possible to rent directly from your hotel or guesthouse, so ask about packages that include lodging and a car rental. If you plan to head out to remote beaches, seriously consider a four-wheel-drive vehicle.

On Vieques, try Island Car Rental, Maritza Car Rental, or Martineau Car Rental. On Culebra, Carlos Jeep Rental has an office in the airport.

There are only a handful of major roads on Vieques and Culebra. On Vieques, Route 200 leads from the airport to Isabel Segunda, and Route 997 leads from Isabel Segunda to Esperanza. There's also a longer, more scenic route between the two towns: from Isabel Segunda, take Route 200 west to Route 201 south. After about 1 mi, take Route 996 to Esperanza.

Culebra has two major roads. Route 250 leads east and south of the airport. Route 251 leads northeast to Playa Flamenco.

EMERGENCY SERVICES
Rental-car agencies usually give customers emergency road-service numbers to call. There's no AAA service in Puerto Rico.

GASOLINE
Gas stations are found only in Isabel Segunda on Vieques and Dewey on Culebra. There are often gas shortages on the islands, especially during high season. Even during low season there can be long lines at gas stations.

ROAD CONDITIONS
The main roads are in fairly good shape, but many highway-exit and other signs have been blown down by hurricanes and may or may not have been replaced. When it rains, be alert for flash flooding, even on the major roads.

🚩Agencies **Carlos Jeep Rental** ⊠ Aeropuerto Benjamin Rivera Noriega, Culebra ☎787/742-3514 ⊕ www.carlosjeeprental.com. **Island Car Rental** ⊠ Rte. 201, Vieques ☎787/741-1666 ⊕ www.enchanted-isle.com/islandcar. **Maritza's Car Rental** ⊠ Rte. 201, Vieques ☎787/741-0078. **Martineau Car Rental** ⊠ Rte. 200, Km 3.4, Vieques ☎787/741-0087 ⊕ www.martineaucarrental.com.

BY FERRY

The Puerto Rico Ports Authority runs passenger ferries from Fajardo to Culebra and Vieques. Service is from the ferry terminal in Fajardo, about a 90-minute drive from San Juan. A municipal parking lot next to the ferry costs $5 a day—handy if you are going to one of the islands for the day. On Culebra the ferry pulls right into a dock in downtown Dewey. The Vieques ferry dock is in downtown Isabel Segunda.

A more convenient way to get to Vieques and Culebra, especially if you are departing from San Juan, is the catamaran operated by Island High-Speed Ferry. It departs from Pier 2, next to the cruise-ship docks in Old San Juan.

FARES & SCHEDULES
The Fajardo–Vieques ferry departs from Vieques weekdays at 6:30 AM, 11 AM, 3 PM, and 6:30 PM, returning at 9:30 AM, 1 PM, 4:30 PM, and 8 PM. On weekends ferries depart from Vieques at 6:30 AM, 1 PM, and 4:30 PM, returning at 9 AM, 3 PM, and 6 PM. Tickets for the 45-minute journey are $2 each way.

The Fajardo-Culebra ferry leaves Culebra daily at 6:30 AM, 1 PM, and 5 PM, returning at 9 AM, 5 PM, and 7 PM. The 90-minute trip is $2.25.

Ferry schedules change with alarming frequency. Call to confirm before you plan your trip, especially if you are planning to travel on the weekend.

The Island High-Speed Ferry departs from Old San Juan on Monday, Tuesday, Wednesday, Thursday, and Saturday at 8 AM. It departs on Friday and Sunday at 8 AM and 3 PM. Round-trip tickets are between $68 and $78. The ferry runs only during the high season, from December through April.

🚢 **Island High-Speed Ferry** ☎ 787/724–6600 ⊕ www.islandhighspeedferry.com. **Puerto Rico Ports Authority** ☎ 787/863-0705.

🚢 **Ferry Terminals Culebra Terminal** ☎ 787/742-3161. **Fajardo Terminal** ☎ 787/863–4560. **Vieques Terminal** ☎ 787/741-4761.

BY TAXI

You can flag down taxis on the street, but it's faster and safer to have your hotel call one for you. Either way, agree on how much the trip will cost before you get inside the taxi.

🚕 **Lolo Felix Tours** ✉ Vieques ☎ 787/485–5447. **Willy's Taxi** ✉ Culebra ☎ 787/742–3537.

Contacts & Resources

BANKS & EXCHANGE SERVICES

There are only a handful of banks on Vieques and Culebra, but they have 24-hour ATMs (or ATHs, as they're known here). The local branches of Banco Popular are open weekdays from 9 to 5.

🏦 **Banco Popular** ✉ 115 Calle Muñoz Rivera, Isabel Segunda, Vieques ☎ 787/741-2071 ✉ 15 Calle Pedro Marquez, Dewey, Culebra ☎ 787/742–0220

EMERGENCIES

Vieques has a pharmacy and a hospital, but there are neither on Culebra. Make sure you stock up on all supplies—such as allergy medications, contact-lens solution, or tampons—before heading to the island.

🚨 **Emergency Numbers General Emergencies** ☎ 911.

🏥 **Hospitals Hospital Susana Centeno** ✉ Rte. 997, Isabel Segunda, Vieques ☎ 787/741-3283.

💊 **Pharmacies Farmacia Isla Nena** ✉ Calle Muñoz Rivera, Isabel Segunda, Vieques ☎ 787/741-1906.

ENGLISH-LANGUAGE MEDIA

On Vieques, look for the monthly *Vieques Events,* which includes everything from the latest news to a calendar of cultural events.

Its counterpart on Culebra is the monthly *Culebra Calendar.* Put together by publisher Jim Petersen on the terrace of his wife's restaurant, it has plenty of news and even more opinion. It's a great way to bone up on local politics. You might also want to pick up a copy of the colorful *Culebra Guide,* available for $3 at most local shops. The map in its centerfold is especially helpful.

INTERNET, MAIL & SHIPPING

Internet cafés are a rare commodity once you leave San Juan. On Culebra there are a few terminals at Excétera. You can get online for $15 an hour.

Vieques has a post office on the main street in Isabel Segunda, and Culebra has one on the main street in Dewey. Culebra's post office functions as a town center, and usually has a group of locals out front chewing the fat. It's in an older building with a hand-carved front door.

🚩 InternetCafé **Excétera** ⊠ 126 Calle Escudero, Dewey ☎ 787/742-0844.

🚩 Post Offices **Culebra Post Office** ⊠ Calle Pedro Marquez, Dewey, Culebra ☎ 787/742-3288. **Vieques Post Office** ⊠ 97 Calle Muñoz Rivera, Suite 103, Isabel Segunda, Vieques ☎ 787/741-3891.

SAFETY

Although crime isn't as prevalent on Vieques as it is in San Juan, be on your guard. Avoid bringing valuables with you to the beach; if you must do so, be sure not to leave them in view in your car. Rental agencies advise that you leave your car unlocked when parked at a beach so thieves won't break the windows to get inside. There's very little crime on Culebra.

VISITOR INFORMATION

The island's tourism offices are hit and miss when it comes to helpful material. The Vieques Tourism Office, across from the main square in Isabel Segunda, has a friendly staff that will give you armloads of brochures. If you need more, they'll print out a complete list of local businesses. It's open Monday to Saturday 8 to 4:30.

The Culebra Tourism Office, near the ferry dock, has very little information on hand. The staffers will help you as best they can, even recommending restaurants that are off the beaten path. The office is open weekdays 9 to 5.

🚩 **Culebra Tourism Office** ⊠ 250 Calle Pedro Marquez, Dewey, Culebra ☎ 787/742-3521. **Vieques Tourism Office** ⊠ 449 Calle Carlos Lebrón, Isabel Segunda, Vieques ☎ 787/741-5000.

WEB SITES

The Web site Enchanted Isle has plenty of information about Vieques and Culebra; the Web site Isla Vieques has information about Vieques only.

🚩 **Enchanted Isle** ⊕ www.enchanted-isle.com. **Isla Vieques** ⊕ www.isla-vieques.com.

Ponce & the Southern Coast

WORD OF MOUTH

"San Germán, Guánica, and La Parguera are all no more than an hour's drive from each other. San Germán can be just a half-day stop. Walk a little around the center of town to enjoy the architecture and stop for a meal."

—PRnative

"La Parguera's main economy is tourism and fishing, so expect to find an area with a number of hotels alongside the main coast and also parts that are used by locals for their daily fishing activities. It has become very popular . . . so it can get very crowded during the weekends. Snorkeling in La Parguera is superb; certainly better than any snorkeling in the north side of the island."

—Maira

Revised and
Updated by
Mark Sullivan

FROM LUSH TROPICAL MOUNTAINS to arid seacoast plains, Puerto Rico's southern region lets you sample the island from a local's perspective. The south is where San Juan families escape the hustle and bustle of the city for weekends on the beach. Though rich in history, the area also provides ample opportunities for golf, swimming, hiking, and cave exploration. Snaking roads between major highways reveal a glimpse of how rural Puerto Ricans enjoy life. Every mile or so you'll see a café or bar, which is the local social center. The only traffic jams you'll likely encounter will be caused by slow-moving farmers taking their goods to the local market.

At the center of everything is Ponce, a city called the "Pearl of the South." Ponce was founded in 1692 by farmers attracted to the rich soil, which was perfect for growing sugarcane. Evidence found at the Tibes Indian ceremonial site, just north of Ponce, suggests that people have been living here as far back as 400 BC. Many residents still carry the last names of the dozens of European pioneer families who settled here during the 19th century. The region's largest city, Ponce is home to some of the island's most interesting architecture and one of its most important art museums. Nearby San Germán, the second-oldest city in Puerto Rico, is known for its two historic main squares well preserved in a wide variety of architectural styles.

On the coast, Guayama and Patillas show off their splendors as little-known destinations for beachgoers. But the real beach party is at La Parguera, which attracts a young but noisy crowd. If you're willing to explore beyond the casinos, high-rises, and daily traffic congestion of the island's capital, the south is a wise escape from Puerto Rico's usual tourist fare. Don't be surprised by the help many of its residents will offer whether you ask for it or not. Southern *puertorriqueños* are known for their friendliness as well as their hospitality.

Exploring Ponce & the Southern Coast

The southeastern part of the island has a rugged shoreline, where cliffs drop right into the water. This is a little-explored section of the coast, which means that on one hand the beaches aren't crowded, but on the other there aren't many places to find a decent meal or a place to bed down for the night. Covered with dry vegetation, the southwest's ragged coast has wonderful inlets and bays and jagged peninsulas that make for breathtaking views. This region is a popular destination for Puerto Rican families, so expect crowds on weekends.

About the Restaurants

Not all the culinary hot spots are in San Juan. In fact, people from the capital drive to Ponce or Guánica to see what's new on the horizon. Some of the more ambitious restaurants in this part of Puerto Rico are experimenting with fusion cuisine, which means you might find pork with tamarind glaze or guava sauce or snapper in a plantain crust. But what you'll mostly find is open-air eateries serving simple, filling fare. The southern coast is known for seafood. A 15% to 20% tip is customary; most restaurants won't include it in the bill, but it's wise to check.

TOP 5 PICKS FOR THE SOUTHERN COAST

- Marvel at the Parque de Bombas, a century-old firehouse whose red-and-black color scheme has inspired thousands of photographers.
- Hike through the Bosque Estatal de Guánica, where the cactus may make you think you're in the American Southwest.
- Sample a cup of the local brew at historic Hacienda Buena Vista, a beautifully restored coffee plantation outside of Ponce.
- Stroll around San Germán, whose cobblestone streets are lined with architectural treasures.
- Step back in time at Casa Cautiño, a lovingly restored colonial-era residence in the sleepy community of Guayama.

4

WHAT IT COSTS In U.S. dollars				
$$$$	$$$	$$	$	¢
AT DINNER over $30	$20–$30	$12–$20	$8–$12	under $8

Prices are per person for a main course at dinner.

About the Hotels

Modest, family-oriented establishments near beaches or in small towns are the most typical accommodations. Southern Puerto Rico doesn't have the abundance of luxury hotels and resorts found to the north and east; however, the Hilton Ponce & Casino and the Copamarina Beach Resort are self-contained complexes with a dizzying array of services.

WHAT IT COSTS In U.S. dollars				
$$$$	$$$	$$	$	¢
FOR 2 PEOPLE over $350	$250–$350	$150–$250	$80–$150	under $80

Prices are for a double room in high season, excluding 9% tax (11% for hotels with casinos, 7% for paradores) and 5%–12% service charge.

Timing

The resort towns of Patillas, Guánica, and La Parguera are also popular with Puerto Ricans during Easter and Christmas and during the summer, when children are out of school. Ponce's spirited pre-Lenten Carnival, held the week before Ash Wednesday, draws many visitors. Note that during busy times some *paradores* and hotels require a minimum two- or three-night stay on weekends.

Numbers in the text correspond to numbers in the margin and on the Southern Puerto Rico, Ponce Centro, Greater Ponce, and San Germán maps.

PONCE

34 km (21 mi) southwest of Coamo.

"Ponce is Ponce and the rest is parking space" is the adage used by the residents of Puerto Rico's second-largest city (population 194,000) to express their pride in being a *ponceño*. The rivalry with the island's capital began in the 19th century, when European immigrants from England, France, and Spain settled here. Because the city's limits extend from the Caribbean to the foothills of the Cordillera Central, it's a lot hotter in climate than San Juan. Another contrast is the architecture of the elegant homes and public buildings that surround the main square.

Many of the 19th-century buildings in Ponce Centro, the downtown area, have been renovated, and the Museo de Arte de Ponce—endowed by its late native son and former governor Luis A. Ferré—is considered one of the Caribbean's finest art museums. Just as famous is Ponce's pre-Lenten carnival. The

> ## GETTING AROUND
>
> Getting around Ponce couldn't be easier. You can catch a free, city-run trolley or *"chu chu"* train from Plaza las Delicias to the major attractions. On weekends there are free horse-and-carriage rides around the plaza, or if the weather is pleasant, as it often is, you could just walk. All the downtown sites are within a few blocks of the main square.

colorful costumes and *vejigante* (mischief maker) masks worn during the festivities are famous throughout the world. The best dining in Ponce is just west of town. Seafood restaurants line the highway in an area known as Las Cucharas, named for the spoon-shape bay you'll overlook as you dine.

Exploring Ponce

Las Delicias Plaza (Plaza of Delights) with its trees, benches, and famous lion fountain is a perfect people-watching square in which to spend an hour or two on a Sunday afternoon. The old red-and-black firehouse is right on the plaza and has a fire-fighting museum on its second floor. Ponce is known for its museums and has several dedicated to music, art, history, sports, and architecture. Ponceños are proud of their city, called the "Pearl of the South," and offer all visitors a warm welcome.

Ponce Centro

At the heart of Ponce Centro is the Plaza las Delicias, with trees, benches, and the famous lion fountain. Several interesting buildings are on this square or the adjacent streets, making the area perfect for a leisurely morning or afternoon stroll.

A GOOD WALK

Start on the tree-lined Plaza las Delicias. (You'll find parking nearby on Calle Marina, Calle Isabel, and Calle Reina.) Dominating it is the **Catedral Nuestra Señora de Guadalupe** ❶ ⊢, dating from 1835. Across the street is the **Casa Armstrong-Poventud** ❷, home of the Institute of Culture's Ponce branch. Leaving Armstrong-Poventud, cross back to the plaza,

IF YOU LIKE

BEACHES
On Puerto Rico's southern coast you'll find surfing beaches and calm bays for swimming. Ballena Bay, near Guánica, has oft-deserted sandy stretches. Boat operators make trips to such uninhabited cays as Gilligan's Island off the coast of Guánica and Caja de Muertos off Ponce.

DIVING & SNORKELING
Southern Puerto Rico is an undiscovered dive destination, which means unspoiled reefs and lots of fish. You can arrange for dive boats at Caribe Playa Beach Resort in the southeast, Ponce's La Guancha, and the Copamarina Beach Resort in the southwest. Shore diving and snorkeling are best around islands or cays or along the southwestern coast.

HIKING
Vegetation in the region is dramatically different from that of the rest of the island. Near Guánica is the 9,900-acre Bosque Estatal de Guánica, a rare dry tropical forest. With more than 100 species of birds, it's known for its excellent bird-watching. There are good trails throughout the area, but printed guides and trail maps are hard to come by. Ask locals for directions to their favorite paths.

4

circle south by the Alcaldía, and continue to the plaza's east side to visit the red-and-black striped fire station, **Parque de Bombas** ❸.

From the intersection of Calles Marina and Cristina, take Calle Cristina a block east to one of the city's first restoration projects, **Teatro La Perla** ❹, at the corner of Cristina and Mayor. One block north of the theater, at Calles Mayor and Isabel, is a former home that's now the **Museo de la Historia de Ponce** ❺. A block east, at the corner of Calles Salud and Isabel, is the **Museo de la Música Puertorriqueña** ❻. Four blocks west (you will go by Plaza las Delicias again, and Calle Isabel will turn into Calle Reina) is the 1911 architectural masterpiece **Casa Wiechers-Villaronga** ❼. For more early-20th-century architecture, continue west on Calle Reina, where you'll see examples of *casas criollas,* wooden homes with the spacious front balconies that were popular in the Caribbean during the early 1900s.

TIMING   Although it's possible to see Ponce Centro in one morning or afternoon, it's best to devote a full day and evening to it. Explore the streets and museums during daylight, then head for the plaza at night when the lion fountain and street lamps are lighted and townspeople stroll the plaza.

WHAT TO SEE   **Casa Armstrong-Poventud.** Banker and industrialist Carlos Armstrong and
❷   his wife Eulalia Pou lived in this neoclassical house designed and built for them in 1901 by Manuel V. Domenech. The house is known for its ornate facade, which is chock-full of columns, statues, and intricate moldings. It now houses the offices of the Institute of Puerto Rican Culture. Note the high, pressed-tin ceilings and the decorative glass doors in the foyer. ⊠ *Calle Union at Catedral, Ponce Centro* ☎ *787/844–2540 or 787/840–7667* 🖭 *Free* ☉ *Weekdays 8–4:30.*

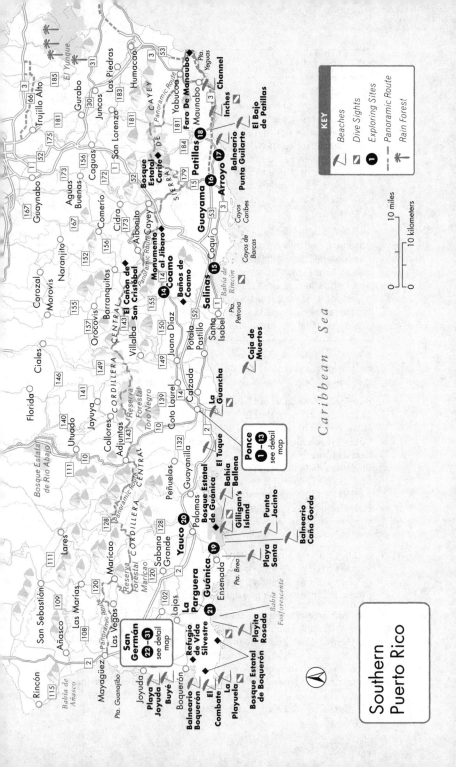

Southern Puerto Rico

KEY

🏖 Beaches

◼ Dive Sights

1 Exploring Sites

- - - Panoramic Route

🌴 Rain Forest

0 — 10 miles

0 — 10 kilometers

Caribbean Sea

Rincón • Bahía de Añasco • Pta. Guanajibo • Mayagüez • San Sebastián • Añasco • Las Marías • Lares • Maricao • *Reserva Forestal Maricao* • Las Vegas • *Panoramic route* • San Germán **22–31** *see detail map* • Lajas • La Parguera **21** • Guánica **19** • Ensenada • *Bahía Fosforescente* • Joyuda • **Playa Joyuda** • Boquerón • **Balneario Boquerón** • Buyé • El Combate • La Playuela • **Bosque Estatal de Boquerón** • **Refugio de Vida Silvestre** • Playita Rosada

Florida • Ciales • Corozal • Morovis • Naranjito • Barranquitas • Orocovis • Villalba • *Reserva Forestal Toro Negro* • *CORDILLERA CENTRAL* • Adjuntas • Jayuya • Utuado • *Bosque Estatal de Río Abajo* • Collores • *CORDILLERA CENTRAL* • *Panoramic Route* • Peñuelas • Guayanilla • Yauco **20** • Palomas • **Bosque Estatal de Guánica** • Ptas. Brea • Playa Santa • **Balneario Caña Gorda** • Punta Jacinto • Gilligan's Island • **Bahía Ballena** • **El Tuque** • **Ponce 1–13** *see detail map*

Corozal • Comerío • Cidra • Aibonito • Coamo • **El Cañón de San Cristóbal** • **Monumento al Jíbaro** • *Panoramic Route Cayey* • **Baños de Coamo** • Santa Isabel • Pastillo • Potala • Juana Díaz • Calzada • Coto Laurel • **La Guancha** • Pta. Petrona • *Bahía de Rincón* • **Caja de Muertos** • Salinas **15** • Coquí • *Cayos de Borcas* • *Cayos Caribes* • Guayama • Arroyo **16** • **Balneario Punta Guilarte** • Patillas **17** • **El Bajo de Patillas** • Maunabo • Inches **Channel** • **Faro De Manaubo** • Yabucoa • Pta. Yeguas

Trujillo Alto • *El Yunque* • Gurabo • Juncos • Las Piedras • Humacao • San Lorenzo • *SIERRA DE CAYEY* • *Panoramic Route* • **Bosque Estatal Carite** • Aguas Buenas • Caguas • Guaynabo

Roads: 115, 2, 108, 109, 111, 120, 102, 128, 10, 111, 140, 141, 146, 149, 155, 143, 10, 139, 150, 149, 132, 1, 52, 2, 53, 3, 15, 179, 184, 181, 183, 3, 53, 185, 66, 3, 31, 30, 175, 181, 173, 156, 172, 167, 173, 152, 157, 156, 165, 167

GREAT ITINERARIES

IF YOU HAVE 1 DAY

Many residents of San Juan think nothing of a day trip to **Ponce ❶-⓭**. If you head south on Route 52 you'll reach the city called the "Pearl of the South" in less than two hours. There's plenty to do here, including a tour of the Museo de Arte de Ponce. The best way to spend an hour or two is to stroll around the lovely Plaza de las Delicias. Make sure to dine in one of the outstanding restaurants, especially Mark's at the Meliá.

IF YOU HAVE 3 DAYS

From San Juan, head south on Route 52 until you reach **Ponce ❶-⓭**, the Pearl of the South. Spend the afternoon strolling around the Plaza de las Delicias, poking into the beautiful Catedral de Nuestra Señora de Guadalupe and the striking Parque de Bombas. On the following day, visit some of the other attractions in and around the city, perhaps the Museo de Arte de Ponce, the Castillo Serrallés, or Hacienda Buena Vista. Dedicate your final day to **Guánica ⓱**, where you'll find wonderful beaches and deserted cays; spend the night here before heading back to San Juan. If you are in the mood for hiking, there's the Bosque Estatal de Guánica.

IF YOU HAVE 5 DAYS

Make a leisurely trip south from San Juan on Route 52, spending a night in **Coamo ⓮**. These hot springs were thought by some to be Ponce de León's Fountain of Youth. Continue on your second day to **Ponce ❶-⓭** for two days of exploring. Travel west along the coast and settle at a waterfront hotel in **Guánica ⓱**. In the evening you can take a boat trip to the bioluminscent bay at **La Parguera ㉑**. On your last day explore the beautifully preserved colonial city of **San Germán ㉒-㉛**, making sure to see the lovely colonial-era chapel known as the Capilla de Porta Coeli.

4

❼ **Casa Wiechers-Villaronga.** In a city filled with neoclassical confections, this is one of the most elaborate. It was designed by Alfredo B. Wiechers, who returned to his native Ponce after studying architecture in Paris. This house, though small in scale, makes a big impression with details like huge arched windows and a massive rooftop gazebo. No wonder that soon after it was completed it 1911 the Villaronga-Mercado family decided to make it their own. Check out the stained-glass windows and other fanciful touches. Inside you'll find original furnishings and exhibits on Wiechers and other Ponce architects of his era. ⊠ *Calle Reina and Calle Meléndez Vigo, Ponce Centro* ☎ 787/843–3363 🗐 *Free* ⊙ *Wed.–Sun. 8:30–4:30.*

FodorsChoice ★

❶ **Catedral de Nuestra Señora de Guadalupe.** This cathedral dedicated to the Virgin of Guadalupe is built on the site of a 1670 chapel destroyed by earthquakes. Part of the current structure, where mass is still held, dates from 1835. After another earthquake in 1918, new steeples and a roof were put on and neoclassical embellishments were added to the facade. Inside you'll see stained-glass windows, chandeliers, and two al-

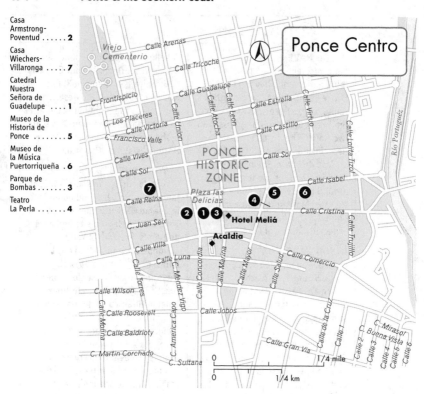

abaster altars. ⊠ *Plaza las Delicias, Ponce Centro* ☎ *787/842–0134* ☉ *Services daily 6 AM and 11 AM.*

⑤ Museo de la Historia de Ponce. Housed in two adjoining buildings, this museum has 10 exhibition halls covering Ponce's development from the Taíno Indians to the present. Hour-long guided tours in English and Spanish give an overview of the city's history. ⊠ *51–53 Calle Isabel, Ponce Centro* ☎*787/844–7071 or 787/843–4322* 🔳*$3* ☉*Tues.–Fri. 9–5, weekends 10–6.*

⑥ Museo de la Música Puertorriqueña. At this museum you'll learn how Puerto Rican music has been influenced by African, Spanish, and Native American cultures. On display are instruments, such as the *triple* (a small string instrument resembling a banjo), and memorabilia of local composers and musicians. The small museum takes up several rooms in a neoclassical former residence. ⊠ *Calle Isabel and Calle Salud, Ponce Centro* ☎ *787/848–7016* 🔳 *Free* ☉ *Wed.–Sun. 8:30–4:30.*

🌙 **❸ Parque de Bombas.** After El Morro, this distinctive red-and-black striped
Fodor'sChoice building may be the most photographed building in Puerto Rico. Built
★ in 1882 as a pavilion for an agricultural and industrial fair, it was converted the following year into a firehouse. Today it's a museum tracing the history—and glorious feats—of Ponce's fire brigade. Kids love the

Masked Mischief

CLOSE UP

A WEEK BEFORE ASH WEDNESDAY, *vejigantes* (pronounced veh-hee-GAN-tays), wearing long, colorful robes and brightly painted horned masks, turn the normally placid city of Ponce into a hotbed of rowdiness. These masked mischief makers prowl city streets for a week, scaring anyone in their path. Some historians date this tradition to a Spanish one of the 1600s that targeted lapsed Christians. Men in long robes and grotesque masks waved cow bladders, or *vejigas*, on long sticks at passersby, attempting to frighten them back into churches for Lent. Today balloons and plastic bottles have replaced cow bladders, and the playful masks present the face of Ponce's exquisite folk art to the world.

Unlike carnival masks from other parts of the island, which are made of coconut shells *(Loíza)* or fine metallic

screening *(Hatillo)*, Ponce masks are made of papier-mâché. Many have African and Native American elements; it's even possible to detect influences from ancient Greece and Rome. All masks have at least two horns, but most have several protruding from the forehead, chin, and nose. Some antique masks have been known to have more than 100 horns.

At the beginning of the 20th century, masks were usually painted red with yellow dots or vice versa, but today they come in every color and pattern imaginable. You'll also find them for sale at crafts stores and arts festivals. Small, simple masks start at around $20 or $30; larger ones by well-known makers cost as much as $100. One of the best-known mask-making families today is the Caraballo family from the Playa de Ponce area.

4

antique fire trucks. Short tours in English and Spanish are given on the half hour. There's a small tourist information desk just inside the door. ✉ *Plaza las Delicias, Ponce Centro* ☎ *787/284–3338* 🎟 *Free* 🕙 *Wed.–Mon. 9:30–6.*

NEED A BREAK?

An institution for more than 40 years, **King's** (✉ 9223 Calle Marina ☎ 787/843–8520), across from Plaza las Delicias, is *the* place for ice cream in Ponce. It serves 12 varieties, from tamarind and passion fruit to classic chocolate and vanilla. A bench in the tiny storefront seats three, but most folks take their cups and cones across the street and stake out shady plaza benches. King's is open daily from 8 AM to midnight.

❹ **Teatro La Perla.** This theater was restored in 1941 after an earthquake and fire damaged the original 1864 structure. The striking interior contains seats for 1,047 and has excellent acoustics. It's generally open for a quick look on weekdays. ✉ *Calle Mayor and Calle Cristina, Ponce Centro* ☎ *787/843–4322* 🎟 *Free* 🕙 *Weekdays 8–4:30.*

Greater Ponce

The greater Ponce area has some of Puerto Rico's most notable cultural attractions, including one of the island's finest art museums and its most important archaeological site.

A GOOD TOUR

The **Museo de Arte de Ponce** ⑧ ⌐ is on Avenida Las Américas, south of Plaza las Delicias and not far from the Luis A. Ferré Expressway (Route 52). Anyone with a taste for art can happily while away many hours in its galleries. East of the museum you can pick up Route 14 south to the Caribbean and **La Guancha** ⑨, a boardwalk with food kiosks, a playground, and a child-friendly public beach. It's a good place to relax and let the younger generation work off energy. From here, if you retrace your path north past downtown you'll be heading to Calle Bertoly and El Vigía (Vigía Hill), where the **Cruceta El Vigía** ⑩ towers over the city and the **Castillo Serrallés** ⑪, a former sugar baron's villa, is a popular attraction.

Farther north on Route 503 is the **Centro Ceremonial Indígena de Tibes** ⑫, which displays native artifacts dating back more than 1,500 years. You'll have to backtrack to reach Route 10, then head north to **Hacienda Buena Vista** ⑬, a former coffee plantation that's been restored by the Puerto Rican Conservation Trust. (Call ahead to arrange a tour.)

You can drive to all these sights or hop on the free trolleys or *chu chu* trains that run from Plaza las Delicias to the museum, La Guancha, and El Vigía. You'll need a car or a cab to reach the Centro Ceremonial Indígena de Tibes or Hacienda Buena Vista.

TIMING   To visit all the sights mentioned above you'll need at least 2 days. If you don't want to devote that much time, visit only the sights that have the most appeal for you personally.

WHAT TO SEE   **Castillo Serrallés.** This lovely Spanish-style villa—such a massive house
⑪   that people in the town below referred to it as a castle—was built in the 1930s for Ponce's wealthiest family, the makers of Don Q rum. Guided tours give you a glimpse into the lifestyle of a sugar baron. A highlight is the dining room, which has the original hand-carved furnishings. A permanent exhibit explains the area's sugarcane and rum industries. The extensive garden, with sculptured bushes and a shimmering reflection pool, is considered the best kept on the island. ⊠ *17 El Vigía, El Vigía* ☎ *787/259–1774* ⊕ *home.coqui.net/castserr* ⌐ *$6, $9 includes admission to Cruceta El Vigía* ☉ *Tues.–Thurs. 9:30–5, Fri.–Sun. 9:30–5:30.*

⑫   **Centro Ceremonial Indígena de Tibes.** The Tibes Indian Ceremonial Center, discovered after flooding from a tropical storm in 1975, is the island's most important archaeological site. The pre-Taíno ruins and burial grounds date from AD 300 to 700. Be sure to visit the small museum before taking a walking tour of the site, which includes nine ceremonial playing fields used for a ritual ball game that some think was similar to soccer. The fields are bordered by smooth stones, some engraved with petroglyphs that researchers believe might have ceremonial or astro-

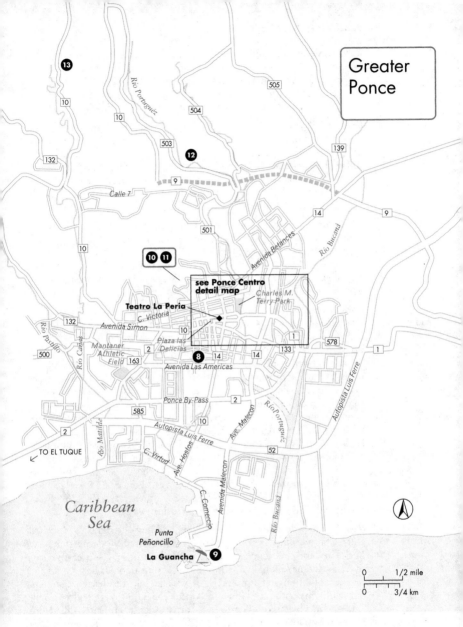

Greater Ponce

13

10

Río Portuguéz

505

504

10

503

132

12

9

Calle 7

501

14

9

10

Avenida Bétances

Río Bucaná

10 11

see Ponce Centro
detail map

Charles M.
Terry Park

Teatro La Peria

132

C. Victoria

Río Pastillo

Avenida Simón

10

1

Río Cañas

Mantaner
Athletic
Field

163

Plaza las
Delicias

2

8

14

14

133

578

1

500

Avenida Las Américas

Autopista Luis Ferré

Ponce By-Pass

2

585

10

2

Autopista Luis Ferre

Río Matilde

Ave. Malecón

Río Portuguéz

52

TO EL TUQUE

C. Virtud

Ave. Hostos

Avenida Malecón

Caribbean
Sea

Punta
Peñoncillo

C. Comercio

Río Bucaná

La Guancha

9

0   1/2 mile

0   3/4 km

nomical significance. Enough mutilated corpses have been found here for researchers to speculate that the residents practiced human sacrifice. A village with several thatch huts has been reconstructed in an original setting. ⊠ *Rte. 503, Km 2.8, Barrio Tibes* ☎ *787/840–2255 or 787/840–5685* ⊕ *ponce.inter.edu/tibes/tibes.html* 🖃 *$2* ☉ *Tues.–Sun. 9–4.*

⑩ Cruceta El Vigía. At the top of Cerro Vigía—a hill where the Spanish once watched for ships, including those of marauding pirates—is this colossal concrete cross. You can climb the stairs or take an elevator to the top of the 100-foot cross for a panoramic view across the city. Purchase tickets at the nearby Castillo Serrallés. ⊠ *Across from Castillo Serrallés, El Vigía* ☎ *787/259–3816* ⊕ *home.coqui.net/castserr* 🖃 *$4* ☉ *Tues.–Sun. 9–5:30.*

☾ ⑨ La Guancha. Encircling the cove of a working harbor, the seaside boardwalk features kiosks where vendors sell local food and drink. The adjacent park has a large children's area filled with playground equipment and on weekends, live music. The nearby public beach has restrooms, changing areas, a medical post, and plenty of free parking. ⊠ *End of Rte. 14, La Guancha* ☎ *787/844–3995.*

☾ ⑬ Hacienda Buena Vista.
Fodor'sChoice
★
Built by Salvador de Vives in 1838, Buena Vista was one of the area's largest coffee plantations. It's a technological marvel—water from the nearby Río Canas was funneled into narrow brick channels that could be diverted to perform any number of tasks, including turning the waterwheel. (Seeing the two-story wheel slowly begin to turn is thrilling, especially for kids.) Nearby is the two-story manor house, filled with furniture that gives a sense of what it was like to live on a coffee plantation nearly 150 years ago. Make sure to take a look in the kitchen, dominated by a massive hearth. In 1987 the plantation was restored by the Puerto Rican Conservation Trust, which leads four tours a day (one in English). The tours are by reservation only, so make sure to call several days ahead. After seeing the plantation, you can buy coffee beans and other souvenirs at the gift shop. Allow yourself an hour to travel the winding road from Ponce. ⊠ *Rte. 123, Km 16.8, Sector Corral Viejo* ☎ *787/722–5882 weekdays, 787/284–7020 weekends* 🖃 *$5* ☉ *Fri.–Sun., by reservation only.*

⑧ Museo de Arte de Ponce.
Fodor'sChoice
★
This interesting building—designed by Edward Durrell Stone, who designed the original Museum of Modern Art in New York City and the Kennedy Center in Washington, DC—is easily identified by the hexagonal galleries on the second floor. It has one of the best art collections in Latin American, which is why residents of San Juan frequently make the trip down to Ponce. The 3,000-piece collection includes works by famous Puerto Rican artists such as Francisco Oller, represented by a lovely landscape called *Hacienda Aurora*. There are plenty of European works on display, including paintings by Peter Paul Rubens and Thomas Gainsborough. The highlight of the European collection is the Pre-Raphaelite paintings, particularly the mesmerizing *Flaming June,* by Frederick Leighton, which has become the museum's unofficial symbol. Watch for special exhibits, such as a recent one examining the work of Frida Kahlo. ⊠ *2325 Av. Las Américas, Sector Santa María* ☎ *787/848–0505* ⊕ *www.museoarteponce.org* 🖃 *$5* ☉ *Daily 10–5.*

Beaches

Caja de Muertos (Coffin Island). This island a few miles off the coast has the best beaches in the Ponce area and is, perhaps, the second-best area in southern Puerto Rico for snorkeling, after La Parguera. Ask one of the many boatmen at La Guancha to take you out for about $30 round-trip. ⊠ *Boats leave from La Guancha, at the end of Rte. 14, Ponce.*

La Guancha. Ponce's public beach is small, but the shallow water makes it nice for children. There's some shade under thatched umbrellas, but bring sunscreen. ⊠ *At the end of Rte. 14, Ponce.*

El Tuque. This beach has a swimming area and picnic tables. ⊠ *Rte. 2, approx. 5 km (3 mi) west of Ponce.*

Where to Eat

$$–$$$$ ✕ **Mark's at the Meliá.** Hidden behind an etched-glass door, this discreet
Fodor'sChoice restaurant is one of the best on the island. Chef Mark French has won
★ praise for his creative blend of European cooking techniques and local ingredients. That skill results in appetizers like terrine of foie gras with dried cherry compote and smoked salmon topped with caramelized mango. The menu changes often, but you're likely to see such entrées as plantain-crusted dorado and rack of lamb with a goat cheese crust. The chocolate truffle cake draws fans from as far away as San Juan. This is a family-run business, so Mark's wife, Melody, is likely to greet you at the door. ⊠ *Hotel Meliá, 75 Calle Cristina, Ponce Centro, Ponce* ☎ 787/284–6275 ⌨ *Reservations essential* ▭ *AE, MC, V* ⊙ *Closed Mon. and Tues.*

$$–$$$$ ✕ **Rincón Argentina.** Housed in a beautifully restored criollo-style house, Rincón Argentina is one of the city's most popular restaurants. Completely unpretentious, this is the kind of steak house you find all over South America. The specialty of the house is *parrilladas,* meaning just about anything that comes off the grill. Don't pass up the skirt steak, served here with the best chimichurri you'll find anywhere. On cool evenings take a table on the terrace. Otherwise, wander through the maze of dining rooms until you find a table you like. ⊠ *69 Calle Salud, at Calle Isabel, Ponce Centro, Ponce* ☎ 787/840–3768 ⌨ *Reservations essential* ▭ *AE, MC, V.*

$–$$$ ✕ **El Ancla.** Families favor this laid-back restaurant, whose dining room sits at the edge of the sea. The kitchen serves generous and affordable plates of fish, crab, and other fresh seafood with tostones, french fries, and garlic bread. Try the shrimp in garlic sauce, salmon filet with capers, or the delectable mofongo. Finish your meal with one of the fantastic flans. The piña coladas—with or without rum—are exceptional. ⊠ *9 Av. Hostos Final, Ponce Playa* ☎ 787/840–2450 ▭ *AE, MC, V.*

$–$$$ ✕ **Pito's Seafood.** Choose from the waterfront terrace or one of the enclosed dining rooms at this longtime favorite east of Ponce in Las Cucharas. No matter where you sit, you'll have a view of the ocean. The main attraction is the freshly caught seafood, ranging from lobster and crab to salmon and red snapper. To indulge yourself, try the shrimp wrapped in bacon—a specialty of the house. There's also a wide range of chicken and beef dishes. From the expansive wine cellar you can select more than 25 different wines by the glass. There's live music on Friday and Saturday nights. ⊠ *Rte. 2, Sector Las Cucharas* ☎ *787/841–4977* ▤ *AE, MC, V.*

¢ ✕ **Café Tompy.** The prices are right at this no-frills cafeteria, which draws a lot of locals for lunch. You can sample such down-home Puerto Rican cuisine as roasted chicken marinated with local spices or slices of roast pork in a honey-sweet glaze. You can pile on the side dishes, which include toasted plantains and creamy potato salad. There's also a selection of sandwiches piled high with meats and cheeses. It's open daily for lunch and dinner, and for breakfast every day except Sunday. ⊠ *56 Calle Isabel, Ponce Centro* ☎ *787/840–1965* ▤ *MC, V.*

Where to Stay

$$–$$$ ⊞ **Hilton Ponce Golf & Casino Resort.** The south coast's biggest resort sits on a black-sand beach about 6 km (4 mi) south of Ponce. Everything on this 80-acre property is massive, beginning with the open-air lobby. Constructed of reinforced concrete, like the rest of the hotel, it requires huge signs to point you in the right direction. All its bright, spacious rooms are decorated in a lush, tropical motif and have balconies overlooking the sea. A large pool is surrounded by palm trees and has a spectacular view of the Caribbean. Golf lovers will appreciate the 27-hole course at the adjacent Costa Caribe Resort, which has a clubhouse with its own restaurant and lounge. ⊠ *1150 Av. Caribe, La Guancha* ⓓ *Box 7419, Ponce 00732* ☎ *787/259–7676 or 800/445–8667* 🖷 *787/259–7674* ⊕ *www.hiltoncaribbean.com* ⏎ *253 rooms* ♨ *4 restaurants, room service, in-room safes, some in-room hot tubs, minibars, cable TV with movies and video games, Wi-Fi, 3 9-hole golf courses, driving range, 4 tennis courts, pool, gym, hot tub, sauna, spa, beach, bicycles, basketball, Ping-Pong, volleyball, 3 bars, casino, dance club, video game room, shops, babysitting, children's programs (ages 8–12), playground, business services, convention center, meeting rooms, parking (fee)* ▤ *AE, D, DC, MC, V* ⍟ *EP.*

> ### WORD OF MOUTH
>
> "Ponce Hilton disappoints the uninformed—their facilities have a casino, nice grounds, but no beach whatsoever. This is posted many places in the Internet, including guidebooks. Their staff is very nice, but again, I wouldn't stay there if looking to swim in the ocean."
>
> –Viajero2.

$ ⊞ **Holiday Inn Ponce.** Perched on a hilltop, this hotel has a sweeping view of the southern coast. In exchange for that view from your private balcony, however, you give up direct access to the beach. The pair of pools, one for the kids, is a bit of a consolation. Romantic music wafting from the lobby bar and the dance beat that pulsates from the disco lend considerable Latin flair to the hotel. Adding to the energy is the sound of slot machines that echoes through the lobby. The Tanama restaurant serves Spanish, Puerto Rican, and nouvelle cuisine; several seafood restaurants are also in the nearby Las Cucharas area. ⊠ *3315 Ponce Bypass, El Tuque, 00731* ☎ *787/844–1200 or 800/465–4329* 🖷 *787/841–8683* ⊕ *www.ichotelsgroup.com* ⏎ *116 rooms* ♨ *Restaurant, room service, refrig-*

erators, cable TV, in-room data ports, Wi-Fi, 2 pools, gym, 2 bars, casino, dance club, video game room, dry cleaning, laundry service, business services, convention center, meeting rooms, free parking ⊟ AE, D, DC, MC, V ⦿ EP.

★ $ ⌸ **Hotel Meliá.** In the heart of the city, this family-owned hotel has long been a local landmark. Its neoclassical facade, with flags from a dozen countries waving in the breeze, will remind you of the small lodgings in Spain. The lobby, with wood-beamed ceilings and blue-and-beige tile floors, is well worn but extremely charming. The best rooms have French doors leading out to small balconies; the six suites have terrific views of the main square. Breakfast is served on the rooftop terrace, which overlooks the mountains. A waterfall drops into the beautiful tiled swimming pool. The restaurant, Mark's at the Meliá, is one of the best on the island. ⊠ 75 Calle Cristina, Ponce Centro ⌑ Box 1431, Ponce 00733 ☎ 787/842–0260 or 800/448–8355 🖶 787/841–3602 ⊕ www. hotelmeliapr.com ⇄ 72 rooms, 6 suites ⌕ Restaurant, cable TV, pool, bar, Internet room, parking (fee) ⊟ AE, MC, V ⦿ CP.

$ ⌸ **Howard Johnson.** Near the airport, this hotel is a good choice if you have an early morning flight. The rooms are pretty much what you'd expect from a chain hotel, but all have balconies overlooking a palm-shaded pool. There's not much in the way of amenities, but the smiling staff provides little extras like coffeemakers with an unlimited supply of freshly ground beans. ⊠ 103 Turpó Industrial Park, Airport, 00715 ☎ 787/841–1000 🖶 787/841–2560 ⊕ www.hojo.com ⇄ 120 rooms ⌕ Restaurant, room service, some microwaves, some refrigerators, cable TV, in-room broadband, Wi-Fi, 2 pools, hot tub, gym, video game room, bar, business services, meeting rooms ⊟ AE, D, DC, MC, V ⦿ EP.

¢–$ ⌸ **Fox Delicias.** The facade of this hotel—an art–deco fantasy with streamlined columns soaring heavenward and brightly colored mosaics swirling above the front door—once graced a movie palace. Don't be surprised if you stop and stare the moment you step into the cozy, brick courtyard. The interior could only pale by comparison. Once a shopping mall, this boutique hotel still feels like it should be filled with boutiques. The restaurants are behind windows where locals used to browse. The rooms are clean and comfortable, although a few of the smaller ones don't have windows. ⊠ 6963 Calle Isabel, Ponce Centro, 00728 ☎ 787/ 290–5050 🖶 787/259–6413 ⊕ www.foxdeliciashotel.com ⇄ 30 rooms ⌕ 2 restaurants, cable TV, hair salon, 2 bars, business services ⊟ AE, MC, V ⦿ EP.

¢ ⌸ **Hotel Bélgica.** Near the central square, this hotel is both comfortable and economical. A stairway off the large 1940s-era lobby leads to clean rooms with wrought-iron headboards and other furnishings. Those on the front of the building have balconies with wooden shutter-style doors. The rooms vary widely in size (Room 3 is one of the largest), so ask to see a few before you decide. The friendly staff makes up for the lack of amenities. The hotel has no restaurant, but there are plenty of options in the neighborhood. ⊠ 122 Calle Villa, Ponce Centro, 00731 ☎ 787/ 844–3255 ⊕ www.hotelbelgica.com ⇄ 20 rooms ⌕ Cable TV, some pets allowed ⊟ MC, V ⦿ EP.

Nightlife & the Arts

Nightlife

BARS & CLUBS Catering mostly to a gay crowd, **Backstage** (✉ Off Rte 123, Ponce Centro ☎ 787/448–8112) has a huge dance floor surrounded by intimate lounges where groups of friends inevitably gather. Don't get here before midnight, or you might arrive before the staff. On the main square, **Café Palermo** (✉ Calle Union at Calle Villa, Ponce Centro ☎ 787/448–8112) is a hole in the wall. Still, locals can be found crowding around the bar every night of the week. **Fusion** (✉ 28 Calle Isabel, Ponce Centro ☎ 787/842–254) has a laid-back lounge area that makes you want to order a fancy cocktail. You can also belly up to the chic bar. With live music most nights, **Hollywood Café** (✉ Blvd. Miguel Pou, Km 5.5, Ponce Centro ☎ 787/843–6703) draws a college-age crowd.

> **TAKE A WALK**
>
> In downtown Ponce, people embrace the Spanish tradition of the *paseo*, an evening stroll with family and friends around Plaza las Delicias, which is spectacular at night when its old-fashioned street lamps glow and the fountain is lit. The boardwalk at La Guancha is also a lively scene with bands playing on weekends.

CASINOS The casinos in Ponce can't hold a candle to their counterparts in San Juan. **Hilton Ponce Golf & Casino Resort** (✉ Rte. 14, 1150 Av. Caribe, La Guancha ☎ 787/259–7676) has a rather cramped casino that stays open nightly until 4 AM. **Holiday Inn Ponce** (✉ 3315 Ponce Bypass, El Tuque ☎ 787/844–1200) has a small casino just off the lobby. It is open nightly until 4 AM.

The Arts

The **Museo de Arte de Ponce** (✉ 2325 Av. Las Américas, Sector Santa María ☎ 787/848–0505) occasionally sponsors chamber-music concerts and recitals by members of the Puerto Rico Symphony Orchestra. Check for Spanish-language theater productions and concerts at the **Teatro La Perla** (✉ Calle Mayor and Calle Cristina, Ponce Centro ☎ 787/843–4322).

Sports & the Outdoors

Diving & Snorkeling

You'll see many varieties of coral, parrotfish, angelfish, and grouper in the reefs around the island of Caja de Muertos. Snorkeling around La Guancha and the beach area of the Ponce Hilton is also fairly good.

Rafi Vega's **Island Venture** (☎ 787/842–8546 ⊕ www.islandventurepr.com) offers two-tank dive excursions for $65, as well as snorkeling trips for $35. The company also takes day-trippers from La Guancha to Caja de Muertos—a 45-minutes boat ride—for a day of relaxing on the beach.

Shopping

On holidays and during festivals, artisans sell wares from booths in the Plaza las Delicias. Souvenir and gift shops are plentiful in the area around the plaza, and Paseo Atocha, a pedestrian mall with shops geared to residents, runs north of it.

Den Cayá (⊠ 72 Calle Isabel, Ponce Centro ☎ 787/649–7763), a fun and funky store, has a wide variety of crafts from around the island as well as around the world.

Mi Coquí (⊠ 9227 Calle Marina, Ponce Centro ☎ 787/841–0216) has shelves filled with Carnival masks, colorful hammocks, freshly ground coffee, and bottles and bottles of rum.

Plaza del Caribe Mall (⊠ Rte. 2, Km 224.9 ☎ 787/259–8989), just outside town, is one of the island's largest malls and has such stores as Sears, JCPenney, and the Gap.

Ponce Mall (⊠ Rte. 2, Km 225.8 ☎ 787/844–6170), with more than 25 stores, is an older shopping center with many local clothing and discount stores.

Utopia (⊠ 78 Calle Isabel, Ponce Centro ☎ 787/848–8742) sells carnival masks and crafts.

THE SOUTHEASTERN COAST

As you cross the Cordillera Central, the scenery becomes drier and more rugged. The Caribbean sparkles in the distance, and the plain between the sea and the mountains, once the heart of the sugarcane industry, is now the domain of cattle. Tucked into the foothills is Coamo, a popular hot-springs resort since the early 1900s. Closer to the coast is Guayama, with a tree-lined square surrounded by many historic buildings.

Coamo

⑭ *34 km (21 mi) northeast of Ponce, 33 km (20 mi) southwest of Cayey; 20 km (13 mi) northwest of Salinas.*

Founded by the Spanish in 1579, Coamo was the third city established in Puerto Rico. It dominated the south of the island until the mid-1880s, when political power shifted to Ponce. Coamo town, however, remained an important outpost; several decisive battles were fought here during the Spanish-American War in 1898.

The thermal springs outside Coamo are believed by some to be the Fountain of Youth for which Ponce de León was searching. In the mid-1800s a fashionable resort was built nearby, and people have been coming for a soak in the waters ever since. Coamo is also famous for the San Blas Half-Marathon, which brings competitors and spectators from around the world. The race, held in early February, covers 18 km (13 mi) of the city's hilly streets.

> **WORD OF MOUTH**
>
> "If you decide to rent a car, just be aware that most of the road signs are solely in Spanish. While the roads were pretty well marked, if you don't know left (*izquierda*) from right (*derecho*), you'll face a few challenges!"
>
> —Callaloo

On Coama's main square, the **Iglesia Católica San Blás** has a gorgeous neoclassical facade. Dating from 1563, the whitewashed building is one of the oldest churches on the island. ⊠ *Calle Mario Braschetti* ☎ *787/825–1122* ◷ *Daily 6:30–noon.*

Off the main square, the **Museo Histórico de Coamo** is appropriately housed in the former residence of one of the city's illustrious citizens, Clotilde Santiago, a wealthy farmer and merchant born in 1826. The museum is on the second floor of this sprawling, tangerine-colored building that dates from 1863. Several rooms are decorated with colonial-style furnishings; photographs of the town and the Santiago family line the walls. ⊠ *29 Calle José I. Quintón* ☎ *787/825–1150* ⊠ *Free* ◷ *Weekdays 8–4:30.*

Outside Coamo on Route 546 you can take a dip at the famous **Baños de Coamo,** thermal springs that are said to have curative powers. Parador Baños de Coamo allows day-trippers to bathe in its own warm pool for $5 (parador guests enjoy it on the house). There's also a free public bathing area at the end of a path behind the parador. ⊠ *Rte. 546, Km 1* ☎ *787/ 825–2186* ⊠ *$5* ◷ *Daily 10–5:30.*

Where to Eat

¢–$ ✕ **La Ceiba.** The highway leading to Coama is lined by dozens of fast-food restaurants. Luckily, there are a few family-owned eateries worth stopping for, one of the best of which is this open-air cantina. You'll find the usual tacos, burritos, quesadillas, and fajitas, as well as some interesting Puerto Rican dishes like chicken breast stuffed with shrimp. World-class margaritas are served at the bar. ⊠ *Rte. 153* ☎ *787/825– 2299* ▤ *MC, V.*

Where to Stay

$ ▥ **Parador Baños de Coamo.** On weekends musicians play in the central courtyard of this rustic country inn. Rooms—in four modern, two-story buildings—have soaring ceilings and open onto latticed wooden verandahs. Thermal water flows from natural springs into a swimming pool a few steps away from a cool-water pool, where you can still see walls dating from 1843. The oldest building still standing is the 19th-century dining room, which serves huge portions of tasty *churrasco* (skirt steak) along with rice and beans. The open-air bar is popular in the afternoons. ⊠ *Rte. 546, Km 1, Box 1867, 00769* ☎ *787/825–2186 or 787/825–2239* ⊟ *787/825–4739* ◪ *48 rooms* ⌂ *Restaurant, cable TV, 2 pools, bar, video game room* ▤ *AE, D, MC, V* ⍾ *EP.*

Sports & the Outdoors

GOLF The **Coamo Springs Golf Club & Resort** (⊠ Rte. 546 ☎ 787/825–1370) is popular for its rugged beauty. It's the only 18-hole, par-72 course with Bermuda grass on the island. When it's raining in the capital, sanjuaneros may drive down here for a day of play. The 6,647-yard course, designed by Ferdinand Garbin, is open daily.

Salinas

⑮ *41 km (27 mi) east of Ponce.*

Most visitors are familiar with this town only from seeing its name on an exit sign along Route 52. Islanders, however, know that the road from the expressway exit to Salinas leads to some of Puerto Rico's best seafood restaurants. Most of them are along the seafront in the Playa de Salinas area, reached by heading south on Route 701.

> **SALINAS HAS THE MOJO**
>
> When you stop in Salinas—and you should—be sure to try local seafood with *mojo isleño,* a popular sauce made from tomatoes, onions, and spices, which was created here.

Where to Eat

$–$$$ ✕ **Costa Marina.** At the Marina de Salinas, this seafood restaurant has porthole windows that look out onto the dozens of sailboats anchored nearby. From the steeply sloped ceiling hang strings of semaphore flags and huge model ships. Some of the specialties include *ensalada de carrucho* (conch salad) and *arroz mamposteao de jueyes* (rice with crab). Make sure to try fish with the local mojo isleño. ⊠ *Calle Chapin G-8* ☎ *787–824–647* ⊟ *AE, MC, V.*

Where to Stay

$ 🏨 **Posada El Náutico.** Several different types of mangroves shade this hotel at the Marina de Salinas. Many guests arrive by private yacht, but there's no reason you can't show up in a car. The spacious rooms are cheerfully decorated with tropical colors. Your dining options include Costa Marina, a restaurant that's also in the marina, or a string of seafood restaurants along the road. It's a bit difficult to find; follow the signs leading to the PLAYA DE SALINAS. ⊠ *Calle Chapin G-8, 00751* ☎ *787/ 824–3185 or 787/752–8484* ✉ *jarce@coqui.net* ☞ *32 rooms* ⚐ *Restaurant, snack bar, cable TV, pool, marina, bar, meeting room* ⊟ *AE, MC, V* ⏛ *EP.*

Guayama

⑯ *29 km (18 mi) east of Salinas, 28 km (17 mi) southeast of Cayey; 49 km (31 mi) southeast of Barranquitas.*

Guayama was founded in 1736, but the city was destroyed by fire in the early 1800s. It quickly recovered when the sugarcane industry grew by leaps and bounds, and the wealth that the surrounding plantations brought to town is evident in the number of striking neoclassical homes on the streets surrounding the main square. Some have been beautifully restored, whereas others are crumbling. One of the finest 19th-century homes, Casa Cautiño, is now a museum.

The nearby countryside is home to Paso Fino horses. Each March at the Marcelino Blondet Stadium you can watch these high-stepping show horses strut their stuff during the Feria Dulce Sueño, a fair named after one of the island's most famous Thoroughbreds. Folk music and crafts are part of the festivities.

★ Built for sugar, cattle, and coffee baron Genaro Cautiño Vázquez and his wife Genoveva Insúa, **Casa Cautiño** is an elegant neoclassical home dating from 1887. A balcony with ornate grillwork graces the painstakingly restored exterior. You'll be swept back in time walking through the home's rooms, which are filled with the original Victorian-era furnishings. Don't miss the modern-for-its-time bathroom, complete with a standing shower. The museum in on the main square. ⊠ *1 Calle Palmer, at Calle Vicente Palé Matos* ☎ *787/864–9083* ⚏ *Free* ☉ *Tues.–Fri. 9–4:30, weekends 10–4.*

The fruit-flavored ice cream at **Rex Cream** (⊠ 24 Calle Derkes ☎ No phone) is hard to pass up. Flavors vary, depending on what's in season, but often include lime, pineapple, tamarind, and *guanábana* (soursop). You can also get milk shakes—the mango shake is outstanding.

Just a few blocks from the main square, the **Centro de Bellas Artes** is housed in a beautifully restored neoclassical building. Its 11 rooms are filled with paintings by local artists. ⊠ *Calle McArthur* ☎ *787/864–7765* ⚏ *Free* ☉ *Tues.–Fri. 9–4:30, Sat. 10–4:30.*

One of the prettiest churches on the southern coast, **Iglesia San Antonio de Padua** was begun in 1827 but not completed until 40 years later. Don't set your watch by the time on the clock; the hand-painted face forever reads 11:30, the time the church was "baptized." The bells in the tower were cast in gold and bronze in 1835. ⊠ *5 Calle Ashford* ☎ *787/864–7765.*

Where to Eat

¢ ✕ **El Suarito.** You're surrounded by history at this restaurant in a building that dates from 1862. The site has seen life as a repair shop for horse-drawn buggies, a gas station, and—since the mid-1950s—a restaurant. The place is always hopping with townspeople who stop by at all hours for a meal or a drink. You can get eggs and toast for breakfast, sandwiches throughout the day, and roasted chicken or liver and onions for dinner. ⊠ *6 Calle Derkes, at Calle Hostos* ☎ *787/864–1820* ⊟ *MC, V* ☉ *Closed Sun.*

Where to Stay

$ ⊞ **Molino Inn.** This tidy hotel is on the outskirts of Guayama, near the ruins of a Spanish *molino* (sugar mill). Nine acres of grounds—including flower beds and a large pool—surround its two buildings. Although the grounds are attractive and lush, the rooms are plain and provide only the basics. Join the local business crowd for the international and Caribbean cuisines at the Molinito restaurant. There's often live music on weekends. ⊠ *Av. Albizu Campos at Rte. 54, Box 2393, 00785–2393* ☎ *787/866–1515* ⌨ *787/866–1510* ⇴ *20 rooms* ⚐ *Restaurant, cable TV, tennis court, pool, basketball, lounge, laundry service* ⊟ *AE, MC, V* ⵏ *EP.*

Sports & the Outdoors

GOLF Running through an old sugar plantation, the **Aguirre Golf Club** (✉ Rte. 705, Km 3, Aguirre ☎ 787/853–4052) was built in 1925 for the executives of a local sugar mill. Open daily, the 9-hold course is short but tough. The **El Legado Golf Resort** (✉ Rte. 153 at intersection 713 ☎ 787/ 866–8894 ⊕ www.ellegadogolfresort.com), designed by golf legend and native son Chi Chi Rodríguez, is one of the island's best new courses. The 7,213-yard 18-hole course has 12 lakes.

Arroyo

17 *6 km (4 mi) east of Guayama.*

Arroyo is popular for its nearby beaches, especially Punta Guilarte, as well as its many fiestas. The festival honoring the Virgin of Carmen, patron saint of fishermen, is held every July; a fish festival is in October. Most of the events take place on the boardwalk along the *malecón* (sea wall), officially known as Paseo de Las Américas.

In 1855 Arroyo was a small but bustling port surrounded by cane fields. Today remnants of its past are scattered throughout the town. The old customs house is now a museum, and a refurbished sugarcane train, which runs on weekends and holidays, is one of the main attractions. Arroyo also contributed to the development of modern communications. Samuel F. B. Morse installed a telegraph machine in his son-in-law's farm on the outskirts of town in 1858 and connected it to another in the center of town, creating what is believed to be the Caribbean's first telegraph line. The main street is named after Morse, and there's a monument to the inventor in the main plaza. A trolley makes a scenic tour of the town with stops along the way.

An ornate pink building next to the city hall, the **Museo Antigua Aduana de Arroyo** (Museum of the Old Customs House of Arroyo), traces the history of the town and some of its well-known inhabitants, including Samuel F. B. Morse. It also has a small display of Indian artifacts and revolving exhibits of contemporary works by local artists. ✉ *65 Calle Morse* ☎ *787/839–8096* ▣ *Free* ☉ *Wed.–Fri. 9–noon and 1–4:30, weekends 9–4:30.*

NEED A BREAK? Near the waterfront walk, the ice-cream parlor **Jodymar** (✉ 46 Calle Morse ☎ No phone) is a great place to beat the heat. Try a scoop or two of one of the old-fashioned flavors like butter pecan and butter rum. It's closed Sunday.

⟳ **El Tren del Sur** (The Train of the South) takes passengers for one-hour trips along an old rail line between Arroyo and Guayama. The train carried cane from the fields to the mills from 1915 to 1958; today it's one of the island's few working trains. Call in advance; service is frequently disrupted. ✉ *Rte. 3, Km 130.9* ☎ *787/271–1574* ▣ *$3* ☉ *Trains run hrly on weekends and holidays 9:30–4:30.*

Beach

Balneario Punta Guilarte. East of Arroyo's city center, this is one of the south coast's most popular beaches. There are palm trees for shade, changing facilities, picnic tables, and barbecue grills. In summer it's crowded with locals, especially on weekends and holidays; in winter it's almost deserted. ⊠ *Off Rte. 3, 2 mi east of Arroyo.*

Where to Eat

$–$$ ✕ **La Llave del Mar.** This casual restaurant sits across from the Arroyo's waterfront walk. In the evening, tables spill out onto a tiled terrace. Popular with locals, it serves seafood dishes like broiled red snapper as well as grilled steaks. ⊠ *Paseo de Las Américas* ☎ *787/839–6395* ☴ *AE, MC, V* ⊘ *Closed Mon. and Tues.*

Patillas

⑱ *6 km (4 mi) northeast of Arroyo.*

Patillas, the so-called "Emerald of the South," is a tranquil city of about 22,000, with a small plaza and steep, narrow streets. The best sightseeing is along the coast east of town, where Route 3 skirts the Caribbean. This stretch passes rugged cliffs and beautiful beaches, many of which have not yet been discovered by visitors.

Where to Eat

$$–$$$ ✕ **El Mar de la Tranquilidad.** Get a table on the terrace at the edge of the Caribbean. You'll find good Puerto Rican cuisine and lots of seafood, including lobster, red snapper, and *mofongo* (mashed plantains with seafood). Be sure to sample one of the restaurant's daiquiris—there's a huge list from which to choose. ⊠ *Rte. 3, Km 118.9* ☎ *787/839–6469* ☴ *AE, MC, V* ⊘ *No dinner Mon.–Wed.*

Where to Stay

$ ▦ **Caribbean Paradise.** It's not right on the beach, but this family-oriented hotel is just a block away. Many of the second-floor rooms have views of the water, and all of them look out onto the little pool. The staff here can be a bit brusque. ⊠ *Rte. 3, Km 114.3* ⌂ *Box 1092, 00723* ☎ *787/839–5885* 🖷 *787/271–0069* ⊕ *www.caribbeanparadisepr.com* ⇨ *23 rooms* ⌂ *Restaurant, cable TV, pool, playground* ☴ *AE, MC, V* ⍾ *EP.*

★ $ ▦ **Caribe Playa Beach Resort.** A good base from which to explore the southeastern coast, this small hotel sits on a crescent-shaped beach that's a little rocky but still good for a refreshing dip. Unwind by the pool, in a hammock tied between coconut trees, or in the informal library. You can arrange for boat rides, fishing trips, and scuba-diving excursions. Beachfront rooms are spacious and have small kitchenettes. The Seaview Terrace is open for breakfast, lunch, and dinner; reservations are required for dinner. The hotel is close to the highway, but traffic noise is seldom a problem. ⊠ *Rte. 3, Km 112.1* ⌂ *HC 764, Box 8490, 00723* ☎ *787/839–7719 or 787/839–6339* 🖷 *787/839–1817* ⊕ *www.caribeplaya.com* ⇨ *32 rooms* ⌂ *Restaurant, kitchenettes, refrigerators, cable TV, pool, wading pool, hot tub, massage, beach, dive shop, boating, fishing, library, playground, some pets allowed* ☴ *AE, MC, V* ⍾ *EP.*

OFF THE
BEATEN
PATH **FARO DE MAUNABO** – Route 3 going eastward intersects with Route 901, the eastern portion of the cross-island Ruta Panorámica. Along the way you'll pass animals grazing in fields and cliffs that drop straight down to the ocean. If you turn off on Route 760 and take it to the end, you'll be rewarded by a dramatic view of the Faro de Maunabo (Maunabo Lighthouse, not open to the public) at Punta Tuna.

THE SOUTHWESTERN COAST

With sandy coves and palm-lined beaches tucked in the coastline's curves, southwestern Puerto Rico fulfills everyone's fantasy of a tropical paradise. The area is popular with local vacationers on weekends and holidays, but many beaches are nearly deserted on weekdays. Villages along the coast are picturesque places where oysters and fresh fish are sold at roadside stands.

Guánica

19 *38 km (24 mi) west of Ponce.*

Juan Ponce de León first explored this area in 1508, when he was searching for the elusive Fountain of Youth. Nearly 400 years later, U.S. troops landed first at Guánica during the Spanish-American War in 1898. The event is commemorated with an engraved marker on the city's malecón. Sugarcane dominated the landscape through much of the 1900s, and the ruins of the old Guánica Central sugar mill, closed in 1980, loom over the town's western area, known as Ensenada. Today most of the action takes place at the beaches and in the forests outside of Guánica.

FodorśChoice
★
The 9,900-acre **Bosque Estatal de Guánica** (Guánica State Forest), a United Nations Biosphere Reserve, is a great place for hiking expeditions. It's an outstanding example of a tropical dry coastal forest, with some 700 species of plants ranging from the prickly pear cactus to the gumbo limbo tree. It's also one of the best places on the island for bird-watching, since you can spot more than 100 species, including the pearly eyed thrasher, the lizard cockoo, and the nightjar.

> **WORD OF MOUTH**
>
> "While [in Guánica] we did some hiking in the Guánica tropical dry forest, and a little kayaking in the bay. We also had an unexpectedly fantastic lobster dinner at a little hole-in-the wall restaurant just down the street from Mary Lee's called San Jacinto Seafood Restaurant."   –trekker.

One of the most popular hikes is the **Ballena Trail,** which begins at the ranger station on Route 334. This easy 2-km (1¼-mi) walk, which follows a partially paved road, takes you past a mahogany plantation to a dry plain covered with stunted cactus. A sign reading GUAYACÁN CENTENARIO leads you to an extraordinary guayacán tree with a trunk that measures 6 feet across. The moderately difficult **Fuerte Trail** takes you on a 5 ½-km (3½-mi) hike to an old fort built by the Spanish Armada.

It was destroyed during the Spanish-American War in 1898, but you can still see the ruins of the old observatory tower.

In addition to the main entrance on Route 334, you can enter on Route 333, which skirts the forest's southwestern quadrant. You can also try the less-explored western section, off Route 325. ⊠ *Enter along Rte. 334, 333, or 325* ☎ 787/821–5706 ⊠ *Free* ⊙ *Daily 9–5.*

Off the southwest coast, near Guánica, is **Gilligan's Island,** a palm-ringed cay skirted by gorgeous beaches. You'll find picnic tables and restrooms but few other signs of civilization on this tiny island, officially part of the Bosque Estatal de Guánica. Wooden boats line up at the small dock in the San Jacinto section of Guánica, off Route 333 just past the Copamarina Beach Resort. Boats depart every hour from 10 to 5 (except Monday, when rangers close the island to visitors). Round-trip passage is $6. The island is often crowded on weekends and around holidays, but during the week you can find a spot to yourself. Nearby **Isla de Ballena,** reached by the same ferry, is much less crowded. ⊠ *Rte. 333 or 334* ☎ 787/821–5706 ⊠ *Free* ⊙ *Daily 9–5.*

Beaches

Balneario Caña Gorda. The gentle water at this beach on Route 333 washes onto a wide swath of sand fringed with palm trees. There are picnic tables, restrooms, showers, and changing facilities. ⊠ *Rte. 333, west of Copamarina Beach Resort.*

Playa Jaboncillo. Rugged cliffs make a dramatic backdrop for this little cove off Route 333, but the water can be rough. ⊠ *Rte. 333, west of Copamarina Beach Resort.*

Playa Santa. You can rent Jet Skis, kayaks, and pedal boats at this beach at the end of Route 325 in the Ensenada district. ⊠ *Rte. 325, west of Guánica.*

Where to Eat

$$–$$$$ ╳ **Alexandra.** Puerto Ricans drive for miles to reach this restaurant in the
Fodor'sChoice Copamarina Beach Resort. You won't find such creative cuisine anywhere
★ else west of Ponce. The kitchen takes traditional dishes and makes them something special; take the free-range chicken with cumin and thyme butter, for example, or the grilled pork chops with pineapple chutney. A standout is the risotto, which surrounds tender mussels with rice flavored with saffron, basil, and tomatoes. The elegant dining room looks out onto well-tended gardens; if you want to get closer to the flora, take a table outside on the terrace. The only disappointment may be noisy children, who tend to run in and out. ⊠ *Rte. 333, Km 6.5* ☎ 787/821–0505 Ext. 766 ⌂ *Reservations essential* ⊟ *AE, MC, V.*

$–$$$ ╳ **La Concha.** This family favorite specializes in all types of seafood. Mofongo leaves the kitchen overflowing with shrimp, lobster, or conch. The hearty *asopao* (a thick soup) is made with shrimp or chicken. There's also fried chicken with rice and beans and skirt steak covered with mushrooms. The restaurant is west of Guánica, past the western section of the Bosque Estatal de Guánica. From Route 116, take Route 325 to the end. ⊠ *End of Rte. 325, Playa Santa, Ensenada* ☎ 787/821–5522 ⊟ *AE, MC, V.*

$-$$$ ✕ **San Jacinto.** Popular with day-trippers to Gilligan's Island, this modest restaurant sits right at the ferry terminal. This doesn't mean, however, that the dining room has views of the Caribbean. For those, grab one of the concrete picnic tables outside. The menu is almost entirely seafood, running the gamut from fried snapper to broiled lobster. When it's not high season the menu can be limited to two or three items. ⊠ *Off Rte. 333* ☎ *787/821–4941* ▤ *MC, V.*

Where to Stay

🕒 $$–$$$ 🏨 **Copamarina Beach Resort.** Without a doubt the most beautiful resort
Fodor'sChoice on the southern coast, the Copamarina is set on 16 palm-shaded acres
★ facing the Caribbean Sea. The fruit trees and other plants are meticulously groomed, especially around the pair of swimming pools (one popular with kids, the other mostly left to the adults). All the guest rooms are generously proportioned, especially in the older building. Wood shutters on the windows and other touches lend a tropical feel. New in 2005 was a small spa whose Asian-influenced design blends seamlessly with the rest of the hotel. Both the elegant Alexandra and more casual, alfresco Las Palmas Café serve good food. All-inclusive packages, which include all meals and activities, are available. ⊠ *Rte. 333, Km 6.5, Box 805, 00653* ☎ *787/821–0505 or 800/468–4553* 🖷 *787/821–0070* ⊕ *www. copamarina.com* 🛏 *104 rooms, 2 villas* ⚷ *2 restaurants, room service, in-room safes, refrigerators, cable TV, Wi-Fi, 2 tennis courts, 2 pools, 2 wading pools, gym, 2 hot tubs, massage, spa, 2 steam rooms, beach, dive shop, snorkeling, windsurfing, boating, volleyball, 2 bars, playground, laundry facilities, business services, meeting rooms* ▤ *AE, MC, V* ⭢| *EP.*

$-$$ 🏨 **Mary Lee's by the Sea.** This me-
Fodor'sChoice andering cluster of apartments sits
★ in quiet grounds full of brightly colored flowers. It's home to Mary Lee Alvarez, and she'll make you feel like it's yours as well. Most units have ocean views; in the others you'll catch a glimpse of the mangroves by the shore as well as

> **WORD OF MOUTH**
>
> "Mary Lee's is the best."
>
> –tripster

of the cactus growing in the nearby Bosque Estatal de Guánica. Each of the one-, two-, and three-bedroom units is decorated in bright colors. Each is different, but most have terraces hung with hammocks and outfitted with barbecue grills. You can rent kayaks to drift along the coast or hop a boat bound for Gilligan's Island. ⊠ *Rte. 333, Km 6.7* ⛫ *Box 394, 00653* ☎ *787/821–3600* 🖷 *787/821–0744* ⊕ *www. maryleesbythesea.com* 🛏 *8 apartments* ⚷ *Some kitchens, some kitchenettes, 2 docks, boating, coin laundry, laundry service, some pets allowed; no room phones, no room TVs* ▤ *MC, V* ⭢| *EP.*

Sports & the Outdoors

DIVING & Dramatic walls created by the continental shelf provide great diving off
SNORKELING the Guánica coast. There are also shallow gardens around Gilligan's Island and Cayo de Caña Gorda (off Balneario Caña Gorda) that attract both snorkelers and divers. **Dive Copamarina** (⊠ Copamarina Beach Resort, Rte. 333, Km 6.5 ☎ 787/821–0505) offers instruction and trips.

Yauco

 8 km (5 mi) north of Guánica.

The picturesque town of Yauco in the southern foothills of the Cordillera Central is known for its festival celebrating the end of the coffee harvest, held each year in February. It's rumored to be the birthplace of *chuletas can-can* (twice-cooked pork chops), called "can-can" because of the resemblance the pork chop's edges have to dancers' skirts.

Where to Eat

$–$$ ✕ **La Guardarraya.** In an old-fashioned country-style house, this extremely popular restaurant serves some of the best chuletas can-can that you'll find anywhere. Other traditional dishes include stewed rice and pork, steak with onions, and fried chicken. Save room for the vanilla flan, which is the specialty of the house. This is a good place to stop for lunch or dinner when you're traveling along the southern coast on Route 2. ⊠ *Rte. 127, Km 6.0* ☎ *787/856–4222* ⊟ *AE, MC, V* ☉ *Closed Mon.*

Sports & the Outdoors

HORSEBACK **Gaby's World** (⊠ Rte. 127, Km 5.1 ☎ 787/856–2609) is a 204-acre horse
RIDING ranch that conducts ½-hour, 1-hour, and 2-hour rides through the hills surrounding Yauco. There are also pony rides for children. The on-site steak house serves Yauco's specialty, chuletas can-can.

La Parguera

 13 km (8 mi) west of Guánica; 24 km (15 mi) southwest of Yauco.

La Parguera is best known for its bioluminescent bay. Although it is not nearly as spectacular as the one of the island of Vieques, it's still a beautiful sight on a moonless night. Glass-bottom boats lined up at the town dock depart several times each evening for 45-minute trips across the bay. During the day, you can explore the nearby mangrove forest.

The town bursts at the seams with vacationers from other parts of the island on long holiday weekends and all during the summer. The town's dock area feels a bit like Coney Island, and not in a good way. Vendors in makeshift stalls hawk cheap souvenirs, and ear-splitting salsa music pours out of the open-air bars. There are signs warning people not to drink alcoholic beverages in the street, but these are cheerfully ignored.

If you're driving through the area between February and April, keep your eyes open for roadside vendors selling the area's famous pineapples, called *piñas cadezonas*. In late June there's the colorful Fiesta de San Pedro, honoring the patron saint of fishermen.

On moonless nights, large and small boats line up along the dock to take visitors out to view the **Bahía de Fosforescente** (Phosphorescent Bay) Microscopic dinoflagellates glow when disturbed by movement, invading the waves with thousands of starlike points of light. The bay's glow has diminished substantially from pollution—both light pollution from the nearby communities and water pollution from toxic chemicals being dumped into the bay. (And, yes, the smoke-belching boats that take tourists to the bay are doing damage, too.) If you've seen the bioluminescent bay in Vieques, give this one a pass. If not, you may find it mildly interesting. ⊠ *East of La Parguera.*

The eastern section of the **Bosque Estatal de Boquerón** (Boquerón State Forest) is made up of miles of mangrove forests that grow at the water's edge. Boats from the dock in La Parguera can take you on cruises through this important breeding ground for seabirds. You can also organize a kayak trip. ⊠ *East of La Parguera.*

Beaches

Cayo Caracoles. You can take a boat to and from this island for $5 per person. There are mangroves to explore as well as plenty of places to swim and snorkel. ⊠ *Boats leave from marina at La Parguera, off Rte. 304.*

Isla Mata de la Gata. For about $5 per person boats will transport you to and from this small island just off the coast for a day of swimming and snorkeling. ⊠ *Boats leave from marina at La Parguera, off Rte. 304.*

Playita Rosada. The small beach doesn't compare to some of the longer beaches on the southwestern coast, but it's a convenient place for a quick swim. ⊠ *At the end of Calle 7.*

Where to Eat

$$–$$$ ✕ **La Pared.** Many restaurants in La Paraguera sit beside the bay, but very few have an actual view. This elegant, second-floor dining room at the rear of Posada Porlamar overlooks a lovely stretch of coastline ringed by mangrove trees. The menu is the best in town, going well beyond the standard surf-and-turf offerings. There's rack of lamb, for example, but here you'll find it topped with goat cheese. The lobster tail is as fresh as anywhere else on the strip, but is topped with a tasty guanabana sauce. ⊠ *Posada Porlamar, Rte. 304, Km 3.3* ☎ *787/899–4015* ☐ *MC, V.*

$$ ✕ **La Casita.** The so-called "Little House" isn't little at all—it's a sizeable establishment that sits smack in the middle of the town's main road. Generous portions make this family-run restaurant one of the town's favorites. Try the *asopao*, which is made with shrimp, lobster, or other types of seafood. You can take a table in the rather bland ground-floor dining room or on the second-floor terrace, which has a view of the water. ⊠ *Rte. 304, Km 3.3* ☎ *787/899–1681* ☐ *MC, V* ☯ *Closed Mon.*

Where to Stay

$ ☐ **Posada Porlamar.** You might not realize it at first, but this small hotel is all about the water. Most of the comfortable rooms have views of the mangrove-ringed bay, as do the restaurant, café, and bar. In the rear you'll find a dock where you can rent a boat to explore the coastline, as well as a full-service dive shop where you can arrange snorkeling and diving excursions. And when you're finished exploring, you can relax by the pretty pool. The hotel is on La Paraguera's main drag, but far enough from the action that it's quiet at night. ⊠ *Rte. 304, Km 3.3* ⬠ *Box 3113, Lajas 00667* ☎ *787/899–4343* 🖶 *787/899–4015* ⊕ *www. parguerapuertorico.com* ⤳ *38 rooms* ⬠ *Restaurant, café, cable TV, pool, boating, dive shop, dock, lounge, bar, meeting rooms* ⊟ *MC, V* ⦿| *EP.*

★ $ 🏠 **Villa del Mar.** What sets this family-run inn apart is the warmth of the staff, which promises to take care of anything you need. The hotel, painted refreshing shades of lemon and lime, sits on a hill overlooking the boats in the bay. Not all of the squeaky clean rooms have views, so make sure to specify when you call for reservations. You'll find an open-air lounge area near the reception desk and a shimmering pool in the courtyard. You can arrange for very tasty, reasonably priced meals in the small restaurant. To find the place, take the first left as you drive into La Paraguera. ⊠ *3 Av. Albizu Campos* ⬠ *Box 1297, San Germán* ☎ *787/899–4265* ⊕ *www.pinacolada.net/villadelmar* ⤳ *25 rooms* ⬠ *Restaurant, cable TV, pool, lounge; no room phones* ⊟ *AE, MC, V* ⦿| *EP.*

$ 🏠 **Villa Parguera.** The rooms in this rambling hotel are clustered around small courtyards filled with bright tropical flowers. Many have balconies overlooking the bay, so make sure to look at a few rooms before you decide. A spacious dining room overlooking the pool serves excellent Puerto Rican and international dishes. On Saturday night there's live music and a floor show in the dance club. The staff can be a little brusque at times. ⊠ *Rte. 304, Km 3.3* ⬠ *Box 273, Lajas 00667* ☎ *787/899–7777* 🖶 *787/899–6040* ⊕ *www.villaparguera.net* ⤳ *70 rooms* ⬠ *Restaurant, cable TV, pool, dock, lounge, bar, dance club, video game room, meeting rooms* ⊟ *AE, D, DC, MC, V* ⦿| *EP.*

Nightlife & the Arts

La Parguera's dock area heats up after sunset, when crowds come to take excursions to the Bahía de Fosforescente. On weekends **Mar y Tierra** (⊠ Rte. 304, Km 3.3 ☎ 787/899–4627) is the most popular place in the strip. The open-air establishment has a couple of pool tables that are always in use. Pay attention to the sign that tells you not to put your feet on the wall.

The live floor show at **Villa Parguera** (⊠ Rte. 304, Km 2.3 ☎ 787/899–7777 or 787/899–3975) includes a buffet. The show changes frequently, but includes live music, dancing, and a comedy of the seltzer-in-your-pants variety.

Sports & the Outdoors

DIVING & SNORKELING Endangered leatherback turtles, eels, and an occasional manatee can be seen from many of the sites that attract divers and snorkelers from all parts. There are more than 50 shore-dive sites off La Parguera. **Paradise Scuba** (⊠ Hostal Casa Blanca, Rte. 304, Km 3.5 ☎ 787/899–7611) has classes and trips, including night snorkeling excursions in phosphorescent waters. **Parguera Divers** (⊠ Posada Porlamar, Rte. 304, Km 3.3 ☎ 787/899–4171 ⊕ www.pargueradivers.com) offers scuba and snorkeling expeditions and basic instruction.

FISHING You can spend a day or half-day fishing for blue marlin, tuna, or reef fish with Captain Mickey Amador at **Parguera Fishing Charters** (⊠ Rte. 304, Km 3.8 ☎ 787/382–4698 or 787/899–4698). Lunch in included in the price.

Shopping

Outdoor stands near Bahía Fosforescente sell all kinds of souvenirs, from T-shirts to beaded necklaces. In La Parguera's center, there are several small souvenir shops, including **Nautilus** (⊠ Rte. 304 ☎ 787/899–4565), which sell posters, mugs, and trinkets made from shells.

San Germán

4

10 km (6 mi) north of La Parguera, 166 km (104 mi) southwest of San Juan.

During its early years, San Germán was a city on the move. Although debate rages about the first settlement's exact founding date and location, the town is believed to have been established in 1510 near Guánica. Plagued by mosquitoes, the settlers moved north along the west coast, where they encountered French pirates and smugglers. In the 1570s they fled inland to the current location, but they were still harassed. Determined and creative, they dug tunnels and moved beneath the city (the tunnels are now part of the water system). Today San Germán has a population of 39,000, and its intellectual and political activity is anything but underground. It's very much a college town, and students and professors from the Inter-American University often fill the bars and cafés.

Around San Germán's two main squares—Plazuela Santo Domingo and Plaza Francisco Mariano Quiñones (named for an abolitionist)—are buildings done in every conceivable style of architecture found on the island including mission, Victorian, creole, and Spanish colonial. The city's tourist office offers a free guided trolley tour. Most of the buildings are private homes; two of them—the Capilla de Porta Coeli and the Museo de Arte y Casa de Estudio—are museums. The historical center is surrounded by strip malls, and the town is hemmed to the south and west by busy seaside resorts.

▌A GOOD
TOUR

The best place to start is Plazuela Santo Domingo, the sun-baked park in the center of the historic district. At the eastern edge of the park is the **Capilla de Porta Coeli** ㉒ ☛, perched at the top of an imposing set of stairs. From the top you get a good view of the rest of the city. Several historic homes, none of them open to the public, are within a block of the Capilla de Porta Coeli. Across the street is the **Casa Morales** ㉓, striking for its Victorian-style gables. It would not look out of place in any New England hamlet. Half a block north on Calle Dr. Santiago Veve are two criollo-style houses, **Casa Kindy** ㉔ and **Casa Acosta y Forés** ㉕. A block south of the Capilla de Porta Coeli is one of the most beautiful homes in San Germán, **Casa Perichi** ㉖.

Head west through Plazuela Santo Domingo. The hulking yellow building you see at the northwest corner of the park is the rear of the **Alcaldía Antigua** ㉗. It faces the town's other park, the Plaza Francisco Mariano

Quiñones. This park is more popular with locals, as the tree-shaded benches are a pleasant place to watch the world go by. On the park's northern edge is **La Casona** ㉘, one of the town's best-preserved criollo-style buildings. The most imposing structure on the park, however, is the **Iglesia de San Germán de Auxerre** ㉙.

A block and a half west of the church is the **Casa de Lola Rodríguez de Tió** ㉚, on Calle Dr. Santiago Veve. It's one of the best examples of criollo-style architecture in the city. Backtrack to Calle Esperanza and head two blocks south to where you'll find the **Museo de Arte y Casa de Estudio** ㉛.

TIMING   San Germán's historic district is compact, so you can cover all the sights in about 1½ hours. You'll want to budget a bit more time to stroll around the nearby streets. Be sure to wear comfortable shoes, as there will be a lot of walking uphill and downhill on cobbled streets.

What to See

㉗ **Alcaldía Antigua** (Old Municipal Building). At the eastern end of Plaza Francisco Mariano Quiñones, this Spanish colonial–style building served as the town's city hall from 1844 to 1950. Once used as a prison, the building is now the headquarters for the police department. ✉ *East end of Plaza Francisco Mariano Quiñones.*

★ ㉒ **Capilla de Porta Coeli** (Heaven's Gate Chapel). One of the oldest religious buildings in the Americas, this mission-style chapel overlooks the long, rectangular Plazuela de Santo Domingo. It's not a grand building, but its position at the top of a stone stairway gives it a noble air. Queen Isabel Segunda decreed that the Dominicans should build a church and monastery in San Germán, so a rudimentary building was built in 1609, replaced in 1692 by the structure that can still be seen today. (Sadly, most of the monastery was demolished in 1866, leaving only a vestige of its facade.) The chapel now functions as a museum of religious art, displaying painted wooden statuary by Latin American and Spanish artists. ✉ *East end of Plazuela Santo Domingo* ☎ *787/892–5845* ⊕ *www.icp. gobierno.pr* ☞ *Free* ⊗ *Wed.–Sun. 8:30–noon and 1 to 4:15.*

㉕ **Casa Acosta y Forés.** A few doors down from Casa de los Kindy is this beautiful yellow-and-white wooden house dating from 1918. Although the front of the house is typical criollo architecture, the side entrance is covered with an ornate Victorian-style porch. The house isn't open to the public. ✉ *70 Calle Dr. Santiago Veve.*

㉚ **Casa de Lola Rodríguez de Tió** On the National Registry of Historic Places, this house bears the name of poet and activist Lola Rodríguez de Tió. A plaque claims she lived in this creole-style house, though town officials believe it actually belonged to her sister. Rodríguez, whose mother was a descendent of Ponce de León, was deported several times by Spanish authorities for her revolutionary ideas. She lived in Venezuela and then in Cuba, where she died in 1924. The museum, which contains Rodríguez's desk and papers, isn't open regular hours; call ahead to schedule a tour. ✉ *13 Calle Dr. Santiago Veve* ☎ *787/892–3500* ☞ *Free* ⊗ *By appointment only.*

㉔ **Casa Kindy.** East of the Plazuela de Santo Domingo, this 19th-century home is known for its eclectic architecture, which mixes neoclassical and criollo elements. Note the elegant stained-glass windows over the front windows. It's now a private residence. ✉ *64 Calle Dr. Santiago Veve.*

㉓ **Casa Morales.** Facing Plazuela de Santo Domingo, this Victorian-style house was designed in 1913 by architect Pedro Vivoni for his brother, Tomás Vivoni. The gleaming white structure has numerous towers and gables. The current owners have kept it in mint condition. It is not open to the public. ✉ *38 Calle Ramos.*

㉖ **Casa Perichi.** You'll find an excellent example of Puerto Rican ornamental architecture in this elegant mansion, which sits a block south of Plazuela Santo Domingo. This gigantic white home, on the National Register of Historic Places, was built in 1920. Note the sensuous curves of the wraparound balcony and wood trim around the doors. It's not open to the public. ✉ *94 Calle Luna.*

㉘ **La Casona.** On the north side of Plaza Francisco Mariano Quiñones, this two-story home was built in 1871 for Tomás Agrait. (If you look closely, you can still see his initials in the wrought-iron decorations.) For many years it served as a center of cultural activities in San Germán. Today it holds several shops. ✉ *Calle José Julien Acosta and Calle Cruz.*

CLOSE UP

Lives of the Santos

WHEN THEY ARRIVED ON PUERTO RICO, Spanish missionaries spread the word of God and fostered a spirited folk art. Since few people were literate, the missionaries often commissioned local artisans to create pictures and statues depicting Bible stories and saints or *santos*. These figures—fashioned of wood, clay, stone, or even gold—are still given a place of honor in homes throughout the island.

Early *santeros* (carvers) were influenced by the Spanish baroque style. Later figures are simple and small, averaging about 8 inches tall. The carving of santos is usually a family tradition, and most of today's santeros have no formal art training. San Germán has been associated with santos-making since the origins of the art form, and the Rivera family has been known for its carvings for more than 150 years.

Each santo has a traditional characteristic. You can spot the Virgin by her blue robes, St. Francis by the accompanying birds and animals, St. Barbara by her tower, and the Holy Spirit by its hovering dove. St. John, the island's patron saint, is an ever-popular subject, as is the Nativity, which might be just the Holy Family, or the family with an entire cast of herald angels, shepherds, and barnyard animals.

Carvings of Los Santos Reyes (The Three Kings) are also popular. Their feast day, January 6, is important on Puerto Rico. Celebrations often continue for days before or after the actual holiday, when it's difficult to find a home without these regal characters. In Puerto Rico one king is often strumming the *cuatro*, an island guitar.

㉘ **Iglesia de San Germán de Auxerre.** Dating from 1739, this neoclassical church has seen many additions over the years. For example, the impressive crystal chandelier was added in 1860. Be sure to take a look at the carved-wood ceiling in the nave. This church is still in use, so the only time you can get a look inside is during services. ✉ *West side of Plaza Francisco Mariano Quiñones* ☎ *787/892–1027* ☉ *Mass Mon.–Sat. at 7* AM *and 7:30* PM *and Sun. at 7, 8:30, 10* AM, *and 7:30* PM.

㉛ **Museo de Arte y Casa de Estudio.** This early-20th-century home—built in the criollo style with some obvious neoclassical influences—has been turned into a museum. Displays include colonial furnishings, religious art, and artifacts of the indigenous peoples; there are also changing exhibits by local artists. ✉ *7 Calle Esperanza* ☎ *787/892–8870* 🎟 *Free* ☉ *Wed.–Sun. 10–noon and 1–3.*

Where to Eat

$–$$ ✕ **Chaparritas.** On San Germán's main drag, this place certainly feels like a traditional cantina. The Mexican food here is the real deal. Although you'll find some dishes that are more Tex than Mex, such as the cheesy nachos, the kitchen does best with more authentic tacos, burritos, and enchiladas. For something a bit more off the wall, try the shrimp fried in tequila. ⊠ *Calle Luna 171* ☎ *787/892–1078* ☉ *Closed Sun.–Wed.*

★ ¢–$ ✕ **Tapas Café.** One of the biggest surprises in San Germán is this wonderful little restaurant facing Plaza Santo Domingo. The dining room looks like a Spanish courtyard, complete with blue stars swirling around the ceiling. Don't expect tiny portions just because it serves tapas—several of the dishes, including the medallions of beef topped with a dab of blue cheese, could pass as full entrées anywhere. You'll find old favorites on the menu, including spicy sausage in red wine, but some new creations as well, such as the yam and codfish fritters. ⊠ *50 Calle Dr. Santiago Veve* ☎ *787/264–0610* ▤ *MC, V* ☉ *Closed Mon. and Tues. No lunch Wed. and Thurs.*

Where to Stay

$ ▦ **Villa del Rey.** On a quiet country road, Villa del Rey is set among banana and papaya trees. This family-run inn couldn't be simpler, but it's clean and comfortable. The rooms are larger than you'll find in most of the region's lodgings. The patio around the pool is a bit rundown, but the pool itself is refreshing on a hot afternoon. A restaurant and bar are planned for the future. ⊠ *Rte. 361, Km 0.8, off Rte. 2* ⌂ *Box 3033, 00667* ☎ *787/264–2542 or 787/642–2627* 🖷 *787/264–1579* ⊕ *www. villadelrey.net* ⇆ *19 rooms* ⓖ *Some kitchenettes, pool, meeting room* ▤ *MC, V* ❌ *EP.*

¢ ▦ **Parador Oasis.** The only hotel in the center of San Germán is a 200-year-old hacienda. This description makes the place sound prettier than it is, as an ill-considered addition takes away all the charm. Many of the rooms are small and dark, so ask to see a few before you decide. The restaurant's menu hasn't changed for years, but it serves generous portions of Puerto Rican food. ⊠ *72 Calle Luna, Box 1063, 00683* ☎ *787/892–1175* 🖷 *787/892–4546* ⇆ *52 rooms* ⓖ *Restaurant, cable TV, in-room data ports, pool, bar* ▤ *AE, D, DC, MC, V* ❌ *EP.*

Shopping

In the yellow-and-green La Casona, **Casa Vieja** (⊠ Calle José Julien Acosta and Calle Cruz ☎ 787/264–3954) is a small shop that carries an interesting selection of Caribbean antiques.

PONCE & THE SOUTHERN COAST ESSENTIALS

To research prices, get advice from other travelers, and book travel arrangements, visit www.fodors.com.

Transportation

BY AIR

Aeropuerto Mercedita (PSE) is about 8 km (5 mi) east of Ponce's downtown. The airport is so tiny that between flights there may be nobody in the terminal besides you and a bored-looking security guard. Needless to say, there are almost no amenities. The only international flights are on Continental, which shuttles between Ponce and Newark. Cape Air flies several times a day from San Juan.

Taxis at the airport operate under a meter system, so expect to pay about $6 to get downtown Ponce. Some hotels have shuttles from the airport, but you must make arrangements in advance.

🛪 **Airlines Cape Air** ☎ 800/525-0280 ⊕ www.flycapeair.com. **Continental** ☎ 800/231-0856 ⊕ www.continental.com.

🛪 **Airport Aeropuerto Mercedita** PSE ⊠ Rte. 506 off Rte. 52, Ponce ☎ 787/842-6292.

BY BUS

There's no easy network of buses linking the towns in southern Puerto Rico with the capital of San Juan or with each other. Some municipalities and private companies operate buses or *públicos* (usually large vans) that make many stops. Call ahead; although reservations aren't usually required, you'll need to check on schedules, which change frequently. The cost of a público from Ponce to San Juan is about $15 to $20; agree on a price before you start your journey.

🛪 **Choferes Unidos de Ponce** ⊠ Terminal de Carros Públicos, Calle Vives and Calle Mendéz Vigo, Ponce Centro, Ponce ☎ 787/842-1222. **Línea Sangermeña** ⊠ Terminal de Carros Públicos, Calle Luna at entrance to town, San Germán ☎ 787/722-3392.

BY CAR

A car is pretty much a necessity if you are exploring Puerto Rico's southern coast. Without one you'd find getting anywhere—even to the beach or to a restaurant—frustrating. You can rent cars at the Luis Muñoz Marín International Airport and other San Juan locations. There are also car-rental agencies in some of the larger cities along the south coast. Rates run about $35 to $45 a day, depending on the car. You may get a better deal if you rent a car for a week or more. Test your vehicle before heading out to be sure it runs properly.

A road map is essential in southern Puerto Rico. So is patience: allow extra time for twisting mountain roads and wrong turns. Some roads, especially in rural areas, aren't plainly marked. The fastest route through the region is the Luis Ferré Expressway (Route 52), a toll road that runs from San Juan to Ponce, crossing the island's central mountain range. The trip takes about 1½ hours.

🛪 **Avis** ⊠ Mercedita Airport, Ponce ☎ 787/842-6154. **Budget** ⊠ Mercedita Airport, Ponce ☎ 787/848-0907. **Dollar** ⊠ Av. Los Caobos and Calle Acacia, Ponce ☎ 787/843-6940. **Leaseway of Puerto Rico** ⊠ Rte. 3, Km 140.1, Guayama ☎ 787/864-8149 ⊕ www.leasewaypr.com 🖃 Ponce ☎ 787/843-4330.

EMERGENCY SERVICES There's no AAA service in Puerto Rico, but independent tow trucks regularly scout the Luis A. Ferré Expressway (Route 52) looking for disabled vehicles. Police also patrol the expressway. A number of towing companies will send trucks on request.

🛪 **Alfredo Towing Service** ☎ 787/251-6750. **Dennis Towing** ☎ 787/504-5724.

GASOLINE Gas stations are plentiful, particularly near expressway exits and at town entrances on secondary roads. Some stations are open 24 hours, but many close at around midnight or 1 AM. Prices in Puerto Rico are given in liters.

PARKING You can find free on-street parking in most southern cities; metered parking is rare. Larger communities have lots in their downtown areas. Prices are usually less than $1 an hour.

ROAD CONDITIONS Major highways in southern Puerto Rico are well maintained. You may encounter some construction on Highway 2 between Ponce and Guánica. Watch out for potholes on secondary roads, especially after heavy rains.

BY PUBLIC TRANSPORTATION

Ponce offers free transportation to its major attractions on its *"chu chu"* train. (It's actually a tram.) They run daily from 8:30 AM to about 7:30 PM, and leave from Plaza las Delicias. On Sunday, Guayama has a free trolley that runs to many sights. Arroyo's free trolley operations on Saturday and Sunday, and a trolley tour of San Germán is available by appointment.

Arroyo Trolley ⊠ Acaldía de Arroyo, 64 Calle Morse, Arroyo ☎ 787/721-1574. **Guayama Trolley** ⊠ Acaldía de Guayama, Calle Vicente Pales, Guayama ☎ 787/864-7765. **Ponce Trolley & Chu Chu** ⊠ Plaza las Delicias, Ponce Centro, Ponce ☎ 787/841-8160. **San Germán Trolley** ⊠ Acaldía de San Germán, 136 Calle Luna, San Germán ☎ 787/892-3500.

BY TAXI

In Ponce you can hail taxis in tourist areas and outside hotels. In smaller towns it's best to call a taxi. You can also hire a car service (make arrangements through your hotel); often you can negotiate a rate that's lower than what you would pay for a taxi.

Borinquen Taxi ☎ 787/843-6000 in Ponce. **Ojeda Taxi** ☎ 787/259-7676 in San Germán.

Contacts & Resources

BANKS & EXCHANGE SERVICES

You'll find plenty of banks in the region, and many supermarkets, drug stores, and gas stations have ATMs. Banks are normally open weekdays from 9 AM to 3 PM or 4 PM. Some banks—such as the Scotiabank branch in Ponce—are also open until noon on Saturday. You can exchange foreign currency in Banco Popular branches; Scotiabank exchanges Canadian currency. Western Union service is available at Pueblo Supermarkets.

Banco Popular ⊠ Plaza Guayama, Rte. 3, Km 134.9, Guayama ☎ 787/866-0180 ⊠ Plaza las Delicias, Ponce Centro, Ponce ☎ 787/843-8000. **Scotiabank** ⊠ Plaza las Delicias, Ponce Centro, Ponce ☎ 787/259-8535.

EMERGENCIES

Emergency Number General Emergencies ☎ 911.

Hospitals Hospital de la Concepción ⊠ 41 Calle Luna, San Germán ☎ 787/892-1860. **Hospital de Damas** ⊠ 2213 Ponce Bypass Rd., Villa Grillasca, Ponce ☎ 787/840-8686.

Pharmacies Walgreens ⊠ 1 Calle Marginal, Guayama ☎ 787/864-5355 ⊠ 13 Av. Fagot, Ponce Centro, Ponce ☎ 787/841-2135 ⊠ 64 Calle Luna, San Germán ☎ 787/892-1170.

INTERNET, MAIL & SHIPPING

Internet cafés are few and far between in this part of the island. If you'll need to be wired on your trip, make sure that your hotel has an Internet connection.

There are branches of the U.S. Post Office throughout the region. You can buy stamps in Pueblo Supermarkets and in many gift shops.

🖪 Post Offices **Guayama Post Office** ✉ 151 Calle Ashford, Guayama ☎ 787/864-1150. **Ponce Post Office** ✉ 94 Calle Atocha, Ponce Centro, Ponce ☎ 787/842-2997.

OVERNIGHT SERVICES Express delivery services are available at the U.S. Post Office. Some shops are authorized to handle Federal Express (FedEx) packages, and there are FedEx stations in Ponce and Guayama. Note that there's no Saturday pick-up service in the area. You can drop off packages and U.S. mail at area PostNet stores, which also sell envelopes and boxes.

🖪 **FedEx** ✉ Plaza Guayama, Rte. 3, Km 134.9, Guayama ☎ 877/838-7834 ✉ Mercedita Airport, Ponce ☎ 877/838-7834.

TOUR OPTIONS

Alelí Tours and Encantos Ecotours Southwest in La Parguera offer ecological tours of the southwestern area, including two- or three-hour kayak trips that cost about $25.

🖪 **Alelí Tours** ✉ Rte. 304, Km 3.2, La Parguera ☎ 787/390-6086. **Encantos Ecotours Southwest** ✉ El Muelle Shopping Center, Av. Pescadores, La Parguera ☎ 787/808-0005.

VISITOR INFORMATION

In Ponce the municipal tourist office is open weekdays from 8 to 4:30, as is the small information desk in the Parque de Bombas. The Puerto Rico Tourism Company's office in the Paseo del Sur plaza is open weekdays from 8 to 5. Smaller cities generally have a tourism office in the city hall that's open weekdays from 8 to noon and 1 to 4.

🖪 **Ponce Municipal Tourist Office** ✉ 2nd fl. of Citibank, Plaza las Delicias, Ponce Centro, Ponce ☎ 787/841-8160 or 787/841-8044. **Puerto Rico Tourism Company** ✉ 291 Av. Los Caobos, Sector Vallas Torres, Ponce ☎ 787/843-0465 ⊕ welcome.topuertorico.org.

Rincón & the Porta del Sol

5

WORD OF MOUTH

"I like Rincon, a little surfing town on the West side of the island. Many restaurant options & a very nice laid-back vibe."

—SAnParis

"Boquerón is a glorious little village on the west coast of PR."

—tripster

Revised and
Updated by
Mark Sullivan

THE "GATEWAY TO THE SUN" is how tourism officials describe the island's western coast. Although the name calls to mind well-developed, well-traveled vacations spots like Spain's Costa de Sol, the Porta del Sol is neither. Unlike the area around San Juan, the Porta del Sol is relatively undiscovered. Even around Rincón, which has the lion's share of the lodgings, the beaches are delightfully deserted. And in places like Aguadilla and Isabela, two sleepy towns on the northwestern corner of the island, it's easy to find a stretch of shoreline all to yourself.

Adventurers since the time of Christopher Columbus have been drawn to the jagged coastline of northwestern Puerto Rico. Columbus made his first stop here on his second voyage to the Americas in 1493. His exact landing point is the subject of ongoing dispute: both Aguadilla on the northernmost tip of the coast and Aguada, just to Aguadilla's south, claim the historic landing, and both have monuments honoring the explorer.

Less than a century ago, western Puerto Rico was still overwhelmingly rural. Some large fruit plantations dotted the coast, while farther inland coffee was grown on hillside *fincas* (farms). The slow pace began to change during the mid-20th century. New roads brought development to the once-isolated towns. They also brought surfers, who were amazed to find some of the best waves in the Caribbean. There are also long beaches of golden sand. Now there are top-notch hotels, interesting natural areas to explore, and almost every kind of water sport imaginable.

Exploring Rincón & the Porta del Sol

The speedy Highway 22 and the more meandering Highway 2 head west from San Juan and swing around the northwestern part of the island, skirting the beaches of the northern coast. A short 45 minutes from the capital you'll pass through the resort town of Dorado; after Arecibo, Highway 2 continues along the coast, where the ragged shoreline holds some of the island's best surfing beaches, and a steady contingent of surfers in Aguadilla and Rincón gives the area a laid-back atmosphere. Past Mayagüez, Highway 100 leads to an area known as Cabo Rojo, where you'll find seaside communities like Joyuda, Boquerón, and El Combate.

Numbers in the text correspond to numbers in the margin and on the Northwestern Puerto Rico map.

About the Restaurants

Throughout northwestern Puerto Rico you'll find wonderful *criollo* cuisine, interspersed with international restaurants ranging from French to Japanese. You can enjoy five-course meals in elegant surroundings at night, then sip coffee on an outdoor balcony the next morning. Tips, normally 15% to 20%, are usually not included in the bill, but it's always wise to double-check.

WHAT IT COSTS In U.S. dollars				
$$$$	$$$	$$	$	¢
AT DINNER over $30	$20–$30	$12–$20	$8–$12	under $8

Prices are per person for a main course at dinner.

TOP 5 PICKS FOR RINCÓN & THE PORTA DEL SOL

- Hiking to the lighthouse at El Combate, a peninsula that juts out into the Caribbean Sea.
- Relaxing in your private plunge pool at the Horned Dorset Primavera, perhaps the most romantic inn in the Caribbean.
- Sampling fresh seafood at any of the dozens of oceanfront eateries along Joyuda's "Golden Mile."

- Challenging the waves at Playa Tres Palmas or any other of Rincón's world-famous surfing spots.
- Island-hopping to Desecheo Island or Mona Island.

About the Hotels

Lodging in the area runs the gamut from posh resorts offering wind-surfing lessons to rustic cabins in the middle of a forest reserve. The western part of the island near Rincón has a variety of hotels, from furnished apartments geared toward families to colorful small hotels. In the central mountains a few old plantation homes have been turned into wonderful country inns that transport you back to slower and quieter times.

WHAT IT COSTS In U.S. dollars					
	$$$$	$$$	$$	$	¢
FOR 2 PEOPLE	over $350	$250–$350	$150–$250	$80–$150	under $80

Prices are for a double room in high season, excluding 9% tax (11% for hotels with casinos, 7% for paradores) and 5%–12% service charge.

Timing

In winter the weather is at its best, but you'll have to compete with other visitors for hotel rooms; book well in advance. Winter is also the height of the surfing season on the west coast. In summer many family-oriented hotels fill up with *sanjuaneros* escaping the city for the weekend—some hotels require a two-night stay. Larger resorts normally drop their rates in summer by at least 10%. The weather gets hot, especially in August and September, but the beaches help keep everyone cool.

RINCÓN

❶ *150 km (93 mi) southwest of San Juan*

Jutting out into the ocean along the rugged western coast, Rincón, meaning "corner" in Spanish, may have gotten its name because of how it's nestled in a corner of the coastline. Some, however, trace the town's name to Gonzalo Rincón, a 16th-century landowner who let poor families live on his land. Whatever the history, the name suits the town, which is like a little world unto itself.

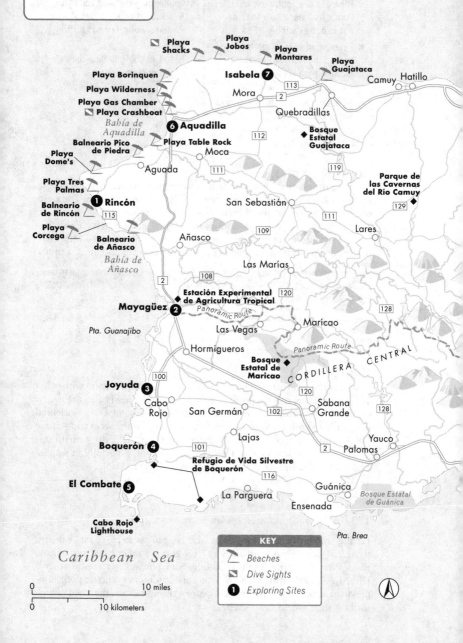

Rincón & the Porta del Sol

ATLANTIC OCEAN

Playa Shacks

Playa Jobos

Playa Montares

Playa Guajataca

Isabela **7**

Camuy   Hatillo

Playa Borinquen

Playa Wilderness

Playa Gas Chamber

Playa Crashboat

Mora

113

2

Quebradillas

Bahía de Aquadilla

6 Aquadilla

Playa Table Rock

112

Bosque Estatal Guajataca

Balneario Pico de Piedra

Moca

111

119

Parque de las Cavernas del Río Camuy

Playa Dome's

Aguada

Playa Tres Palmas

San Sebastián

129

Balneario de Rincón

1 Rincón

115

Añasco

109

111

Lares

Playa Corcega

Balneario de Añasco

Bahía de Añasco

Las Marías

2

108

120

Estación Experimental de Agricultura Tropical

Mayagüez **2**

Panoramic Route

128

Pta. Guanajibo

Las Vegas

Marícao

Panoramic Route

CENTRAL

Hormigueros

Bosque Estatal de Marícao

CORDILLERA

Joyuda **3**

100

120

Cabo Rojo

San Germán

102

Sabana Grande

128

Lajas

Boquerón **4**

101

2

Palomas

Yauco

Refugio de Vida Silvestre de Boquerón

116

Guánica

Bosque Estatal de Guánica

El Combate **5**

La Parguera

Ensenada

Cabo Rojo Lighthouse

Pta. Brea

Caribbean Sea

KEY	
⊼	*Beaches*
◱	*Dive Sights*
1	*Exploring Sites*

0 ——————— 10 miles

0 ——————— 10 kilometers

The most famous hotel in the region is the Horned Dorset Primavera—the only Relais & Chateaux property in Puerto Rico. It's one of the most luxurious resorts on the island, not to mention the Caribbean. A couple of larger hotels, including the Rincón of the Seas and Rincón Beach Resort, have been built, but Rincón remains a laid-back place. The town is still a mecca for wave-seekers, particularly surfers from the East Coast of the United States, who can make the relatively quick flight to Aguadilla airport direct from New York–area airports instead of the long haul to the Pacific. The town continues to cater to all sorts of travelers, from budget-conscious surfers to families to honeymooners seeking romance.

The beat picks up from October through April, when the waves are the best, but tourists can be found here year-round, and many American mainlanders have settled here.

Surrounding the Punta Higuera Lighthouse, **Parque Pasivo El Faro** has small kiosks at the water's edge with telescopes you can use to look for whales. (Have patience, though, even during the "season," from December through February; it could take days to spot one.) You can also glimpse the rusting dome of the defunct Bonus Thermonuclear Energy Plant from here; it has been closed since 1974, but is being resurrected as a nuclear-energy museum. The park is a nice place to take in sunsets, and there are also benches, a shop, and a refreshment stand on the grounds. The lighthouse is closed to the public, but it's hard to walk away without taking a photo of the stately white structure. Half a block up the street are a playground and a paintball course. ⊠ *End of Calle 4413, off Rte. 413* 🖹 *Free* ⊙ *Daily 8 AM–midnight.*

For divers, **Desecheo Island,** about 20 km (13 mi) off the coast of Rincón, has abundant reef and fish life. A rocky bottom sloping to 120 feet rims the island; one formation known as Yellow Reef is distinguished by long tunnels and caverns covered with purple hydrocoral. There are other sites with plentiful fish and coral in the shallower water just off Rincón's shores.

Beaches

The best beaches north of Rincón are lined up along Route 413 and Route 4413 (the road to the lighthouse). South of town the only beach worth noting is Playa Córcega, off Route 115. The beaches below are in geographical order, north to south.

Balneario de Rincón. Swimmers can enjoy the tranquil waters at this beach. The beautiful facility has a playground, changing areas, restrooms, and a clubhouse. It's within walking distance of the center of town. Parking is $2. ⊠ *Rte. 115.*

Domes. Named for the eerie green domes on a nearby power plant, this beach is extremely popular with

CAUTION

The waves in the Rincón area run the gamut from gentle, low waves suitable for novice surfers to expert-only breaks. It's a good idea to talk with other surfers about which beaches would be suitable for your skill level.

surfers. It's also a great whale-watching spot in winter. To get here, head north on Route 4413. The beach is just north of the lighthouse. ⊠ *Rte. 4413, north of the lighthouse.*

Maria's. This surf spot, south of Domes, can get crowded when the waves are high. It's popular with locals, as much for its breakers as for its proximity to the Calypso Café. To get here, look for the street sign reading SURFER CROSSING. ⊠ *Rte. 4413, south of the lighthouse.*

Playa Córcega. The long stretch of yellow sand in front of Villa Cofresí is considered one of the best swimming beaches in Rincón. ⊠ *Rte. 115, Km 12.0.*

Steps. A set of concrete steps sitting mysteriously at the water's edge gives this beach its name. The waves here can get huge. It's hard to find—look for the turnoff at a whale-shaped sign indicating PLAYA ESCALERA. ⊠ *Rte. 413, north of turnoff for Black Eagle Marina.*

Tres Palmas. When the surf is on here—which may be only a handful of days each year, at best—this epic wave spot is one of the world's best. At other times, it's an excellent snorkeling spot. It is on the same road at Steps. ⊠ *Rte. 413, north of turnoff for Black Eagle Marina.*

Where to Eat

In addition to the restaurants recommended below, the Villa Confresí and the Lazy Parrot hotels also have good restaurants serving fresh seafood.

$$$$ ✕ **Horned Dorset Primavera.** People come from all over the island for a
FodorśChoice meal at the Horned Dorset Primavera, and it's easy to see why. A pair
★ of stone stairways sweep you up to the elegant dining room, with black-and-white marble floors and chandeliers with ruby-red shades. From the terrace you'll hear the constant crash of the waves. Chef Aaron Wratten has been doing double duty since he bought the restaurant in 2005, but you can't tell from the delights that stream out of the kitchen. The five-course daily menu and the nine-course tasting menu change daily, but might include pan-seared scallops with asparagus risotto or roasted grouper with pumpkin purée. Dress is formal by island standards, meaning that no shorts are allowed. One disappointment: the wine list is well-traveled, but not to budget destinations. ⊠ *Rte. 429, Km 3, Box 1132, 00677* ☎ *787/823–4030* ⌂ *Reservations essential* ☰ *AE, MC, V.*

$–$$ ✕ **Rincón Tropical.** Don't be scared off by the cheap plastic tables and chairs. What you should notice is that they are almost always full of locals enjoying the area's freshest seafood. The kitchen keeps it simple, preparing dishes with the lightest touch. Highlights include the mahimahi with onions and peppers, or fried red snapper with beans and rice. Fried plantains make a nice accompaniment to almost anything. ⊠ *Rte. 115, Km 12* ☎ *787/823–2017* ☰ *AE, MC, V.*

IF YOU LIKE

EATING WELL

If you like seafood, you're in the right place. Simply stop at one of the seafood shacks in Joyuda—a place so well-known for its fresh fish that people come here from as far away as Ponce and San Juan. You'll do no better anywhere else on the island. In Boquerón people line up at pushcarts where vendors sell oysters on the half shell. (Hot sauce is optional.) If you're in Rincón, the Horned Dorset Primavera has one of the most elegant eateries in the Caribbean.

ECOTOURISM

The concept of ecotourism is catching on in Puerto Rico. Not surprisingly, many outfits are based in Rincón and center around trips to Mona Island. This protected island has world-class diving as well as a series of trails that wind their way along the edge of steep cliffs.

SURFING

The waves of northwestern Puerto Rico have long served as siren-song for traveling surfers. Spared the trade winds that can limit surf in other areas, its beaches have some of the best waves in the world, especially in winter. Rincón first drew international attention when it hosted the World Surfing Championship in 1968. Other areas on the north coast, such as Aguadilla, have impressive waves as well. The area around Isabela has some well-known breaks but this stretch of coast can reveal some hidden gems to those willing to explore a little.

¢–$ ✕ **Tamboo.** Here is a bar and grill that doesn't fall too much into either category. The open-air kitchen prepares any number of unusual items, from king-crab sandwiches to chicken-and-basil wraps. The bar, also open to the elements, serves a mean margarita. Happy hour sometimes starts dangerously early—at 10 AM on Saturday. The deck is a great place to watch the novice surfers wipe out on the nearby beach. ⊠ *Rte. 413, Km 4.7* ☎ *787/823–3210* ▭ *MC, V.*

¢ ✕ **Cowabunga's.** This little place is Rincón's answer to Ben & Jerry's. (It even borrowed the trademark cow spots for its facade.) The 16 flavors, especially the creamy butter pecan, are a blast from the past. After taking on the town's legendary waves, you can sit down to a juicy hamburger or hot dog while surfing though cyberspace at one of the lightning-fast terminals or thumbing through a tome from the lending library. ⊠ *Rte. 115, Km 11.6* ☎ *787/823–5225* ▭ *AE, MC, V.*

Where to Stay

$$$$ ▢ **Horned Dorset Primavera.** This is, without a doubt, the most luxuri-
Fodor'sChoice ous hotel in Puerto Rico. The 22 whitewashed villas scattered around
★ throughout the tropical gardens are designed so you have complete privacy whether you are relaxing in your private plunge pool or admiring the sunset from one of your balconies. The furnishings in each of the two-story suites are impeccable, from the hand-carved mahogany table in the downstairs dining room to the four-poster beds in the upstairs

bedroom. The marble bathroom has a footed porcelain tub that's big enough for two. (There's a second bath downstairs that's perfect for showering off after a walk on the beach.) Breakfast is served in your room, and lunch is available on a terrace overlooking the ocean. Dinner in the elegant restaurant is a must. A place to unplug from the rest of the world, the hotel has no radios or televisions, and does not allow children younger than 12. ✉ *Rte. 429, Km 3, Box 1132, 00677* ☎ *787/823–4030, 787/823–4050, or 800/633–1857* 🖷 *787/725–6068* 🌐 *www.horneddorset.com* *22 villas* *Restaurant, fans, 2 in-room safes, kitchenettes, 2 pools, gym, massage, beach, croquet, library, bar; no room TVs, no kids under 12* 💳 *AE, MC, V* 🍽 *EP.*

HORNED DORSET PRIMAVERA

"If you want an amazing beach, entertainment or nightlife, I'd seek elsewhere. If you want fabulous accomodations, excellent service, and amazing dining, seek no further." –Ben, from Chicago, IL.

$$–$$$ **Rincón Beach Resort.** Although it's a bit off the beaten path, that's part of the allure of this oceanfront hotel. The South Seas–style decor begins in the high-ceilinged lobby, where hand-carved chaises invite you to enjoy the view through the almond trees. The rooms continue the theme with rich fabrics and dark-wood furnishings. A variety of activities are available, including whale- and turtle-watching in season. At the end of the infinity pool, a boardwalk leads down to the sand. Unlike many of the beaches just a few miles north, the waters here are calm—not great for surfing, but perfect for a dip if you're staying here. The resort is tucked away in Añasco, about halfway between Rincón to the north and Mayagüez to the south. ✉ *Rte. 115, Km 5.8, Añasco 00610* ☎ *787/589–9000* 🖷 *787/589–9010* 🌐 *www.rinconbeach.com* *112 rooms* *Restaurant, room service, fans, in-room safes, some kitchenettes, refrigerators, cable TV, in-room data ports, pool, gym, beach, dive shop, snorkeling, boating, 2 bars, babysitting, business services, free parking* 💳 *AE, D, DC, MC, V* 🍽 *EP.*

$$–$$$ **Rincón of the Seas.** Tucked at the end of a palm-lined drive, this hotel feels like it could be in Miami Beach. The gentle curve of the facade and the elegant railings on the balconies give it a vaguely art–deco feel. Of course, the free-form pool has a swim-up bar where you can order drinks with umbrellas. The open-air lobby takes full advantage of the lush foliage in the courtyard. A U-shaped design gives every room a wall of windows facing the beach. ✉ *Rte. 115, Km 12.2, 00677* ☎ *787/823–7500* 🖷 *787/823–7503* 🌐 *www.rinconoftheseas.com* *109 rooms* *2 restaurants, room service, fans, in-room safes, cable TV, in-room data ports, pool, beach, 2 bars, shop, business services, convention center, Internet room, meeting rooms* 💳 *AE, MC, V* 🍽 *EP.*

★ **$–$$** **Casa Isleña.** With its barrel-tiled roofs, wall-enclosed gardens, and open-air dining room, Casa Isleña might remind well-traveled souls of a villa on the coast of Mexico. The secret of its charm is that this little inn retains a simplicity without compromising the romantic flavor of its setting. Several of the terra-cotta floored rooms have balconies overlooking the pool and the palm-shaded stretch of beach. Others have ter-

GREAT ITINERARIES

IF YOU HAVE 1 DAY
If you just have a day to spend in the Porta del Sol, make the drive to Joyuda ❸ for some of Puerto Rico's freshest seafood. You probably won't be the only ones driving from San Juan for this feast.

IF YOU HAVE 3 DAYS
If you have a few days to explore the region, start in **Rincón ❶**. There are accommodations here for every taste, from compact inns to sprawling resorts. There isn't too much to see, other than the lighthouse at Parque Pasivo El Faro, but you will find plenty of beautiful beaches. Most have been discovered, however. If you crave complete solitude, you're more likely to find empty beaches in the communities of **Aguadilla ❻** or **Isabela ❼**. On Day 2 drive south to the coastal communities in the Cabo Rojo. Your first stop should be Joyuda ❸, where you can choose

from among dozens of seaside restaurants. After lunch, continue past **Boquerón ❹** to **El Combate ❺**. This is the end of the line, quite literally. The road ends at the lighthouse that once warned sea captains about the treacherous waters around the island's southwestern tip. On Day 3 you can explore more of this windswept landscape, or head offshore for a look at Mona Island.

IF YOU HAVE 5 DAYS
After spending three days along the western coast, you may be tempted to set sail to one of the islands off the coast. On Day 4, head out on an overnight trip to **Mona Island,** a 14,000-acre paradise known as the "Galápagos of the Caribbean." You'll have to camp on this deserted island, but the opportunity to gaze off the 200-foot cliffs on the northern shore makes it all worth it.

races that face the courtyard. There's also a hot tub and an indoor patio with a soothing, burbling fountain. ⊠ *Rte. 413, Km 4.8, Barrio Puntas, 00677* ☎ *787/823–1525 or 888/289–7750* 📠 *787/823–1530* 🌐 *www.casa-islena.com* 🛏 *9 rooms* 🍴 *Restaurant, some refrigerators, cable TV, pool, hot tub, beach, snorkeling, shop, free parking* 🖃 *AE, MC, V* 🍴 *EP.*

$ 🏨 **Beside the Pointe.** This perennial favorite sits right on Sandy Beach, where the waves are big, but not too big for novice surfers. The tropical-themed rooms—ranging from studios to two-bedroom apartments with full kitchens—have some charmingly kitschy touches like murals of palm trees. These can't compare to the real thing, which you can see from your balcony. Downstairs, the popular bar and grill Tamboo is a good place to dine. Whales can sometimes be spotted from the sun deck. ⊠ *Rte. 413, Km 4.7, 00677* 📠 *787/823–8550* 🌐 *www.besidethepointe. com* 🛏 *4 rooms, 4 apartments* 🍴 *Restaurant, fans, some kitchens, refrigerators, cable TV, bar* 🖃 *MC, V* 🍴 *CP.*

★ **$** 🏨 **Lazy Parrot.** Painted an eye-popping shade of pink, this mountainside hotel doesn't take itself too seriously. Colorful murals of the eponymous bird brighten the open and airy lobby. The accommodations are a bit more more subdued, though they continue the tropical theme. (The Dolphin Room has—what else?—a stuffed dolphin.) Each has a balcony where you can enjoy the view. There are two restaurants that share a similar theme—Sloppy Joe's on the lower level serves sandwiches and other light fare, while Smilin' Joe's upstairs serves red snapper and other excellent seafood dishes. At the bar you can sample a parrot-themed concoction. The only downside: you're not on the beach. ⊠ *Rte. 413, Km 4.1, 00677* ☎ *787823–5654 or 800/294–1752* 🖷 *787/823–0224* ⊕ *www.lazyparrot.com* ⟿ *11 rooms* ⚇ *2 restaurants, refrigerators, cable TV, pool, hot tub, 2 bars, shop* ⊟ *AE, D, MC, V* ⏐◯⏐ *CP.*

$ 🖼 **Lemontree Waterfront Cottages.** Sitting right on the beach, these two buildings hold six apartments of various sizes. Choose from one three-bedroom unit, one two-bedroom unit, two one-bedroom units, or two studios. No matter which you pick, each has a kitchen and private balcony with views of the coastline. Ted and Jane Davis, who bought the place in 2005, have added amenities not so common in this price range, such as plasma televisions, DVD players, and free Wi-Fi. There is a dive shop on the premises and a massage therapist on call. This is one of the few gay-friendly places in Rincón. ⊠ *Rte. 429, Km 4.1, Box 200, 00677* ☎ *787/823–6452* ⊕ *www.lemontreepr.com* ⟿ *6 apartments* ⚇ *Kitchens, cable TV, in-room DVDs, Wi-Fi, beach, dive shop, massage* ⊟ *MC, V* ⏐◯⏐ *EP.*

$ 🖼 **Villa Cofresí.** On one of the best swimming beaches in Rincón, Villa Cofresiá is extremely popular with families. Parents can keep an eye on the kids while they enjoy the beachfront bar or restaurant. The guest rooms are more spacious than most, especially those that have kitchenettes. Rooms on the second floor are preferable, since those surrounding the pool can get a bit noisy; second-floor rooms have better views, too. The hotel can arrange a host of water sports. ⊠ *Rte. 115. Km 12.0, 00677* ☎ *787/823–2450* 🖷 *787/823–1770* ⊕ *www.villacofresi. com* ⟿ *51 rooms* ⚇ *Restaurant, some kitchenettes, refrigerators, cable TV, pool, beach, bar, shop, meeting room* ⊟ *AE, D, MC, V* ⏐◯⏐ *CP.*

¢–$ 🖼 **Rincón Surf & Board.** All the rooms here have surfboard racks, which should give you a clue as to who is drawn to this out-of-the-way guest-house. Two hostel-type rooms with bunk beds—remains of the original lodging concept—are available at $20 per person. One- to three-bed private rooms are ample size and have a clean and fresh feel; some are like small apartments. Common areas are fun and friendly, but not conducive to late-night partying, as the best surfing is for the early birds. ⊠ *Off Rte. 413, Barrio Puntas, 00677* ☎ *787/823–0610* 🖷 *787/823–6440* ⊕ *www.surfandboard.com* ⟿ *13 rooms, 2 hostel rooms* ⚇ *Restaurant, some refrigerators, cable TV, pool, hot tub, beach, snorkeling, shop, free parking* ⊟ *AE, MC, V* ⏐◯⏐ *EP.*

Nightlife

Rincón attracts a younger crowd, so there are plenty of options for fun after dark. On weekends the **Calypso Café** (⊠ Rte. 4413, Maria's Beach ☎ 787/823–4151) often has live rock-and-roll bands. The open-air establishment, more bar than grill, is also a good place to go after you've had your fill of the beach. Don't miss the second floor of the **Sandy Beach Surf Club** (⊠ Rte. 413, Km 4.3, Sandy Beach ☎ 787/823–1146), which has a fantastic view of the town's lights.

Sports & the Outdoors

DIVING & SNORKELING Most of the region's dive operators also run fishing charters around Desecheo Island and whale-watching trips in season.

Along with organizing whale-watching trips, **Moondog Charters** (⌧ Black Eagle Marina, off Rte. 413 ☎ 787/823–3059 ⊕ www.moondogcharters.com) will take a minimum of four people on a snorkeling or diving trip to Desecheo Island. Prices are from $45 to $95 per person. The company also does fishing charters. **Oceans Unlimited** (⌧ Rte. 115, Km 11.9 ☎ 787/823–2340 ⊕ www.oceans-unlimited.com) has snorkeling trips for $50, including lunch. The company also offers day-trips to Desecheo Island and Mona Island. **Taíno Divers** (⌧ Black Eagle Marina, off Rte. 413 ☎ 787/823–6429 ⊕ www.tainodivers.com) has daily snorkeling, diving, and fishing trips. The cost is $55 and $99, including lunch. It also has daily trips to Desecheo Island, charters to Mona Island, and scuba PADI certification courses.

> **WORD OF MOUTH**
>
> "The best snorkeling by far was our beginners' Discover Scuba trip with Taino Divers to Desecheo Island, which is a 45-minute boat trip from Rincón. The snorkeling was incredible."   –KGates.

> **WHALE-WATCHING**
>
> If you visit between December and February, you might get a glimpse of the humpback whales that winter off the Puerto Rican coast.

SURFING **Rincón Surf School** (⌧ Rincón Surf & Board, Rte. 413 ☎ 787/823–0610) offers full-day lessons for $89, which includes board rental and transportation. You can also arrange two-, three-, and five-day surfing seminars for $169 to $369. Boards can be rented for $20 without a lesson. Diego Montoya of **West Coast Surf Shop** (⌧ Calle Muñoz Rivera at Calle Comercio ☎ 787/823–3935 ⊕ www.westcoastsurf.com) can teach you to surf—the basics, at least—for $35. Board rental is an additional $25.

WATER SPORTS **Desecheo Surf & Dive Shop** (⌧ Rte. 413, Km 2.5 ☎ 787/823–0390 ⊕ www.desecheoinn.com) rents snorkeling equipment ($10 a day), boogie boards ($20 a day) and a variety of short and long surfboards ($25 to $30 a day). The company also organizes diving and snorkeling trips and rents Jet Skis.

Shopping

Eco-Logic-Co (⌧ Parque Pasivo El Faro, end of Rte. 413 ☎ 787/823–1252) has fun and ecologically oriented souvenirs.

MAYAGÜEZ

❷ *24 km (15 mi) southeast of Rincón.*

"Me encanta" is what most people from Puerto Rico say when you ask them about Mayagüez. But you are likely to be less than enchanted by the city. With more charming communities in every direction, there's no real reason to stop in this traffic-clogged city. But if you have some spare time, the city known as the "Sultan of the West" is fun to explore. Its tree-lined main square, called Plaza Colón, is dominated by a large statue of Christopher Columbus. On the surrounding streets you'll find the domed Teatro Yagüez, which dates from 1902, and a mishmash of buildings that run the gamut from neoclassical to baroque to art deco.

Puerto Rico's only zoo, the **Zoológico de Puerto Rico,** is just north of downtown. The older section of the park has undergone an extensive renovation, so now most of the cages have been replaced by fairly natural-looking environments. Kids love the zebras, giraffes, and hippopotomi at the African savannah exhibit. There is a $2 charge for parking. ☒ *Rte. 108, north of Rte. 65* ☎ *787/834–6330* ⊕ *www.parquesnacionalespr.com* ☜ *$6* ☽ *Wed.–Sun. 8:30–4.*

Founded in 1901 on a 235-acre farm on the outskirts of Mayagüez, the **Estación Experimental de Agricultura Tropical** (Tropical Agriculture Research Station) is run by the U.S. Department of Agriculture and contains a tropical plant collection that has been nurtured for more than a half century. More than 2,000 plant species from all over the tropical world are found here, including teak, mahogany, cinnamon, nutmeg, rubber, and numerous exotic flowers. Free maps are available for self-guided tours. ☒ *Hwy. 2 and Rte. 108* ☎ *787/831–3435* ☜ *Free* ☽ *Weekdays 7–4.*

The **Teatro Yagüez** is an extravagant yellow-and-white theater dating from 1902 that's famed throughout the island for its lavish, columned facade and domed roof. The structure, a little over the top, is still the main venue for theater in Mayagüez. As this writing, it was closed for renovations until sometime in 2006. ☒ *Calle McKinley at Calle Dr. Basora* ☎ *787/834–0523* ☜ *Free* ☽ *Daily, except when rehearsals are scheduled.*

Beaches

Balneario de Añasco. Mayagüez isn't famous for its beaches—you'll find better stretches in Rincón, about 25 minutes north—but the this beach, also called Tres Hermanos Beach, is 10 minutes north of town via Highway 2 and Routes 115 and 401. Dotted with palm trees, it's good for swimming and has changing facilities and restrooms.

Where to Eat

$$–$$$ ✕ **El Estoril.** The elegant tiled dining room calls to mind the old world, while the friendly, relaxed service is all about the new one. Seafood is the specialty: order a traditional paella or the unusual lobster wrapped in mozzarella and bacon and flambéed. If you're in the mood for something lighter, you can order tapas in the wood-and-brick bar. Call ahead, as private parties sometimes close the place to visitors. ☒ *100 Calle Méndez Vigo* ☎ *787/834–2288* ▤ *AE, MC, V* ☽ *Closed Sun.*

¢ ✕ **Ricomini Bakery.** This popular bakery, open daily from 6 AM to midnight, is a good spot to try one of the city's trademark delicacies, a *brazo gitano* (literally "gypsy arm"). These gigantic jellyrolls are filled with anything from guava to lemon to sweet cheese. You can also find another famous local product here, Fido's Sangría, made from the closely guarded secret recipe of Mayagüez resident Wilfredo Aponte Hernández. There are also tasty pastries, freshly baked bread, and a selection of sandwiches. ⊠ *202 Calle Méndez Vigo* ☎ *787/832–0565* 🖃 *AE, MC, V.*

Where to Stay

$$ 🏨 **Holiday Inn Mayagüez & Tropical Casino.** Everything seems shoehorned into this big box on the northern edge of Mayagüez. The sound of slot machines is impossible to escape in the extremely popular casino, which is adjacent to the lobby, as well as the bar and restaurant. The rooms are a bit larger than usual, but otherwise nothing special. Holly's Restaurant serves Caribbean cuisine with a Sunday "South American" brunch. The easy-to-reach location puts the hotel about 10 minutes from the downtown historic district and 5 minutes from the airport. ⊠ *2701 Hwy. 2, Km 149.9, 00681* ☎ *787/833–1100* 🖶 *787/833–1300* ⊕ *www.hidpr. com* 🛏 *141 rooms* ♿ *Restaurant, room service, cable TV, in-room data ports, 2 pools, gym, bar, lounge, casino, dance club, video game room, shop, dry cleaning, laundry facilities, laundry service, Internet room, business services, meeting rooms* 🖃 *AE, D, MC, V* ⊠ *CP.*

$$ 🏨 **Mayagüez Resort & Casino.** The center of the city's social life, this old-fashioned hotel is packed with elegantly dressed men and women all weekend. Some are trying their luck in the casino, some are dancing the tango in the lounge, and some are sipping cocktails on the long, sweeping terrace. The nicely decorated guest rooms look out onto 20 acres of lush gardens. El Castillo specializes in seafood. The public beach in Añasco is 10 minutes away. ⊠ *Rte. 104, Km 0.3, off Hwy. 2, Box 3781, 00681* ☎ *787/832–3030 or 888/689–3030* 🖶 *787/265–1430* ⊕ *www. mayaguezresort.com* 🛏 *140 rooms* ♿ *Restaurant, cable TV with movies, 3 tennis courts, pool, wading pool, gym, hot tub, bar, lounge, casino, playground, business services, meeting rooms, parking (fee)* 🖃 *AE, D, DC, MC, V* ⊠ *EP.*

$ 🏨 **Howard Johnson Downtown Mayagüez.** Set in a former monastery, this downtown hotel still has stained-glass windows in some rooms and a stone cross on the roof. The rooms are mostly small (they were originally for monks, after all), but more stylish than those in your standard chain hotel. The downtown location is near some good restaurants. ⊠ *70 Calle Méndez Vigo, 006810* ☎ *787/832–9191* 🖶 *787/832–9122* ⊕ *www. hojo.com* 🛏 *39 rooms* ♿ *Cable TV, pool, business services* 🖃 *AE, D, MC, V.*

¢–$ 🏨 **Parador El Sol.** In the heart of downtown, this modern high-rise is a block or so from the main square. The spacious rooms have fairly standard decor, but they also have some much-appreciated extras such as refrigerators. The palm-shaded pool makes the Mayagüez heat a bit more bearable. ⊠ *9 Calle Santiago Riera Palmer, 00680* ☎ *787/834–0303 or 866/765–0303* 🖶 *787/265–7567* ⊕ *www.hotelelsol.com* 🛏 *52 rooms* ♿ *Restaurant, refrigerators, cable TV, pool, bar, business services* 🖃 *AE, D, MC, V* ⊠ *CP.*

Nightlife & the Arts

A block from Plaza Colón, **Dom Pepe** (⊠ 56 Calle Méndez Vigo ☎ 787/834–4941) has live eclectic music upstairs.

Shopping

Small stores and pharmacies dot downtown Mayagüez. For heavy-duty shopping, the **Mayagüez Mall** (⊠ Hwy. 2, Km 159.4 ☎ 787/834–2760) has local stores, a food court, and stateside chains such as JCPenney.

CABO ROJO

Named for its pinkish cliffs, "Red Cape" was used in the late 18th century as a port for merchant vessels—and for the smugglers and pirates who inevitably accompanied ocean-going trade. Today the miles of coastline to the west and north of this tiny curl of land jutting into the Atlantic Ocean are a destination for families. Many small, inexpensive hotels can be found in the small communities of Joyuda, Boquerón, and El Combate. (There's also a town with the name of Cabo Rojo, but there's little of interest here.) Outdoor activities are quite popular, from sailing out of Boquerón to hiking to the lighthouse near El Combate.

Joyuda

❸ *21 km (14 mi) south of Mayagüez*

Known as the *Milla de Oro* (Golden Mile) because of its string of more than 30 seaside restaurants, the community of Joyuda is a must for seafood lovers. The same can't be said for those in search of a beautiful beach, as erosion has taken a terrible toll, leaving in some places only a sliver of sand. But that doesn't stop hoards of local families from making a beeline to the bit of beach that is left.

★ About 50 mi off the coast of Cabo Rojo, **Mona Island** sits brooding in the Atlantic Ocean. Known as the Galápagos of the Caribbean, the 14,000-acre island has long been a destination for adventurous travelers. It's said to have been settled by the Taíno and visited by both Christopher Columbus and Juan Ponce de León. Pirates were known to use the small island as a hideout, and legend has it that there is still buried treasure to be found here. Today, however, Mona's biggest lure is its distinctive ecosystem. It is home to a number of endangered species, such as the Mona iguana and leatherback sea turtle. A number of seabirds, including red-footed boobies, also inhabit the island. Off its coast are reefs filled with 270 species of tropical fish, black coral, and purple seafans. There are plenty of places to explore, such as the 200-foot cliffs on the north side of the island or the abandoned lighthouse that once protected ships off the southern coast. Travelers must get there by boat—planes aren't permitted to land. Several tour operators in Joyuda and Boquerón, as well as companies in Mayagüez and Rincón, offer overnight camping trips to the island; they will help you with the camping permits from the Department of Natural and Environmental Resources. You need to reserve at least a few weeks ahead for an overnight stay on the island. ☎ 787/724–3724 *for Department of Natural and Environmental Resources.*

Where to Eat

★ **$$–$$$** ✕ **Tino's.** The colorful neon sign outside this restaurant touts its signature dish: AN EARTHENWARE GOBLET OVERFLOWING WITH MASHED PLANTAINS AND SEAFOOD. It comes in two sizes, but the smaller one is usually enough to satisfy all but the biggest appetites. There are plenty of other dishes on the menu, from red snapper in a spicy sauce to lobster with butter. There's no ocean view, but the elegant dining makes up for it. ⊠ *Rte. 102, Km 13.6* ☎ *787/851–2976* ▭ *AE, DC, MC, V.*

$$ ✕ **El Bohío.** Watch seagulls dive for their dinner while you dine on a covered deck extending out into the bay. The long list of seafood is prepared in a variety of ways: shrimp comes breaded, stewed, or skewered; conch is served as a salad or cooked in a butter and garlic sauce. And the lobster can be prepared in just about any way you can imagine. ⊠ *Rte. 102, Km 9.7* ☎ *787/851–2755* ▭ *AE, DC, MC, V.*

Where to Stay

$ ▦ **Parador Joyuda Beach.** Talk about truth in advertising: the beach in question is so close that the water laps against the seawall. Rooms here are spic and span, with terra-cotta tile floors. Ask for one of the sunset suites, which have ocean views. There's an open-air restaurant by the beach and a snack bar by the pool. ⊠ *Rte. 102, Km 11.7* ☍ *Box 18410, 00623* ☎ *787/851–5650 or 800/981–5464* 🖷 *787/255–3750* ⊕ *www.joyudabeach.com* ↶ *41 rooms* ঌ *Restaurant, snack bar, cable TV, pool, beach, bar, meeting room* ▭ *AE, MC, V* ⦿ *EP.*

¢ ▦ **Joyuda Plaza.** Across the road from the beach, this three-story is one of the best deals in Joyuda. you don't come here for the ambience—the building is little more than a box, and the rooms make only a vague attempt at decor. But if you're on a budget, this place has nice touches you don't always get in this price range, like a pair of kidney-shaped pools sitting side by side in a pretty courtyard. Dozens of bars and restaurants are nearby. ⊠ *Rte. 102, Km 14.5* ☍ *Box 18410, Joyuda 00623* ☎ *787/851–8800* 🖷 *787/851–2638* ⊕ *www.joyudaplaza.com* ↶ *55 rooms* ঌ *2 restaurants, room service, cable TV, 2 pools, bar* ▭ *AE, MC, V.*

Nightlife

Overlooking a bit of the bay, the open-air **Bayside** (⊠ Rte. 102, Km 14.9 ☎ 787/882–0790) often has live music.

Sports & the Outdoors

DIVING & SNORKELING Several reef-bordered cays lie off the Cabo Rojo area near walls that drop to 100 feet. A mile-long reef along Las Coronas, better known as Cayo Ron, has a variety of hard and soft coral, reef fish, and lobster. You can arrange snorkeling and scuba-diving trips with Captain Elick Hernández Garciá, who runs **Tour Marine Adventures** (⊠ Rte. 101, Km 14.1 ☎ 787/375–2625 ⊕ www.tourmarinepr.com). They cost between $35 and $75 per person. He'll also arrange trips out to Mona Island for $115 per person.

GOLF Get in 18 holes at the **Club Deportivo del Oeste** (⊠ Rte. 102, Km 15.4 ☎ 787/851–8880). Jack Bender incorporated the region's rolling hills in his design to provide golfers with panoramic views. The nicely tended course is open daily; greens fees are $30.

Boquerón

❹ *5 km (3 mi) south of Joyuda.*

Once a quiet fishing village, Boquerón still has its share of seaside shanties. Its narrow streets are quiet during the week, but come alive on the weekend, when vendors appear with carts full of clams and oysters you can slurp down on the spot—wedges of lemon of provided, of course. Bars and restaurants throw open their doors—if they have any, that is. Many of the establishments here are open to the breeze. Boquerón is also a water-sports center,

> **WORD OF MOUTH**
>
> "Boquerón, about ½ hour south of Rincon, has a great, well-maintained beach on the bay. The sleepy fishing village also provides a great atmosphere. Be sure to take a drive a bit further south of Boquerón to the Cabo Rojo Lighthouse (the southwestern tip of PR)."   –Adrienne.

many companies operating from or near the docks of the imposing Club Nautico de Boquerón, which is easy to find at the end of Route 100.

The **Refugio de Vida Silvestre de Boquerón** (Boquerón Wildlife Refuge) encompasses three tracts of land at the island's southern tip. The first is about 1 mi (2 km) south of Boquerón. There is a trail that leads through three different types of mangroves to picnic areas and a dock where you can launch a canoe or kayak. Note: hunting is allowed in the reserve between November and January. ⊠ *Rte. 101, Km 1.1* ☎ *787/851–4795* 🖙 *Free* ⊙ *Weekdays 7:30–4.*

Beaches

Balneario Boquerón. The long stretch of sand at this beach off Route 101 is a favorite with islanders, especially on weekends. You'll find changing facilities, cabins, showers, restrooms, and picnic tables; it costs $3 to enter with a car. ⊠ *Off Rte. 101.*

Playa Buyé. The white-sand beach has swaying palm trees and crystal-clear water. ⊠ *Rte. 307, north of Boquerón.*

Where to Eat

$–$$$ ✕ **Galloway's.** From a covered deck overlooking Bahía Boquerón, catch the sunset while enjoying seafood—caught fresh from local waters, of course. There's a lively happy hour and occasional live music. This place is along the main drag, but is set back from the street so you don't have to be a part of the passing parade. ⊠ *12 Calle José de Diego* ☎ *787/254–3302* ▤ *AE, MC, V* ⊙ *Closed Mon.–Wed.*

Where to Stay

$–$$ ▥ **Cofresí Beach Hotel.** A favorite with families, this place puts you a few blocks from the hustle and bustle of Boquerón. Its four floors—practically a high-rise in these parts—are filled with one-, two-, and three-bedroom apartments complete with full kitchens. They didn't forget a thing, as there's even nice china and flatware in the cupboards. The pool is small, but very much appreciated on hot afternoons. ⊠ *57 Calle Muñoz Rivera* ⊡ *Box 1209, Boquerón 00622* ☎ *787/254–3000* 🖷 *787/254–1048*

⊕ *www.cofresibeach.com* ⤳ *12 apartments* ⌂ *Restaurant, kitchens, microwaves, refrigerators, cable TV, pool* ☰ *AE, D, DC, MC, V.*

$ ▣ **El Muelle Guest House.** Near the Club Nautico de Boquerón, this buttery yellow house has rooms that are clean and spacious. The weekly rates are cheaper, so it's a good choice if you're planning to stay a while. ⊠ *Calle Jose de Diego, 00623* ☎ *787/254–2801* 🖷 *802/609–9105* ⊕ *www.elmuelleguesthouse.com* ⤳ *8 rooms* ⌂ *Some kitchenettes* ☰ *AE, MC, V.*

$ ▣ **Parador Boquemar.** Even though it's a hike from Balneario Boquerón, families flock to this friendly parador on weekends. Rooms on the first floor are so cramped that people tend to leave their doors open; for room to breathe, ask for a third-floor room with a balcony overlooking the water. The seafood restaurant, La Cascada, has an actual waterfall along one wall. On weekends the lounge is filled with live music. ⊠ *Calle Gill Buyé* ✉ *Box 133, Boquerón 00622* ☎ *787/851–2158* 🖷 *787/851–7600* ⊕ *www.boquemar.com* ⤳ *75 rooms* ⌂ *Restaurant, refrigerators, cable TV, pool, boating, jet skiing, bicycles, lounge, meeting rooms* ☰ *AE, D, DC, MC, V* ¶⊙¶ *EP.*

Nightlife

A curvy bar distinguishes **Boquerón Bay** (⊠ Calle Jose de Diego ☎ 787/640–3820) from its straightforward neighbors. The open-air establishment has a second floor where you can catch a glimpse of the sunset.

Sports & the Outdoors

DIVING & SNORKELING Snorkeling and scuba-diving trips are the speciality at **Mona Aquatics** (⊠ Calle Jose de Diego ☎ 787/851–2185 ⊕ www.monaaquatics.com). Night dives are available as well. You'll find the crew in a wooden shack painted an eye-popping shade of blue next to the Club Nautico de Boquerón. The company has weekly trips to Mona Island.

FISHING You can arrange fishing trips with Captain Francisco "Pochy" Rosario, who runs **Light Tackle Adventure** (☎ 787/849–1430 ⊕ www.lighttackleadventure.8k.com). His specialty is tarpon, which are plentiful in these waters.

El Combate

❺ *3 km (2 mi) south of Boquerón.*

This is the end of the earth—or the end of the island, anyway. El Combate sits in the southwest corner of Puerto Rico, a bit removed from everything. The travel industry hasn't figured out how to market this place, so they've left it mostly to the locals, who have built small but elaborate weekend homes—some with grandiose touches like fountains—along the narrow streets. On the road closest to the beach, which for some reason is called Calle 3, is a cluster of seafood shacks. The more prosperous ones have added second stories.

You're probably wondering about the town's odd name, which literally means "The Combat." It seems that some unscrupulous characters had their eyes on the salt flats just outside town. They were repelled by the machete-wielding villagers who were to live forever in local lore. Is it a true story? Residents of El Combate swear it is.

The **Refugio de Vida Silvestre de Cabo Rojo** (Cabo Rojo Wildlife Refuge) has an interpretive center with exhibits of live freshwater fish and sea turtles. You see as many as 100 species of birds along the trails, even the elusive yellow-shouldered blackbird. The entrance is about 1 mi north of the turnoff for El Combate. ⊠ *Rte. 301, Km 1.2* ☎ *787/851–7260* ☒ *Free* ☼ *Weekdays 8–4.*

The **Centro Interpretativo Las Salinas de Cabo Rojo** (Cabo Rojo Sal Flats Interpretive Center) has a small display about the salt flats and their importance to the local economy. (Remember that the name of the town comes from a battle over control of the salt flats.) The best part of the center is a massive observation tower that lets you scan the outline of Cabo Rojo itself. ⊠ *End of Rte. 301* ☎ *787/851–2999* ⊕ *proambientepr.org* ☒ *Free* ☼ *Wed.–Sat. 8:30–4:30, Sun. 9:30–5:30.*

<table>
<tr><td></td><td>CAUTION</td></tr>
<tr><td></td><td>It's a good idea to rent a four-wheel-drive vehicle if you are headed to Cabo Rojo Lighthouse, as it is reached via a truly terrible dirt road.</td></tr>
</table>

★ The area's most popular attraction is the neoclassical **Cabo Rojo Lighthouse,** dating from 1881. The magnificent structure is not open to the public, but you are free to hike around the rugged terrain or relax on La Playuela or one of the other pink-sand beaches. ⊠ *End of Rte. 301, El Combate* ☎ *787/851–7260* ☒ *Free* ☼ *24 hrs.*

Beaches

Fodor'sChoice
★ **El Combate Beach.** This great beach draws college students to its rustic waterfront eateries. You can rent small boats and kayaks here, and in summer there are often concerts and festivals. ⊠ *At the end of Rte. 3301.*

La Playuela. The crescent-shaped strand is the most secluded of the area's beaches. ⊠ *Rte. 301, past the vast salt flats.*

Where to Eat

$–$$$ ✕ **Annie's.** A dining room with windows facing the ocean is a fitting place to try some of the southwest coast's best seafood. You can snack on *empanadillas* (deep-fried fritters), then move on to red snapper with rice and beans or plantains stuffed with seafood. This place, in an unmistakable orange building on the main drag, is casual and friendly. ⊠ *Calle 3* ☎ *787/254–2553* ⊟ *AE, MC, V* ☼ *Closed Mon.–Wed.*

¢–$ ✕ **Los Chapines.** This rustic seaside shack—painted, like Annie's, a vivid shade of orange—sells a variety of fish and chicken dishes. Be sure to try one of the specialty sandwiches, which are made with deep-fried plantains instead of bread. The deck in back is a perfect place to catch the breeze. ⊠ *Calle 3* ☎ *787/254–4005* ⊟ *MC, V.*

Where to Stay

★ $–$$ ☐ **Bahía Salinas Beach Hotel.** The Cabo Rojo Lighthouse is this resort's closest neighbor. You can wander along the boardwalk or down the garden paths, bask in the sun on a deck or terrace, or relax in the pool that was added to the property in 2005. Another addition is a spa offering a wide range of massages and other treatments. The hotel's restaurant, Agua al Cuello, serves freshly caught seafood; don't overlook the giant tostones. The guest rooms are spacious and have reproduction antiques. At this writing, about 100 more rooms were slated to open by the end of 2006. Note that on weekends a two-night stay is required. ⊠ *End of Rte. 301* ⌂ *Box 2356, El Combate 00622* ☎ *787/254–1212 or 877/ 205–7507* 🖷 *787/254–1215* ⊕ *www.bahiasalinas.com* ⋑ *22 rooms* ⌂ *Restaurant, cable TV, pool, gym, hot tub, massage, spa, bar, lounge, playground; no room phones* ▭ *MC, V* ⭐ *BP.*

¢ 🖾 **Combate Beach Hotel.** On a quiet side street, this little hotel puts you within walking distance of the main drag. It's not right on the beach, but the second-floor rooms all have views of the water through the palm trees. The downstairs restaurant serves seafood, including tasty mofongo. ⊠ *Rte. 3301* ⌂ *Box 1138, El Combate 00622* ☎ *787/254–7053 or 787/254–2358* 🖷 *787/254–2358* ⋑ *20 rooms* ⌂ *Restaurant, refrigerators, cable TV, pool, bar; no room phones* ▭ *MC, V* ⭐ *EP.*

Nightlife

Check in at **Tropicoro Sports Bar** (⊠ Calle 3 ☎ 787/254–2466), a lively spot with billiard tables, to see whether there's a band playing.

THE NORTHWESTERN COAST

North of Rincón you'll find a string of beaches that have yet to be discovered. You won't find much large-scale development along this stretch of shoreline. Instead, the area is populated with modest hotels that cater to local families. Many surfers say that the waves here are better than those in Rincón itself.

Aguadilla

❻ *18 km (12 mi) north of Rincón*

Resembling a fishing village, downtown Aguadilla has narrow streets lined with small wooden homes. Weathered but lovely, the faded facades recall the city's long and turbulent past. Officially incorporated as a town in 1775, Aguadilla subsequently suffered a series of catastrophes, including a devastating earthquake in 1918 and strong hurricanes in 1928 and 1932. Determined to survive, the town rebuilt after each disaster, and by World War II it became known for the sprawling Ramey Air Force Base. The base was an important link in the U.S. defense system throughout the Cold War. Ramey was decommissioned in 1973; today the former base has an airport, a golf course, and some small businesses, although many structures stand empty.

> **WORD OF MOUTH**
>
> "I lived for three years in Rincón, and as far as surfing I would recommend Wilderness Beach in Aguadilla. Take note, though, it is for advanced surfers. I have seen Wilderness go off at 40-foot ground swells before." –caribedon

Along Route 107—an unmarked road crossing through a golf course—you'll find the ruins of **La Ponderosa,** an old Spanish lighthouse, as well as its replacement Punta Borinquen at Puerto Rico's northwest point. The original was built in 1889 and destroyed by an earthquake in 1918. The U.S. Coast Guard rebuilt the structure in 1920. ⊠ *Rte. 107.*

Parque Actuático las Cascades has a large wave pool, giant slides, and the "Crazy River," a long, free-flowing river pool. ⊠ *Hwy. 2, Km 126.5* ☎ *787/819–1030* ⊙ *Mar.–Aug., weekdays 10–5, weekends 10–6.*

Beaches

Fodor'sChoice **Playa Crashboat.** This is where you'll find the colorful fishing boats that
★ are found on postcards all over the island. The sand here is soft and sugary, and the water is as smooth as glass. Named after rescue boats used when Ramey Air Force Base was in operation, this *balneario* has picnic huts, showers, parking, and restrooms. There's a modest food stand run by local fishermen where the catch of the day is served with cold beer. ⊠ *Off Rte. 458.*

Playa Gas Chamber. This beach with crashing waves is favored by surfers. ⊠ *Rte. 107, north of Playa Crashboat.*

Playa Wilderness. This undeveloped beach north of Playa Gas Chamber is recommended only for experienced surfers, as it can have dangerous breaks. ⊠ *Rte. 107, north of Playa Gas Chamber.*

Where to Stay & Eat

$ ╳▥ **Hotel Cielomar.** Just north of the town of Aguadilla, this hotel is perched on a bluff high above the water. The good news is that nearly every room has a jaw-dropping view of the coastline; the bad news is that the beach is far, far away. The accommodations are comfortable, if a bit old-fashioned. The hotel's restaurant, El Bohío ($–$$), specializes in lobster, as well as other types of seafood. The open-air dining room is extremely pleasant, especially in the evening. There's often live music on weekends. ⊠ *84 Av. Montemar, off Rte. 111, 00605* ☎ *787/ 882–5959 or 787/882–5961* 🖷 *787/882–5577* ⊕ *www.cielomar.com* ⇖ *72 rooms* ◊ *Restaurant, refrigerators, cable TV, pool, bar, video game room, playground, business services, meeting rooms* ▤ *AE, MC, V* ⑩ *EP.*

$ ╳▥ **El Faro.** This family-friendly resort isn't close to the lighthouse that gives it a name, or to any of the beaches. But it's a good place to stop if you're driving along the coast and need a place to stop for the night. (Keep a sharp eye out for the PARADOR sign on Route 107, as it's easy to miss.) Cheerfully decorated rooms surround a pair of pools. There are two restaurants on the premises, including the popular Tres Amigos ($$–$$$), one of the most highly regarded in the area. Its specialty is steaks and other meats that come sizzling from the grill. ⊠ *Rte. 107, Km 2.1, Box 5148, 00605* ☎ *787/882–8000 or 866/321–9191* 🖷 *787/ 882–1030* ⊕ *www.farohotels.net* ⇖ *70 rooms, 5 suites* ◊ *2 restaurants, cable TV, tennis court, pool, basketball, playground, coin laundry, Internet, business services, meeting rooms, airport shuttle* ▤ *AE, D, DC, MC, V* ⑩ *EP.*

$ ⬚ **JB Hidden Village.** This family-friendly hotel is in Aguada, about halfway between Aguadilla and Rincón. There's plenty here to keep the kids occupied. If you have your heart set on the beach, however, the land-locked location won't be ideal. The modern rooms and suites all have balconies, most overlooking the sparkling pool. There's a well-regarded restaurant and bar on the premises. ⊠ *Rte. 4416, Km 9.5, Aguada 00602* ☎ *787/868–8686* 🖷 *787/868–8701* ⬐ *45 rooms* ♨ *Restaurant, cable TV, pool, game room, bar, meeting room* ▤ *MC, V* ⭗ *EP.*

Sports & the Outdoors

DIVING & SNORKELING Near Gate 5 of the old Ramey Air Force Base, **Aquatica Underwater Adventures** (⊠ Rte. 110, Km 10 ☎ 787/890–6071) offers scuba-diving certification courses as well as snorkeling and surfing trips. You can also rent any gear you need. It's open Monday through Saturday from 9 to 5, Sunday from 9 to 3.

GOLF The 18-hole **Punta Borinquen Golf Course** (⊠ Rte. 107, Km 2 ☎ 787/890–2987 ⊕ www.puntaborinquengolfclub.com), on the former Ramey Air Force Base, was a favorite of President Dwight D. Eisenhower. Now a public course, the beachfront course is known for its tough sand traps and strong cross winds. The course is open daily.

Isabela

⑦ *20 km (13 mi) east of Aguadilla.*

Founded in 1819 and named for Spain's Queen Isabella, this small, white-washed town on the northwesternmost part of the island skirts tall cliffs that overlook the rocky shoreline. Locals have long known of the area's natural beauty, and lately more and more off-shore tourists have begun coming to this niche, which offers secluded hotels, fantastic beaches, and, just inland, hiking through one of the island's forest reserves.

Explore karst topography and subtropical vegetation at the 2,357-acre **Bosque Estatal Guajataca** (Guajataca State Forest) between the towns of Quebradillas and Isabela. On more than 46 walking trails you can see 186 species of trees, including the royal palm and ironwood, and 45 species of birds—watch for red-tailed hawks and Puerto Rican woodpeckers. Bring a flashlight and descend into the **Cueva del Viento** to find stalagmites, stalactites, and other strange formations. At the entrance to the forest there's a small ranger station where you can pick up a decent hiking map. (Get here early, as the rangers don't always stay until the official closing time.) A little farther down the road is a recreational area with picnic tables and an observation tower. ⊠ *Rte. 446, Km 10* ☎ *787/872–1045* 🎫 *Free* ☉ *Ranger station weekdays 8–5.*

OFF THE BEATEN PATH **PALACETE LOS MOREAU** – In the fields south of Isabela toward the town of Moca, a French family settled on a coffee and sugar plantation in the 1800s. The grand two-story house, trimmed with gables, columns, and stained-glass windows, was immortalized in the novel *La Llamarada,* written in 1935 by Puerto Rican novelist Enrique A. Laguerre. In Laguerre's novel about conditions in the sugarcane industry, the house belonged to his fictional family, the Moreaus. Although it doesn't have many

CLOSE UP

The Abominable Chupacabra

THE HIMALAYAS HAVE THEIR YETI, Britain has its crop circles, New Jersey has its legendary Jersey Devil . . . and Puerto Rico has its Chupacabra. This "goat sucker" (as its name translates) has been credited with strange attacks on goats, sheep, rabbits, horses, and chickens since the mid-1970s. The attacks happen mostly at night, leaving the animals devoid of blood, with oddly vampirelike punctures in their necks.

Though the first references to these attacks were in the 1970s, the biggest surge of reports dates to the mid-1990s, when the mayor of Canóvanas received international attention and support from local police for his weekly search parties equipped with a caged goat as bait. The police stopped short of fulfilling the mayor's request for a special unit devoted to the creature's capture.

Sightings offer widely differing versions of the Chupacabra; it has gray, scraggly hair and resembles a kangaroo or wolf, or walks upright on three-toed feet. Some swear it hops from tree branch to tree branch, and even flies, leaving behind, in the tradition of old Lucifer, the acrid stench of sulphur. It peers through large, oval, sometimes red eyes, and "smells like a wet dog" as its reptilian tongue flicks the night air. It has, according to some, attacked humans, ripped through window screens, and jumped family dogs at picnics.

According to a 1995 article in the *San Juan Star*, island lore abounds with monsters predating the Chupacabra. The *comecogollo* was a version of bigfoot—but smaller and a vegetarian. It was particularly sweet on *cogollo*, a baby plantain that springs up near its parent plant. In the early 1970s the Moca vampire also attacked small animals, but opinion differed on whether it was alien, animal, or really a vampire. The *garadiablo*, a swamp creature that emerged from the ooze at night to wreak havoc on the populace also struck fear in the early 1970s. This "sea demon" was described as having the face of a bat, the skin of a shark, and a humanlike body.

The Chupacabra has also been active in other spots with large Hispanic communities—Mexico, southern Texas, and Miami—and its scope is pretty wide. The list of reported sightings at ⊕ www.elchupacabra.com includes such unlikely locales as Maine and Missouri. And the Chupa's coverage on the Web isn't limited to sci-fi fan sites: Princeton University maintains a Web site meant to be a clearinghouse for Chupa information.

What to make of Chupa? Above the clamor of the fringe elements, one hears the more skeptical voice of reason. Zoologists have suggested that the alleged condition of some Chupacabra victims may actually be the result of exaggerated retelling of the work of less mysterious animals, such as a tropical species of bat known to feed on the blood of small mammals. Even some bird species are known to eat warm-blooded animals. Skeletal remains of an alleged Chupacabra found in Chile were determined to be those of a wild dog. This, however, doesn't explain the sightings of the hairy, ravenous beast. Then again, there's no accounting for the Loch Ness Monster either.

—Karl Luntta

furnishings, you can walk through the house and also visit Laguerre's personal library in the mansion's basement. On the grounds is an old steam engine once used to transport surgarcane. ✉ *Hwy. 2, Km 115.9* ☎ *787/877–3390* ✑ *Free* ⊙ *Tues.–Sat. 8–4:30.*

Beaches

Playa de Guajataca. Stretching by what is called El Tunel—part of an old tunnel used by a passenger and cargo train that ran from San Juan to Ponce from the early to mid-1900s—this beach is lined with kiosks selling local snacks and souvenirs. On weekends you'll hear live music playing around the area. Just before El Tunel is El Merendero de Guajataca, a picnic area with cliffside trails for a spectacular view of the coastline. ✉ *Off Rte. 113.*

Playa de Jobos. This beach is famous for surfing, but it can have dangerous breaks. On the same stretch there are a couple of restaurants with oceanfront decks serving light fare and drinks. Down the road, the dunes and long stretches of golden sand are gorgeous for walks or running. Route 466 runs parallel, and there are narrow accesses to the beach scattered all along the road. ✉ *Rte. 466.*

Playa Montones. Not far from Playa de Jobos on Route 466, this is a beautiful beach for swimming and frolicking in the sand; it has a natural protected pool where children can splash safely. An outcropping of coral creates a huge wave spray on the ocean side. ✉ *Rte. 466.*

Playa de Shacks is known for its surfing and horseback riding. It also has an area called the Blue Hole that is popular with divers. ✉ *Rte. 4446.*

Where to Eat

In addition to the restaurant listed below, the restaurants at Villa Montaña and Villas del Mar Hau are known for having good food.

$–$$$ ✕ **Happy Belly's.** If you're in the mood for a hamburger or club sandwich, this laid-back restaurant is a good choice. The seating is comfortable wooden booths that overlook Playa Jobos—the wind that whips up the waves may also blow away your napkin. In the evening the menu changes to more substantial fare, everything from shrimp scampi to baby back ribs. But many people just come for the socializing and the sunsets. ✉ *Rte. 4466, Km 7.5* ☎ *787/872–6566* ▭ *AE, MC, V.*

Where to Stay

$$$ 🏨 **Villa Montaña.** This secluded cluster of villas, situated on a deserted stretch of beach between Isabela and Aguadilla, feels like a little town. You can pull your car into your own garage, then head upstairs to your airy studio or one-, two-, or three-bedroom suite with hand-carved mahogany furniture and canopy beds. Studios have kitchenettes, while the larger suites have full-size kitchens and laundry rooms. Eclipse, the open-air bar and restaurant, serves Caribbean-Asian fusion cuisine. Playa de Shacks, a popular beach, is nearby. ✉ *Rte. 4466, Km 1.9, Box 530, 00662* ☎ *787/872–9554 or 888/780–9195* 🖷 *787/872–9553* ⊕ *www.villamontana.com* ✐ *56 suites* ⚷ *Restaurant, cable TV, in-room*

DVDs, 2 tennis courts, 2 pools, beach horseback riding, gym, laundry facilities, business services, meeting rooms ▭ AE, D, MC, V ¡⊙¡ EP.

$$ ▥ **Villas de Costa Dorada.** Painted cheerful shades of pink, blue, and yellow, this cluster of buildings certainly gets your attention. The studios and one- and two-bedroom apartments, all with spacious balconies overlooking the ocean, have a homey feel. The complex has a pool and hot tub, but shares most of its facilities with the older hotel next door. ⊠ Rte. 466, Km 0.1, 00662 ☎ 787/830–0303 or 800/981–5693 ⊟ 787/830–0311 ⊕ www. costadoradabeach.com ↩ 24 rooms ⌂ Restaurant, room service, cable TV, 2 pools, hot tub, 2 tennis courts, hot tub, bar, playground, shop, meeting rooms ▭ AE, MC, V ¡⊙¡ EP.

$–$$ ▥ **Villas del Mar Hau.** One-, two-, and three-bedroom cottages—
Fodor'sChoice painted in cheery pastels and trimmed with gingerbread—are the
★ heart of this beachfront resort. The accommodations aren't luxurious, but if you're looking for an unpretentious atmosphere, you'll have a hard time doing better. If you are planning on cooking, you should consider one of the studios, all of which have a full kitchens. Otherwise, the open-air Olas y Arena is known for its excellent fish and shellfish; the paella is especially good. The hotel also has a stable of horses reserved for guests. ⊠ Rte. 466, Km 8.9, Box 510, 00662 ☎ 787/ 872–2045 or 787/872–2627 ⊟ 787/872–0273 ⊕ www. paradorvillasdelmarhau.com ↩ 40 cottages ⌂ Restaurant, fans, some kitchens, tennis court, pool, basketball, horseback riding, laundry facilities ▭ AE, MC, V ¡⊙¡ EP.

$ ▥ **El Guajataca.** Perched on a bluff overlooking the Atlantic, this unassuming inn between Quebradillas and Isabela makes the most of its location. Its rooms are modest but have nice views. The palm-lined swimming pool overlooks the ocean as well, and paths lead to Guajataca Beach. There's peeling paint here and there, but, hey, this is a budget accommodation. ⊠ Hwy. 2, Km 103.8, Quebradillas ⓓ Box 1558, 00678 ☎ 787/895–3070 ⊟ 787/895–2204 ↩ 38 rooms ⌂ Restaurant, cable TV, 2 tennis courts, pool, beach, basketball, bar, playground ▭ AE, MC, V ¡⊙¡ EP.

Sports & the Outdoors

HORSEBACK **Tropical Trail Rides** (⊠ Rte. 4466, Km 1.9 ☎ 787/872–9256 ⊕ www.
RIDING tropicaltrailrides.com) has two-hour morning and afternoon rides along the beach and through a forest of almond trees. Groups leave from Playa Shacks.

DIVING & Beginning and advanced divers can explore the submerged caves off Playa
SNORKELING Shacks through **La Cueva Submarina Dive Shop** (⊠Rte. 466, Km 6.3 ☎787/ 872–1390 ⊕ www.lacuevasubmarina.com), which also offers certification courses and snorkeling trips.

RINCÓN & THE PORTA DEL SOL ESSENTIALS

To research prices, get advice from other travelers, and book travel arrangements, visit www.fodors.com.

Transportation

BY AIR

Aguadilla is a convenient gateway to western Puerto Rico, thanks to several daily international flights. Continental Airlines flies from Newark to Aguadilla, and JetBlue has daily service from New York–JFK to Aguadilla. American Eagle and Cape Air fly between San Juan and Mayagüez.

🛪 **American Eagle** ☎ 787/749-1747 ⊕ www.aa.com. **Cape Air** ☎ 800/525-0280 ⊕ www.flycapeair.com. **Continental** ☎ 800/433-7300 ⊕ www.continental.com. **Jet-Blue** ☎ 800/538-2583 ⊕ www.jetblue.com.

AIRPORTS & TRANSFERS Aguadilla's Aeropuerto Internacional Rafael Hernández (BQN) is on the old Ramey Air Force Base. The renovated structure, as modern as any on the island, has a tourist information office, car-rental agencies, and a handy ATM. Tiny Aeropuerto Eugenio María de Hostos (MAZ), just north of Mayagüez on Highway 2, looks a bit like a strip mall. There's little inside besides the car-rental counters and a handy ATM. There are no airport shuttles in either Aguadilla or Mayagüez. A taxi from either airport into town is about $6 to $10, but if you are going any farther, you should rent a car.

🛪 **Aeropuerto Eugenio María de Hostos** ✉ Hwy. 2, Km 148.7, Mayagüez ☎ 787/833-0148 or 787/265-7065. **Aeropuerto Internacional Rafael Hernández** ✉ Hwy. 2, Km 148.7, Aguadilla ☎ 787/891-2286.

BY BOAT & FERRY

Ferry service by Ferries del Caribe shuttle between Mayagüez and Santo Domingo. Trips are overnight leaving at 8 PM and arriving at 8 AM. Small cabins with sleeping accommodations for two, three, and four persons are provided. Tickets are usually available, but reserve well in advance if you're bringing your car. Ships leave from the Zona Portuaria, past the Holiday Inn on Route 2.

🛪 **Ferry Reservations** ☎ 787/832-4800 ⊕ www.ferriesdelcaribe.com.

BY BUS & VAN

There's no easy network of buses linking the towns in the Porta del Sol region of northwestern Puerto Rico. Some municipalities and private companies operate buses and large, shared vans *(públicos)* from one city to another, but schedules are loose. It's not wise to count on them as your primary means of transportation. That said, if you're adventurous and not easily frustrated, it's possible to arrange cheap transportation from San Juan to Aguadilla, Rincón, and Mayagüez, among other towns. Prices from terminal to terminal are set, but drivers may go to another destination if arranged beforehand.

Choferes Unidos travels from San Juan to Aguadilla for about $10 per person. Linea Sultana has vans from San Juan to Mayagüez that also drop off passengers along Highway 2 in Aguada, Quebradillas, and Isabela; the price is about $12 per person. Línea Caborrojeña travels between San Juan and Cabo Rojo.

Choferes Unidos ☎ 787/751-7622. **Linea Sultana** ☎ 787/765-9377. **Línea Caborrojeña** ☎ 787/723-9155.

BY CAR

You really need a car to see northwestern Puerto Rico, especially the mountain area. The toll road, Highway 22, makes it easy to reach Arecibo from San Juan. Highway 22 turns into Highway 2 just after Arecibo, swings by the northwestern tip of the island, then heads south to Mayagüez.

If you are not flying into San Juan, you can rent a car in Aguadilla or Mayagüez. Prices vary from $35 to $65 per day.

Avis ☎ 787/890-3311 in Aguadilla, 787/832-0406 in Mayagüez. **Budget** ☎ 787/890-1110 in Aguadilla, 787/823-4570 in Mayagüez. **Hertz** ☎ 787/890-5650 in Aguadilla, 787/832-3314 in Mayagüez. **L & M Rent a Car** ☎ 787/890-3010 in Aguadilla. **Leaseway of Puerto Rico** ☎ 787/833-1140 in Mayagüez. **Thrifty** ☎ 787/834-1590 in Mayagüez.

GASOLINE Prices are measured in liters instead of gallons and are not terribly different from those in the United States. The chain gas stations, Esso and Shell, are open 24 hours. Locally owned stations in small towns generally close before 6 PM.

PARKING Parking is usually available on the street, though downtown Mayagüez can become congested, especially in the historic district, where streets are narrower. At tourist or commercial sites, parking is normally provided.

ROAD CONDITIONS The major highways throughout the northwest region, Highways 22 and 2, are well maintained. The Ruta Panorámica throughout the central mountains is also in good condition and has amazing vistas, but its twists and turns should be driven with caution. Road signs in the mountains may be missing—some have been blown down by storms or hurricanes and have yet to be replaced.

EMERGENCY SERVICES **Gruas Sanchez** ⊠ Hwy. 2, Km 149.7, Bo Algarrobo, Mayagüez ☎ 787/832-6704. **Junker Nazario** ⊠ Rte. 105, Km 1.1, Bo Limón, Mayagüez ☎ 787/833-2755.

BY TAXI

Taxis can be hailed near the main plaza in Mayagüez, but in the smaller towns they may be hard to come by. Check with your hotel or restaurant, and they may be able to call one for you. In Mayagüez, White Taxi is reliable and charges flat rates—no meters—by location. Fares to or from San Juan are steep: for example, service is $120 from Mayagüez.

Arecibo Taxi Cab ☎ 787/878-2929.

Contacts & Resources

BANKS & EXCHANGE SERVICES

Banks are plentiful in larger cities, and smaller towns usually have at least one; banks are sometimes attached to grocery stores. All banks have

ATMs (called ATHs), and many businesses accept ATM cards. If you need to change money into U.S. dollars, you can do that in banks in either Aguadilla or Mayagüez.

🖪 **Banco Popular** ⊠ Calle Mercedes Moreno, corner of Munoz Rivera, Aguadilla ☎ 787/891–2085 🖾 Mayagüez Mall, Hwy. 2, Km 159.4, Mayagüez ☎ 787/834–4750 🖾 13 Av. Agustín Ramos Calero, Isabela ☎ 787/872–3100 🖾 1 Calle Commercio, Rincón, ☎ 787/823–2055.

EMERGENCIES
🖪 **General emergencies** ☎ 911.

🖪 **Hospitals General Hospital Dr. Ramón Emeterio Betances** ⊠ Hwy. 2, Km 157, Mayagüez ☎ 787/834–8686. **Hospital Bellavista** ⊠ Rte. 349, Km 2.7, Mayagüez ☎ 787/831–2048. **Hospital Subregional Dr. Pedro J. Zamora** ⊠ Hwy. 2, Km 141.1, Aguadilla ☎ 787/791–3000.

🖪 **24-hour Pharmacies Walgreens** ⊠ Hwy. 2, Km 129.7, Aguadilla ☎ 787/882–8005 🖾 Mayagüez Mall, Hwy. 2, Km 159.4, Mayagüez ☎ 787/831–9249 🖾 Plaza Universitaria, Mayagüez ☎ 787/805–4005.

INTERNET, MAIL & SHIPPING
Getting connected is a bit difficult in this part of the island. Most lodgings don't have any way for you to get online. There are only a handful of Internet cafés. The best bet is Cowabunga's, an ice-cream shop in Rincón. It's open Tuesday to Sunday noon to 9.

Larger towns like Arecibo and Mayagüez have a main post office with smaller branches throughout the city. You can often buy stamps in grocery and drug stores. Generally, post offices are open weekdays from 7 or 8 AM until 5 or 6 PM and for a few hours Saturday morning.

🖪 **Internet Cafés Cowabunga's** ⊠ Rte. 115, Km 11.6, Rincón ☎ 787/823–5225.

🖪 **Post Offices Cabo Rojo Post Office** ⊠ 64 Calle Carbonell, Cabo Rojo ☎ 787/851–1095. **Mayagüez Main Office** ⊠ 60 Calle McKinley W, Mayagüez 00680 ☎ 787/265–3138. **Rincón Main Office** ⊠ 100 Rte. 115, Rincón 00677 ☎ 787/823–2625.

OVERNIGHT SERVICES — Express Mail, overnight, and two-day service is available at all main post offices. FedEx has offices in Aguadilla at the Borinquen Airport (Hangar 404) and in Arecibo (Rte. 10, Km 83.2). There are drop boxes at the Holiday Inn Mayagüez and the Mayagüez Resort & Casino. UPS has a branch in Mayagüez at Airport El Maní, which closes at 5 PM.

🖪 **FedEx** ☎ 877/838–7834. **UPS** ☎ 800/742–5877 or 787/253–2877.

SAFETY
Unless you're camping in a recreational area, it's best to go to forest reserves during daylight hours only. Outside metro areas there's little crime, but you should take normal precautions: remember to lock your car and don't leave valuables unattended.

TOUR OPTIONS
The Mayagüez-based AdvenTours offers bird-watching, biking, and kayaking trips.

🖪 **AdvenTours** ⊠ 17 Calle Uroyán, Mayagüez ☎ 787/831–6447 ⊕ www.adventourspr.com.

VISITOR INFORMATION

The Puerto Rico Tourism Company has an office at the Rafael Hernández Airport in Aguadilla. The Cabo Rojo branch is open Monday through Saturday from 8 to 4:30. The town of Rincón has a tourism office on Route 115; it's open weekdays from 9 to 4. Mayagüez has a tourism office in city hall.

🖪 **Mayagüez City Hall** ⊠ 8 McKinley St., Mayagüez ☏ 787/834-8585. **Puerto Rico Tourism Company** ⊠ Rafael Hernández Airport, Aguadilla ☏ 787/890-3315. **Rincón Tourism Office** ⊠ Rte. 115, Rincón ☏ 787/823-5024.

The Cordillera Central

WORD OF MOUTH

" . . .you can go caving at Rio Camuy, one of the largest underground cave systems in the world and visit Arecibo (the huge telescope featured in the movies *Golden Eye* and *Contact*). There's lots of great dining options too."

—TravelFamily4

"Jayuya in the center of the island, in the middle of the mountains (Cordillera Central Mountains) . . .is an amazing destination for really adventurous people who want to get a real feeling of the island."

—Maira

Revised and
Updated by
Mark Sullivan

THERE'S MORE TO PUERTO RICO THAN BEAUTIFUL BEACHES, as anyone who lives on the island will tell you. When they want to escape the heat, islanders head to the Cordillera Central. This mountain range, which runs for most of the length of the island, seems impossibly lush. Towering trees lean over the narrow roadways that crisscross the region, often brushing branches with those across the pavement. In the shade below, impatiens in shades of pink and purple bloom in profusion.

Agriculture is very important to the economy of the Cordillera Central. Bananas, pineapples, and plantains are grown throughout the region. Coffee was once a dominant crop along hillsides between Utuado and Maricao, and it can still be seen growing in small plots today. A few of the old plantation homes have been turned into quaint country inns, all of them stocked with plenty of blankets for cool evenings, when temperatures—especially in higher elevations—can drop into the 40s.

In the east you'll find several attractive colonial towns, such as Aibonito and Barranquitas. Farther west is karst country—terrain built up by limestone deposits in which erosion has produced fissures, sinkholes, and underground streams and rivers. The peaks above are often astounding. It's in the Bosque Estatal de Toro Negro that the island's highest peak, Cerro de Punta, rises 4,398 feet above sea level. It may not measure up to many around the world, but on this island it seems as tall as Mount Everest.

Visitors to the Cordillera Central often arrive via the island's northern coast. There's little to keep you in Arecibo, but the dusty little town makes a perfect gateway to such unmissable attractions as the Observatorio de Arecibo and Parque de las Cavernas del Río Camuy. And if you want your trip to combine hiking in the mountains with walking on the beach, you couldn't do better than stop in the cozy coastal town of Dorado.

Exploring the Northern Coast & Cordillera Central

The speedy Highway 22 and the more meandering Highway 2 head west from San Juan and swing around the northwestern part of the island, skirting the beaches of the northern coast. A short 45 minutes from the capital are the resort town of Dorado and, shortly thereafter, Arecibo. From the north, Route 10 speeds you from Arecibo to the mountain town of Utuado and the Cordillera Central, at an elevation of 3,000 feet.

If you want to get anywhere else in the Cordillera Central, you're going to have to take the narrow roads that traverse the rugged mountain range. Driving here takes patience; some roads aren't clearly marked, and others twist and turn for what seems an eternity. Towns such as Cayey, Aibonito, and Barranquitas can be reached on these twisting roads between Highway 10 and Highway 52, the other main route down from San Juan.

The Ruta Panorámica, which runs horizontally across the island, passes through this area. The grandiose name may lead you to think that the Ruta Panorámica is a highway. Don't be fooled. It's a network of mountain roads that snakes through the region. Some are nicely maintained, others are little more than gravel. But the Panoramic

TOP 5 PICKS FOR THE NORTHERN COAST & CORDILLERA CENTRAL

- Hiking in the Bosque Estatal de Toro Negro, home to the island's highest lake and tallest mountain.
- Feasting on roasted suckling pig at one of the roadside *lechoneras* near Cayey.
- Reliving scenes from the movie *Contact* at the Observatorio de Arecibo, the world's largest radar–radio telescope.
- Bird-watching in the Bosque Estatal de Maricao, where you can see more species than anywhere else on the island.
- Looking for blue-eyed river crabs and long-legged tarantulas in the Parque de las Cavernas del Río Camuy.

Route does live up to its name, providing eye-catching vistas around every bend of the road.

Numbers in the text correspond to numbers in the margin and on the Cordillera Central map.

About the Restaurants

Traditional Puerto Rican cooking is the norm in this part of the island. But that's not to say you won't find anything memorable. Along Route 184, not far from Cayey, look for restaurants serving slow-roasted *lechón* (suckling pig), a local delicacy cooked outdoors over coals.

	$$$$	**$$$**	**$$**	**$**	**¢**
AT DINNER	over $30	$20–$30	$12–$20	$8–$12	under $8

Prices are per person for a main course at dinner.

About the Hotels

In this part of the island there's seldom more than two or three options in any given town. Sometimes there's one hotel—take it or leave it. You'd better take it, especially if you're traveling on a weekend. The best lodgings, rustic retreats set beside a river or on acres of lush forest, are often booked solid. Make sure to call ahead, as it's a long way between towns.

	$$$$	**$$$**	**$$**	**$**	**¢**
FOR 2 PEOPLE	over $350	$250–$350	$150–$250	$80–$150	under $80

Prices are for a double room in high season, excluding 9% tax (11% for hotels with casinos, 7% for paradores) and 5%–12% service charge.

Timing

The temperate climate of the mountainous central zone makes it a pleasure to visit year-round. Locals especially like to head up to this area in summer, when Aibonito holds its Flower Festival (late June or July) and Barranquitas hosts its Artisans Fair (July). The weather gets hot in August and September, but the north-coast beaches help everyone stay cool. Note that during busy times some hotels require a minimum two- or three-night stay on weekends.

THE NORTH COAST

West of San Juan, large tracts of coconut palms silhouette Dorado and its environs, the scenic remnants of large coconut and fruit plantations. Farther west, near Arecibo, the island's limestone karst country is distinguished by haystack-shaped hills (called *mogotes* by locals) and underground rivers and caves. One of the island's most fascinating geological wonders is the Río Camuy cave system, one of the largest such systems in the Western Hemisphere. Nearby, science takes center stage at the Arecibo Observatory, the largest radar–radio telescope in the world.

Dorado

❶ *27 km (17 mi) west of San Juan.*

This small and tidy town has a definite festive air about it, even though more and more it's turning into a suburb for San Juan's workers. It's one of the oldest vacation spots on the island, having gotten a boost in 1955 when Laurance Rockefeller bought the pineapple, coconut, and grapefruit plantation of Dr. Alfred Livingston and his daughter Clara, and built a resort on the property. Sadly, the Hyatt Dorado Beach Resort & Country Club closed in May 2005. But its excellent golf courses— among the best-known in Puerto Rico—are still open. The town of Dorado itself is fun to visit; its winding road leads across a bridge to a main square, and there are small bars, restaurants, and shops nearby. Most visitors, however, don't stray too far from the beach.

Beaches

Playa Breñas. The exceptional stretch of beachfront near the Hyatt resort is known for its surfing; adventurous swimmers also enjoy the waves. ⊠ *Rte. 693, Km 10.8.*

Playa Cerro Gordo. The 2,500-foot-long beach at the end of Route 690 is lined with cliffs. It's very popular and can get crowded on weekends. ⊠ *At the end Rte. 690.*

Playa Los Tubos. This beach is popular for both swimming and surfing. It holds a summer festival with live music and water-sports competitions, normally the first week of July. ⊠ *Rte. 687, Vega Baja.*

Playa Sardinera. This Dorado beach is suitable for swimming and has shade trees, changing rooms, and restrooms. ⊠ *At the end of Rte. 697.*

IF YOU LIKE

BOATING
On any weekend, people from all over Puerto Rico make a beeline for Lago Dos Bocas, a beautiful reservoir north of Utuado. Take the ferry leaving from the main dock to any of the seafood shacks on the opposite shore. These boats, which are used as public transportation for the locals, have spectacular views of the mountains.

COLONIAL TOWNS
Although the island's southern edge has the best-known colonial capitals, the Cordillera Central has several little-known gems. Towns such as Aibonito, Barranquitas, and Cayey have lovely central squares.

And don't miss Jayuya, which has Casa Canales, a replica of a 19th-century coffee plantation.

HIKING
The Cordillera Central has a number of forest reserves that rival the better-known El Yunque. The Bosque Estatal de Río Abajo has trails in the island's "karst country." The cloud-covered Bosque Estatal de Toro Negro has waterfalls, natural pools, and the island's tallest mountain peak, Cerro de Punta, which rises to 4,398 feet. The drier Bosque Estatal de Maricao is known for its numerous species of birds, including many on the endangered list.

Where to Eat

$$$–$$$$ ✗ **El Ladrillo.** This cozy spot covers its brick walls (*ladrillo* means "brick") from floor to ceiling with original paintings. Many of the dishes on the menu are Spanish, which might account for the many portraits of Don Quixote. There's a wide selection of seafood—try the *zarzuela*, a combination of lobster, squid, octopus, and clams. Lobster is a specialty, and you can order it *a la criolla* (in a spicy stew), *a la parrilla* (from the grill), or *ajillo* (with a garlic sauce). The steaks are also good, especially the filet mignon. The red-jacketed waiters really know their stuff. ⊠ *Calle Méndez Vigo 334* ☎ *787/796–2120* ▭ *AE, MC, V.*

$$–$$$$ ✗ **Mangére.** Any night of the week you're likely to find this place packed with locals, who come for the convivial atmosphere as much as the delicious Italian fare. The glassed-in dining room gets noisy, so you may have to shout when you order the veal medallions with portobello and porcini mushrooms or the salmon with capers. Unusual for these parts, there's even a good selection of vegetarian options, including a hearty broccoli alfredo. The wine list, which naturally focuses on Italian vintages, is impressive. ⊠ *Rte. 693, Km 8.5* ☎ *787/796–4444* ▭ *AE, D, MC, V.*

$$–$$$ ✗ **A La Brasa.** Argentine-style steak houses have become quite popular, and this modest little place is no exception. You can watch as the cook tosses your meat on the grill, flipping it with a casual flair. The selections are many, from the 12-ounce flank steak to the 18 ounces of beef short ribs. A delicious dessert selection is the *panqueque de dulce de leche*, a caramel-filled crepe. ⊠ *Rte. 693, Km 8.5* ☎ *787/796–4477* ▭ *AE, D, MC, V.*

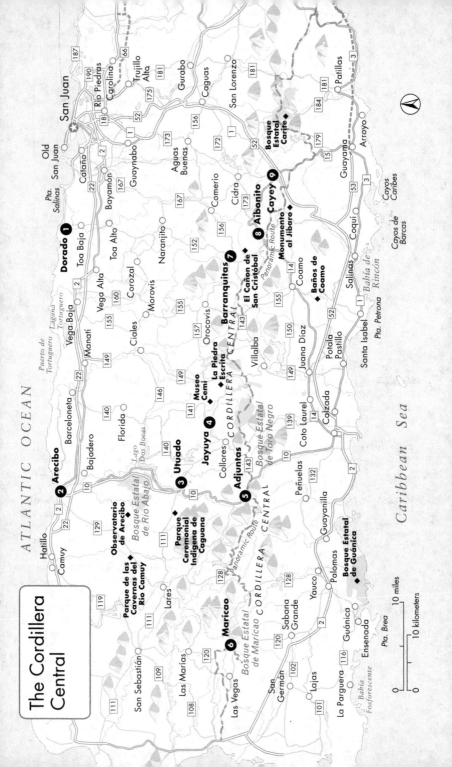

The Cordillera Central

ATLANTIC OCEAN

Caribbean Sea

San Juan
Old San Juan
Río Piedras
Carolina
Trujillo Alto
Cataño
Guaynabo
Bayamón
Aguas Buenas
Comerío
Cidra
Gurabo
Caguas
San Lorenzo

Dorado 1

Toa Baja
Toa Alta
Vega Alta
Naranjito
Corozal
Morovis

Arecibo 2

Barceloneta
Bajadero
Florida
Manatí
Vega Baja

Utuado 3

Jayuya 4

Adjuntas 5

Maricao 6

Barranquitas 7

Aibonito 8

Cayey 9

Museo Cemi
La Piedra Escrita
El Cañon de San Cristóbal
Monumento al Jíbaro
Baños de Coamo

Observatorio de Arecibo
Parque de las Cavernas del Río Camuy
Parque Ceremonial Indígena de Caguana

Bosque Estatal de Río Abajo
Bosque Estatal de Toro Negro
Bosque Estatal de Maricao
Bosque Estatal de Guánica

Bosque Estatal Carite

Laguna Tortuguero
Puerto de Tortuguero
Pta. Salinas

Hatillo
Camuy

Ciales
Orocovis
Villalba
Collores
Adjuntas

Coamo
Juana Díaz
Coto Laurel
Colzada
Peñuelas
Guayanilla
Guánica
Palomas
Yauco
Sabana Grande
Lajas
La Parguera
Ensenada

San Sebastián
Las Marías
Lares
Las Vegas
San Germán

Coamo
Salinas
Santa Isabel
Potala Pastillo

Guayama
Arroyo
Patillas

Bahía de Rincón
Pta. Petrona
Bahía Fosforescente
Pta. Brea

Cayos Caribes
Cayos de Barcas

CORDILLERA CENTRAL

Panoramic Route

10 miles

10 kilometers

GREAT ITINERARIES

IF YOU HAVE 1 DAY

If you feel like escaping from San Juan for a day, head to one of the resorts in **Dorado ❶**. Because so many of *sanjuaneros* do just that, this pretty little town has some of the best restaurants on the island.

IF YOU HAVE 2 DAYS

If you have another day, you can still base yourself by the lovely Dorado beaches. If you tire of beach-bumming and feel like a feast, head to **Cayey ❾**. Along Route 184 you will find a string of open-air eateries serving suckling pig. On weekends the roads are jammed with people from San Juan and Ponce sampling the Puerto Rican version of comfort food. To burn off a few calories, you might go for a stroll in the 7,000-acre

Bosque Estatal Carite. If you're spending the night, head to **Aibonito ❽** or **Barranquitas ❼**, or just return to Dorado.

IF YOU HAVE 3 DAYS

For your base camp, head to one of the converted coffee plantations near **Utuado ❸**. Make sure to explore the area's sights, such as Parque Ceremonial Indigena de Caguana. If it's a weekend, take a boat ride across Lago Dos Bocas. On Day 2 explore the trails that crisscross Bosque Estatal de Toro Negro, a state forest near **Jayuya ❹**. On Day 3 head to **Maricao ❻**, where you'll find the spectacular Bosque Estatal de Maricao. This state forest is one of the island's most important bird-watching destinations.

Where to Stay

$$ 🖭 **Embassy Suites Dorado del Mar Beach & Golf Resort.** Kids love the free-form pool that shimmers in the courtyard of this beachfront resort. All the suites have separate bedrooms and living rooms but are otherwise uninteresting. Golfers can take in the mountains and the sea at the same time while playing the course designed by the legendary Chi Chi Rodríguez. The Paradise Café serves Caribbean favorites such as crusted sea bass with mango butter. ⊠ *201 Dorado del Mar Blvd., 00646* ☎ *787/796–6125* 🖷 *787/796–6145* ⊕ *www.embassysuitesdorado.com* ⟿ *174 suites, 35 condos* ⚹ *2 restaurants, room service, kitchenettes, cable TV with movies, in-room data ports, 18-hole golf course, 2 tennis courts, pool, gym, hot tub, bar, video game room, shop, dry cleaning, laundry facilities, laundry service, meeting rooms* ▤ *AE, D, DC, MC, V* ❦❖ *BP.*

Sports & the Outdoors

DIVING & SNORKELING The north coast has several good areas for snorkeling and diving, including an underwater "aquarium" full of tropical fish and coral just off Cerro Gordo Beach. For trips aboard a six-person catamaran, contact **Pez Vela** (☎ 787/215–3806). Two hour trips cost $75 per person.

GOLF ★ Originally sketched out by Robert Trent Jones Sr., the four 18-hole golf courses at the **Dorado Beach Country Club** (⊠ Rte. 693, Km 10.8 ☎ 787/796–1234) all got a face-lift in 2005. Six new holes and six redesigned holes mean that the **Pineapple** and the **Sugar Cane** courses feel completely different. Jack Niklaus has said that the 4th hole at the **East Course** is one of the top-10 holes in the world. The **West Course** is buffeted by constant breezes off the Atlantic, making it tough to negotiate. All golfers can use the Plantation Club, a 45,000-square-foot pro shop completed in 2005. Prices vary from $105 to $160 for guests and $130 to $195 for nonguests.

The 7,100-yard **Dorado del Mar** (✉ Rte. 693, west of Dorado city center ☎ 787/796–3065) is a Chi Chi Rodríguez signature course with narrow fairways that can be a challenge to hit when the wind picks up. Greens fees are $102 in the morning and $87 in the afternoon.

HORSEBACK   **Tropical Paradise Horse Back Riding** (✉ Off Rte. 690, west of Hyatt Ha-
RIDING   cienda del Mar ☎ 787/720–5454) arranges rides along the beach on beautiful Paso Fino horses.

Shopping

About 20 minutes from Dorado via Highway 22 at Exit 55 is Puerto Rico's first factory outlet mall. **Prime Outlets Puerto Rico** (✉ Hwy. 2, Km 54.8, Barceloneta ☎ 787/846–9011) is a pastel village of more than 40 stores selling discounted merchandise from such familiar names as Liz Claiborne, Polo, Calvin Klein, Brooks Brothers, the Gap, Reebok, and Tommy Hilfiger.

Arecibo

❷ *60 km (38 mi) west of Dorado.*

As you approach Arecibo on Highway 22, you see its white buildings glistening in the sun against an ocean backdrop. The town was founded in 1515 and is known as the "Villa of Captain Correa" because of a battle fought here by Captain Antonio Correa and a handful of Spanish soldiers to repel a British sea invasion in 1702. Today it's a busy manufacturing center, and serves as a link for visits to two of the island's most fascinating sights—the Parque de las Cavernas del Río Camuy and the Observatorio de Arecibo, both south of the city—and for deeper exploration of the central mountain region. For one of the best ocean drives on the island, get off the main road at Barceloneta and take Route 681 into Arecibo's waterfront district.

Ⓒ A beautiful example of Spanish colonial architecture, the **Faro de Arecibo** (Arecibo Lighthouse) is among the loveliest on the island. Dating from 1897, it sits on a bluff high above Arecibo. Although the museum inside the lighthouse has maritime treasure that will interest everyone in your group, the rest of the park is strictly kid stuff. There are scaled-down replicas of Christopher Columbus's *Niña, Pinta,* and *Santa María* and replicas of the huts used by the island's original inhabitants, the Taíno Indians. On weekends, groups in traditional costumes play live music; there's a café with a sitting area where you can watch the revelry. Follow the signs from Highway 2. ✉ *End of Rte. 655, off Rte. 681* ☎ *787/817–1936* 🖃 *$9* ⊙ *Weekdays 9–6, weekends 10–7.*

Fodor'sChoice   Hidden among pine-covered hills is the **Observatorio de Arecibo,** the world's
★   largest radar–radio telescope. Operated by the National Astronomy

Modern Day Taínos?

PUERTO RICO'S FIRST INHABITANTS—today known as *Arcaicos* (Archaics)—appear to have traveled on rafts from Florida around AD 500. These hunter-gatherers lived near the shore and subsisted on fish and fruit. By AD 1000, the Arawak, who came from South America by canoe, were replacing the Arcaicos. The agrarian Taíno (a subgroup of the Arawak) established thatched villages on the island, which they called Boriquén.

In his journal Columbus describes the Taíno as "beautiful and tall, with a gentle, laughing language." Although this language was unwritten, it still echoes in some island place names and in everyday items such as *casabe* (a kind of bread). Many Taíno folktales have also survived, as have some art and artifacts. They were adept at wood,

shell, and stone carving, and the small figures they made of people and animals had great significance. Known as *cemí* (or *zemí*), the diminutive statues were believed to have the power to protect villages and families.

Studies suggest that there are still islanders with Taíno genes. In some isolated communities in the mountains of Maricao, around 70% of subjects with dark skin and straight black hair had traces of Amerindian DNA. A study in Mayagüez found that 50% of the subjects had such traces. Although it's been long thought the Taíno died out after their 1493 encounter with Columbus, it's possible the Taínos survived much longer or were more numerous than previously thought.

—Karen English and John Marino

and Ionosphere Center of Cornell University, the 20-acre dish lies in a 563-foot-deep sinkhole in the karst landscape. If the 600-ton platform hovering eerily over the dish looks familiar, it may be because it can be glimpsed in scenes from the movie *Contact*. (And yes, the dish has been used to seach for extraterrestrial life.) You can walk around the viewing platform and explore two levels of interactive exhibits on planetary systems, meteors, and weather phenomena in the visitor center. ⊠ *Rte. 625, Km 3.0* ☎ *787/878-2612* ⊕ *www.naic.edu* 🖃 *$5* ☉ *Wed.–Fri. noon–4, weekends 9–4.*

Fodor'sChoice
★

The 268-acre **Parque de las Cavernas del Río Camuy** contains one of the world's largest cave networks. A tram takes you down a trail shaded by bamboo and banana trees to Cueva Clara, where the stalactites and stalagmites turn the entrance into a toothy grin. Hour-long guided tours in English and Spanish lead you on foot through the 180-foot-high cave, which is teeming with wildlife. You're likely to see blue-eyed river crabs and long-legged tarantulas. More elusive are the more than 100,000 bats that

CAUTION

If it's rainy, call ahead before making the long drive to Parque de las Cavernas del Río Camuy. The caves are sometimes closed during wet weather, when the paths can get slippery.

make their home in the cave. They don't come out until dark, but you can feel the heat they generate at the cave's entrance. The visit ends with a tram ride to Tres Pueblos sinkhole, where you can see the third-longest underground river in the world passing from one cave to another. Tours are first-come, first-served; plan to arrive early on weekends, when local families join the crowds. Tours are sometimes canceled if it is raining, as the steep walkways can get slippery. There's a picnic area, cafeteria, and gift shop. ⊠ *Rte. 129, Km 18.9* 🕾 *787/898–3100* 🖃 *$10* ⊙ *Wed.–Sun. 8–4; last tour at 3:45.*

Where to Eat

$–$$ ✕ **El Buen Café.** Halfway between Arecibo and Hatillo, this diner is packed with locals, especially on weekends. You can sit at the curvy counter or at one of the cozy booths. A favorite dish on the long menu is *carne mechada* (stuffed pot roast). Breakfast is also served starting at 5 AM. ⊠ *381 Hwy. 2, Km 84, Hatillo* 🕾 *787/898–3495* 🖃 *AE, MC, V.*

Where to Stay

¢ 🏨 **Hotel Villa Real.** Near the eastern edge of Arecibo, the Hotel Villa Real is a good choice if you're heading to any of the attractions in the mountains or along the coast. It's nothing fancy, but it's one of the few options in the area. The rooms are clean and spacious; for a few dollars more you can get one with a hot tub. The restaurant serves local fare. ⊠ *Hwy. 2, Km 67.2, Box 344, 00613* 🕾 *787/881–4134* 🖷 *787/881–1992* 🖅 *40 rooms, 4 villas, 13 apartments* ⌂ *Restaurant, cable TV, pool, hair salon* 🖃 *AE, MC, V* ⦿� *EP.*

THE CORDILLERA CENTRAL

The Cordillera Central is for those who like to get off the well-traveled roads and spend time exploring small towns, rural areas, and unspoiled nature. It's here, in several large forest reserves, that Puerto Rico has its greatest ecotourism potential. The area's natural beauty has attracted people for centuries, including pre-Columbian Indians, who have left behind remnants of earlier civilizations. You can explore these at the Parque Ceremonial Indígena de Caguana, near Utuado. There are also some forests that rival El Yunque: Bosque Estatal de Toro Negro in Jayuya and Bosque Estatal de Río Abajo in Utuado.

> **CAUTION**
>
> Give yourself plenty of time when navigating the Ruta Panorámica, the so-called "Panoramic Route" that runs through the Cordillera Central. Almost all parts of the route are marked by hairpin curves and bridges originally built for horsedrawn carts.

Utuado

❸ *32 km (20 mi) south of Arecibo, 24 km (15 mi) northwest of Jayuya.*

Utuado was named after a local Taíno chief, Otoao. Surrounded by mountains and dotted with blue lakes, the town of Utuado sits in the middle of lush, natural beauty. Just driving on Route 10 between Arecibo and Utuado is an experience—imposing brown limestone cliffs flank the road, and clouds often hover around the tops of the surrounding hills. The town's narrow and sometimes busy streets lead to a double-steepled church on the main plaza. The best sights, however, are outside town along winding side roads.

In the middle of karst country, the **Bosque Estatal de Río Abajo** (Río Abajo State Forest) spans some 5,000 acres and includes huge bamboo stands and native silk-cotton trees. It also has several plantations of Asian teaks, Dominican and Honduran mahogany, and Australian pines, which are part of a government tree management program that supplies wood for the local economy (primarily for artisans and fence building). Walking trails wind through the forest, which is one of the habitats of the rare Puerto Rican parrot. An information office is near the entrance, and a recreation area with picnic tables is farther down the road. ⊠ *Rte. 621, Km 4.4* ☎ *787/817–0984* ⌣ *Free* ☉ *Daily dawn–dusk.*

East of Bosque Estatal de Río Abajo is **Lago Dos Bocas,** one of several man-made lakes near Utuado. Government-operated boats take you around the U-shaped lake from a dock, called El Embarcadero, near the intersection of Routes 123 and 146. Although the boats are used primarily as a means of public transit for residents, the 45-minute ride around the lake is pleasant and scenic, and gets you to four shoreline restaurants known for criollo cuisine and seafood. The boats are free and leave daily between 7 and 5. Trips after 3 PM are usually reserved for residents and returning passengers. The lake is stocked with sunfish, bass, and catfish; you can also fish from the shore. ⊠ *Off Rte. 10, accessed via Rtes. 621, 123, 146, and 612* ☎ *787/879–1838 for El Embarcadero* ⌣ *Free* ☉ *Boats daily 7–5.*

The 13 acres of **Parque Ceremonial Indígena de Caguana** were used more than 800 years ago by the Taíno tribes for worship and recreation, including a game—thought to have religious significance—that resembled modern-day soccer. Today you can see a dozen *bateyes* (ball courts) of various sizes, as well as some large stone monoliths carved with petroglyphs. Archaeologists believe this may have been one of the most important ceremonial sites for the Taíno people. ⊠ *Rte. 111, Km 12.3* ☎ *787/894–7325* ⌣ *$2* ☉ *Daily 8:30–4:30.*

Where to Eat

$–$$$ ✕ **El Fogón de Abuela.** This rustic restaurant on the edge of Dos Bocas Lake would make any Puerto Rican grandmother envious. The menu features stews, red snapper (whole or filleted), and fricassees, including pork chop, goat, and rabbit. You arrive either by taking the public boat from El Embarcadero on Route 612, by calling the restaurant from the dock and requesting a boat be sent to pick you up (free of charge), or by driving to the south side of the lake. From Utuado, take Route 111 to Route 140 to Route 612 and follow that to its end. The restaurant is open weekends only. ⊠ *Lago Dos Bocas* ☎ *787/894–0470* ▭ *MC, V* ☉ *Closed Mon.–Thurs.*

CLOSE UP

Hit That Perfect Beat

MUSIC IS THE HEART AND SOUL of Puerto Rico. Take the instruments from the days of the Taíno Indians—the *guiro* (scratch gourd) and the *fotuto* (conch shell)—and blend them with the drums and rhythms of Africa that took root on the island's sugarcane-lined coasts. To this mixture, stir in the Spanish-Moorish-influenced music of the inland farmers and mountain folk—the *trovadores,* who still perform their improvised songs accompanied by the *cuatro* (ten-string Puerto Rican guitar). Let all this simmer for a couple of centuries, and there you have it.

The island's brash Latin sound is best exemplified by the highly danceable salsa, especially as interpreted by such entertainers as the late, great Tito Puente and pop sensation Ricky Martin. Salsa, Spanish for "sauce" (as in the sauce that energizes the party) is a fusion of West African percussion and jazz with a swing beat. Two of its predecessors, *bomba* and *plena,* can still be heard today. Bomba is African-based drum and dance music in which a lead singer often leads a chorus of singers in a call-and-response interplay, similar to Cuba's rumba music. Plena is a more melodic country music that makes use of the cuatro as well as scratch gourds.

Other Latin beats heard on the island, with origins in the Caribbean, Latin America, and Spain, are mambo, merengue, flamenco, cha-cha, and rumba. Increasingly, young musicians are experimenting with new forms. Salsón and reggaetón, high-energy versions of salsa and reggae, are the new beat of the island. You hear them everywhere, from bars to beaches.

Where to Stay

$ FodorśChoice ★ **Casa Grande Mountain Retreat.** This isn't sleeping in a tree house, but it's close. The guest rooms here are in five wooden buildings that sit on platforms high above the varied vegetation. When you lie in the hammock on your private porch, all you can see is mountains in every direction. The furnishings couldn't be simpler—little more than a bed and a dresser—but that's part of the rustic charm. Leave the windows open at night to hear the chorus of tiny tree frogs sing cantatas. If this doesn't relax you, yoga classes are offered every morning. Even people who aren't staying here stop to dine on the terrace at Jungle Jane's restaurant, which features Puerto Rican specialties. ✉ *Rte. 612, Km 0.3, Box 1499, 00641* ☎ *787/894–3939 or 800/343–2272* 🖷 *787/894–3900* 🌐 *www.hotelcasagrande.com* *20 rooms* *Restaurant, fans, pool, fitness classes, hiking; no a/c, no room phones, no room TVs, no smoking* 💳 *AE, MC, V* 🍴 *EP.*

Sports & the Outdoors

HIKING **Expediciones Tanamá** (✉ Rte 111, Km 14.5, Barrio Angeles ☎ 787/894–7685) leads half-day or full-day excursions into the Río Tanamá underground-cave system. Guides speak limited English but are friendly and eager. Lunch is included. There's a free camping site adjacent to the office, which provides electricity and bathrooms.

HORSEBACK RIDING Across from Casa Grande Mountain Retreat, **Rancho de Caballos** (⊠ Rte. 612, Km 0.3 ☎ 787/894–0240) offers three- to four-hour horse rides through mountain forests.

KAYAKING Jenaro Colón at **Locura Arecibeña** (⊠ End of Rte. 612 ☎ 787/878–1809) can arrange for rentals and guided tours of Lago Dos Bocas.

Jayuya

❹ *24 km (15 mi) southeast of Utuado.*

This small town of 15,000 is in the foothills of the Cordillera Central, Puerto Rico's tallest mountain range. Cerro de Punta, the island's highest peak, looms to the south of the town center. Named after the Indian chief Hauyua, Jayuya is known for preserving its Indian heritage and draws people from all over the island for its yearly Indigenous Festival in November, which features crafts, exhibits, parades, music, and dancing. Coffee is still grown in the area—look for the locally produced Tres Picachos.

★ The main attraction of the 7,000-acre **Bosque Estatal de Toro Negro** (Toro Negro State Forest) is the island's crowning glory: 4,398-foot Cerro de Punta. The Black Bull State Forest also has the island's highest lake, Lago Guineo, and one of the most impressive waterfalls, 200-foot Doña Juana Falls). The best place to start exploring this vast park is at the ranger station on Route 143. Make sure to ask the friendly staffers for a trail map, although it's certain to be a copy of a copy of a copy. The trails, such as one from the ranger station that leads to an observation tower with views of the northern and southern sides of the island, are not always well marked. East of the ranger station, at the Doña Juana Recreational Area, there are more trails. Keep an eye out for exotic birds such as the Guadalupe woodpecker. The reserve also contains a huge, but often out-of-service, swimming pool built into the side of a mountain. ⊠ *Rte. 143, Km 32.4* ☎ *787/867–3040* ☒ *Free* ☉ *Ranger station daily 6–6.*

You'll want to relax on the front porch of the charming **Casa Canales**, a re-creation of the home of Jayuya's first mayor, Rosario Canales. Like the original building, dating from the late 19th century, it has tiny bedrooms surrounding a central parlor. Windows on all sides can be flung open to catch the breeze. There are lots of period furnishings, such as the hand-carved wooden chairs. Even the china on the dining room table belonged to the family. ⊠ *Rte. 144, Km 9.3* ☎ *787/828–4094* ☒ *$1* ☉ *Weekdays 12:30–4, weekends noon–4.*

This is definitely the weirdest building in Puerto Rico. The tiny **Museo Cemí** (Cemí Museum) is named for a Taíno artifact believed to have religious significance. This structure resembles the snail-like cemí, and you enter through its mouth. The collection, however, is pretty dull. On display are religious and ceremonial objects found on the island. ⊠ *Rte. 144, Km 9.3* ☎ *787/828–1241* ☒ *Free* ☉ *Weekdays 8–4:30, weekends 10–3:30.*

6

La Piedra Escrita (Enscribed Rock) is a huge boulder with handful of highly visible Taíno petroglyphs, located in a stream among several other large rocks. The area has been completely renovated, so now there are several viewing areas and a shady spot for a picnic lunch. Don't worry, the boulder in the parking lot painted a lurid shade of blue is *not* La Piedra Escrita. ⊠ *Rte. 144, Km 7.8* ⊠ *Free.*

Where to Stay & Eat

$ ✕⊞ **Parador Hacienda Gripiñas.**

Fodor'sChoice Built on the grounds of a coffee
★ plantation, this 19th-century inn is
surrounded on all sides by mountain peaks. Several of the clapboard-walled rooms in the red-roofed manor house have private balconies overlooking lush gardens and the spring-fed pool; the nicest are Numbers 4 and 5. There are plenty of small parlors where you can relax with a drink from the bar. Breakfast and dinner are included in the room rates. The dining area, which meanders through three different rooms, serves criollo fare such as chicken with rice and beans. Nonguests are welcome for dinner, too. One hiking trail near the property leads to Cerro de Punta, about a 2½-hour climb. ⊠ *Rte. 152, Km 1.7, Box 387, 00664* ☎ *787/828–1717* 🖷 *787/ 828–1719* ⊕ *www.haciendagripinas.com* ⟿ *19 rooms* ♻ *Restaurant, cable TV, 2 pools, hiking, bar* ⊟ *AE, MC, V* ❍*❙ MAP.*

> **WORD OF MOUTH**
>
> "My parents, who are in their sixties and not the rustic type of traveler at all, have stayed at [Parador] Hacienda Gripiñas and enjoyed it."   –PRnative.

Adjuntas

❺ *27 km (17 mi) southwest of Jayuya.*

The coffee-growing town of Adjuntas sits north of Puerto Rico's Ruta Panorámica. Although known for its coffee, it's also the world's leading producer of citron, a fruit whose rind is processed here and then shipped for use in sweets, especially fruitcakes. Few tourists do more than drive through the town itself, but it has a quaint central plaza and a sporadic trolley used mostly by locals and school children.

Hiking trails, surrounded by wild-growing impatiens, lead up to the 3,900-foot Pico Guilarte and into other areas of **Bosque Estatal de Guilarte** (Guilarte State Forest). Bird-watchers have 26 different species to look for, including the carpenter bird. Or if your interest is botany, you can find a variety of trees, including candlewood, trumpet, Honduran mahogany, and Honduran pine. There's a pleasant picnic area near a eucalyptus grove. ⊠ *Rte. 518 at Rte. 131* ☎ *787/829–5767* ⊠ *Free* ⊙ *Information Center weekdays 7–3:30, weekends 9–5:30.*

Where to Stay & Eat

$ ✕⊞ **Villas de Sotomayor.** Covering more than 14 acres, this complex of modern villas has a summer-camp atmosphere. The focus is on horseback riding, and there are stables on the premises. You can also take horse-and-carriage rides around the grounds. Freestanding villas range in size from one bedroom with a refrigerator only to two bedrooms with a kitchenette. The on-site restaurant ($$) is open daily and serves international and criollo cuisine—it's known for its *mofongo relleno* (stuffed mashed plantains). ⊠ *Rte. 123, Km 36.8, Box 28, 00601* ☎ *787/829–1717* ⊠ *787/829–1774* ⊃ *35 villas* ♧ *Restaurant, some kitchenettes, some refrigerators, cable TV, 2 tennis courts, 2 pools, badminton, basketball, horseback riding, meeting room* ⊟ *AE, D, MC, V* ⟨◯⟩ *EP.*

Maricao

❻ *59 km (37 mi) west of Adjuntas; 43 km (27 mi) east of Mayagüez.*

Puerto Rico's smallest municipality (pop. 6,200), Maricao is part of the island's coffee country and hosts a well-known Coffee Harvest Festival each February. Although not far from Mayagüez—the third-largest urban area on the island—Maricao feels completely isolated.

Drier than other forest reserves found near the central mountains, ★ **Bosque Estatal de Maricao** (Maricao State Forest) is known as one of the island's most important bird-watching destinations. The 60 species found here—29 of which are endangered—include the Puerto Rican vireo and the elfin woods warbler. You'll find an information center and a stone observation tower about ½ mi beyond the forest entrance. The Centro Vacacional Monte de Estado has rustic cabins for rent. ⊠ *Rte. 120 at Rte. 366* ☎ *787/838–1040* ⬚ *Free* ⟳ *Park daily dawn–dusk.*

Part of the Bosque Estatal de Maricao is the **Vivero de Peces de Maricao.** The Maricao Fish Hatchery contains a collection of ponds and tanks where fish are raised to stock the island's lakes and streams. The carefully tended grounds are better groomed than most golf courses. ⊠ *Rte. 410, Km 1.7* ☎ *787/838–3710* ⬚ *Free* ⟳ *Thurs.–Sun., 8:30–11:30 and 1–3:30.*

Where to Stay & Eat

★ $ ✕⬚ **Parador La Hacienda Juanita.** Part of a coffee plantation dating from the 1800s, the hotel exudes the slower pace of days gone by. Rooms are in four wooden buildings, some with four-poster beds and antiques from the coffee industry's heyday. The accommodations are rustic—most have classic wooden shutters instead of glass windows. La Casona de Juanita ($$–$$$) serves up criollo cuisine, including *sancocho*, a hearty soup made with meat and root vegetables. Meals are served on a sweeping balcony where you can reach up and pull fruit off the trees. ⊠ *Rte. 105, Km 23.5, Box 777, 00606* ☎ *787/838–2550* ⊠ *787/838–2551* ⊕ *www.haciendajuanita.com* ⊃ *21 rooms* ♧ *Restaurant, fans, cable TV, tennis court, pool, hiking; no a/c* ⊟ *AE, MC, V* ⟨◯⟩ *MAP.*

Barranquitas

❼ *66 km (41 mi) east of Adjuntas, 15 km (9 mi) northwest of Aibonito.*

Founded in 1804, the small mountain town of Barranquitas appears to have changed little over the years. Its steep streets and quaint plaza seem light years away from the frenetic energy of Puerto Rico's larger cities. Its tranquillity has made Barranquitas a popular location for summer homes. One of the most beautiful, **El Cortijo** (on Route 162 at Km 9.9), was built in 1938 and is said to be haunted by a former servant. Although it's closed to the public, consider stopping to admire the sprawling white structure from the road. You *can* visit the former home and mausoleum of two of Barranquitas' most famous residents: Luis Muñoz Rivera, a politician and newspaperman, and his son, Luis Muñoz Marín, the island's first elected governor. In July craftspeople gather in Barranquitas for the annual Feria Nacional de Artesanías (National Artisans Fair), one of the most popular such events on the island.

Museo Luis Muñoz Rivera, one block west of the main square, occupies the house where Luis Muñoz Rivera—a politician, poet, and journalist famous for his support of Puerto Rican autonomy—was born in 1859. Many personal belongings and the manuscripts of his political writings and poems are housed here. There's also a friend's car—a 1912 Pierce Arrow—which transported Muñoz to political events. The small wooden house is considered a superb example of 19th-century rural architecture. It's wise to call in advance; the museum doesn't always stick to its posted hours. ⊠ *10 Calle Muñoz Rivera, at Calle Padre Berríos* ☎ *787/ 857–0230* 🖼 *Free* ⊙ *Wed.–Sun. 8:30–4:20.*

Steps away from Luis Muñoz Rivera's birthplace you'll find the **Mausoleo de la Familia Muñoz** (⊠ Calle Padre Berríos, 2 blocks west of main plaza), where Muñoz Rivera and his son, Luis Muñoz Marín, are buried with other members of their family. It's in a small, parklike area.

Where to Eat

$–$$ ✕ **Casa Bavaria.** Enjoy a bit of Germany at this out-of-the-way eatery outside the town of Orocovis, about 16 km (10 mi) northwest of Barranquitas. Casa Bavaria is a kitschy blend of biergarten and casual country restaurant. Choose bratwurst and sauerkraut or chicken with rice and beans. On weekends, patrons spend a good part of the day enjoying the view from the terrace, singing along with the jukebox, and joking with the waiters, some of whom speak German as well as English and Spanish. ⊠ *Rte. 155, Km 38.3* ☎ *787/862–7818* 🖃 *AE, MC, V* ⊙ *Closed Mon.–Wed.*

Where to Stay

$ 🏨 **Hacienda Margarita.** This secluded hotel just north of Barranquitas is known for its sweeping mountain views. Seventeen modern rooms— each with a balcony—are in a concrete building. Smaller wooden buildings house 10 more rustic rooms that can accommodate up to four people bunkhouse-style. Watch the sun go down from the outdoor terrace or dine in the restaurant, well known for its Puerto Rican cuisine. It's open

Puerto Rico's Black Gold

CLOSE UP

WHEN THE LATE ISLAND POET Tomás Blanco wrote that coffee should be "black as the devil, hot as hell, and sweet as sin," he may well have had Puerto Rican brews in mind. Cultivated at high altitudes in a swirl of cool, moist air and mineral-rich soil, the island's beans are like gold—the black and aromatic sort.

Introduced in the mid-18th century from nearby Martinique, coffee started its life in Puerto Rico as a minor cash crop, cultivated mainly for consumption. But by the end of the 1700s Puerto Rico was producing more than a million pounds of coffee a year, and by the late 19th century, the island was the world's seventh largest producer of coffee.

Puerto Rican coffee benefited from the labors and experimentation of immigrants experienced in coffee production, and it was highly respected by connoisseurs in Europe and the Americas. Its status grew, yet Puerto Rican coffee suffered after Spain ceded the island to the United States in 1898, and after several major hurricanes. Today, Puerto Rican beans have once again taken their place next to the Jamaica Blue Mountain and Hawaiian Kona varieties as one of the world's premium coffees.

The secret is in the coffee bean itself (called "cherry"). The island's dominant bean is the *arabica*; it has a more delicate and lower-yielding cherry and produces half the caffeine of the prolific *robusta* bean found on the mega-plantations of Central and South America. The arabica cherry, in the proper conditions, is known as the richest and most flavorful among the coffee varieties. Cloud cover, tree shade, soil composition, and the

altitude at which the coffee bushes are grown—higher than 3,000 feet above sea level—combine to produce a slow-ripening bean that stays on the bush at least two months longer than at lower elevations. This lengthy ripening process acts as a sort of "pre-brew," imbuing the bean with a rich flavor and a slightly sweet aftertaste.

As the beans ripen, they turn from green to yellow to red, and the trees produce a white flower with a pleasant aroma similar to jasmine. Coffee-picking season starts in August and continues through February. The process is slow and delicate because workers pick through bushes manually to collect only the cherries that are fully ripe. Small, family-run pulperies are the norm. The ripened beans are pulped (shelled) to remove the outer covering, then fermented to remove a thin layer that covers the bean, called the "mucilago." The beans are then dried, roasted, and packed. The main coffee-growing areas of the island lie in the wet, mountainous regions of Yauco, Lares, and Las Marís, where the limited suitable terrain makes large-scale production impossible, making the coffee all the more precious a commodity.

Look for local brands: Yauco Selecto, Rioja, Yaucono, Cafe Rico, Crema, Adjuntas, Coqui, and Alto Grande Super Premium. Alto Grande has gained the most fame off the island and is guaranteed to have been grown at high altitudes. It's best consumed straight up as espresso, though many prefer to cut it with hot milk, the traditional *café con leche*, a local equivalent of café au lait.

–Karl Luntta

6

Friday for dinner and Saturday and Sunday for lunch and dinner. Regular rates include breakfast; all-inclusive rates are available. ⊠ *Rte. 152, Km 1.7, Box 100, 00794* ☎ *787/857–0414* 🖷 *787/857–1265* ⊕ *www. hotelhm.com* 🖙 *27 rooms* ⚷ *Restaurant, cable TV, pool, meeting rooms* ▤ *MC, V* ◉ *BP.*

Aibonito

❽ *15 km (9 mi) southeast of Barranquitas, 20 km (12 mi) northwest of Cayey.*

Legend has it that Aibonito got its name when a Spaniard exclaimed "¡Ay, que bonito!" ("Oh, how pretty!") upon seeing the valley where the town now stands. At 1,896 feet above sea level, it's Puerto Rico's highest city. Aibonito is known as "The Queen of Flowers" because flowering plants thrive in its temperate climate. The city hosts a flower festival every year, usually in late June or July, and gives awards for blossoms and garden design. Live music and craft stalls add to the festivities. A double-steeple cathedral graces the charming town square, which is surrounded by shops and restaurants. Local guides organize outings to nearby Cañon de San Cristóbal.

♺ **Mirador Piedra Degetau** (Degetau Lookout Rock) is a scenic point near Aibonito. From the tower, use the telescope to get a closer look at the surrounding mountains. You'll find picnic tables under gazebos and a playground nearby. ⊠ *Rte. 7718, Km 0.7* ☎ *787/735–3880* 🖃 *Free* ☉ *Wed.–Sun. 9–6.*

★ The **Cañon de San Cristóbal** is difficult to find, but it's well worth the effort. Trails of tropical vegetation lead to a breathtaking waterfall. Félix Rivera, a local guide, heads expeditions to the canyon (*see* Tour Options *in* Northern Coast & Cordillera Central Essentials, *below*). ⊠ *Rte. 725, Km 5.1* ☎ *787/857–2065* 🖃 *Free* ☉ *Daily.*

> **WORD OF MOUTH**
>
> "If you get a chance to hike the Cañon San Cristóbal by Aibonito, arrange it in advance with a guide, but we only saw it from a distance and it's very steep and beautiful."
> –lilipad.

Where to Stay & Eat

$–$$$ ✕ **La Piedra.** Near the Mirador Piedra Degetau, this hilltop restaurant has a panoramic view of Aibonito. You can see the lights of the city through the floor-to-ceiling windows. The food is abundant, from the chicken with tamarind sauce to the pork loin in an orange glaze. Even the side dishes, including the fried plantains, are memorable. If you're in the area on Sunday, drop by for the excellent buffet. ⊠ *Rte. 7718, Km 0.8* ☎ *787/735–1034* ▤ *D, MC, V* ☉ *Closed Mon. and Tues. No dinner Wed. and Thurs.*

¢ ▥ **El Coquí.** This shoebox-size hotel is much better than you'd expect in a small town. The rooms are spacious and have kitchenettes with more cabinet space than most people have at home. There are even small private balconies. ⊠ *Rte. 722, Km 7.3, 00705* ☎ *787/735–3150* 🖷 *787/ 735–2225* 🛏 *13 rooms* 🕭 *Restaurant, room service, cable TV, kitch- enettes, microwaves, refrigerators* ▤ *AE, D, MC, V* ¶ *CP.*

Cayey

❾ *19 km (12 mi) east of Aibonito, 50 km (30 mi) south of San Juan.*

Since it was founded in 1773, Cayey has attracted both visitors and set- tlers. Early on, the Spanish realized that the valley surrounding it was perfect for growing coffee and tobacco. Later, people were simply drawn by the refreshing breezes. Today its population of some 56,000 swells— particularly on weekends—with *sanjuaneros* (residents of San Juan) who shop in the strip malls on its outskirts, dine in its hillside restau- rants, or picnic in the nearby Bosque Estatal Carite.

In the 7,000-acre **Bosque Estatal Carite,** 40 km (25 mi) of trails run through stands of palms, Honduras mahogany, and Spanish cedars— many of which host orchids. One trail leads to Charco Azul (Blue Pond), whose cool waters appeal to overheated hikers. Before setting out, get hiking information at the park manager's office near the entrance on Route 184. If you'd like a space in one of the two campgrounds, be sure to get a permit in advance from the Puerto Rico Department of Natural Resources in San Juan. Picnic tables are scattered through- out the forest, and bathroom facilities are available near the camp- grounds. ⊠ *Rte. 184, Km 27.5* ☎ *787/747–4545* 🖾 *Free* ☉ *Office open weekdays 7–3.*

NEED A BREAK?

Mouthwatering marinated lechón, slow-roasted over open pits, is offered at a string of **lechoneras** along Route 184 just before the entrance to the Bosque Estatal Carite. They also serve slow-roasted chicken and a variety of compati- ble side dishes. Traffic jams are legendary on Sunday, when locals gather here along the strip to spend the day eating and listening to local bands.

Where to Eat

$$–$$$ ✕ **Sand and the Sea.** In the open-air dining room, the south-coast views are breathtaking, and the evening breezes are cool enough that you might find the fireplace ablaze. Nightly piano performances of show tunes and Puerto Rican ballads take away any remaining chill, especially when they become sing-alongs. Grilled churrasco and seafood dominate the menu, which changes so often that it's posted on a blackboard. Try the "Russ- ian" *tostones* (fried green plantains with sour cream and caviar). The place is open only on weekends. ⊠ *Rte. 715, Km 5.2* ☎ *787/738– 9086* ▤ *AE, D, MC, V* ☉ *Closed Mon.–Thurs.*

¢–$ ✕ **Martin's BBQ.** Locals come to this restaurant for a quick fix of tradi- tional slow-roasted chicken with all the trimmings—rice and beans, to- stones, and yucca. You order your food at the counter, choosing precisely how much chicken and which side dishes you want. There are picnic tables outside, tables inside, and take-out service. ⊠ *Rte. 1 at Cayey exit off Rte. 52* ☎ *787/738–1144* ▤ *MC, V.*

THE CORDILLERA CENTRAL ESSENTIALS

To research prices, get advice from other travelers, and book travel arrangements, visit www.fodors.com.

Transportation

BY AIR

Arecibo has a small airport for light planes but no regularly scheduled service. There are no airports in the Cordillera Central. Depending on your destination, you can fly into the airports in San Juan, Fajardo, Ponce, Mayagüez, or Aguadilla.

BY BUS

There's no easy network of buses linking the towns in the Cordillera Central. You'll have to depend on *públicos* (usually large vans) that make many stops. These vans usually stop near a town's main squar. Linea de Utuado travels between San Juan and Utuado daily. Prices are $12 per person. Trips to nearby Jayuya and Lares are also possible.

🚗 **Linea Utuado** ☎ 787/765-1908.

BY CAR

The well-maintained and scenic Route 10, which can be accessed in Arecibo, is a main link to the central mountain region. The Ruta Panorámica runs east–west across the island and near some of the central mountain towns. It's made up of a number of small roads, many of which can be hilly and curving. With few public transportation options, a car is essential if you want to see this area.

A road map is essential in the Cordillera Central. Most signs in the region give a route number, rather than the name of a town. You'll also need patience in navigating the twisting mountain roads.

Your best bet is to arrange for a rental car in one of the large cities on the coast, as there are only a handful of agencies in the Cordillera Central itself. If you are coming from the northern coast, you could rent a car from one of the major agencies in Arecibo or Dorado. If you arrive here and find you need a rental car, try Barranquitas Car Rental in Barranquitas or Payless Car Rental in Cayey and Utuado.

🚗 **Major Agencies Avis** ☎ 787/796-7243 in Dorado. **Hertz** ☎ 787/879-1132 in Arecibo.
🚗 **Local Agencies Barranquitas Car Rental** ✉ Barranquitas ☎ 787/857-7283. **Lease-way of Puerto Rico** ☎ 787/878-1606 in Arecibo. **Payless Car Rental** ✉ Cayey ☎ 787/738-7420 ✉ Utuado ☎ 787/894-5015.

GASOLINE Except for on major highways such as Route 52 (which runs past Cayey) and Route 10 (which leads from Arecibo to Utuado), gas stations are rare. Most towns will have at least one, but they are sometimes difficult to find. Locals are glad to point you in the right direction.

ROAD CONDITIONS Major highways in the Cordillera Central are well maintained. Watch out for potholes on secondary roads, especially after heavy rains.

EMERGENCY SERVICES   🚩 **Arecibo Towing Service** ✉ 313 Av. Juan Rosado, Arecibo ☎ 787/879–2902.

BY TAXI

In Arecibo, try Arecibo Taxi Cab, but note that they close at midnight. Fares to or from San Juan are steep: for example, service is $50 from Arecibo.

🚩 **Arecibo Taxi Cab** ☎ 787/878-2929.

Contacts & Resources

BANKS & EXCHANGE SERVICES

You'll find few banks in the region, although many supermarkets, drug stores, and gas stations have ATMs. Banks are normally open weekdays from 9 AM to 3 PM or 4 PM.

🚩 **Banco Popular** ✉ 55 Calle Degetau, Aibonito ☎ 787/735-6191 ✉ Rte. 156, Km 7.1, Barranquitas ☎ 787/857-4380 ✉ Rte. 14, Km 70.6, Cayey ☎ 787/738-2828 ✉ 84 Guillermo Esteves, Jayuya ☎ 787/828-4120 ✉ Calle Zuzuaregui at Calle Baldorioty, Maricao ☎ 787/838-3660 ✉ 59 Calle Cueto, Utuado ☎ 787/894-2700.

EMERGENCIES

🚩 **General emergencies** ☎ 911.

🚩 **Hospitals Centro de Salud** ✉ Calle Isaac González Martínez, Utuado ☎ 787/894-2875. **Hospital Menonita De Cayey** ✉ 4 Calle Mendoza, Cayey ☎ 787/263-1001. **Hospital Regional Dr. C. Coll y Toste** ✉ Rte. 129, Km 0.7, Arecibo ☎ 787/878-7272.

🚩 **24-hour Pharmacies Walgreens** ✉ Rte. 123. Bldg. 940, Utuado ☎ 787/894-0100 ✉ 4210 Rte. 693, Dorado ☎ 787/728-5800 ✉ Calle del Mar 547, Hatillo ☎ 787/880-0290.

INTERNET, MAIL & SHIPPING

There are practically no Internet cafés in this part of the island. If you need to be wired, make sure that your hotel has a connection.

There are branches of the U.S. Post Office throughout the region. Generally, post offices are open weekdays from 7 or 8 AM until 5 or 6 PM and for a few hours Saturday morning.

🚩 **Post Offices Arecibo Main Office** ✉ 10 Av. San Patricio, Arecibo 00612 ☎ 787/878-2775. **Dorado Main Office** ✉ 100 Rte. 698, Dorado 00646 ☎ 787/796-1052. **Utuado Main Office** ✉ 41 Av. Fernando L. Ribas, Utuado 00641 ☎ 787/894-2940.

TOUR OPTIONS

Atlantic Sun San Juan Tours has several different tours of the region. It has an office in Utuado. Félix Rivera, a local guide, heads expeditions to the Cañón de San Cristóbal.

🚩 **Atlantic San Juan Tours** 🗁 Box 215, Utuado 00611 ☎ 787/644-9841 ⊕ www.puertoricoexcursions.com. **Felix Rivera** ✉ Aibonito ☎ 787/644-5122.

VISITOR INFORMATION

Arecibo, Jayuya, Maricao, and Utuado have tourism offices in their town halls.

🚩 **Arecibo City Hall** ☎ 787/879-2232. **Jayuya** ☎ 787/282-5010. **Maricao** ☎ 787/838-2290. **Utuado** ☎ 787/894-3505.

UNDERSTANDING PUERTO RICO

PUERTO RICO AT A GLANCE

Fast Facts

Capital: San Juan
National anthem: *La Borinquéña (The Borinquen Anthem)*
Type of government: U.S. commonwealth, with a local governor, bicameral legislature, and a nonvoting commissioner to the U.S. House of Representatives, all elected. Local municipalities each have a mayor and an assembly. Foreign affairs are dealt with by the United States.
Administrative divisions: 78 municipalities
Constitution: July 25, 1952
Legal system: Based on Spanish civil code, but within the U.S. Federal System of Justice
Suffrage: 18 years of age, universal; indigenous inhabitants are U.S. citizens, but residents of Puerto Rico do not vote in U.S. presidential elections
Legislature: Bicameral Legislative Assembly consists of the Senate (28 seats; members are directly elected by popular vote to serve four-year terms) and the House of Representatives (51 seats; members are directly elected by popular vote to serve four-year terms)
Population: 3.9 million
Median age: female: 35.9, male: 32.5
Life expectancy: female: 82.4, male: 74.4
Infant mortality rate: 8.2 deaths per 1,000 live births
Literacy: 94.1%
Language: Spanish, English (both official languages)
Ethnic groups: White (mostly Spanish origin) 80.5%; other 10.9%; black 8%; Amerindian 0.4%; Asian 0.2%
Religion: Roman Catholic 85%; Protestant and other 15%
Discoveries & Inventions: Cuatro guitar (1800s), coconut cream (1948), piña colada (1954)

Geography & Environment

Land area: 3,459 square mi
Coastline: 311 mi
Terrain: Mountains, with coastal plain belt in north, mountains precipitous to sea on west coast, 28,000-acre Caribbean National Forest (known as El Yunque), sandy beaches along most coastal areas (highest point: Cerro de Punta at 4,389 feet)
Islands: Vieques, Culebra, Desecheo, Mona
Natural resources: Copper, nickel, potential for onshore and offshore oil
Natural hazards: Periodic droughts, hurricanes
Environmental issues: Erosion, occasional drought causing water shortages

Economy

Currency: U.S. dollar
GDP: $69 billion
Per-capita income: $17,700
Inflation: 5%
Unemployment: 12%
Workforce: 1.3 million; services 77%; industry 20%; agriculture 3%
Major industries: Apparel, electronics, food products, pharmaceuticals, tourism
Agricultural products: Bananas, chickens, coffee, livestock products, pineapples, plantains, sugarcane
Exports: $46.9 billion

Major export products: Apparel, beverage concentrates, canned tuna, chemicals, electronics, medical equipment, rum
Export partners: U.S. 90.3%; U.K. 1.6%; Netherlands, 1.4%, Dominican Republic 1.4%

Imports: $29.1 billion
Major import products: Apparel, chemicals, food, fish, machinery and equipment, petroleum products
Import partners: U.S. 55%; Ireland 23.7%; Japan 5.4%

Political Climate

The issue of statehood, or independence is perennial in Puerto Rican politics. Nonbinding referendums on the island's independence were held in 1967, 1993, and 1998, but each time a majority favored keeping Puerto Rico as a commonwealth. In 2001 the federal government agreed to halt live ammunition training on the island of Vieques, conceding to local pressures in an enduring battle. Puerto Rico elected its first female governor in 2000, Sila Marìa Calderón.

Did You Know?

• Puerto Ricans have a unique national identity. No resident pays federal taxes, but all natives can be U.S. citizens. They can be called to serve in the military, but cannot vote in U.S. presidential elections as long as they reside in Puerto Rico.

• The average daily temperature in Puerto Rico is 74 degrees.

• The Puerto Rican flag is almost identical to the Cuban flag for a reason. It was created in 1895 by Puerto Rican members of the Cuban Revolutionary Party to bind both nations in the fight against Spanish rule. Before Puerto Rico gained official status as a U.S. commonwealth, anyone displaying the flag could be arrested on charges of insubordination against the United States.

• Puerto Rico produces 75% of all rum sold in the United States. Among the island's largest distillers is the Bacardí company, which produces most of its rum in Puerto Rico. With sales of more than 240 million bottles annually, it's the fourth-largest spirits company in the world, and the world's largest family-owned spirits company.

• The Sierra de Luquillo Mountains southeast of San Juan are the wettest place on the island. More than 1,700 rain showers drop 170 inches of rain a year. The precipitation keeps land in the north part of the island well watered, benefiting Puerto Rico's many farms.

• Plena is some of Puerto Rico's best-known native music. Drawing on indigenous Taíno traditions, the music was created by a merger with African singing, clapping, and dancing traditions in the city of Ponce and became a "singing newspaper" for the black slaves. Today it's played at Christmas and on other holidays.

COCINA CRIOLLA

PUERTO RICAN *COCINA CRIOLLA*—literally, the creole kitchen—is a relative of other Caribbean cuisines, sharing basic ingredients common to Cuban, Dominican, and to some extent even Brazilian culinary traditions. Still, it has its own distinct flavorings.

The origins of contemporary Puerto Rican cuisine can be traced to the Taíno people, who inhabited the island in the 15th century. Taíno staples still used today include yucca, peppers, and corn. The Taíno used yucca to make *casabe,* a flat bread, and also a variety of vinegar that they used for seasoning instead of salt. Taínos also are believed to have grown guava, pineapple, and soursop.

When the Spaniards arrived on the island, they brought other ingredients, including olives, eggplant, onion, garlic, rice, and cilantro. Wheat would not grow on the island, so yucca remained a staple, as did rice. Regional culinary specialties from Spain, such as paellas, came out of the Spanish-influenced kitchen. These specialties played an important role in the development of Puerto Rican recipes, recognizable today in such dishes as *arroz con pollo.* Lacking olive oil, early Puerto Ricans often used lard as a fat. Back in those days, shortly after the Spanish arrived in the late 15th century, the bubbling cauldron of a hungry soldier welcomed any ingredient that was available. So a typical Spanish recipe might be transformed with yucca and pumpkin and colored with the red of achiote.

African slaves brought by the Spanish from Guinea and the Gold Coast of Africa during the 16th century to toil in the sugar fields also left their marks on the Puerto Rican table. The slaves brought plantains, bananas, pigeon peas, okra, and yams. The Taínos used corn husks to wrap foods, but the Africans replaced them with plantain leaves. The African population developed a variety of coconut-based dishes and preferred frying foods to stewing them.

Other important ingredients were the result of Spanish exploration of the world. For example, breadfruit was brought in from Tahiti and has remained a staple. But Puerto Ricans have also adopted the mango from South Asia and oranges from China.

A wooden *pilon,* which the Taínos used to mash ingredients and paints, is still used today, particularly in the preparation of *mofongo* (mashed plantains with garlic and olive oil), which is of both African and Spanish origin.

Puerto Rican cookery constantly reveals a rich, historical blend. Dishes often feature pepper, lime rind, cinnamon, cloves, fresh ginger, garlic, and the juice of the sour orange. Two popular herb seasonings are cilantro (coriander) and oregano. These ingredients, along with small sweet peppers, are commonly used to flavor soups and meats. The conventional wisdom says that the real secret of the cocina criolla depends on the use of sofrito, achiote, lard, and the *caldero* (cooking pot).

Plátanos, or plantains, are related to bananas but are larger and starchier. They are served mostly as side dishes and may be eaten green (as *tostones,* which are salty) or ripe (as *amarillos,* which are sweet). They can be fried, baked, boiled, or roasted and served either whole or in slices. Sometimes whole amarillos are served with cinnamon as a dessert. *Pasteles,* boiled plantain leaves wrapped with fillings, tamale-style, are a Christmas specialty but can be eaten anytime.

* * *

RICE IS OMNIPRESENT ON THE PUERTO RICAN PLATE. It can be served "white" with kidney beans, or prepared with *gandules* (pigeon peas) or garbanzos (chick peas); most often rice is simply served with *habichuelas* (red beans). Whatever the case, the accompaniment for rice is almost always some kind of bean, always richly seasoned. Rice stuck to the pot, known as *pegao*, is the most highly prized, full of all the ingredients that have sunk to the bottom.

Popular soups include the *sopón de pollo con arroz* (chicken soup with rice), *sopón de pescado* (fish soup), and *sopón de garbanzos con patas de cerdo* (chick pea soup with pig's feet). More than a soup, but maybe less than a stew, is the *asopao*. *Asopao de pollo,* the most popular variety, is made with a whole chicken, flavored with spices such as garlic, paprika, and oregano, as well with salt pork, cured ham, green peppers, chili peppers, onions, tomatoes, chorizo, and pimentos. A remarkable number of ingredients go into the *sancocho*, a hearty soup that includes vegetables, plantains, meats, and anything the poor man could find.

The *lechón asado* (a roasted or barbecued pig) is the quintessential Puerto Rican Christmas tradition. The whole pig is roasted in an open pit, a process that takes several hours. It's basted with sour orange juice and achiote coloring. The lechón asado is best when the pig's skin is golden and absolutely crisp. The traditional dressing served with the dish is the *aji-li-mojili*, a combination of garlic, sweet seeded chili peppers, vinegar, lime juice, salt, and olive oil.

Snacks—particularly different kinds of fritters—are an important part of the Puerto Rican diet. All-time favorite street snacks include *bacalaítos fritos* (deep-fried codfish fritters), *pastelillos* (deep-fried cheese and meat turnovers), and *alcapurrias* green plantain croquettes stuffed with beef or pork. *Piononos,* made from ripe bananas, are also high-ranking fritters.

Tropical fruits often wind up at the table in the form of delicious juices. A local favorite is pineapple juice from crops grown in the north of the island. Coconut, mango, papaya, lime, and tamarind are other local favorites. Puerto Rico is home to lesser known fruits that are worth trying if you find them; these include the caimito (which is also called a star apple and has a mild, grapelike flavor), quenepa (also called a Spanish lime, which has yellow sweet-tart pulp surrounded by a tight, thin skin), and zapote (a plum-size fruit that tastes like a combination of peach, avocado, and vanilla). The Plaza del Mercado in the Santurce sector of San Juan is a good place to look for the unusual.

Popular Puerto Rican desserts include the pudding or custard flan and the coconut tembleque. Guava paste or papaya cubes cooked in sugar and cinnamon must be accompanied by *queso blanco* (white cheese). *Arroz con dulce* is made of cooked rice, coconut cream, sugar, and cinnamon.

Until the 19th century, sugar and coffee were the most important of the island's crops and the backbone of the economy. Puerto Rican coffee is still the source of pride for many; Pope John-Paul II was said to like Puerto Rican coffee. A sip's worth of strong black coffee in a small cup is known as *puya*; when mixed with hot milk, it's *café con leche*.

Likewise a source of pride is a by-product of the sugar industry: rum. Puerto Rico makes first-rate rum, including the most popular, Bacardí. The best rums can be sipped like a fine cognac, but lesser white and golden rums make great mixed drinks. The piña colada is a well-known Puerto Rican invention—a blend of coconut cream, pineapple juice, and rum. A lesser-known but potent local rum specialty is *bilí*, made from quenepas soaked in rum and marinated in the bottle for weeks. *Coquito* is the Puerto Rican version of Christmas rum eggnog.

Puerto Rican cuisine has been experiencing a boom of sorts, with innovative, gourmet restaurants opening around the island. Today, more chefs and restaurateurs are developing menus in the line of a

Nuevo Latino cuisine. Joyfully departing from traditional continental and Puerto Rican recipes, these chefs nevertheless include traditional ingredients and update old favorites. Traditional meats like chicken, fish, and lamb are given an added zest by sauces made from such tropical fruits as tamarind, mango, or guava. Take your palate out for a few adventures. Puerto Rican cuisine may surprise and delight you with both new and old tastes.

—Isabel Abislaimán

THE STATE OF THE ARTS IN PUERTO RICO

ALTHOUGH SPANIARDS LANDED IN PUERTO RICO in the late 15th century (Columbus was guided to the island by the Taíno Indians of Guadeloupe in 1493), several hundred years passed before what could be considered an authentically Puerto Rican art movement was born on the island in the 18th century. Notwithstanding the Taínos and their pre-Columbian works of art that are now highly prized among collectors, most of the existing paintings that came after the Spanish were part of the larger European tradition of Renaissance painting and sculpture.

A 16th-century religious mural, discovered in 1978 in Old San Juan's Iglesia de San José, is among the oldest artworks—aside from those by the Taínos, of course—to have been discovered in Puerto Rico. It is, however, widely considered insignificant in the development of the fine arts on the island. According to art historian Osiris Delgado, this anonymous repertoire of religious images continued uneventfully throughout the 17th century. In the 18th century, sculptor Tiburcio Espada (1798–1852), along with his father Felipe (c. 1754–1818), created some of the oldest surviving *santos* in the San Germán tradition (*see* "Lives of the Santos" *in* chapter 3). With them, and with portrait painter José Campeche (1752–1809), an indigenous tradition of Puerto Rican art, separate from the traditions of Europe of the time, began to emerge.

Another turning point for Puerto Rican artists occurred in the 19th century with the paintings of Francisco Oller (1833–1917). Oller, who was educated in Europe in the company of Gustave Courbet, Camille Pissarro, and Paul Cézanne, may be the first truly modern painter in Puerto Rico. (Oller's *El estudiante* is in the permanent collection of the Musée d'Orsay in Paris.) Unlike his peers, Oller painted realistic scenes of island life,

though his use of light and color was heavily influenced by the impressionists. His most important work, *El velorio,* is the cornerstone of the collection in the Museo de la Universidad de Puerto Rico. Depicting a scene of mourning in a rural setting, the painting is one of the first attempts to create a Puerto Rican cultural identity. Such was his commitment to promoting the arts on the island that around 1870 Oller personally opened the first art gallery in Old San Juan, which exhibited his own works and those of his friends and pupils, all of whom were island natives.

Throughout the first half of the 20th century, most Puerto Rican artists followed Oller's aesthetic and grounded their works in the love of the rural landscape and lifestyle. The *jíbaro* (a poor, usually illiterate, mountain man) and the ideal of the lone house on the mountain became the affirmation of the Puerto Rican identity.

In the 1940s the government started to support the arts by providing artists with studio spaces. Shortly after, art institutions began to flourish, with the Museo de la Universidad de Puerto Rico opening in 1946. Also around this time, carvings of wooden saints (*santos de palo*) became cherished collectors items.

* * *

DURING THE 1950S ARTISTS BEGAN to shift their interests from the agrarian ideal toward social justice and the urban proletariat, and artists of this period focused their eyes on slums, poverty, and hardships of the city. You can see this contrast in the work Ramon Frade's *Nuestro pan* (a celebration of rural life) and Rafael Tufino's *Goyita* (focusing on dignified urban poverty). The artists of the 1950s made art with social impact and wide distribution. Murals were widely commissioned during the 1950s and '60s for government buildings and factories. One example is *La*

Plena, a mural by Rafael Tufiño celebrating the African roots of Puerto Rican folk music in the Centro de Bellas Artes.

The 1950s also saw two specific developments. The Instituto de Cultura Puertorriqueña (ICP) was established in 1955 to promote Puerto Rican artists; today the agency oversees many museums and art programs all over the island. And in 1959 the Museo de Arte de Ponce (MAP) was founded by former governor and philanthropist Luis A. Ferré. MAP houses a private collection of more than 2,400 cataloged works from the 14th through 19th centuries, including paintings by El Greco, Goya, Rubens, Cranach, Murillo, and Delacroix. The collection is particularly strong in Italian baroque and Pre-Raphaelite works, with good representation by Latin American and Puerto Rican artists from the 18th century to the present. Myrna Báez, Julio Rosado del Valle, and Antonio Martorell are included in the collection.

In the 1960s, as the art world moved away from socially committed art, Puerto Rican artists still struggled with nationalism and identity issues. Locally, this struggle resulted in a battle between abstraction and avant-garde expression (with artists such as Julio Rosado Del Valle, Olga Albizu, and Luis Hernández Cruz) on the one hand, and figurative and socially minded art considered "genuinely" Puerto Rican on the other.

Finally, in the 1980s, abstract expressionists and other stylistic experimenters were granted a place at the table of Puerto Rican identity. These years opened art to the irreverent humor of Carmelo Sobrino, to the environmental activism of Carlos Marcial, and to aspects of the fantastic, as in the works of Marta Pérez, Jorge Zeno, and Rafi Trelles. Also, in the early 1980s the Puerto Rican landscape was deemed to include El Barrio in New York City and issues related to migration, poverty, colonialism, and crime. Broadening their geographic horizons also prompted Puerto Rican artists to use the self-portrait as a means of exploring politics, race, the psyche, sexuality, and gender, as seen in the works of Arnaldo Roche and Mari Mater O'Neill.

By 1988 a group of artists, professors, critics, collectors, and art lovers, had come together to establish the Museo de Arte de Contemporáneo de Puerto Rico. The museum's collection comprises mostly works donated by the artists themselves. The museum finally moved to its own new building in 2003. By 1989 even the Puerto Tourism Company recognized that art can be an important way to present Puerto Rico to the world, so it began acquiring its own collection.

In the 1990s sculpture started playing a more significant role. The most visible evidence were the large investments in public art in the city of San Juan and the Sculpture Symposium of the Universidad de Puerto Rico, whose works are permanently exhibited at the Botanical Garden.

Although the government has done a lot to promote the arts in Puerto Rico, it was only in 2000 that the Museo de Arte de Puerto Rico opened, the island's first government-sponsored museum of international caliber. Since it has relatively few pieces in its permanent collection—relying largely on loans from other institutions—the museum is primarily a collection of collections.

The state of the arts is looking up. Puerto Rico's Public Art Project promises to make the whole island an indoor and outdoor showcase of international and Puerto Rican art. The project consists of works in various urban and rural settings around the island—from the stations of the new Urban Train in the San Juan metropolitan area to beach benches in the shape of surfboard-petals by Aaron Salabarrias in Rincón to festive mosaic murals by Daniel Lind in Loíza.

—Isabel Abislaimán

CHRONOLOGY

ca. AD 500   The first human inhabitants arrive in Puerto Rico, apparently on primitive rafts from Florida. Known today as Arcaicos (Archaics), these hunter-gatherers live near the shore, where they subsist on fish and fruit.

ca. 1000   The Arcaico are replaced by more advanced Arawak Indians who arrive by canoe from South America. The agrarian Taíno (a subgroup of the Arawak) name the island Boriquén, and thrive there in thatched villages.

1493   Christopher Columbus, on his second voyage to the New World, meets a group of Taíno on the island of Guadeloupe. The Taíno guide him to Boriquén. On November 19, Columbus claims the island for Ferdinand and Isabella of Spain, and christens it "San Juan Bautista."

1508   Caparra, the first Spanish settlement, is founded on the south shore of the island's largest bay. Juan Ponce de León, a soldier who had accompanied Columbus on his second voyage, is appointed governor by the Spanish crown.

1510   The Spanish begin mining and smelting gold on the island. In an effort to Christianize the Taíno, they also institute a program of virtual slavery: the Indians are required to work for the settlers in return for religious instruction. In November, a group of Taíno loyal to a *cacique* (chieftain) named Urayoan set out to determine whether the Spanish are gods. By drowning a young settler in a river, the Taíno prove the Spanish to be mortal.

1511   The Spanish crown grants the island a coat of arms. The town of Caparra is renamed Puerto Rico (Rich Port). The Taíno rebel against the conquistadors, but are no match for European armament. In a brutal act of reprisal, the Spanish hunt down and kill as many as 6,000 Taíno Indians.

1512   Ferdinand II of Spain issues the Edict of Burgos, intended to protect the island's surviving Indians from abuse by the settlers.

1513   The first African slaves are introduced. Setting sail from the settlement of San Germán on the island's west coast, Ponce de León heads north across the Caribbean and discovers Florida.

1521   The island's primary town moves across the bay from its original, mosquito-plagued site. The island is renamed Puerto Rico, and its capital becomes known as San Juan, instead of the other way around.

1523   The first sugarcane processing plant is built.

1532   Puerto Rican gold mines cease to be profitable, and Spanish settlers leave in droves for Peru. Governor Francisco Manuel de Lando declares emigration a crime punishable by the amputation of a leg.

1539   To help protect their Caribbean trade routes from pirates and competing colonial powers, the Spanish begin building the massive fortress of San Felipe del Morro (El Morro).

1542 The coconut palm is introduced.

1595 English privateer Sir Francis Drake, assigned to disrupt Spanish colonial trade, attempts unsuccessfully to capture the town of San Juan.

1598 Another Englishman, George Clifford, 3rd Earl of Cumberland, attacks the island and occupies San Juan with 4,000 men. He's forced to withdraw a few months later, when his troops are decimated by disease.

1625 San Juan is again invaded, this time by Dutch forces under Bowdoin Hendrick. The attack fails when Hendrick is unable to conquer El Morro.

1680 The town of Ponce is founded on the south coast.

1736 Coffee is first cultivated in the central highlands.

1760 The west-coast town of Mayagüez is founded.

1765 The Spanish crown sends Field Marshal Alejandro O'Reilly to inspect military and social conditions. He conducts a census and reports that Puerto Rico's races mix "without any repugnance whatsoever."

1776 Coffee becomes a major export item.

1797 When France and Spain declare war on England, 7,000 British troops under Sir Ralph Abercromby invade Puerto Rico. The British are driven back after a two-week campaign.

1809 After Napoléon Bonaparte deposes the King of Spain, the Spanish Cortes (parliament) permits representatives from Spain's New World colonies to participate in the drafting of a new constitution.

1810 Ramón Power y Giralt is selected as Puerto Rico's first delegate to Spain.

1812 The Cádiz Constitution is adopted, granting Puerto Rico and other Spanish colonies the rank of provinces and extending Spanish citizenship to colonials. A brief period of social and economic optimism reigns on the island, and Puerto Rico's first newspaper is founded.

1815 With the fall of Napoléon, the monarchy is restored in Spain, and the Cádiz Constitution is revoked. Puerto Rico reverts to being merely a Spanish colony.

1825 Notorious Puerto Rican pirate Roberto Cofresi is captured by the U.S. Navy in the Caribbean and handed over to Spanish authorities, who execute him by firing squad at El Morro.

1843 Puerto Rico's first lighthouse is constructed at El Morro. The first town is founded on the outer island of Vieques.

1868 Inspired by Puerto Rican separatist Ramón Emetrio Betances, several hundred revolutionaries attempt a coup against Spanish rule. The rebels successfully occupy the town of Lares before authorities crush the revolt. The uprising comes to be known as the Grito de Lares (Cry of Lares).

1873   Slavery is abolished on Puerto Rico by decree of the Spanish king, Amedeo I de Saboya.

1876   The mountain rain forest of El Yunque is designated as a nature reserve.

1887   Journalist and patriot Luis Muñoz Rivera helps form the Puerto Rican Autonomous Party.

1897   Just prior to the Spanish-American War, Spain approves the Carta Autonómica, granting the island administrative autonomy.

1898   In February Puerto Rico's first autonomous local government is inaugurated. In April the Spanish-American War breaks out. In July American troops invade, conquering the island in 17 days with minimal casualties. In December, after 405 years of continuous rule, Spain officially cedes Puerto Rico (along with the Philippines and Guam) to the United States. No member of Puerto Rico's autonomous government is consulted.

1899   Hurricane San Ciriaco kills 3,000 people and leaves 25% of the population homeless.

1900   The U.S. Congress passes the Foraker Act, which declares Puerto Rico to be a U.S. territory. The island's elected civil government remains under the control of a U.S.-appointed governor.

1903   President Theodore Roosevelt gives the U.S. Navy control over the out-island of Culebra. The navy later uses it as a gunnery range.

1904   Luis Muñoz Rivera establishes the Unionist Party of Puerto Rico to combat the widely unpopular regulations imposed by the Foraker Act.

1912   As dissatisfaction with American rule increases, the Independence Party is formed. This is the first political party to claim Puerto Rican independence as its primary goal.

1917   President Woodrow Wilson signs the Jones Act, which grants U.S. citizenship to Puerto Ricans.

1930   With economic conditions bleak on the island, militant separatist Pedro Albizu Campos forms the Nationalist Party. The party demands immediate independence for Puerto Rico.

1933   Cockfighting is legalized.

1935   After a visit to the island, President Franklin Roosevelt establishes the Puerto Rican Reconstruction Administration in an effort to rehabilitate Puerto Rico's economy.

1937   A decade of occasional political violence culminates with La Masacre de Ponce (The Ponce Massacre). During a Palm Sunday parade of Nationalist Party blackshirts, police open fire on the crowd, killing 19 and injuring some 100 others.

1938   Luis Muñoz Marín, son of Luis Muñoz Rivera, creates the Democratic Popular Party.

1941   The U.S. military establishes bases on Vieques and Culebra, relocating a portion of the islands' population to St. Croix, Virgin Islands.

1945   Large numbers of Puerto Ricans begin to emigrate to the mainland United States, particularly to Florida and the New York City area.

1948   The U.S. Congress grants Puerto Ricans the right to elect their own governor. In November, Luis Muñoz Marín is voted in as the island's first elected native governor. Gambling is legalized.

1950   In July President Harry Truman signs a law permitting Puerto Rico to draft its own constitution as a commonwealth, but radical nationalists are far from satisfied. In October violence breaks out throughout the island, leaving 31 people dead. A few days later, two Puerto Rican nationalists from New York attempt to assassinate Truman in Washington.

1952   Puerto Rican voters approve the new constitution, and the Commonwealth of Puerto Rico is born. The island's flag, based on a patriotic design dating from the time of Spanish colonialism, is officially adopted.

1953   In this peak year of emigration to the U.S. mainland, nearly 70,000 people leave the island.

1961   Puerto Rican actress Rita Moreno wins an Academy Award for her performance in the hit film *West Side Story*.

1964   Luis Muñoz Marín steps down as governor after 16 years. His career is remembered as brilliantly successful: under his governorship, the percentage of Puerto Rican children attending school rose from 50% to 90%, and per-capita income increased sixfold.

1967   The question of Puerto Rico's political status is put before its voters for the first time. A 60% majority votes to maintain the commonwealth, rather than push for complete independence or U.S. statehood.

1972   Beloved Puerto Rican baseball star Roberto Clemente, an outfielder for the Pittsburgh Pirates, dies in a plane crash. He's inducted into the Baseball Hall of Fame the following year.

1974   A radical nationalist organization called the Fuerzas Armadas Liberación Nacional Puertorriqueña (Armed Forces of Puerto Rican National Liberation, or FALN) claims responsibility for five bombings in New York. Over the next decade, the group commits dozens of acts of terrorism in the United States, causing five deaths and extensive property damage.

1981   Members of the Macheteros, another radical nationalist group similar to the FALN, infiltrate a Puerto Rican Air National Guard base and blow up 11 planes, causing some $45 million in damage.

1993 In a second referendum on Puerto Rico's political status, voters again choose to maintain the commonwealth.

1998 Hurricane Georges leaves 24,000 people homeless and causes an estimated $2 billion in damage. In a third referendum on the political status issue, voters once more opt to maintain the commonwealth, although the pro-statehood vote tops 46%.

1999 Puerto Ricans of all political stripes are unified in protest against the U.S. Navy bombing range on Vieques after a civilian security guard is killed by a stray bomb. Dozens of protesters occupy the range and disrupt naval exercises. President Bill Clinton offers clemency to 16 FALN members serving time in federal prisons for a string of bombings in the U.S. during the 1970s and '80s.

2000 In May, 2000 protesters encamped on the Vieques naval bombing range are forcibly removed by federal agents.

2001 In January Sila Maria Calderón becomes the island's first woman governor. In March Puerto Rican actor Benicio del Toro wins an Academy Award for Best Supporting Actor for his role in *Traffic*. In May beauty Denise Quiñones, from the mountain town of Lares, becomes Miss Universe. Also that month, President George W. Bush announces that the Navy will end training on Vieques by May 2003. After the September 11 terrorist attacks, however, congress passes legislation allowing the military to stay until another suitable site is found.

2003 In May the U.S. Navy withdraws its fleet from the training grounds off the coast of Vieques.

2004 Anibal Acevido Vilá is elected governor in November's hotly contested election. El Tren Urbano, a light-rail communter train, opens with much fanfare in San Juan. Ridership is below expectations—partly because of the island's love affair with the car.

2005 At year's end President George W. Bush asks Congress to schedule another referendum for the island's voters on whether to remain a commonwealth.

–Stephen Fowler.

SPANISH VOCABULARY

Words and Phrases

English	Spanish	Pronunciation
Basics		
Yes/no	Sí/no	see/no
Please	Por favor	pohr fah-vohr
May I?	¿Me permite?	meh pehr-mee-tay
Thank you (very much)	(Muchas) gracias	(moo-chas) grah-see-as
You're welcome	De nada	day nah-dah
Excuse me	Con permiso	con pehr-mee-so
Pardon me	¿Perdón?	pair-dohn
Could you tell me?	¿Podría decirme?	po-dree-ah deh-seer-meh
I'm sorry	Lo siento	lo see-en-to
Good morning!	¡Buenos días!	bway-nohs dee-ahs
Good afternoon!	¡Buenas tardes!	bway-nahs tar-dess
Good evening!	¡Buenas noches!	bway-nahs no-chess
Goodbye!	¡Adiós!/ ¡Hasta luego!	ah-dee-ohss/ah-stah-lwe-go
Mr./Mrs.	Señor/Señora	sen-yor/sen-yohr-ah
Miss	Señorita	sen-yo-ree-tah
Pleased to meet you	Mucho gusto	moo-cho goose-to
How are you?	¿Cómo está usted?	ko-mo es-tah oo-sted
Very well, thank you.	Muy bien, gracias.	moo-ee bee-en, grah-see-as
And you?	¿Y usted?	ee oos-ted
Hello (on the telephone)	Diga	dee-gah

Numbers

1	un, uno	oon, oo-no
2	dos	dohs
3	tres	tress
4	cuatro	kwah-tro
5	cinco	sink-oh
6	seis	saice

7	siete	see-et-eh
8	ocho	o-cho
9	nueve	new-eh-vey
10	diez	dee-es
11	once	ohn-seh
12	doce	doh-seh
13	trece	treh-seh
14	catorce	ka-tohr-seh
15	quince	keen-seh
16	dieciséis	dee-es-ee-saice
17	diecisiete	dee-es-ee-see-et-eh
18	dieciocho	dee-es-ee-o-cho
19	diecinueve	dee-es-ee-new-ev-eh
20	veinte	vain-teh
21	veinte y uno/ veintiuno	vain-te-oo-noh
30	treinta	train-tah
32	treinta y dos	train-tay-dohs
40	cuarenta	kwah-ren-tah
43	cuarenta y tres	kwah-ren-tay-tress
50	cincuenta	seen-kwen-tah
54	cincuenta y cuatro	seen-kwen-tay kwah-tro
60	sesenta	sess-en-tah
65	sesenta y cinco	sess-en-tay seen-koh
70	setenta	set-en-tah
76	setenta y seis	set-en-tay saice
80	ochenta	oh-chen-tah
87	ochenta y siete	oh-chen-tay see-yet-eh
90	noventa	no-ven-tah
98	noventa y ocho	no-ven-tay-o-choh
100	cien	see-en
101	ciento uno	see-en-toh oo-noh
200	doscientos	doh-see-en-tohss
500	quinientos	keen-yen-tohss
700	setecientos	set-eh-see-en-tohss
900	novecientos	no-veh-see-en-tohss
1,000	mil	meel
2,000	dos mil	dohs meel
1,000,000	un millón	oon meel-yohn

Colors

black	negro	neh-groh
blue	azul	ah-sool
brown	café	kah-feh
green	verde	ver-deh
pink	rosa	ro-sah
purple	morado	mo-rah-doh
orange	naranja	na-rahn-hah
red	rojo	roh-hoh
white	blanco	blahn-koh
yellow	amarillo	ah-mah-ree-yoh

Days of the Week

Sunday	domingo	doh-meen-goh
Monday	lunes	loo-ness
Tuesday	martes	mahr-tess
Wednesday	miércoles	me-air-koh-less
Thursday	jueves	hoo-ev-ess
Friday	viernes	vee-air-ness
Saturday	sábado	sah-bah-doh

Months

January	enero	eh-neh-roh
February	febrero	feh-breh-roh
March	marzo	mahr-soh
April	abril	ah-breel
May	mayo	my-oh
June	junio	hoo-nee-oh
July	julio	hoo-lee-yoh
August	agosto	ah-ghost-toh
September	septiembre	sep-tee-em-breh
October	octubre	oak-too-breh
November	noviembre	no-vee-em-breh
December	diciembre	dee-see-em-breh

Useful Phrases

Do you speak English?	¿Habla usted inglés?	ah-blah oos-ted in-glehs
I don't speak Spanish	No hablo español	no ah-bloh es-pahn-yol

I don't understand (you)	No entiendo	no en-tee-en-doh
I understand (you)	Entiendo	en-tee-en-doh
I don't know	No sé	no seh
I am American/ British	Soy americano (americana)/ inglés(a)	soy ah-meh-ree-kah-no (ah-meh-ree-kah-nah)/in-glehs (ah)
What's your name?	¿Cómo se llama usted?	koh-mo seh yah-mah oos-ted
My name is . . .	Me llamo . . .	meh yah-moh
What time is it?	¿Qué hora es?	keh o-rah es
It is one, two, three . . . o'clock.	Es la una. . . . Son las dos, tres	es la oo-nah/sohn lahs dohs, tress
Yes, please/No, thank you	Sí, por favor/No, gracias	see pohr fah-vor/no grah-see-ahs
How?	¿Cómo?	koh-mo
When?	¿Cuándo?	kwahn-doh
This/Next week	Esta semana/ la semana que entra	es-tah seh-mah-nah/lah seh-mah-nah keh en-trah
This/Next month	Este mes/el próximo mes	es-teh mehs/el prok-see-moh mehs
This/Next year	Este año/el año que viene	es-teh ahn-yo/el ahn-yo keh vee-yen-ay
Yesterday/today/ tomorrow	Ayer/hoy/mañana	ah-yehr/oy/mahn-yah-nah
This morning/ afternoon	Esta mañana/tarde	es-tah mahn-yah-nah/tar-deh
Tonight	Esta noche	es-tah no-cheh
What?	¿Qué?	keh
What is it?	¿Qué es esto?	keh es es-toh
Why?	¿Por qué?	por keh
Who?	¿Quién?	kee-yen
Where is . . . ?	¿Dónde está . . . ?	dohn-deh es-tah
the train station?	la estación del tren?	la es-tah-see-on del train
the subway station?	la estación del tren subterráneo	la es-ta-see-on del trehn soob-tair-ron-a-o
the bus stop?	la parada del autobus?	la pah-rah-dah del oh-toh-boos
the post office?	la oficina de correos?	la oh-fee-see-nah deh-koh-reh-os
the bank?	el banco?	el bahn-koh
the hotel?	el hotel?	el oh-tel
the store?	la tienda?	la tee-en-dah

the cashier?	la caja?	la kah-hah
the museum?	el museo?	el moo-seh-oh
the hospital?	el hospital?	el ohss-pee-tal
the elevator?	el ascensor?	el ah-sen-sohr
the bathroom?	el baño?	el bahn-yoh
Here/there	Aquí/allá	ah-key/ah-yah
Open/closed	Abierto/cerrado	ah-bee-er-toh/ ser-ah-doh
Left/right	Izquierda/derecha	iss-key-er-dah/ dare-eh-chah
Straight ahead	Derecho	dare-eh-choh
Is it near/far?	¿Está cerca/lejos?	es-tah sehr-kah/ leh-hoss
I'd like . . .	Quisiera . . .	kee-see-ehr-ah
a room	un cuarto/una habitación	oon kwahr-toh/ oo-nah ah-bee-tah-see-on
the key	la llave	lah yah-veh
a newspaper	un periódico	oon pehr-ee-oh-dee-koh
a stamp	un sello de correo	oon seh-yo deh koh-reh-oh
I'd like to buy . . .	Quisiera comprar . . .	kee-see-ehr-ah kohm-prahr
cigarettes	cigarrillos	ce-ga-ree-yohs
matches	cerillos	ser-ee-ohs
a dictionary	un diccionario	oon deek-see-oh-nah-ree-oh
soap	jabón	hah-bohn
sunglasses	gafas de sol	ga-fahs deh sohl
suntan lotion	loción	loh-see-ohn-brohn-seh-ah-do-rah
a map	un mapa	oon mah-pah
a magazine	una revista	oon-ah reh-veess-tah
paper	papel	pah-pel
envelopes	sobres	so-brehs
a postcard	una tarjeta postal	oon-ah tar-het-ah post-ahl
How much is it?	¿Cuánto cuesta?	kwahn-toh kwes-tah
It's expensive/ cheap	Está caro/barato	es-tah kah-roh/ bah-rah-toh
A little/a lot	Un poquito/ mucho	oon poh-kee-toh/ moo-choh
More/less	Más/menos	mahss/men-ohss
Enough/too much/too little	Suficiente/ demasiado/ muy poco	soo-fee-see-en-teh/ deh-mah-see-ah-doh/moo-ee poh-koh

Telephone	Teléfono	tel-ef-oh-no
Telegram	Telegrama	teh-leh-grah-mah
I am ill	Estoy enfermo(a)	es-toy en-fehr-moh(mah)
Please call a doctor	Por favor llame un medico	pohr fah-vor ya-meh oon med-ee-koh
Help!	¡Auxilio! ¡Ayuda! ¡Socorro!	owk-see-lee-oh/ ah-yoo-dah/ soh-kohr-roh
Fire!	¡Encendio!	en-sen-dee-oo
Caution!/Look out!	¡Cuidado!	kwee-dah-doh

On the Road

Avenue	Avenida	ah-ven-ee-dah
Broad, tree-lined boulevard	Bulevar	boo-leh-var
Fertile plain	Vega	veh-gah
Highway	Carretera	car-reh-ter-ah
Mountain pass, Street	Puerto Calle	poo-ehr-toh cah-yeh
Waterfront promenade	Rambla	rahm-blah
Wharf	Embarcadero	em-bar-cah-deh-ro

In Town

Cathedral	Catedral	cah-teh-dral
Church	Templo/Iglesia	tem-plo/ee-glehs-see-ah
City hall	Casa de gobierno	kah-sah deh go-bee-ehr-no
Door, gate	Puerta portón	poo-ehr-tah por-ton
Entrance/exit	Entrada/salida	en-trah-dah/sah-lee-dah
Inn, rustic bar, or restaurant	Taverna	tah-ver-nah
Main square	Plaza principal	plah-thah prin-see-pahl
Market	Mercado	mer-kah-doh
Neighborhood	Barrio	bahr-ree-o
Traffic circle	Glorieta	glor-ee-eh-tah
Wine cellar, wine bar, or wine shop	Bodega	boh-deh-gah

Dining Out

A bottle of . . .	Una bottella de . . .	oo-nah bo-teh-yah-deh
A cup of . . .	Una taza de . . .	oo-nah tah-thah deh
A glass of . . .	Un vaso de . . .	oon vah-so deh
Ashtray	Un cenicero	oon sen-ee-seh-roh
Bill/check	La cuenta	lah kwen-tah
Bread	El pan	el pahn
Breakfast	El desayuno	el deh-sah-yoon-oh
Butter	La mantequilla	lah man-teh-key-yah
Cheers!	¡Salud!	sah-lood
Cocktail	Un aperitivo	oon ah-pehr-ee-tee-voh
Dinner	La cena	lah seh-nah
Dish	Un plato	oon plah-toh
Menu of the day	Menú del día	meh-noo del dee-ah
Enjoy!	¡Buen provecho!	bwehn pro-veh-cho
Fixed-price menu	Menú fijo o turistico	meh-noo fee-hoh oh too-ree-stee-coh
Fork	El tenedor	ehl ten-eh-dor
Is the tip included?	¿Está incluida la propina?	es-tah in-cloo-ee-dah lah pro-pee-nah
Knife	El cuchillo	el koo-chee-yo
Large portion of savory snacks	Raciónes	rah-see-oh-nehs
Lunch	La comida	lah koh-mee-dah
Menu	La carta, el menú	lah cart-ah, el meh-noo
Napkin	La servilleta	lah sehr-vee-yet-ah
Pepper	La pimienta	lah pee-me-en-tah
Please give me	Por favor déme	pohr fah-vor deh-meh
Salt	La sal	lah sahl
Savory snacks	Tapas	tah-pahs
Spoon	Una cuchara	oo-nah koo-chah-rah
Sugar	El azúcar	el ah-thu-kar
Waiter!/Waitress!	¡Por favor Señor/Señorita!	pohr fah-vor sen-yor/sen-yor-ee-tah

SMART TRAVEL TIPS

There are planners and there are those who, excuse the pun, fly by the seat of their pants. We happily place ourselves among the planners. Our writers and editors try to anticipate all the issues you may face before and during any journey, and then they do their research. This section is the product of their efforts. Use it to get excited about your trip to Puerto Rico, to inform your travel planning, or to guide you on the road should the seat of your pants start to feel threadbare.

ADDRESSES

Addresses in Puerto Rico, especially in and around San Juan, can be confusing because Spanish terms like *avenida* and *calle* are used interchangeably with English terms like avenue and street. This means that the shopping strip in Old San Juan may be called Calle Cristo or Cristo Street. (And it might just be called Cristo, as it is on many maps.) A highway is often called a *expreso*, and an alley or pedestrian-only street is labeled a *paseo*.

Outside a metropolitan area, addresses are most often given by the kilometer mark along the road. That means that the address for Parque de las Cavernas del Río Camuy, south of Arecibo, is given as Route 129, Kilometer 18.9.

AIR TRAVEL

There are many daily flights to Puerto Rico from the United States, and connections are particularly good from the East Coast, although there are a few nonstop flights from the Midwest as well. San Juan's international airport is a major regional hub, so many travelers headed elsewhere in the Caribbean make connections here. Because of the number of flights, fares to San Juan are among the most reasonably priced to the region.

Nonstop flights to San Juan from New York are 3¾ hours; from Miami, 2½ hours; from Atlanta, 3½ hours; from Boston, 4 hours; from Chicago, 4¾ hours; from Los Angeles, 8 hours; from the United Kingdom, 5 hours; from Germany, 9¾ hours.

CARRIERS

San Juan's busy Aeropuerto Internacional Luis Muñoz Marín is the Caribbean hub of American Airlines, which flies nonstop from Baltimore, Boston, Chicago, Dallas, Fort Lauderdale, Miami, Newark, New York–JFK, Orlando, Philadelphia, Tampa, and Washington, D.C.–Dulles. Continental Airlines flies nonstop from Houston and Newark. Delta flies nonstop from Atlanta, Orlando, and New York–JFK. JetBlue flies nonstop from New York–JFK. Spirit Air flies nonstop from Fort Lauderdale and Orlando. United flies nonstop from Chicago, New York–JFK, Philadelphia, and Washington, D.C.–Dulles. US Airways flies nonstop from Baltimore, Boston, Charlotte, Chicago, Philadelphia, and Washington, D.C.–Dulles. International carriers serving San Juan include Air Canada from Toronto, Air France from Paris, Iberia from Madrid, and British Airways from London.

San Juan is no longer the only gateway to Puerto Rico. If you're headed to the western part of the island, you can fly directly into Aguadilla. Continental flies here from Newark, and JetBlue flies here from New York–JFK. If the southern coast is your goal, Continental flies to Ponce from Newark.

If you are flying on to Vieques or Culebra, you no longer have to transfer to Aeropuerto Fernando L. Rivas Dominici. Now all the carriers servicing the islands also have flights from the international airport, including Air Flamenco, Isla Nena Air Service, and Vieques Air Link; of course, these airlines do still fly daily from Isla Grande airport as well. American Eagle and Cape Air fly between the international airport and Vieques.

Puerto Rico is also a good spot from which to hop to other Caribbean islands. American Eagle serves many islands in the Caribbean; Cape Air connects San Juan to St. Thomas and St. Croix. Seaborne Airlines has seaplanes departing from San Juan Piers 6 and 7 to St. Thomas and St. Croix.

📶 **International Airlines Air Canada** ☎ 888/247-2262 ⊕ www.aircanada.com. **Air France** ☎ 800/237-2747 ⊕ www.airfrance.com. **American Air-**lines/American Eagle ☎ 800/433-7300 ⊕ www.aa.com. **British Airways** ☎ 800/247-9297 ⊕ www.britishairways.com. **Continental Airlines** ☎ 800/523-3273 for U.S. and Mexico reservations, 800/231-0856 for international reservations ⊕ www.continental.com. **Delta Airlines** ☎ 800/221-1212 for U.S. reservations, 800/241-4141 for international reservations ⊕ www.delta.com. **Iberia** ☎ 787/725-7000 ⊕ www.iberia.com. **jetBlue** ☎ 800/538-2583 ⊕ www.jetblue.com. **Northwest Airlines** ☎ 800/225-2525 for U.S. reservations, 800/447-4747 for international destinations ⊕ www.nwa.com. **Spirit Airlines** ☎ 800/772-7117 or 586/791-7300 ⊕ www.spiritair.com. **United Airlines** ☎ 800/864-8331 for U.S. reservations, 800/538-2929 for international reservations ⊕ www.united.com. **USAirways** ☎ 800/428-4322 for U.S. and Canada reservations, 800/622-1015 for international reservations ⊕ www.usairways.com.

📶 **Regional Airlines Air Flamenco** ☎ 787/724-1818 ⊕ www.airflamenco.net. **Cape Air** ☎ 800/525-0280 ⊕ www.flycapeair.com. **Isla Nena Air Service** ☎ 787/741-6362 or 877/812-5144 ⊕ www.islanena.8m.com. **Seaborne Airlines** ☎ 888/359-8687 ⊕ www.seaborneairlines.com. **Vieques Air Link** ☎ 787/722-3736 or 888/901-9247 ⊕ www.vieques-island.com/val.

CHECK-IN & BOARDING

Double-check your flight times, especially if you made your reservations far in advance. Airlines change their schedules, and alerts may not reach you. Always **bring a government-issued photo I.D. to the airport** (even when it's not required, a passport is best), and **arrive when you need to and not before.** Check in usually at least an hour before domestic flights and two to three hours for international flights. But many airlines have more stringent advance check-in requirements at some busy airports. The TSA estimates the waiting time for security at most major airports and publishes the information on its Web site. Note that if you aren't at the gate at least 10 minutes before your flight is scheduled to take off (sometimes earlier), you won't be allowed to board.

Don't stand in a line if you don't have to. Buy an e-ticket, check-in at an electronic kiosk, or—even better—check in on your airline's Web site before you leave home. If you don't need to check luggage, you could bypass all but the security lines. These days most domestic airline tickets are electronic; international tickets may be either electronic or paper.

You usually pay a surcharge (usually at least $25) to get a paper ticket, and its sole advantage is that it may be easier to endorse over to another airline if your flight is cancelled and the airline with which you booked can't accommodate you on another flight. With an e-ticket the only thing you receive is an e-mailed receipt citing your itinerary and reservation and ticket numbers. Be sure to carry this with you, as you'll need it to get past security. If you lose you receipt, though, you can simply print out another copy or ask the airline to do it for you at check-in.

Particularly during busy travel seasons and around holiday periods, if a flight is oversold, the gate agent will usually ask for volunteers and will offer some sort of compensation if you are willing to take a different flight. **Know your rights.** If you are bumped from a flight *involuntarily*, the airline must give you some kind of compensation if an alternate flight can't be found within one hour. If your flight is delayed because of something within the airline's control (bad weather doesn't count), then the airline has a responsibility to get you to your destination on the same day, even if they have to book you on another airline and in an upgraded class if necessary. Read your airline's Contract of Carriage; it's usually buried somewhere on the airline's Web site.

Be prepared to quickly adjust your plans by programming a few numbers into your cell: your airline, an airport hotel or two, your destination hotel, your car service, and/or your travel agent. Bring snacks, water, and sufficient diversions, and you'll be covered if you get stuck in the airport, on the tarmac, or even in the air during turbulence.

CUTTING COSTS

It's always good to **comparison shop.** Web sites (aka consolidators) and travel agents can have different arrangements with the airlines and offer different prices for ex-

actly the same flight and day. Certain Web sites have tracking features that will e-mail you immediately when good deals are posted. Other people prefer to stick with one or two frequent-flier programs, racking up free trips and accumulating perks that can make trips easier. On some airlines, perks include a special reservation number, early boarding, access to upgrades, and roomier economy-class seating.

Check early and often. Start looking for cheap fares up to a year in advance, and keep looking until you see something you can live with; you never know when a good deal may pop up. That said, **jump on the good deals.** Waiting even a few minutes might mean paying more. For most people, saving money is more important than flexibility, so the more affordable nonrefundable tickets work. Just remember that you'll pay dearly (often as much as $100) if you must change your travel plans. Check on prices for departures at different times of the day and to and from alternate airports, and look for departures on Tuesday, Wednesday, and Thursday, typically the cheapest days to travel. Remember to **weigh your options,** though. A cheaper flight might have a long layover rather than being nonstop, or landing at a secondary airport might substantially increase your ground transportation costs.

Note that many airline Web sites—and most ads—show prices *without* taxes and surcharges. Don't buy until you know the full price. Government taxes add up quickly. Also **watch those ticketing fees.** Surcharges are usually added when you buy your ticket anywhere but on an airline's own Web site. (By the way, that includes on the phone–even if you call the airline directly—and for paper tickets regardless of how you book).

🎫 **Online Consolidators** AirlineConsolidator.com ⊕ www.airlineconsolidator.com; for international tickets. **Best Fares** ⊕ www.bestfares.com; $59.90 annual membership. **Cheap Tickets** ⊕ www.cheaptickets.com. **Expedia** ⊕ www.expedia.com. **Hotwire** ⊕ www.hotwire.com. **lastminute.com** ⊕ www.lastminute.com specializes in last-minute travel; the main site is for the UK, but it has a link to a U.S. site. **Luxury Link** ⊕ www.luxurylink.com has auctions (surprisingly good deals) as well as offers at the high-end side of travel. **Orbitz** ⊕ www.orbitz. com. **Onetravel.com** ⊕ www.onetravel.com. **Price-line.com** ⊕ www.priceline.com. **Travelocity** ⊕ www.travelocity.com.

ENJOYING THE FLIGHT

Get the seat you want. Avoid those on the aisle directly across from the lavatories. Most frequent fliers say those are even worse than the the the seats that don't recline (e.g., those in the back row and those in front of a bulkhead). For more legroom, you can request emergency-aisle seats, but only do so if you're capable of moving the 35- to 60-pound airplane exit door—a Federal Aviation Administration requirement of passengers in these seats. Seats behind a bulkhead also offer more legroom, but they don't have under-seat storage. Often, you can pick a seat when you buy your ticket on an airline's Web site. But it's not always a guarantee, particularly if the airline changes the plane after you book your ticket; check back before you leave. SeatGuru.com has more information about specific seat configurations, which vary by aircraft.

Fewer airlines are providing free food for passengers in economy class. **Don't go hungry.** If you're scheduled to fly during meal times, verify if your airline offers anything to eat; even when it does, be prepared to pay. If you have dietary concerns, request special meals. These can be vegetarian, low-cholesterol, or kosher, for example. It's a good idea to pack some healthful snacks and a small (plastic) bottle of water in your carry-on bag.

Ask the airline about its children's menus, activities, and fares. On some lines infants and toddlers fly for free if they sit on a parent's lap, and older children fly for half price in their own seats. Also inquire about policies involving car seats; having one may limit where you can sit. While you're at it, ask about seat-belt extenders for car seats. And note that you can't count on a flight attendant to automatically produce an extender; you may have to inquire about it again when you board.

HOW TO COMPLAIN

If your baggage goes astray or your flight goes awry, complain right away. Most carriers require that you **file a claim immediately.** The Aviation Consumer Protection Division of the Department of Transportation publishes *Fly-Rights,* which discusses airlines and consumer issues and is available online. You can also find articles and information on mytravelrights.com, the Web site of the nonprofit Consumer Travel Rights Center.

🚩 **Airline Complaints Office of Aviation Enforcement and Proceedings** (Aviation Consumer Protection Division) ☎ 202/366-2220 ⊕ airconsumer.ost. dot.gov. **Federal Aviation Administration Consumer Hotline** ☎ 866/835-5322 ⊕ www.faa.gov.

AIRPORTS & TRANSFERS

Aeropuerto Internacional Luis Muñoz Marín (SJU) is 20 minutes east of Old San Juan in the neighborhood of Isla Verde. San Juan's other airport is the small Fernando L. Rivas Dominici Airport (SIG) in Isla Grande, near the city's Miramar section. From either airport you can catch flights to Culebra, Vieques, and other destinations on Puerto Rico and throughout the Caribbean. (Note that although the Dominicci airport was still operating at this writing, its ultimate future was uncertain.)

Other Puerto Rican airports include Aeropuerto Internacional Rafael Hernández (BQN) in the northwestern town of Aguadilla, Aeropuerto Eugenio María de Hostos (MAZ) in the west coast community of Mayagüez, Mercedita (PSE) in the south coast town of Ponce, Aeropuerto Diego Jiménez Torres (FAJ) in the east coast city of Fajardo, Antonio Rivera Rodríguez (VQS) on Vieques, and Aeropuerto Benjamin Rivera Noriega (CPX) on Culebra.

🚩 **Aeropuerto Antonio Rivera Rodríguez** ✉ Vieques ☎ 787/741-8358. **Aeropuerto Benjamin Rivera Noriega** ✉ Culebra ☎ 787/742-0022. **Aeropuerto Diego Jiménez Torres** ✉ Fajardo ☎ 787/860-3110. **Aeropuerto Eugenio María de Hostos** ✉ Mayagüez ☎ 787/833-0148. **Aeropuerto Fernando L. Rivas Dominici** ✉ Isla Grande, San Juan ☎ 787/729-8711. **Aeropuerto Mercedita** ✉ Ponce ☎ 787/842-6292. **Aerop-**

uerto Rafael Hernández ⊠ Aguadilla ☎ 787/
891-2286. **Aeropuerto Internacional Luis Muñoz
Marín** ⊠ Isla Verde, San Juan ☎ 787/791-3840.
Airline and Airport Links.com ⊕ www.
airlineandairportlinks.com has links to many of the
world's airlines and airports.

🔂 **Airline Security Issues Transportation Security
Administration** ⊕ www.tsa.gov/public has answers
for almost every question that might come up.

GROUND TRANSPORTATION

Before arriving, check with your hotel
about transfers: some hotels and resorts
provide transport from the airport—free
or for a fee—to their guests; some larger
resorts run regular shuttles. Otherwise,
your best bets are *taxis turísticos* (tourist
taxis). Uniformed officials at the airport
can help you make arrangements. They
will give you a slip with your exact fare to
hand to the driver. Rates are based on
your destination. A taxi turíistico to Isla
Verde costs $10. It's $14 to Condado and
$19 to Old San Juan. There's a 50¢ charge
for each bag handled by the driver.

BOAT & FERRY TRAVEL

The Fajardo Port Authority's 400-passen-
ger ferries run between Fajardo and the
out-islands of Vieques and Culebra; either
trip takes about 90 minutes. The vessels
carry cargo and passengers to Vieques
three times daily ($2 one-way) and to
Culebra twice-daily from Sunday through
Friday, three times a day on Saturday
($2.25 one-way). Get schedules for the
Culebra and Vieques ferries by calling the
Port Authority in Fajardo, Vieques, or
Culebra. You buy tickets at the ferry dock.

Another Vieques and Culebra option is Island Hi-Speed Ferry that leaves from Pier
2 in Old San Juan. During high season, the
ferry makes one daily round-trip (leaving
in the morning, returning in the afternoon). Travel time is 1 hour 45 minutes to
Culebra, 2 hours 15 minutes to Vieques.
Round-trip fares are $68 to Culebra, $78
to Vieques. Reservations are recommended. Ferry service by Ferries del
Caribe runs between Mayagüez and Santo
Domingo. Trips are overnight, leaving at 8
PM and arriving at 8 AM. Small cabins with
sleeping accommodations for two, three,

and four persons are provided. Tickets are
usually available, but reserve well in advance if you're bringing your car. Ships
leave from the Zona Portuaria, past the
Mayagüez Holiday Inn on Highway 2.
🔂 **Autoridad de los Puertos** ☎ 787/788-1155 in
San Juan, 787/863-4560 in Fajardo, 787/742-3161 in
Culebra, 787/741-4761 in Vieques. **Ferries del Caribe**
☎ 787/832-4800 ⊕ www.ferriesdelcaribe.com.

BUSINESS HOURS

BANKS & OFFICES

Bank hours are generally weekdays from 9
to 5, though a few branches are also open
Saturday from 9 to noon or 1. Post offices
are open weekdays from 7:30 to 4:30 and
Saturday from 8 to noon. Government offices are open weekdays from 9 to 5.

GAS STATIONS

Most stations are open daily from early in
the morning until 10 or 11 PM. Numerous
stations in urban areas are open 24 hours.

MUSEUMS & SIGHTS

As a rule, San Juan area museums are
closed on Monday, and in some cases,
Sunday. Hours otherwise are 9 or 10 AM
to 5 PM, often with an hour off for lunch
between noon and 2. Sights managed by
the National Parks Service, such as Fuerte
San Felipe del Morro and San Cristóbal,
are open daily from 9 to 5.

PHARMACIES

In cities, pharmacies are generally open
from 9 to 6 or 7 weekdays and on Saturday. Walgreens operates numerous pharmacies around the island; some are open
24 hours.

SHOPS

Street shops are open Monday through
Saturday from 9 to 6; mall stores tend to
stay open to 9 or sometimes even later.
Count on convenience stores staying open
late into the night, seven days a week. Supermarkets are often closed on Sunday, although some remain open 24-hours, seven
days a week.

BUS TRAVEL

The Autoridad Metropolitana de Autobuses (AMA) operates buses that thread
through San Juan, running in exclusive

lanes on major thoroughfares and stopping at signs marked PARADA. Destinations are indicated above the windshield. Bus B-21 runs through Condado all the way to Plaza Las Américas in Hato Rey. Bus A-5 runs from San Juan through Santurce and the beach area of Isla Verde. Service starts at around 6 AM and generally continues until 9 PM. Fares are 50¢ or 75¢, depending on the route, and are paid in exact change upon entering the bus. Most buses are air-conditioned and have wheelchair lifts and lock-downs.

There is no bus system covering the rest of the island. If you do not have a rental car, your best bet is to travel by *públicos,* which are usually shared 17-passenger vans. They have yellow license plates ending in "P" or "PD," and they scoot to towns throughout the island, stopping in each community's main plaza. They operate primarily during the day; routes and fares are fixed by the Public Service Commission, but schedules aren't set, so you have to call ahead.

🚍 Autoridad Metropolitana de Autobuses
☎ 787/767-7979.

CAR RENTAL

Rates start as low as $35 a day (not including insurance), with unlimited mileage. Discounts are often offered for long-term rentals, for cars that are booked more than 72 hours in advance, and to automobile association members. All major U.S. car-rental agencies are represented on the island, but be sure to look into local companies. Most are reliable and some offer competitive rates.

If you're visiting during peak season or over holiday weekends, reserve your car before arriving on the island—not only because of possible discounts but also to ensure that you get a car and that it's a reliable one. Faced with high demand, the agencies may be forced to drag out the worst of their fleet; waiting unil the last minute could leave you stranded without a car or stranded with one on the side of the road.

You'll find offices for dozens of agencies at San Juan's Aeropuerto Internacional Luis Muñoz Marín, and a majority of them have shuttle service to and from the airport and the pickup point. Most rental cars are available with automatic or standard transmission. Four-wheel-drive vehicles aren't necessary unless you plan to go way off the beaten path or along the steep, rocky roads of Culebra or Vieques; in most cases a standard compact car will do the trick. If you are given a choice, always opt for air-conditioning. You'll be glad you did when it's high noon and you're in a San Juan traffic jam. Don't rent a car on mainland Puerto Rico and expect to take it to Culebra or Vieques.

CUTTING COSTS

Really weigh your options. Find out if a credit card you carry or organization or frequent-renter program to which you belong has a discount program. And check that such discounts really are the best deal. You can often do better with special weekend or weekly rates offered by a rental agency. (And even if you only want to rent for five or six days, ask if you can get the weekly rate; it may very well be cheaper than the daily rate for that period of time.)

Price local car-rental companies as well as the majors. Also investigate wholesalers, which don't own fleets but rent in bulk from those that do and often offer better rates (note you must usually pay for such rentals before leaving home). Consider adding a car rental onto your air/hotel vacation package; the cost will often be cheaper than if you had rented the car separately on your own.

Beware of hidden charges. Those great rental rates may not be so great when you add in taxes, surcharges, cancellation penalties, taxes, drop-off charges (if you're planning to pick up the car in one city and leave it in another), and surcharges (for being under or over a certain age, for additional drivers, or for driving over state or country borders or out of a specific radius from your point of rental).

Note that airport rental offices often add supplementary surcharges that you may avoid by renting from an agency whose office is just off airport property. Don't buy the tank of gas that's in the car when you rent it unless you plan to do a lot of driving. Avoid hefty refueling fees by filling the tank at a station well away from the rental agency (those nearby are often more expensive) just before you turn in the car.

🔣 **Local Agencies AAA Car Rental** ☎ 787/726-7355 in San Juan 🌐 www.aaacarrentalpr.com. **Charlie Car Rental** ☎ 787/728-2418 in San Juan 🌐 www.charliecars.com. **Island Car Rental** ☎ 787/741-1666 in Vieques. **L & M Car Rental** ☎ 787/791-1160 in San Juan, 787/831-4740 in Mayagüez.

🔣 **Major Agencies Alamo** ☎ 800/462-5266 🌐 www.alamo.com. **Avis** ☎ 800/230-4898 🌐 www.avis.com. **Budget** ☎ 800/527-0700 🌐 www.budget.com. **Hertz** ☎ 800/654-3131 🌐 www.hertz.com. **National Car Rental** ☎ 800/227-7368 🌐 www.nationalcar.com.

INSURANCE

Everyone who rents a car wonders about whether the insurance that the rental companies offer is worth the expense. No one—not even us—has a simple answer. It all depends on how much regular insurance you have, how comfortable you are with risk, and whether or not money is an issue.

If you own a car and carry comprehensive car insurance for both collision and liability, your personal auto insurance will probably cover a rental, but read your policy's fine print to be sure. If you don't have auto insurance, then you should probably buy the collision- or loss-damage waiver (CDW or LDW) from the rental company. This eliminates your liability for damage to the car. Some credit cards offer CDW coverage, but it's usually supplemental to your own insurance and rarely covers SUVs, minivans, luxury models, and the like. If your coverage is secondary, you may still be liable for loss-of-use costs from the car-rental company (again, read the fine print). But no credit-card insurance is valid unless you use that card for *all* transactions, from reserving to paying the final bill.

You may also be offered supplemental liability coverage; the car-rental company is required to carry a minimal level of liability coverage that covers all renters, but it's rarely enough to cover claims in a really serious accident if you're at fault. Your own auto insurance policy will protect you if you own a car; if you don't, you have to decide whether you are willing to take the risk.

U.S. rental companies sell CDWs and LDWs for about $15 to $25 a day; supplemental liability is usually over $10 a day. The car-rental company may offer you all sorts of other policies, but they're rarely worth the cost. Personal accident insurance, which is basic hospitalization coverage, is an especially egregious rip-off if you already have health insurance.

Note that you can decline the insurance from the rental company and purchase it through a third-party provider such as Travel Guard (🌐 www.travelguard.com)—$9 per day for $35,000 of coverage. That's sometimes just under half the price of the CDW offered by some car-rental companies. Also, Diner's Club offers primary CDW coverage on all rentals reserved and paid for with the card. This means that Diner's Club's company—not your own car insurance—pays in case of an accident. It *doesn't* mean your car-insurance company won't raise your rates once it discovers you had an accident.

CAR TRAVEL

Several well-marked multilane highways link population centers. Route 26 is the main artery through San Juan, connecting Condado and Old San Juan to Isla Verde and the airport. Route 22, which runs east–west between San Juan and Camuy, and Route 52, which runs north–south between San Juan and Ponce, are toll roads (35¢–50¢). Route 2, a smaller highway, travels along the west coast, and routes 3 and 53 traverse the east shore.

Five highways are particularly noteworthy for their scenery and vistas. The island's tourism authorities have even given them special names. Ruta Panorámica (Panoramic Route) runs east–west through the central mountains. Ruta Cotorra (Puerto Rican Parrot Route) travels along the north coast. Ruta Paso Fino (Paso Fino Horse Route, after a horse breed) takes you north–south and west along the south coast. Ruta Coquí, named for the famous Puerto Rican tree frog, runs along the east coast. Ruta Flamboyán, named after the island tree, goes from San Juan through the mountains to the east coast.

EMERGENCY SERVICES

In an emergency, dial 911. If your car breaks down, call the rental company for a replacement. Before renting, make sure you investigate the company's policy regarding replacement vehicles and repairs out on the island, and ask about surcharges that might be incurred if you break down in a rural area and need a new car.

GASOLINE

All types of fuel—unleaded regular, unleaded super-premium, diesel—are available by the liter. Most stations have both full- and self-service. Hours vary, but stations generally operate daily from early in the morning until 10 or 11 PM; in metro areas many are open 24 hours. Stations are few and far between in the Cordillera Central and other rural areas; plan accordingly. In cities you can pay with cash and bank or credit cards; in the hinterlands cash is often your only option.

ROAD CONDITIONS

Puerto Rico has some of the Caribbean's best roads. That said, potholes, sharp turns, speed bumps, sudden gradient changes, and poor lighting can sometimes make driving difficult. Be especially cautious when driving after heavy rains or hurricanes; roads and bridges might be washed out or damaged. Many of the mountain roads are very narrow and steep, with unmarked curves and cliffs. Locals are familiar with such roads and often drive at high speeds, which can give you quite a scare. When traveling on a narrow, curving road, it's best to honk your horn as you take any sharp turn.

Traffic around cities—particularly San Juan, Ponce, and Mayagüez—is heavy at rush hours (weekdays from 7 to 10 and 4 to 7).

ROAD MAPS

Most car-rental agencies give you a free map with your car; more detailed maps are available in bookstores, drugstores, and souvenir shops. Look for the $6 *Mapa Vial y Turístico* by Metrodata Maps, which features an island map; a large metro map of San Juan; and insets of Aguadilla, Mayagüez, Arecibo, Ponce, and other large towns. The free maps given out at tourism officers and information booths are often outdated or not detailed enough if you're traveling on anything but the major highways.

RULES OF THE ROAD

U.S. driving laws apply in Puerto Rico, and you'll find no problem with signage or directionals. Street and highway signs are most often in Spanish but use international symbols; brushing up on a few key Spanish terms before your trip will help. The following words and phrases are especially useful: *calle sin salida* (dead end street), *cruce de peatones* (pedestrian crossing), *cuidado* (caution), *desvío* (detour), *estación de peaje* (toll booth), *no entre* (do not enter), *prohibido adelantar* (no passing), *salida* (exit), *tránsito* (one way), *zona escolar* (school zone).

Distances are posted in kilometers (1.6 km to 1 mi), whereas speed limits are posted in miles per hour. Speeding and drunk-driving penalties are much the same here as on the mainland. Police cars often travel with their lights flashing, so it's difficult to know when they're trying to pull you over. If the siren is on, move to the right to get out of their way. If the lights are on, it's best to pull over—just be sure that the vehicle is a *marked* police car before doing so.

COMPUTERS ON THE ROAD

Internet cafés are more common than they once were, but are still few and far between. As if that weren't bad enough, many hotels have yet to install high-speed Internet access in their rooms. Your best bet is to use your hotel business center.
🔲 Internet Access **Cowabunga's** ✉ Rte. 115, Km 11.6, Rincón ☎ 787/823–5225. **Cyber Net** ✉ 1128 Av. Ashford, Condado, San Juan ☎ 787/724–4033 ✉ 5980 Av. Isla Verde, Isla Verde, San Juan ☎ 787/ 728–4195. **Internet Active** ✉ Av. Isla Verde and Calle Rosa, Isla Verde, San Juan ☎ 787/791–1916.

CRUISE TRAVEL

Cruising is a relaxing and convenient way to tour this beautiful part of the world. You get all of the amenities of a resort hotel and enough activities to guarantee fun, even on the occasional rainy day. All your important decisions are made long before you board. Your itinerary is set, and you know the basic cost of your vacation beforehand. Ships usually call at several ports on a single voyage but are at each port for only one day. Thus, while you don't get much of a feel for any specific island, you get a taste of what several islands are like and can then choose to vacation on your favorite one for a longer time on a future trip.

If you are planning a Caribbean cruise, consider Fodor's *The Complete Guide to Caribbean Cruises* (available in bookstores everywhere).

🚢 Cruise Lines **Carnival Cruise Line** ☎ 305/599–2600 or 800/227–6482 ⊕ www.carnival.com. **Celebrity Cruises** ☎ 305/539–6000 or 800/647–2251 ⊕ www.celebrity.com. **Clipper Cruise Line** ☎ 314/655–6700 or 800/325–0010 ⊕ www.clippercruise.com. **Costa Cruises** ☎ 954/266–5600 or 800/462–6782 ⊕ www.costacruise.com. **Crystal Cruises** ☎ 800/446–6625 or 310/785–9300 ⊕ www.crystalcruises.com. **Cunard Line** ☎ 661/753–1000 or 800/728–6273 ⊕ www.cunard.com. **Disney Cruise Line** ☎ 407/566–3500 or 800/325–2500 ⊕ www.disneycruise.com. **Holland America Line** ☎ 206/281–3535 or 877/932–4259 ⊕ www.hollandamerica.com. **MSC Cruises** ☎ 954/662–6262 or 800/666–9333 ⊕ www.msccruises.com. **Norwegian Cruise Line** ☎ 800/327–7030 ⊕ www.ncl.com. **Oceania Cruises** ☎ 305/514–2300 or 800/531–5658 ⊕ www.oceaniacruises.com. **Princess Cruises** ☎ 661/753–0000 or 800/774–6237 ⊕ www.princess.com. **Regent Seven Seas Cruises** ☎ 954/776–6123 or 800/477–7500 ⊕ www.rssc.com. **Royal Caribbean International** ☎ 305/539–6000 or 800/327–6700 ⊕ www.royalcaribbean.com. **Seabourn Cruise Line** ☎ 305/463–3000 or 800/929–9391 ⊕ www.seabourn.com. **SeaDream Yacht Club** ☎ 305/856–5622 or 800/707–4911 ⊕ www.seadreamyachtclub.com. **Silversea Cruises** ☎ 954/522–4477 or 800/722–9955 ⊕ www.silversea.com. **Star Clippers** ☎ 305/442–0550 or 800/442–0551 ⊕ www.starclippers.com. **Windjammer Barefoot Cruises** ☎ 305/672–6453 or 800/327–2601 ⊕ www.windjammer.com. **Windstar Cruises** ☎ 206/281–3535 or 800/258–7245 ⊕ www.windstarcruises.com.
🚢 Organizations **Cruise Lines International Association** (CLIA) ✉ 80 Broad St., Suite 1800, New York, NY 10004 ☎ 212/921–0066 ⊕ www.cruising.org.
🚢 Port Information **Autoridad de Puertos de Puerto Rico** ☎ 787/723–2260. **Terminal de San Juan** ☎ 787/729–8714.

CUSTOMS & DUTIES

Puerto Rico is considered to be a part of the U.S. for customs purposes, so you will not pass through customs on arrival if you are coming from the United States. When leaving Puerto Rico for the mainland, you must pass your bag through a checkpoint of the U.S. Department of Agriculture's (USDA) Animal and Plant Health Inspection Service (APHIS). The list of organic products that can be transported from Puerto Rico to the States includes avocados, bananas, breadfruits, citrus fruits, ginger, papayas, and plantains.
🚢 U.S. Information **U.S. Customs and Border Protection** ⊕ www.cbp.gov.

EATING OUT

Throughout the island you'll find everything from French haute cuisine to sushi bars, as well as superb local eateries serving *comidas criollas*, traditional Caribbean-creole meals. Note that the *mesón gastronómico* label is used by the government to recognize restaurants that preserve culinary traditions. For information on food-related health issues *see* Health, *below.*

The restaurants we list are the cream of the crop in each price category. Properties indicated by a ✕🏠 are lodging establishments whose restaurant warrants a special trip.

Was the service stellar or not up to snuff? Did the food give you shivers of delight or leave you cold? Did the prices and portions make you happy or sad? Rate restaurants and write your own reviews in "Travel Ratings" or start a discussion about your favorite places in "Travel Talk" on www.fodors.com. Your comments might even appear in our books. Yes, you, too, can be a correspondent!

MEAL TIMES

Puerto Ricans' eating habits mirror those of their counterparts on the mainland United States: they eat breakfast, lunch, and dinner, though they don't tend to down coffee all day long. Instead, islanders like a steaming, high-test cup in the morning and another between 2 and 4 PM. They may finish a meal with coffee, but they never drink coffee *during* a meal.

Unless otherwise noted, the restaurants listed in this guide are open daily for lunch and dinner. People tend to eat dinner late in Puerto Rico; you may find yourself alone in the restaurant if you eat at 5 PM; at 6, business will pick up a little, and from 7 to 10, it may be quite busy.

RESERVATIONS & DRESS
Regardless of where you are, it's a good idea to make a reservation if you can. In some places it's expected. We only mention specifically when reservations are essential (there's no other way you'll ever get a table) or when they are not accepted. For popular restaurants, book as far ahead as you can (often 30 days), and reconfirm as soon as you arrive. (Large parties should always call ahead to check the reservations policy.) We mention dress only when men are required to wear a jacket or a jacket and tie. Puerto Ricans generally dress up to go out, particularly in the evening. And always remember: beach attire is only for the beach.

WINE, BEER & SPIRITS
Puerto Rico isn't a notable producer of wine, but there are several well-crafted local beers to choose from. Legends trace the birthplace of the piña colada to any number of San Juan establishments, from the Caribe Hilton to a Calle La Fortaleza bar. Puerto Rican rum is popular mixed with cola (known as a *cuba libre*), soda, tonic, juices, or water, or served on the rocks or even straight up. Rums range from light mixers to dark, aged sipping liqueurs. Look for Bacardí, Don Q, Ron Rico, Palo Viejo, and Barrilito. The drinking age in Puerto Rico is 18.

ELECTRICITY
Puerto Rico uses the same 110-volt AC (60-cycle), two-prong-outlet electrical system as in North America. Plugs have two flat pins set parallel to each another. European visitors should bring adapters and converters, or call ahead to to see whether their hotel has them on hand.

EMBASSIES & CONSULATES
Canada and the United Kingdom have consulates in San Juan.
🇫 **British Consulate** ✉ 350 Av. Carlos Chardon, Suite 1236, Hato Rey, San Juan 00918 ☎ 787/758-9828. **Canadian Consulate** ✉ 33 Calle Bolivia, Hato Rey, San Juan 00917 ☎ 787/759-6629.

EMERGENCIES
Emergencies are handled by dialing 911. You can expect a quick response by police, fire, and medical personnel, most of whom speak at least some English. San Juan's Tourist Zone Police are particularly helpful to visitors.
🇫 **Ambulance, police, and fire** ☎ 911. **Air Ambulance Service** ☎ 800/633-3590 or 787/756-3424. **Dental Emergencies** ☎ 787/722-2351 or 787/795-0320. **Fire Department** ☎ 787/343-2330. **Medical Emergency** ☎ 787/754-2222. **Police** ☎ 787/343-2020. **Tourist Zone Police** ☎ 787/726-7020, 787/726-7015 for Condado, 787/728-4770 or 787/726-2981 for Isla Verde.

ENGLISH-LANGUAGE MEDIA
BOOKS
Most bookstores carry books in both English and Spanish, and you'll find the standard English-language paperbacks at supermarkets and drugstores, with prices comparable to those in the United States.
🇫 **Bookstores Bell Book & Candle** ✉ 102 Av. José de Diego, Condado, San Juan ☎ 787/728-5000. **Borders** ✉ Plaza Las Américas, 525 Av. Franklin Delano Roosevelt, Hato Rey, San Juan ☎ 787/777-0916. **The Bookshop** ✉ Mayagüez Mall, Hwy. 2, Km 159.4, Mayagüez ☎ 787/805-3415. **Bookworm** ✉ 1129 Av. Ashford, Condado, San Juan ☎ 787/722-3344. **By the Book** ✉ 1300 Av. Ashford, Condado, San Juan ☎ 787/724-4272. **Cronopios** ✉ 255 Calle San José, Old San Juan, San Juan ☎ 787/724-1815. **Isabel II Books & Magazine** ✉ 66 Calle Isabel, Ponce Centro, Ponce ☎ 787/848-5019. **Librería Thekes** ✉ Plaza Las Américas, 525 Av. Franklin Delano Roosevelt, Hato Rey, San Juan ☎ 787/765-1539.

NEWSPAPERS & MAGAZINES
Puerto Rico's Pulitzer prize–winning *San Juan Star* is printed daily in Spanish and English. It carries local and syndicated columnists as well as a good mix of local and international news. In addition, you can get copies of the *Wall Street Journal, New York Times, USA Today, Miami Herald,* and other nationally distributed U.S. newspapers, most often at hotels and drugstores.

RADIO & TELEVISION

Most local TV programs are in Spanish, and consist of the usual mix of news, game shows, movies, soaps, and music videos. Some local shows broadcast in English, but the majority of English programming comes from cable-transmitted HBO, CNN, and others.

Radio programs run the gamut of Spanish talk shows, Miami-based English news broadcasts, evangelical religious broadcasts, and music of all sorts in both English and Spanish. Radio WOSO (1030 AM) is a local English-language radio station.

ETIQUETTE & BEHAVIOR

In general, islanders have a strong sense of religion—as evidenced by the numerous Catholic patron-saint festivals held throughout the year. Family ties are also strong, and it's not unusual to see families piling onto the beaches on weekends for a day of fun and barbecue. Puerto Ricans tend to proffer a great deal of respect to their elders, in formal greetings, language, and general attitude.

Many islanders are conservative in dress and manners, despite a penchant for frenetic music and dance. Typical greetings between female friends and male and female friends and relatives is a kiss on the cheek, and the greetings *"Buenos días"* ("Good day"), *"Buenos tardes"* ("Good afternoon"), and *"Buenas noches"* ("Good evening") are among a host of formal and less formal colloquial greetings. The phrases are also said in departing.

Although you may be spending a great deal of time on the beach, it's important to wear a shirt and shoes when entering any indoor business establishments. It's considered highly disrespectful to enter a store or a restaurant in a bathing suit or other inappropriate attire.

Islanders' knowledge of U.S. culture is thorough. Many Puerto Ricans have spent a great deal of time stateside, and those who haven't inevitably have relatives or friends living on the mainland. U.S. music, dress, and attitudes have infiltrated the culture, especially among the young, but the overriding cues are Spanish-Caribbean. Indeed, Puerto Ricans have a strong sense of identity, marked by often-ferocious debates over the island's political destiny.

GAY & LESBIAN TRAVEL

In sophisticated San Juan, gays and lesbians will find it easy to mingle. There are many gay-friendly hotels, restaurants, and clubs throughout the city, and the beaches at Condado and Ocean Park tend to attract a gay crowd. The first Sunday in June sees a gay pride parade in Condado that's preceded by a week of events. The bohemian Old San Juan crowd is particularly friendly and—just as in Ocean Park and Condado—many businesses there are owned by gays or lesbians. Some clubs and bars also have a weekly "gay night." Other welcoming areas of the island include Ponce in the South, Boquerón in the southwest, and the town of Fajardo and the out-islands of Vieques and Culebra in the east. To find out more about events and gay-friendly businesses, pick up a copy of the *Puerto Rico Breeze,* the island's gay and lesbian newspaper.

Frank Fournier of Connections Travel—which is a member of the International Gay & Lesbian Travel Association—is a reliable local travel agent for gay and lesbian travelers.

🖪 **Connections Travel** ✉ 257 Calle Tetuán, Old San Juan ☎ 787/721-7090.

HEALTH

Health care in Puerto Rico is among the best in the Caribbean, but expect long waits and often a less-than-pleasant bedside manner. At all hospitals and medical centers you'll find English-speaking medical staff, and many large hotels have an English-speaking doctor on call.

The most common types of illnesses are caused by contaminated food and water. Especially in developing countries, drink only bottled, boiled, or purified water and drinks; don't drink from public fountains or use ice. You should even consider using bottled water to brush your teeth. Make sure food has been thoroughly cooked and is served to you fresh and hot; avoid vegetables and fruits that you haven't washed (in bottled or purified water) or peeled yourself. If you have problems, mild cases of traveler's diarrhea may respond to Imodium (known generically as loperamide) or Pepto-Bismol. Be sure to drink plenty of fluids; if you can't keep fluids down, seek medical help immediately.

Infectious diseases can be airborne or passed via mosquitoes and ticks and through direct or indirect physical contact with animals or people. Some, including Norwalk-like viruses that affect your digestive tract, can be passed along through contaminated food. Condoms can help prevent most sexually transmitted diseases, but aren't absolute and the quality of them varies from country to country. Speak with your physician and/or check the CDC or World Health Organization Web sites for health alerts, particularly if you're pregnant, traveling with children, or have a chronic illness.

Tap water is generally fine on the island; just avoid drinking it after storms (when the water supply can become mixed with sewage). Thoroughly wash or peel produce you buy in markets before eating it.

All the U.S. brands of sunscreen and over-the-counter medicines (Tylenol, Advil, Robitussin, Nyquil, etc.) are available in pharmacies, supermarkets, and convenience stores.

DIVERS' ALERT
Do not fly within 24 hours of scuba diving.
🚩 Health Warnings **National Centers for Disease Control & Prevention** (CDC) ☎ 877/394-8747 international travelers' health line ⊕ www.cdc.gov/travel. **World Health Organization** (WHO) ⊕ www.who.int.

HOLIDAYS
Puerto Rico observes all U.S. federal holidays, as well as many local holidays. Most government offices and businesses shut down on holidays, with the exception of convenience stores and some supermarkets, pharmacies, and restaurants. Public transportation runs on abbreviated schedules, just as on Sunday. Public holidays in Puerto Rico include: New Year's Day, Three Kings Day (Jan. 6), Eugenio María de Hostos Day (Jan. 8), Dr. Martin Luther King Jr. Day (3rd Mon. in Jan.), Presidents' Day (3rd Mon. in Feb.), Palm Sunday, Good Friday, Easter Sunday, Memorial Day (last Mon. in May), Independence Day (July 4), Luis Muñoz Rivera Day (July 16), Constitution Day (July 25), José Celso Barbosa Day (July 27), Labor Day (1st Mon. in Sept.), Columbus Day (2nd Mon. in Oct.), Veterans' Day (Nov. 11), Puerto Rico Discovery Day (Nov. 19), Thanksgiving Day, and Christmas.

INSURANCE
What kind of coverage do you honestly need? Do you even need trip insurance at all? Take a deep breath and read on.

We believe that comprehensive trip insurance is especially valuable if you're booking a very expensive or complicated trip (particularly to an isolated region) or if you're booking far in advance. Who knows what could happen six months down the road? But whether or not you get insurance has more to do with how comfortable you are assuming all that risk yourself.

Comprehensive travel policies typically cover trip-cancellation and interruption, letting you cancel or cut your trip short because of a personal emergency, illness, or, in some cases, acts of terrorism in your destination. Such policies also cover evacuation and medical care. Some also cover you for trip delays because of bad weather or mechanical problems as well as for lost or delayed baggage. Another type of coverage to look for is financial default—that is, when your trip is disrupted because a tour operator, airline, or cruise line goes out of business. Generally you must buy this when you book your trip or shortly thereafter, and it's only available to you if your operator isn't on a list of excluded companies.

If you're going abroad, consider buying medical-only coverage at the very least. Neither Medicare nor some private insurers cover medical expenses anywhere outside of the United States besides Mexico and Canada (including time aboard a cruise ship, even if it leaves from a U.S. port). Medical-only policies typically reimburse you for medical care (excluding that related to pre-existing conditions) and hospitalization abroad and provide for evacuation.

You still have to pay the bills and await reimbursement from the insurer, though.

Expect comprehensive travel insurance policies to cost about 4% to 7% of the total price of your trip (it's more like 12% if you're over age 70). A medical-only policy may or may not be cheaper than a comprehensive policy. Always read the fine print of your policy to make sure that you are covered for the risks that are of the most concern to you. Compare several policies to make sure you're getting the best price and range of coverage available.

Just as an aside: You know you can save a bundle on trips to warm-weather destinations by traveling in rainy season. But there's also a chance that a severe storm will disrupt your plans. The solution? Look for hotels and resorts that offer storm/hurricane guarantees. Although they rarely allow refunds, most guarantees do let you rebook later if a storm strikes.

🛈 Insurance Comparison Sites **Insure My Trip. com** ⊕ www.insuremytrip.com. **Square Mouth.com** ⊕ www.quotetravelinsurance.com.

🛈 Comprehensive Travel Insurers **Access America** ☎ 866/807–3982 ⊕ www.accessamerica.com. **CSA Travel Protection** ☎ 800/729–6021 ⊕ www. csatravelprotection.com. **HTH Worldwide** ☎ 610/254–8700 or 888/243–2358 ⊕ www.hthworldwide. com. **Travelex Insurance** ☎ 888/457–4602 ⊕ www.travelex-insurance.com. **Travel Guard International** ☎ 715/345–0505 or 800/826–4919 ⊕ www.travelguard.com. **Travel Insured International** ☎ 800/243–3174 ⊕ www.travelinsured.com.

🛈 Medical-Only Insurers **International Medical Group** ☎ 800/628–4664 ⊕ www.imglobal.com. **International SOS** ☎ 215/942–8000 or 713/521–7611 ⊕ www.internationalsos.com. **Wallach & Company** ☎ 800/237–6615 or 504/687–3166 ⊕ www.wallach. com.

LANGUAGE

The official languages are Spanish and English, in that order. Spanish prevails in everyday conversation, in commerce, and in the media. And although English is widely spoken, you'll probably want to take a Spanish phrase book along, particularly if you're traveling outside of San Juan. Hotel front-desk staffs and restaurant staffs in large facilities speak English. Most business and government phones are staffed by people who speak English (or will find someone who does), and telephone-answering systems are bilingual.

LANGUAGES FOR TRAVELERS

A phrase book and language-tape set can help get you started. *Fodor's Spanish for Travelers* (available at bookstores everywhere) is excellent.

LODGING

San Juan's high-rise hotels on the Condado and Isla Verde beach strips cater primarily to the cruise-ship and casino crowd, though several target business travelers. Outside San Juan, particularly on the east coast, you'll find self-contained luxury resorts that cover hundreds of acres. In the west, southwest, and south—as well as on the islands of Vieques and Culebra—smaller inns, villas, condominiums, and government-sponsored *paradores* are the norm.

Did the resort look as good in real life as it did in the photos? Did you sleep like a baby, or were the walls paper thin? Did you get your money's worth? Rate hotels and write your own reviews in "Travel Ratings" or start a discussion about your favorite places in "Travel Talk" on www. fodors.com. Your comments might even appear in our books. Yes, you, too, can be a correspondent!

Most hotels and other lodgings require you to give your credit-card details before they will confirm your reservation. If you don't feel comfortable e-mailing this information, ask if you can fax it (some places even prefer faxes). However you book, get confirmation in writing and have a copy of it handy when you check-in.

Be sure you understand the hotel's cancellation policy. Some places allow you to cancel without any kind of penalty—even if you prepaid to secure a discounted rate—if you cancel at least 24 hours in advance. Others require you to cancel a week in advance or penalize you for the cost of one night. Small inns and B&Bs are most likely to require you to cancel far in advance. Most hotels allow children under a certain age to stay in their parents' room at no extra charge, but others charge for them as extra adults; find out the cutoff age for discounts.

Assume that hotels operate on the European Plan (**EP**, no meals) unless we specify that they use the Breakfast Plan (**BP**, with full breakfast), Continental Plan (**CP**, continental breakfast), Full American Plan (**FAP**, all meals), Modified American Plan (**MAP**, breakfast and dinner), or are **all-inclusive** (**AI**, all meals and most activities).

APARTMENT & VILLA RENTALS

If you want a home base that's roomy enough for a family and comes with cooking facilities, consider a furnished rental. These can save you money, especially if you're traveling with a group. Home-exchange directories sometimes list rentals as well as exchanges.

Vacation Home Rentals Worldwide 201/767-9393 or 800/633-3284 www.vhrww.com. **Villas International** 415/499-9490 or 800/221-2260 www.villasintl.com. **Wimco** 800/449-1553 www.wimco.com.

Local Agents Rainbow Realty 787/741-4312 www.enchanted-isle.com/rainbow rents condos and villas on Vieques. **Island West Properties & Beach Rentals** Rte. 413, Km 1.3, Box 700, Rincón 00677 787/823-2323 787/823-3254 www.rinconrealestateforsale.com can help you rent condos in Rincón by the week or the month. **Puerto Rico Vacation Apartments** Calle Marbella del Caribe Oeste S-5, Isla Verde 00979 787/727-1591 or 800/266-3639 787/268-3604 www.sanjuanvacations.com represents some 200 properties in Condado and Isla Verde.

HOME EXCHANGES

With a direct home exchange, you stay in someone else's home while they stay in yours. Some outfits also deal with vacation homes, so you're not actually staying in someone's full-time residence, just their vacant weekend place.

Exchange Clubs HomeLink International 813/975-9825 or 800/638-3841 www.homelink.org; $80 yearly for Web-only membership; $125 with Web access and two directories. **Home Exchange.com** 800/877-8723 www.homeexchange.com charges; $49.95 yearly for a 1-year online listing; this is a Web-based company with no catalog. **Intervac U.S.** 800/756-4663 www.intervacus.com; $128.88 yearly for a listing, online access, and a catalog; $78.88 without catalog.

There's another option for getting all the above plus their second yearly catalogue, for $168.88

HOTELS

In the most expensive hotels your room will be large enough for two to move around comfortably, with two double beds (*camas matrimoniales*) or one queen- or king-sized bed, air-conditioning (*aire acondicionado*), a phone (*teléfono*), a private bath (*baño particular*), an in-room safe, cable TV, a hair dryer, iron and ironing board, room service (*servicio de habitación*), shampoo and toiletries, and possibly a view of the water (*vista al mar*). There will be a concierge and at least one hotel restaurant and lounge, a pool, a shop, and an exercise room or spa. In Puerto Rico's smaller inns rooms will have private baths with hot water (*agua caliente*), air-conditioning or fans, a double to king-sized bed, possibly room service, and breakfast (Continental or full) included in the rates. In some hotels several rooms share baths—it's a good idea to ask before booking. All hotels listed in this guide have private baths unless otherwise noted.

Weigh all your options (we can't say this enough). Join "frequent guest" programs. You may get preferential treatment in room choice and/or upgrades in your favorite chains. Check general travel sites and hotel Web sites, as not all chains are represented on all travel sites. Always research or inquire about special packages and corporate rates. If you prefer to book by phone, note that you can sometimes get a better price if call the hotel's local toll-free number (if one is available) rather than the central reservations number.

If your destination's high season is December through April and you're trying to book, say, in late April, you might save considerably by changing your dates by a week or two. Note, though, that many properties charge peak-season rates for your entire stay even if your travel dates straddle peak and nonpeak seasons. High-end chains catering to businesspeople are often busy only on weekdays and often drop rates dramatically on weekends to fill up rooms. **Ask when rates go down.**

Watch out for hidden costs, including resort fees, energy surcharges, and "convenience" fees for such things as unlimited local phone service you won't use and a free newspaper—possibly written in a language you can't read. Always verify whether local hotel taxes are or are not included in the rates you are quoted, so that you'll know the real price of your stay. In some places taxes can add 20% or more to your bill. If you're traveling overseas, **look for price guarantees,** which protect you against a falling dollar. With your rate locked in, you won't pay more, even if the price goes up in the local currency.

🔢 Discount Hotel Rooms **Accommodations Express** ☎ 800/444-7666 or 800/277-1064. **Hotels.com** ☎ 800/219-4606 or 800/364-0291 ⊕ www.hotels.com. **Quikbook** ☎ 800/789-9887 ⊕ www.quikbook.com. **Turbotrip.com** ☎ 800/473-7829 ⊕ w3.turbotrip.com.

PARADORES

Some paradores are rural inns offering no-frills apartments, and others are large hotels; all must meet certain standards, such as proximity to an attraction or beach. Most have a small restaurant that serves local cuisine. They're great bargains (from $60 to $125 for a double room). You can make reservations by contacting the Puerto Rico Tourism Company. Small Inns of Puerto Rico, a branch of the Puerto Rico Hotel & Tourism Association, is a marketing arm for some 25 small hotels island-wide. The organization occasionally has package deals including casino coupons and LeLoLai (a cultural show) tickets.

🔢 Puerto Rico Tourism Company 📦 Box 902-3960, Old San Juan Station, San Juan 00902-3960 ☎ 787/721-2400 or 800/866-7827 ⊕ www.gotopuertorico.com/parames/paradores. **Small Inns of Puerto Rico** ✉ 954 Av. Ponce de León, Suite 702, 00907 ☎ 787/725-2901 ⊕ www.prhtasmallhotels.com.

MAIL & SHIPPING

Puerto Rico uses the U.S. postal system, and all addresses on the island carry zip codes. The rates to send letters and postcards from Puerto Rico are the same as those everywhere else in the United States.

However, mail between Puerto Rico and the U.S. mainland can take more than a week.

🔢 Major Post Offices **U.S. Post Office** ✉ 153 Calle Fortaleza, Old San Juan, San Juan ✉ 163 Av. Fernández Juncos, San Juan ✉ 102 Calle Garrido Morales, Fajardo ✉ 60 Calle McKinley, Mayagüez ✉ 94 Calle Atocha, Ponce.

SHIPPING PACKAGES

Many shops—particularly those in Old San Juan and Condado—will ship purchases for you. Shipping services are especially common at art galleries. Pay by credit card, and save your receipts. Make sure the proprietor insures the package against loss or damage, and ships it first-class or by courier. Grab a business card with the proprietor's name and phone number so you can readily follow-up with him or her if needed.

Post offices in major Puerto Rican cities offer express mail (next-day) service to the U.S. mainland and to Puerto Rican destinations. In addition, you can send packages via FedEx or UPS. Ask at the concierge desk of your hotel; most have regular courier pick ups or can call for one. Hotels that offer business services will take care of the entire ordeal for you. Caveat emptor: courier delivery and pick-up is not available on Saturday, and even "overnight" packages often take two to three days to reach the U.S. mainland.

🔢 FedEx ☎ 787/793-9300. **UPS** ☎ 787/253-2877.

MONEY MATTERS

Puerto Rico, which is a commonwealth of the United States, uses the U.S. dollar as its official currency. Prices for most items are stable and comparable to those in the States, and that includes restaurants and hotel rates. As in many places, city prices tend to be higher than those in rural areas, but you're not going to go broke staying in the city: soft drinks or a cup of coffee run about $1; a local beer in a bar, $2.75; museum admission, $2.

Prices throughout this guide are given for adults. Substantially reduced fees are almost always available for children, students, and senior citizens. For information on taxes, *see* Taxes.

ATMS

Automated Teller Machines (ATMs; known here as ATHs) are readily available and reliable in the cities; many are attached to banks, but you can also find them in gas stations, drug stores, supermarkets, and larger hotels. Just about every casino has one—the better to keep people in the game—but these can carry large surcharges, so check before you withdraw money. ATMs are found less frequently in rural areas, but there is usually at least one in even the smallest village. Look to local banks, such as Banco Popular.

CREDIT CARDS

Throughout this guide, the following abbreviations are used: **AE**, American Express; **D**, Discover; **DC**, Diners Club; **MC**, MasterCard; and **V**, Visa.

It's a good idea to inform your credit-card company before you travel, especially if you're going abroad and don't travel internationally very often. Otherwise, the credit-card company might put a hold on your card owing to unusual activity—not a good thing halfway through your trip. Record all your credit-card numbers—as well as the phone numbers to call in the if your cards are lost or stolen—in a safe place so you're prepared should something go wrong. Both Mastercard and Visa have general numbers you can call (collect if you're abroad) if your card is lost, but you're better off calling the number of your issuing bank, since Mastercard and Visa usually just transfer you to your bank; your bank's number is usually printed on your card.

🛈 Reporting Lost Cards **American Express** ☎ 800/992-3404 in the U.S. or 336/393-1111 collect from abroad ⊕ www.americanexpress.com. **Diners Club** ☎ 800/234-6377 in the U.S. or 303/799-1504 collect from abroad ⊕ www.dinersclub.com. **Discover** ☎ 800/347-2683 in the U.S. or 801/902-3100 collect from abroad ⊕ www.discovercard.com. **MasterCard** ☎ 800/622-7747 in the U.S. or 636/722-7111 collect from abroad ⊕ www.mastercard.com. **Visa** ☎ 800/847-2911 in the U.S. or 410/581-9994 collect from abroad ⊕ www.visa.com.

TRAVELER'S CHECKS & CARDS

Some consider this the currency of the cave man, and it's true that fewer establishments accept traveler's checks these days. Nevertheless, they're a cheap and secure way to carry extra money, particularly on trips to urban areas. Both Citibank (under the Visa brand) and American Express issue traveler's checks in the United States, but AmEx is better known and more widely accepted; you can also avoid hefty surcharges by cashing AmEx checks at at AmEx offices. Whatever you do, keep track of all the serial numbers in case the checks are lost or stolen.

American Express now offers a stored-value card called a Travelers Cheque Card, which you can use wherever American Express credit cards are accepted, including ATMs. The card can carry a minimum of $300 and a maximum of $2,700, and it's a very safe way to carry your funds. Although you can get replacement funds in 24 hours if your card is lost or stolen, it doesn't really strike us as a very good deal. In addition to a high initial cost ($14.95 to set up the card, plus $5 each time you "reload"), you still have to pay a $2.50 fee each time you use the card in an ATM—add it all up and it can be considerably more than you would pay for simply using your own ATM card. Regular traveler's checks are just as secure and cost less.

🛈 **American Express** ☎ 888/412-6945 in the U.S., 801/945-9450 collect outside of the U.S. to add value or speak to customer service ⊕ www. americanexpress.com.

PACKING

Why do some people travel with a convoy of suitcases the size of large-screen TVs and yet never have a thing to wear? How do others pack a toaster-oven-size duffle with a week's worth of outfits *and* supplies for every possible contingency? We realize that packing is a matter of style—a very personal thing—but there's a lot to be said for traveling light. The tips in this section will help you win the battle of the bulging bag.

Make a list. In a recent Fodor's survey, 29% of respondents said they make lists (and often pack) at least a week before a trip. Lists can be used at least twice—once to pack and once to repack at the end of your trip. You'll also have a record of the contents of your suitcase, just in case it disappears in transit.

Think it through. What's the weather like? Is this a business trip or a cruise or resort vacation? Going abroad? In some places and/or sights, traditions of dress may be more or less conservative than you're used to. As your itinerary comes together, jot activities down and note possible outfits next to each (don't forget those shoes and accessories).

Edit your wardrobe. Plan to wear everything twice (better yet, thrice) and to do laundry along the way. Stick to one basic look—urban chic, sporty casual, etc. Build around one or two neutrals and an accent (e.g., black, white, and olive green). Women can freshen looks by changing scarves or jewelry. For a week's trip, you can look smashing with three bottoms, four or five tops, a sweater, and a jacket you can wear alone or over the sweater.

Be practical. Put comfortable shoes at the top of your list. (Did we need to tell you this?) Pack items that are lightweight, wrinkle resistant, compact, and washable. (Or this?) Try a simple wrinkling test: Intentionally fold a piece of fabric between your fingers for a couple minutes. If it refuses to crease, it will probably come out of your suitcase looking fresh. That said if you stack and then roll your clothes when packing, they'll wrinkle less.

Check weight and size limitations. In the United States you may be charged extra for checked bags weighing more than 50 pounds. Abroad some airlines don't even allow you to check bags weighing more than 50 pounds, or they charge outrageous fees for every pound your luggage is over. Carry-on size limitations can be stringent, too.

Be prepared to lug it yourself. If there's one thing that can turn a pack rat into a minimalist, it's a vacation spent lugging heavy bags over long distances. Unless you're on a guided tour or a cruise, select luggage that you can readily carry. Porters, like good butlers, are hard to find these days.

Lock it up. Several companies sell locks (about $10) approved by the Transportation Safety Administration that can be unlocked by all U.S. security personnel should they decide to search your bags. Alternatively, you can use simple plastic cable ties, which are sold at hardware stores in bundles.

Tag it. Always put tags on your luggage with some kind of contact information; use your business address if you don't want people to know your home address. Put the same information (and a copy of your itinerary) inside your luggage, too.

Don't check valuables. On U.S. flights, airlines are only liable for about $2,800 per person for bags. On international flights, the liability limit is around $635 per bag. But just try collecting from the airline for items like computers, cameras, and jewelry. It isn't going to happen; they aren't covered. And though comprehensive travel policies may cover luggage, the liability limit is often a pittance. Your home-owners' policy may cover you sufficiently when you travel—or not. You're really better off stashing baubles and gizmos in your carry-on—right near those prescription meds.

Report problems immediately. If your bags—or things in them—are damaged or go astray, file a written claim with your airline *before you leave the airport.* If the airline is at fault, it may give you money for essentials until your luggage arrives. Most lost bags are found within 48 hours, so alert the airline to your whereabouts for two or three days. If your bag was opened for security reasons in the United States and something is missing, file a claim with the TSA.

WHAT YOU'LL NEED IN PUERTO RICO

Although "casual" is the operative word for vacation clothes, wearing resort attire outside the hotel or at the casino will peg you as a tourist. Puerto Ricans, particularly in the cities, dress up to go out. Pack some dressy casual slacks and shirts, summer skirts for women, casual clothes for the resort, at least two bathing suits (to avoid having to wear that wet one from yesterday), and sturdy shoes for walking. A light sweater or jacket isn't a bad idea either.

PASSPORTS & VISAS

When traveling internationally, carry your passport even if you don't need one (it's always the best form of ID) and **make two photocopies of the data page** (one for someone at home and another for you, carried separately from your passport). If you lose your passport, promptly call the nearest embassy or consulate and the local police.

ENTERING PUERTO RICO

U.S. citizens don't need passports to visit Puerto Rico, and there is no passport control either to or from Puerto Rico; in this respect, flying here is just like traveling on any domestic flight. Nevertheless, it's always wise to carry some form of identification that proves your citizenship, and we still recommend that you carry a valid passport when traveling to Puerto Rico; it's a necessity if you are making any other trips around the Caribbean, except to the U.S. Virgin Islands, where you will pass through customs but not passport control.

PHONES

All Puerto Rican phone numbers—like those throughout the United States—consist of a three-digit area code and a seven-digit local number. Puerto Rico's area codes are 787 and 939. Toll-free numbers (prefix 800, 888, or 877) are widely used in Puerto Rico, and many can be accessed from North America. You can also access many North American toll-free numbers from the island.

Cell phones are a viable alternative to using local service if you need to keep records of your bills. Call your cell-phone company before departing to get information about activation and roaming charges. Companies that have service on the island include Cellular One, Cingular, and Sprint. For many cell-phone users, Puerto Rico is considered part of their regular nationwide calling area; for others, it's considered international.

LONG-DISTANCE SERVICES

AT&T, MCI, and Sprint access codes make calling long-distance relatively convenient, but you may find the local access number blocked in many hotel rooms.

First ask the hotel operator to connect you. If the hotel operator balks, ask for an international operator, or dial the international operator yourself. One way to improve your odds of getting connected to your long-distance carrier is to travel with more than one company's calling card (a hotel may block Sprint, for example, but not MCI). If all else fails, call from a pay phone.

🔒 Access Codes **AT&T Direct** ☎ 787/725-0300. **Cellular One** ☎ 787/505-2273 or 787/505-4636. **MCI WorldPhone** ☎ 787/782-6244 or 800/939-7624. **Sprint International Access** ☎ 800/473-3037 or 800/298-3266.

PHONE CARDS

Phone cards are widely available. The Puerto Rico Telephone Company sells its "Ring Cards" in various denominations that can be used for both local and international calls. They're available in shops, supermarkets, and drugstores as well as from the phone company.

🔒 **Ring Cards** ☎ 800/981-9105.

PUBLIC PHONES

Pay phones, which are abundant in tourist areas, use coins or prepaid phone cards; some accept credit cards. Local calls are 25¢, and on-island, long-distance calls cost about 50¢.

SAFETY

San Juan, Mayagüez, and Ponce, like most big cities, have their share of crime, so guard your wallet or purse in markets, on buses, and in other crowded areas. Avoid beaches at night, when muggings have been known to occur even in Condado and Isla Verde. Don't leave anything unattended on the beach. If you must keep valuables in your vehicle, put them in the trunk. Always lock your car. The exception is at the beaches of Vieques, where rental-car agencies advise you to leave the car unlocked so thieves don't break the windows to search for valuables. This happens extremely rarely, but it does happen.

Distribute your cash, credit cards, I.D.s, and other valuables between a deep front pocket, an inside jacket or vest pocket, and a hidden money pouch. Don't reach for the money pouch once you're in public.

We recommend that women carry only a handbag that closes completely and wear it bandolier style (across one shoulder and your chest). Open-style bags and those allowed to simply dangle from one shoulder are prime targets for pickpockets and purse snatchers. Avoid walking anywhere alone at night, and don't wear clothing that's skin-tight or overly revealing.

TAXES

You must pay a tax on your hotel room rate: for hotels with casinos it's 11%, for other hotels it's 9%, and for government-approved paradores it's 7%. Ask your hotel before booking. The tax, in addition to each hotel's discretionary service charge (which usually ranges from 5% to 12%), can add a hefty 12% to 23% to your bill. There's no sales tax on Puerto Rico. Airport departure taxes are usually included in the cost of your plane ticket rather than being collected at the airport.

TIME

Puerto Rico operates on Atlantic Standard Time, which is one hour later than the U.S. Eastern Standard Time in winter. The island does not keep U.S. daylight savings time. This means that when it's noon on a winter day in New York, it's 1 PM in Puerto Rico. In summer Puerto Rico and the East Coast of the United States are on the same time, and three hours ahead of the West Coast. Sydney is 14 hours ahead of Puerto Rico, Auckland is 16 hours ahead, and London is 4 hours ahead.

TIPPING

Some hotels automatically add a 5% to 12% service charge to your bill. Check ahead to confirm whether this charge is built into the room rate or will be tacked on at check-out. Tips are expected, and appreciated, by restaurant waitstaff (15% to 20% if a service charge isn't included), hotel porters ($1 per bag), maids ($1 to $2 a day), and taxi drivers (10% to 15%).

TOURS & PACKAGES

VACATION PACKAGES

Packages *are not* guided tours. Packages combine airfare, accommodations, and perhaps a rental car or other extras (theater tickets, guided excursions, boat trips,

reserved entry to popular museums, transit passes), but they let you do your own thing. During busy periods, packages may be your only option because flights and rooms may be otherwise sold out. Packages will definitely save you time. They can also save you money, particularly in peak seasons, but—and this is a really big "but"—you should price each part of the package separately to be sure. And be aware that prices advertised on Web sites and in newspapers rarely include service charges or taxes, which can up your costs by hundreds of dollars.

Note that local tourism boards can provide information about lesser-known and small-niche operators that sell packages to just a few destinations. And don't always assume that you can get the best deal by booking everything yourself. Some packages and cruises are sold only through travel agents.

Each year consumers are stranded or lose their money when packagers—even large ones with excellent reputations—go out of business. How can you protect yourself? First, always pay with a credit card; if you have a problem, your credit-card company may help you resolve it. Second, buy trip insurance that covers default. Third, choose a company that belongs to the United States Tour Operators Association, whose members must set aside funds ($1 million) to cover defaults. Finally choose a company that also participates in the Tour Operator Program of the American Society of Travel Agents (ASTA), which will act as mediator in any disputes. You can also check on the tour operator's reputation among travelers by posting an inquiry on one of the Fodors.com forums.

🖪 Organizations **American Society of Travel Agents** (ASTA) ☎ 703/739–2782 or 800/965–2782 24-hr hotline ⊕ www.astanet.com. **United States Tour Operators Association** (USTOA) ☎ 212/599–6599 ⊕ www.ustoa.com.

TRAIN TRAVEL

The *Tren Urbano,* an elevated light-rail system, travels throughout the metropolitan area, with stops at the University of Puerto Rico and Bayamón, but does not stop near the main tourist areas or at the airport. The fare is $1.50, which includes transfers to city buses. The system runs from 5:30 AM to 11 PM. It's run by the Alternativa de Transporte Integrado, better known as the ATI.

🚩 **Alternativa de Transporte Integrado** ☎ 787/723-3760 ⊕ www.ati.gobierno.pr.

TRAVEL AGENTS

If you use an agent—brick-and-mortar or virtual—you'll pay a fee for the service. And know that the service you get from some online agents isn't comprehensive. For example Expedia or Travelocity don't search for prices on budget airlines like JetBlue, Southwest, or small foreign carriers. That said, some agents (online or not) *do* have access to fares that are difficult to find otherwise, and the savings can more than make up for any surcharge.

A knowledgeable brick-and-mortar travel agent can be a godsend if you're booking a cruise, a package trip that's not available to you directly, an air pass, or a complicated itinerary including several overseas flights. What's more, travel agents that specialize in a destination may have exclusive access to certain deals and insider information on things such as charter flights. Agents who specialize in types of travelers (senior citizens, gays and lesbians, naturists) or types of trips (cruises, luxury travel, safaris) can also be invaluable.

🚩 **Agent Resources** **American Society of Travel Agents** ☎ 703/739-2782 ⊕ www.travelsense.org. 🚩 **Online Agents** **Expedia** ⊕ www.expedia.com. **Onetravel.com** ⊕ www.onetravel.com. **Orbitz** ⊕ www.orbitz.com. **Priceline.com** ⊕ www.priceline.com. **Travelocity** ⊕ www.travelocity.com.

VISITOR INFORMATION

In addition to the Puerto Rico Tourism Company's *Qué Pasa,* pick up the Puerto Rico Hotel and Tourism Association's *Bienvenidos* and *Places to Go.* Among them you'll find a wealth of information about the island and its activities. All are free and available at tourism offices and hotel desks. The Puerto Rico Tourism Company has information centers at the airport, Old San Juan, Ponce, Aguadilla, and Cabo Rojo. Most island towns also have a tourism office in their city hall.

🚩 Tourist Information **Puerto Rico Tourism Company** ⊕ www.gotopuertorico.com ✉ Box 902-3960, Old San Juan Station, San Juan 00902-3960 ☎ 787/721-2400 or 800/866-7827 ✉ 666 5th Ave., 15th fl., New York, NY 10103 ☎ 212/586-6262 or 800/223-6530 ✉ 3575 W. Cahuenga Blvd., Suite 560, Los Angeles, CA 90068 ☎ 213/874-5991 or 800/874-1330 ✉ 901 Ponce de León Blvd., Suite 101, Coral Gables, FL 33134 ☎ 305/445-9112 or 800/815-7391.

WEB SITES

We're really proud of our Web site: Fodors.com is a great place to begin any journey. Scan "Travel Wire" for suggested itineraries, travel deals, restaurant and hotel openings, and other up-to-the-minute info. Check out "Booking" to research prices and book plane tickets, hotel rooms, rental cars, and vacation packages. Head to "Talk" for on-the-ground pointers from travelers who frequent our message boards. You can also link to loads of other travel-related resources.

After your trip, be sure to rate the places you visited and share your experiences and travel tips with us and other Fodorites in "Travel Ratings" and "Talk" on www.fodors.com.

You can get basic information about Puerto Rico from ⊕ www.puertoricowow.com and ⊕ www.gotopuertorico.com. Maps are available at ⊕ www.travelmaps.com. For information on conferences and conventions, see the Puerto Rico Convention Center Web site at ⊕ www.prconvention.com or the Puerto Rico Convention Bureau at ⊕ www.meetpuertorico.com. In addition, many of the hotels and attractions throughout the island have their own Web sites.

🚩 Weather **Accuweather.com** ⊕ www.accuweather.com is an independent weather-forecasting service with especially good coverage of hurricanes. **Weather.com** ⊕ www.weather.com is the Web site for the Weather Channel.

INDEX

PHOTO CREDITS

Cover Photo (Buye Beach near Cabo Rojo): *José Azel/Aurora.* 12, *Joe Viesti/viestiphoto.com.* 13 (left), *Greg Vaughn/Alamy.* 13 (right), *Lucid Images/age fotostock.* 14, *Envision/Corbis.* 15, *Ricardo Ordóñez/ age fotostock.* 16, *Marty Cooper/viestiphoto.com.* 17 (left), *Atlantide S.N.C./age fotostock.* 17 (right), *Philip Coblentz/Medioimages.* 24, *David Sanger Photography/Alamy.* 25 (left), *Joe Viesti/viestiphoto.com.* 25 (right), *Nicholas Pitt/Alamy.* 26, *David R. Frazier Photolibrary, Inc./Alamy.* 27 (left), *Doug Scott/age fotostock.* 27 (right), *Kim Karpeles/Alamy.*

NOTES

NOTES

NOTES

ABOUT OUR AUTHOR

It was a trip to Bahía Mosquito that convinced Mark Sullivan that Puerto Rico was not just another spot in the Caribbean. Diving into the bioluminescent bay—and watching the trail of blue-green sparks he left in his wake—made him realize that this is truly an *isla encantada*. Since that time he's explored every nook and cranny, from the bat-filled caverns of the the Parque de las Cavernas del Río Camuy to the cactus-lined trails of the Bosque Estatal de Guánica. A few of his favorite pastimes? Trying the *lechón* (suckling pig roasted on a spit) at roadside stands near Cayay was an experience, as was eating the *mofongo* (mashed plantains stuffed with lobster and other delicacies) in several of the seafood shacks at Joyuda. He has written or edited dozens of travel guides, including *Fodor's Central America, Fodor's South America,* and *Fodor's Pocket Aruba.* His cultural reporting has also appeared in many magazines, including *Billboard, InStyle,* and *Interview.* When not on the road, he splits his time between a shoebox apartment in New York City and a rambling Victorian in the Catskills.

Acknowledgements

Few travel guides, even ones like this that have a single author, are the work of one person. Many people made this book possible. I'd like to thank Glorimar Alvarez and Nelly Cruz at the offices of the Puerto Rico Tourism Company. They provided me with a stack—quite literally—of information about the island. Several people along the way were especially helpful, introducing me to places I might otherwise have missed, including Estaban Haigler and Emeo Cheung at the Andalucia Guest House, Evy Garcia at the Westin Río Mar Beach Golf Resort & Spa, and Sigrid Velez at the recently closed (and much missed) Hyatt Dorado Beach Resort & Country Club. A big help on Vieques was Hacienda Tamarindo's Burr Vail, who pointed the way to secluded beaches and off-the-beaten-path eateries. Everyone on Culebra seemed to want to lend a hand, but I'm especially grateful to Ginny Tawalski at Posada La Hamaca and Jim Petersen of the *Culebra Calendar.* (His "office," on the sunny patio of his wife's restaurant, is one of the friendliest spots in Puerto Rico.) The biggest thanks goes to my editor, Doug Stallings, whose ability to juggle many projects but still give each writer his full attention is amazing.